A Social Psychology of
Organizing

A Social Psychology of Organizing

PEOPLE, PROCESSES AND CONTEXTS

Dian-Marie Hosking and Ian E. Morley

HARVESTER
WHEATSHEAF

New York   London   Toronto   Sydney   Tokyo   Singapore

First published 1991 by
Harvester Wheatsheaf,
66 Wood Lane End, Hemel Hempstead,
Hertfordshire, HP2 4RG

A division of
Simon & Schuster International Group

Typeset in 10½/12pt Garamond by
Pentacor PLC, High Wycombe, Bucks
Printed and bound in Great Britain at the University Press Cambridge

British Library Cataloguing in Publication Data
Hosking, Dian-Marie
  A social psychology of organizing: People,
  processes and contexts.
  I. Title   II. Morley, Ian E.
  302.3
  ISBN 0-7450-1053-9
  ISBN 0-7450-1054-7 pbk

2   3   4   5   95   94   93   92

Contents

Part 2 Organizing Processes

Part 3 Structure in the Process of Projects

Preface

Many texts speak of person and organization, usually to emphasize one at the expense of the other. In the literatures of Organisational Behaviour (OB) and Human Resource Management (HRM), interest is focused on the characteristics and behaviour of individuals and groups in organization. The relationship between person and organization is seen as analogous to relationships between Russian dolls of different sizes: one doll is placed inside another, and can be removed, with each staying the same. In the literatures of OB and HRM, the organization is often viewed as a context which is independent of the human actor. Further, the underlying concept of organization is not held up for critical examination but is left implicit. Much the same can be said of organization theories which focus on the design and internal functioning of an organization. In such theories, organization is the central interest; an implicit theory of the nature of human nature is articulated but not critically examined.

Our interest in writing this text is to explore seriously relationships between person and organization. Our approach, broadly speaking, is social psychological. To theorize the interrelations, we build throughout the book a language of organizing processes – a language which allows us to speak of person and organization in terms which are commensurate. In this way we hope to avoid the negative consequences of the approach described above, that is, one which theorizes person and organization as *entities* independent of each other. An entitative approach fails to represent what it means to be human, misrepresents the qualities of relational processes and, more generally, grossly distorts the relationships between person and organization.

So far, this adds up to an interest in developing a framework for the appreciation of organizing which reflects the theories and findings of modern psychology. However, a lot follows from this. In terms of the book as a whole, we are keen to construct an argument which is carried throughout, situated in relation to an explicit theoretical framework. Those of you who know the literatures of OB, HRM, and social psychology, will appreciate that such an approach is rare. Notable exceptions are found in Katz and Kahn's

(1978) *The Social Psychology of Organizations*; in Weick's (1979) *The Social Psychology of Organizing*; in Crano and Messé's (1982) *Social Psychology*; in Kelvin's (1970) *The Bases of Social Behaviour* (1970), and in Sherif and Sherif's *Social Psychology* (1969). What might be termed standard texts in OB, in HRM, and in social psychology typically consist of a set of chapters for which no obvious logic exists. In other words, it is not evident why some topics are included or others left out, relationships between the topics are left largely undiscussed, and none can be shown to be more or less important than another.

So, we offer this as an attempt to construct a theoretically integrated text. However, whilst we aim to be integrative we do not aim to be comprehensive. Again, if conventional texts in OB, in social psychology, and in HRM are our standard for comparison, it is impossible to be sure whether or not they intend to be comprehensive, at least within the limited scope of relevant theories and findings. This is important. To judge a perspective, or what claims to be an account of a particular realm of discourse, it is important to have some notion of its limits.

We aim to bring together literatures which normally are kept apart. This would be impossible without a well worked-out theoretical framework. As we struggled with the vast range of literatures that we might include, increasingly it became clear that we were being selective, and we became more aware of the grounds on which we were being so. Our framework deals with concepts central to social psychology. It has allowed us to choose selected areas for detailed attention, that is, those areas which – given our framework – are more important.

Our point of view has a degree of coherence which makes plain what we think important and why we think so. This allows us to ignore topics which we think relatively unimportant and unhelpful, such as traditional theories of motivation. Such a framework also allows us to bring to the foreground arguments about processes, collective action, and leadership – arguments which typically are glossed over in one appalling chapter. Finally, we are able to give appropriate and continuing emphasis to relational processes which usually are ignored, that is sense making and political processes. The result, we believe, constitutes a distinctive approach both to social psychology, and to organization behaviour.

Perhaps most fundamental to our framework is the argument that the relationship between a person and their context is one of *mutual creation*. In other words, persons to some extent make their contexts and, to some extent, are made by them. We shall emphasize how persons make their contexts whilst recognizing that not anything and everything is possible. In other words, they are active and creative but also are constrained in what they may create. Though not anything is possible, they to some extent select their contexts; though constrained, they to some degree adapt to their contexts by changing themselves; though constrained, they to some extent make their contexts. Persons do so with and through their relationships with their contexts, particularly with and through their relationships with other people. These relational processes importantly are characterized by what we shall call the activities of sense-making.

This is a very empowering point of view and one which contrasts markedly with the implied message of much of the writing to which we have referred. For example, OB texts and texts in human resource management (HRM) speak to readers as though they were managers (active) who can manipulate others (passive) as human resources. The picture of 'behaviour in organization' is of people who can (and should) manipulate others who, in turn, rationally should accept manipulation as all share the same or congruent goals. This is not our picture; we will paint another.

As we indicated earlier, the ways in which person and organization are theorized has profound and extensive implications for the ways their relations may be theorized. When person and organization are theorized as entities, independent of each other, each is seen to provide inputs to the other and to experience outcomes. This means that *relational processes* are reduced to more or less complex but, in principle, predictable interactions; these simply connect inputs in ways which are more or less 'instrumental' for the achievement of outcomes. In contrast, when the relationship between person and context is seen as one of mutual creation, the concept of process is very different. This is because outputs cannot be reduced to the inputs of either actor or context, but rather are seen as the emergent product of their interrelation. As a result, processes supplant inputs and outcomes as the centre of interest, and the issue of instrumentality is redefined.

Our arguments about the social processes of organizing take seriously what usually is trivialized. Social processes are the vehicle for political and cognitive processes. They are the means through which organizing is performed. When we say 'take seriously', we mean that we will not reduce social processes to backwards and forwards exchanges of information and other resources, within contexts which are treated as given and therefore as un-problematic. Rather, we view social processes as processes in which participants (in organizing) construct a sense of who they are (identity) in relation to a context, which consists importantly of other people and their constructions. Further, participants construct their contexts through the many ways in which they build their understandings and mobilize influence, pursuing lines of action in relation to what we shall call projects.

Our approach does not see social processes as 'instrumental' in the manner emphasized in entitative perspectives. Rather, we emphasize what others usually leave tacit. This is that a person, and those with whom he or she interacts, *needs the help of others* to construct their sense of self and sense of social order, and needs the help of others to act in relation to them. In its most general and fundamental sense, this is what we mean when we say that an actor needs the help of others to add value to their lives. Beyond this, what counts as 'adding value' varies depending on the particular relationship between an actor and their context.

It is not just that our concept of process is distinctive. When developing our arguments about organizing we seek to make plain that we see organizing as intrinsically political. It may suprise some readers to know that we came to this view out of following the implications of a psychologically adequate concept of person. Political processes are implied by any perspective which takes the view that actors differ from one another in their valuing of their contexts such that they see things differently and differ in their interests. Actors differ in their relationships with their contexts such that some are more able than others to mobilize power in support of their valuations and their interests. We think it impossible to say much that is sensible about organizing without recognizing that relationships, potentially, always are political. Readers of OB and HRM could be forgiven for missing this quality. This is because most texts ignore it. Further, even when they do not, politics simply is seen as a naughty, self serving activity. This view is grounded in an entitative perspective of person and organization. A psychologically adequate picture of persons and their relationships with their contexts – relations of mutual creation – leads to the view that political processes are endemic to organizing.

Readers of OB and HRM texts also could be forgiven for supposing that human behaviour only is cognitive when actors perform tasks which readily can be defined as 'problem solving' or 'decision-making'. Here we use the term cognitive as 'a generic term . . . to designate all processes involved in knowing' (Hilgard, 1980). We see cognitive activity as something that goes on all the time: activity which, when oriented to the present, is so in relation to possible futures and constructions of the past. Organizing processes are intrinsically cognitive as actors, all actors, attempt to make sense of what is, and might be 'going on', what if anything to do about it, and how to translate their understandings into action. In other words, we take a cognitive or decision-making perspective of organizing processes. However, we should emphasize that we view cognitive processes as constructive processes of sense-making in the sense summarized above.

These arguments are brought together in ways which allow us to theorize processes of organizing as more or less skilful. At the start of this preface we observed that often person is emphasized to the neglect of context, or vice versa. In writing this book, our broad intention is to avoid both errors by developing a language to theorize the relationships between persons, processes, and contexts. It is our wish to take seriously what modern psychology has to say about people and their interrelations with their contexts in ways which put processes back into organizational life. For us, the real trick – a trick rarely performed – is to develop ways to discuss these processes whilst, at the same time, not losing the human actor as a contributor to relational processes.

In taking the view that organizing processes are more or less skilful we develop arguments about skill which are not tied to any particular valuational content. We argue, descriptively, that actors 'move around' building their own descriptions and influencing the descriptions and actions of others with whom they are interdependent. We take the view that it is convenient to think of them doing so in relation to 'projects' set partly by person, and partly by their context. We argue prescriptively that these processes are more skilful when participants experience them as legible, coherent, and open-ended.

In Part 1, we lay out our basic arguments about persons, processes, and organising; in Part 2, we discuss in some detail, cognitive, social, and political processes; in Part 3, we apply these arguments to particular projects – teamworking, negotiation, and the projects of top management. We end by bringing our arguments together through a focus on leadership as a more or less collective and skilful process of organizing projects, whatever and whose-ever they might be.

PART 1

Persons, organization, and organizing

This part consists of three chapters in which we detail our basic arguments about the concepts of person, organization, and organizing. In Chapter 1, we develop a picture of person sufficient to support what we wish to say about organizing processes and skilful organizing. The picture contrasts greatly with that which usually is found in texts on organization behaviour; it is very different from the view of human nature implied by many writings on organization. We emphasize the interrelations between persons and their contexts as those of 'mutual creation'. We take the view that actors – individuals and groups – usefully may be understood to perform projects. Projects are set partly by the actor and partly by their context. In performing projects, actors more or less continuously create cultures, what we call 'social order'.

It follows from our concept of person that, for those who are interested to understand the relations between people and organization, any approach which assumes that one can be understood independently of the other is intrinsically flawed. In Chapter 2 we examine approaches to organization which are flawed in this way. We show how treatments of organization as an entity independent of participants' actions and sense-making constructions goes 'naturally' with an entitative concept of person. And yet – as argued in Chapter 1 – such a concept of person does not fit with research and theory in modern psychology.

In these arguments we say a lot about what we wish *not* to do. We do this not because we wish to reject all perspectives but our own. Rather, we do so in the hope that we will help you to appreciate how we view persons and their relations with their contexts. In Chapter 3, we present our first and most general description of people organizing. We develop a language of processes, emphasizing the need to find ways to discuss the ways in which people make their contexts, whilst also being made by them. This relationship is theorized in ways which recognize that not 'anything goes', at the same time stressing that many of the limits are conventional rather than matters of fact. Organizing processes are argued to be ongoing processes which emerge as interdependent actors perform their projects through and in relation to one another. These are processes of social ordering: processes which are cognitive, social, and political. It is through these arguments that Part 1 lays the foundations for our treatment of organizing processes as more or less skilful. Organizing processes are argued to be more skilful – in relation to some project – when they are experienced as legible, coherent, and open-ended.

Chapter 1

Persons

Introduction

Students of business often see little point in studying psychology. One reason is that they see little or nothing which obviously refers to the world of business and management. However, they are often equally disappointed with textbooks of organizational behaviour because they find little which helps them to understand the nature of intelligent social action. Instead, the traditional textbooks have been dominated by three kinds of theory (Hosking, 1988a).

First, there are theories in which almost all of the emphasis is given to the person. Allport (1963) has argued that they commit 'the individualistic fallacy' because they view 'personality as a unit in isolation' without any 'reference to its setting in, and dependence upon, the social environment'. As he has said:

> The person lives and dies in splendid isolation. His (her) behaviour is consistent from situation to situation. Culture, society, role-relations are viewed as mere troublesome details to be brushed aside in favor of character structure, fixed organization, unchanging traits, and a closed selfhood. (p. 192)

All too frequently, students who are willing to take psychology seriously decide that psychologists are all too ready to commit the individualistic fallacy.

In contrast, there are theories in which almost all of the emphasis is given to the context. This means that they commit what Allport has called the 'culturalistic fallacy'. This means that:

> There is a biological organism, yes; but everything this organism does is a product of social, cultural, situational forces. This view denies self-sufficiency to the person but awards self-sufficiency to cultural institutions, to social systems, and to role-relations. From this point of view the individual is a mere nuisance for social science. (p. 192)

The result is textbooks which treat organization as a 'given' because they see organization as something which exists independently of actors and actions.

Those who commit the culturalistic fallacy are unlikely to appreciate the significance of the activities of organizing.

More recently, theories have become more complicated without becoming more sophisticated. The approach taken is most often a contingency theory in which:

1. People are treated as fixed entities, to be described independently of the contexts in which they live and work. This has led to descriptions of people which identify clusters of motives and traits, based on primary needs. The concept of person is static and asocial.

2. Contexts are treated as fixed entities, to be described independently of the people who act in and on them. This has led to descriptions of organizations as physical objects. Such models emphasize the condition of being organized rather than the acts of organizing. The concept of organization is static and apolitical.

All modern textbooks accept that we need to give due weight to both people and contexts, so that in general performance is viewed as the result of variables 'inside' and 'outside' the person. All too often, however, the result has been treated simply as a statistical interaction between 'inputs' from the person and 'inputs' from the context. This has had three serious consequences. First, it has encouraged students to suppose that the main job of psychology is to provide a list of inputs from the person. This is incorrect. Psychology has as its central concern the *scientific study of intelligent action, and what makes it possible*. Second, it has given students a distorted view of the relationship between persons and contexts. Neither people nor contexts are fixed entities. Rather, the relationship is one of mutual creation. Finally, it has meant that too little attention has been given to the systematic analysis of social processes. Even though psychology of this kind has often been called 'interactional psychology' the interaction is just the statistical interaction to which we have already referred. There has been little attempt to produce theories which systematically analyse the nature of the social interaction whereby people make contexts and contexts make people. There has been little appreciation of the fact that social action is an attempt to identify possible projects; to choose between them; and to get others to 'fit in' with projects of one's own (Athay and Darlay, 1981). This means that people have not been given the respect they are due as intelligent social actors. If we are to produce psychological theories which give them this respect it is important to begin by analysing the nature of intelligent social action.

Intelligent social action

It is clear that 'the investigation of intelligence is rapidly becoming central to psychology as a discipline, and to all disciplines involved in the scientific study of the mind' (Sternberg, 1982, p.xi). Although psychologists retain a concern with the measurement of intelligence the study of intelligence is by no means confined to what is measured by intelligence tests. Considerable attention has been given to the study of people who have been highly successful in some sphere of everyday life. It has been very clearly established that:

> Such people tend to share not any one particular ability (such as spatial ability or verbal ability) but rather a higher order ability to capitalize upon whatever abilities they have in their work and to minimize the negative consequences of their weaknesses. Where possible, more intelligent people actively select environments that are more favourable for their adaptive skills . . . To the extent that there is any one aspect of intelligence that transcends particular environments, this aspect would appear to be crucial. (Sternberg, 1985a).

It has also been shown that successful innovation in business requires people who are able to identify their strengths and capitalize upon them (Drucker, 1985). The general lesson to be drawn from this is that the relationship between a person and a context involves accommodation (changing oneself) and assimilation (changing the context).[1] This means that people are both products of their contexts and participants in the shaping of those contexts. They act in contexts and they act on contexts at the same time. The relationship is one of mutual creation.

In recent years considerable attention has been given to the nature of machine intelligence as well as to human intelligence. This has raised the question whether intelligent social activity, such as that involved in office work, could be carried out by computers rather than by people. In the case of office work, at least, the answer seems to be 'no'. Apparently, it proved impossible fully to automate this work because the work was informal (Fikes, 1982). This meant that it was not feasible to think of office procedures as algorithms to operate on some kind of computerized data base. There were always occasions when following the algorithms closed down the options available and prevented the workers from doing sensible things. This led to two conclusions: the first was that programming metaphors were inadequate as a basis for understanding office work (because it was impossible to say in advance what would constitute intelligent social action).[2] The second was that what was required, instead, was an analysis of the social nature of office work.

As we shall see, people use their intelligence to further projects which they hope will add value to their lives (because the activities are intrinsically interesting or because they produce something new). Intelligent social action is needed when people need help from others, singly or collectively, to complete their projects on time, or even to complete them at all.[3] We may, therefore, think of office work, or work in general, as a series of linked projects.

One line of argument then proceeds as follows (Fikes, 1982). When we seek help from others we may be described as clients. When we give help to others we may be described as contractors. Either way, we are negotiating contracts. These define the nature of our relationships with others because they define the terms on which we will 'do business', so to speak. However, because the projects are informal it is not possible to say in advance exactly what will have to be done, nor in what ways. In particular circumstances it may be sensible to do different things, or to use different methods. Consequently, project work will most often involve a series of negotiations and renegotiations.

To understand the nature of these negotiations it is helpful to take what has been called a language-action perspective. The central concepts are an agreed description of the task, and a commitment to some future action. To quote Fikes (1982):

> In order for a task contract to be established, the clients and contractor must agree on the task that is to be performed. The negotiations will produce an agreed upon description of the task, and the commitment will be a statement of intent to do the described task. Therefore, we consider cooperative tasks as being defined by a social process, and as representing a negotiated agreement between the client and the contractor. (p.333)

We prefer the term collaboration to the term cooperation, but Fikes's general point is well taken. Our model of project work is one in which contractors and clients negotiate and renegotiate descriptions of tasks and commitments to action. The negotiations allow the participants to make sense of change, and to decide collectively how to manage it. The process is a continuing one because, whilst statements of intent may be more or less precise, it is never possible to spell out the nature of the arrangement completely and unambiguously. Each of the statements of intent has to be interpreted in the appropriate context. And interpretations change as contexts change. This requires further negotiation, and may lead to a more or less well articulated collection of 'case law'. This is one reason why it is so important not to neglect the historical dimension to social action.

We take the view that each negotiation may be regarded as an historical narrative to be decomposed into open-ended stages. The historical narrative comes in because, when people make commitments, they look for a clear rationale, linking what is happening now to what has happened in the past, and to what needs to happen in the future.[4] The stages are stages of identification, development, selection, and implementation In other words what is negotiated is the *identification* of issues, the *development* of solutions, the *choice* between alternatives, and the *implementation* of policies.[5] Such negotiations affect, and are affected by, the relationships between the participants (considered as individuals or as representatives of groups). They also affect, and are affected by, participants' commitment to other project work. There is thus one further reason why the study of negotiation should not be abstracted from the historical context in which it occurs. It is one of the main ways by which that context is constructed. This is why psychologists and sociologists speak of a negotiated social order (see Chapter 3).

We take the view that each stage of the negotiation poses cognitive and political problems. The cognitive problems arise because the negotiators must organize their intellectual activity and think clearly about the issues. The political problems arise because people have more or less strongly held views about what counts as an issue; what counts as a sensible line of development; what counts as an effective policy; and what counts as a practical way to implement that policy. Some will have competing commitments. Some will not. Some will have more influence than others because they are better able to listen, digest, and construe events, passing on their inferences to others in summary form. Those who treat the relationship between the individual and the social context as a statistical interaction between inputs from the person and inputs from the context entirely fail to appreciate the necessity for intelligent social actors to engage in disputation and to initiate change (see Billig, 1989). Consequently, they have very little to say about the powers, competences, and capabilities required to manage the cognitive and political problems which arise as those actors negotiate contracts for various kinds of project work.

To sum up: our analysis of the nature of intelligent social action has suggested that people are both products of their contexts and participants in the shaping of those contexts. The work they do is informal and is managed through a series of negotiations. Essentially, clients and contractors negotiate task contracts and thereby participate in the construction of a social order.

The purpose of this chapter is to examine how modern psychology construes such interactions between persons and contexts. We shall survey three major areas of psychology: personality theory; cognitive psychology; and social psychology. We shall be looking for an account which does much more than treat the interaction as a statistical relationship between inputs from the person and inputs from the context. We shall be looking for a model of intelligent social action which focuses on the processes through which people make their contexts whilst being made by them. It is only when we have such a model that we will have a psychology which will help us to understand the activities of organizing.

Personality theory

Personality theory is concerned with the search for those attributes of people which are relatively enduring and which help define some important aspect of their individual identities. Personality theorists would like to find personality variables that apply to a large number of people; that are relatively stable over time; and that relate to the different stages of project work. We shall discuss three main approaches to the study of personality: trait approaches; psychodynamic approaches; and phenomenological approaches.

Trait approaches

Traits have been defined in a variety of ways. However, the core of the concept is contained in the idea that traits refer to dispositions to act in certain kinds of ways in certain kinds of contexts. This makes it look as if personality is nothing more than bundles of dispositions, meaning 'tendencies-in-a-situation'. To quote Allport (1963), 'it is not we who are integrated; it is only that the environments in which we move have some stability and therefore elicit characteristic behavior in given situations' (Allport, 1963, p.177). However, Allport went on to argue that this view needed to be modified for two reasons. First, it is quite clear that people seek out situations which encourage the expression of certain traits. Indeed, it is just this sort of argument which is central in theories of occupational choice and career development, as Schein (1980) has shown. Second, traits of personality must not be regarded as fixed entities 'operating mechanically to the same degree on all occasions' (Allport, 1963, p.181). Rather, the possession of a trait implies a range of possible activity. What happens will depend on the demands of the task and the constraints imposed by the context (or relational setting).

Trait theories are of two kinds: those which simply investigate one aspect of personality (single-trait theories) and those which attempt to describe the structure of personality in terms of a relatively small number of traits (multi-trait theories). Typically, the traits are identified by using specially constructed psychometric tests. It is for this reason that the trait approach is sometimes called the psychometric trait approach. It is probably this focus which has led critics to suppose that the typical psychologist treats people as entities with attributes which are fixed and unchanging.

The trait approach has led to an extremely large collection of empirical data although very little of this work relates specifically to management. Nevertheless, we may distil some quite important lessons about the nature of organizing, as Baron (1986) has shown. For example, some people such as Type A personalities are unlikely to be effective members of teams; high self-monitors are more likely than low self-monitors to be effective in boundary roles requiring dialogue between different groups; Machiavellians are more likely to be elected leaders than other people; and they may lead more effective groups.[6]

Nevertheless, it is important to note that there is no single, unified theory integrating the study of personality traits. What is very evident is that the field contains a very wide variety of explanatory frameworks. Some come from psychoanalytic theory; some from neuropsychology; some from cognitive psychology; and some from social psychology. Thus, whilst there is an abundance of findings, we do not have a well established and integrated theory of social action based on what we know of personality in the social process .[7]

The most sophisticated attempt to produce such a theory has been produced by Aronoff and Wilson (1985). For this reason we shall describe their work in some detail. The major source is their *Personality in the Social*

Process, and all page references are to that text.

Aronoff and Wilson's framework

Like more traditional theorists Aronoff and Wilson have considered inputs from the person and inputs from the context. What makes their approach different is that:

1. They have argued that decades of research allow us to identify inputs which are small enough to be manageable but large enough to produce interesting, contrasting, and important results.[8] The inputs from the person have been identified after a review of some of the main theories of personality. The inputs from the context have been taken from a review of work in experimental social psychology. Aronoff and Wilson's framework is an ambitious attempt to integrate work in personality and social psychology.

2. Inputs from the person, inputs from the context, and the interaction between them, have been discussed in terms of a much wider theoretical framework which includes an explicit model of social process. In general, social process has been treated as a series of events performed by certain kinds of people in certain kinds of context. Each social event has been analysed into a cycle of information processing tasks, within which we may identify certain broad lines of development. The cycle begins when someone identifies an issue. What follows next is a more or less well organized series of tasks in which people develop solutions, select a policy, and put it into practice.[9] Thus, talk about inputs is linked to talk about projects.

3. Explicit consideration has been given to individual and to collective levels of analysis. Any part of any cycle may be performed individually or collectively. The collective nature of the process means that:

   > Once members of a group become involved with the demands of the task, they must find a basis for meshing their individual aspirations for what the group will accomplish, their desires for recognition from other members, their expectations of impact on the outcome of the group's work, their preference for group roles and tasks, and the nature of the rewards they hope to attain. In other words, they must develop group processes that permit their initial positions to be integrated into a common social vehicle for meeting the formal task requirements. (pp.81–2)

Group process is defined in terms of four performance styles and four modes of negotiation. The four performance styles are defined in terms of a two-dimensional space with orthogonal task and social-emotional axes.[10] It is supposed that people will tend to use only one of the styles. It is recognized that intelligent social action requires negotiation. That is the 'common social vehicle' which has been described above. The four modes of negotiation are called adversarial; exploitative; ingratiating; and integrative.[11]

4. Explicit consideration has been given to the ways in which people act in and on contexts. For example, social events are seen as information processing tasks defined partly by the people and partly by the context. The general model of group process has the merit that it sees group structure as feeding into group process and being changed by that process.

5. The distribution of inputs from the person has been seen as an important feature of the social context. Thus, the structure of an organization cannot be described entirely in physical terms, without reference to the psychological characteristics of those who make up that organization.[12]

Aronoff and Wilson have identified eleven inputs from the person. They are divided into categories of secondary motives and secondary traits. They constitute learned ways of satisfying primary needs, such as the needs for safety and the needs for esteem. They organize the ways we handle the various cognitive, social, and political tasks involved in project work. Some years ago, Murray referred to such organizing 'forces' as 'psychogenic needs'. He identified twenty such needs (Murray, 1938). Essentially, Aronoff and Wilson have retained nine of these needs, and added two 'broad traits', authoritarianism and Machiavellianism, of more recent origin. What has been achieved is an impressive intellectual synthesis but, as Aronoff and Wilson have themselves warned, six of the nine needs have proved extremely difficult to measure. In some cases the tests do not satisfy the usual criteria for the construction of psychometric tests. In other cases the tests are multidimensional. Thus, some elements of the framework must be treated with a great deal of caution. We shall first describe Aronoff and Wilson's framework, and then provide a critical evaluation of it.

The inputs from the context have been grouped into categories concerned with the physical attributes of the environment; personal inputs from other people; dimensions of the primary task; group process; and group structure. The list represents one attempt to say which aspects of the context have been shown to have important effects on a wide range of cognitive, social, and political phenomena. Few would quarrel with the basic categories. But there would be considerable debate about exactly which elements to include and why.

Personality in the social process: An illustrative example. The style of the analysis may be seen by considering one of the personal inputs in which Aronoff and Wilson place some confidence, namely authoritarianism. The trait is broad in the sense that the core of the construct is contained in the combination of conventionalism, authoritarian submission, and authoritarian aggression.[13] Aronoff and Wilson have argued that these characteristics may be related to primary needs for safety and for esteem.

The first stage of the analysis is to consider how authoritarianism relates to 'situational variables'. Under this heading Aronoff and Wilson have considered characteristics of the physical environment and characteristics of other people. What they have to say is speculative but makes sense in terms of the postulated links with needs for safety and needs for esteem. They expect authoritarians to be sensitive to those aspects of physical space which help to control social interaction, and to use them to their advantage. They also expect authoritarians to be highly sensitive to external cues which indicate others' social status. Presumably, these cues help the authoritarian to decide whether a submissive or an aggressive stance is the more appropriate.

The second stage of the analysis is to examine how authoritarianism relates to dimensions of the primary task. The major predictions which have been made are that authoritarians will be very reluctant to get involved with tasks which are difficult, complex, ambiguous, and important . The reason is that, as a person becomes engaged in a task, the dimensions of the task (difficulty, complexity, ambiguity and importance) *become part of his or her social experience*. In the case of the authoritarian they are likely to threaten fear of failure, leading to various maladaptive forms of disengagement from jobs which need to be done. This means that authoritarians will prefer a performance style which combines initiation with disaffiliation:

> Authoritarianism leads to a blunt, narrowly focused, and socially insensitive assumption of responsibility for the task work of the group. We expect high levels of activity in a few instrumental categories that narrowly move the task toward completion. For example, we expect that this concern, which is based on defensive and fairly inflexible cognitive structure, will lead people to give direction and to disagree. But they will not be able to use broader instrumental strategies such as giving analysis or integrating the work of other group members. Similarly, we expect low levels of positive socioemotional activity and high levels of interpersonal hostility when anxious or frustrated during the group process. (Aronoff and Wilson, 1985, p.101)

There is good evidence that authoritarians will rely heavily on the authority of their position when attempting to influence others. They are impatient for success and will not hesitate to use coercion if they are in the superordinate rather than the subordinate position. Not surprisingly, Aronoff and Wilson have taken the view that authoritarians will prefer differentiated group structures, with a very clear separation of function. Given such structures they may be ambitious to take on leader roles. In any case they are likely to demonstrate a concern with establishing a clear role structure, with clearly defined responsibilities. As we shall see there is some evidence to support these views (although some well informed critics remain extremely sceptical).

The third stage of the analysis is to consider how inputs from the person relate to the demands posed by the different stages of a project. Broadly speaking, Aronoff and Wilson have argued that authoritarians are least able to cope with the early stages of a project and best able to cope with the later stages, particularly if the project is difficult, complex, ambiguous, and important. The authoritarian's ability to identify issues and to develop solutions suffers, first, because they are likely to rely far too much on the suggestions of high status others, and second, because they tend to form concrete, rather than abstract, cognitive structures. These limit their abilities to process information, and to integrate different lines of development. According to Aronoff and Wilson, authoritarians are likely to show their highest levels of task involvement when policies have been agreed and are being put into practice.

The fourth stage of the analysis is to consider the authoritarian's performance styles and modes of negotiation. As we have seen, it seems likely that the authoritarian's preferred performance style will be one which combines initiation with disaffiliation. With respect to negotiation, Aronoff and Wilson have argued that authoritarians will be competitive rather than cooperative, and guarded rather than frank in their communications. This means that they will negotiate in an exploitative mode.

Evaluating Aronoff and Wilson's framework. Aronoff and Wilson have made an excellent start on an extremely important project. Instead of expanding the network of correlations between person and context, and producing an even more complicated contingency theory, they have attempted to produce a theory which is simpler, more systematic, and which gives a more coherent view of personality. Their central assumption has been that a social event occurs when a person anticipates or responds to features of his or her context by taking actions designed to achieve a personal goal. They have then attempted to identify a fairly small number of personality characteristics which help to explain how people adapt, shape, or select the different tasks involved in project work. We have attempted to illustrate the kind of analysis which has been given, using authoritarianism as an example of an input from the person. However, it is important not to forget that Aronoff and Wilson have analysed the ways in which each of the ten other inputs from the person become integrated parts of those processes that construct social events. It is precisely because of this integration that Aronoff and Wilson have said that personality becomes part of the process of social interaction.

Aronoff and Wilson's treatment of personality in the social process is a major attempt to move traditional personality theories in the direction of social psychology. Their primary goal has been to show that knowledge of a 'common core of dispositional elements . . . can help to explain those features of human activity that constitute the primary units of social psychology' (p.xii). What they have to say is frequently illuminating, and always worth serious consideration. Their treatment of personality in the social process represents the current state of the art.

Nevertheless, it is not clear that their treatment has been entirely successful. First, the identification of the common core of dispositional elements remains extremely controversial. In our view much more needs to be done to show that the sub-set of variables taken from Murray's list of needs produces interesting, contrasting, and important consequences. Second, and despite the emphasis on group processes, social processes are reduced to individual processes . Thus, one of Aronoff and Wilson's final conclusions is that 'All personality processes occur within a social context; all social psychological processes occur within an individual' (p.340). We agree with the first part of this conclusion but not the second. Even with an approach of this degree of sophistication there is the danger that inputs from the person will be understood in an entitative fashion. They may be treated as personal properties in a manner which leads to the individualistic fallacy.

Psychodynamic approaches

Various psychodynamic approaches have developed from the work of Freud. Collectively, they are sometimes referred to as depth psychologies, because they emphasize aspects of personality hidden 'deep within the psyche'. The various approaches differ enormously in detail. However, they all assume that people are unaware of some of their most basic motivations. The reason is that such motivations develop in response to traumatic events, which usually occur in childhood, and which evoke extremely painful affects, such as anxiety, guilt, or shame. One possible response is for the person to repress his or her feelings so that they are no longer conscious. However, when the feelings are repressed they do not really disappear. Nor can they be controlled entirely. Nevertheless, various mechanisms of defence operate to mean that they appear in consciousness only in disguised forms. The disguises are systematically related, however, so that dispositions which may look quite different will hang together as part of the same syndrome. In this way, psychodynamic theorists treat personality as a dynamic whole, rather than considering individual differences separately, one at a time.

As a concrete example of the approach let us consider the classic statement of the nature of the authoritarian personality (Adorno, Frenkel-Brunswik, Levinson, and Sanford, 1950). It came from an attempt to establish whether certain kinds of person were attracted to social movements which encouraged anti-semitism. Adorno et al. made two basic assumptions: that anti-semitism was 'not a specific or isolated phenomenon, but part of a broader ideological framework' (known as ethnocentrism); and that a person's 'susceptibility to this ideology depends primarily upon his psychological needs'(Adorno et al., 1950, p.3). Because they were committed to Freudian theory they argued that ethnocentrism was the outward expression of certain anti-democratic tendencies, located deep within the personality so that they were often unconscious, and thus implicit or disguised. It followed that certain kinds of people (those with implicit anti-democratic trends) would be particularly susceptible to anti-democratic propaganda and likely to join social movements which advocated discrimination against minority groups.[14] Such people were said to have authoritarian personalities. Adorno et al. identified nine related traits which seemed to covary in the authoritarian personality. The most important were conventionalism, authoritarian submission, and author-itarian aggression. The covariation was explained in terms of the effects of socialization. Briefly, it was assumed that status anxiety led certain parents strictly to enforce a rigid set of rules based on conventional middle class values. Apparently, this discipline was sufficiently harsh to evoke reactions of hostility, anxiety, and fear of failure. When these feelings were repressed they reappeared in disguised forms, producing the syndrome known as the authoritarian personality.

More recently, Kets de Vries and Miller (1984) have set out what might be taken as part of a manifesto for a psychodynamic approach. 'We believe', they say

> that the human psyche is complex, that it is made up of a broad array of tightly interdependent components that develop in channeled ways over long periods. The psyche is not terribly malleable, nor is it easy to understand without much study. We believe that it simply is not good enough to examine one or two personality dimensions ('along a 7-point scale') if one hopes to obtain any insight into the primary causes of individual, group, or organizational dysfunction. Far more detailed, complex, and encompassing characterizations of mental behavior are needed. We believe these are more common in the psychiatric and psychoanalytic literature than in the traditional behavioristic writings. (pp.4–5)

Research within this tradition is important because it gives us further insight into the relationship between person and context. This has been studied in three rather different ways.

Contexts and their effects

First, there is research which shows that people select certain contexts and are then changed by those contexts. For example, people with authoritarian personalities are attracted to organizations which allow expression of their authoritarian traits (see Greenblatt, Levinson, and Williams, 1957). If the expression of those traits is encouraged they may become even more authoritarian. If it is not they may become less authoritarian. Let us consider a particular example. Levinson and his associates studied staff members in three mental hospitals. They found that people with authoritarian personalities tended to adopt a 'custodial' rather than a 'humanistic' orientation toward the patients. They also found clear differences within and between the hospitals with respect to the degree of custodialism expected of the staff. As Sanford has said:

> Their major conclusion was that there is congruence between the policy requirements of a social system such as a hospital and the modal personality of its members. Authoritarianism in personality helps to determine who will select (and be selected for) a given organizational role and who will remain in it, while life in the role (with which an individual may identify himself) and in

the organization (which may be oppressive or liberating) may increase or decrease authoritarianism in personality. (Sanford, 1973, p.157)

The psyche may not be very malleable, as Kets de Vries and Miller have claimed. Nevertheless, it is important to note that even deep-seated personality structures are sustained by social contexts (relational settings), and may change when the setting changes.[15]

Military incompetence

Second, there is the work of Dixon (1976) on the psychology of military incompetence. He has examined a large number of military fiascoes (from the Crimean War to World War II) and argued that the mistakes made were a direct result of the personalities of the senior commanders. In one respect this thesis is not new. For example, military historians such as Barnett have made considerable efforts to show 'the decisive effect of human character on history' (Barnett, 1963, p.10). What makes Dixon's work original is the argument that the commanders all had the same kind of personality, namely authoritarian personalities. To make this argument plausible he has had to argue that certain kinds of people (those with authoritarian personalities) will be attracted to certain kinds of organizations (those which allow the expression of authoritarian traits). This is a very reasonable position, and Dixon has himself provided evidence that people with authoritarian personalities are attracted to military organizations (Henley, Dixon, and Cartmell, 1977). However, it is much less clear that, once in military organizations, those with authoritarian personalities will be more likely to succeed in them. There is not sufficient evidence to bring in a verdict, but what little evidence there is has produced very mixed results (see Altemeyer, 1981).

The first stage in Dixon's analysis is an attempt to show that when we examine military fiascoes we see the same kinds of mistake being made again and again. The most important of these are: a tendency to underestimate the capabilities of the enemy relative to one's own; an inability to admit mistakes, which motivates attempts to blame others, and makes it difficult to learn from experience; a fundamental conservatism which inhibits change and ignores technical advances; a failure adequately to use reconnaissance; a tendency to discount warning signals which indicate things are going wrong; passivity and procrastination; failure to take the initiative and exploit advantages gained; and finally, a predisposition to use frontal assaults, often against the enemy's main line of defence.

The second stage in Dixon's analysis is to argue that mistakes of this kind cannot be explained without reference to psychological principles.[16] He has argued that the errors go together because each follows naturally from the dynamics of the authoritarian personality. In some instances this works very well. For example, the tendency to underestimate the capabilities of the enemy may be seen as one manifestation of the authoritarian's concern with power and toughness. Furthermore, the inability to admit mistakes is just what we would expect given the authoritarian's repressed fear of failure. In other instances, however, the analysis is less compelling. To take just one example, the fundamental conservatism which Dixon has described is not a defining characteristic of authoritarianism. There is some evidence that authoritarians are conservative in the sense that they will resist changes in existing power structures. This may mean that they will also resist changes in technology, but Dixon has not presented any direct evidence to support his case.

One main difficulty with Dixon's analysis is that it is extremely difficult to decide whether historical figures were or were not authoritarian personalities of the classic type. He has been forced to rely on biographical data, which is sometimes by no means extensive.[17] For what it is worth we would be inclined to go along with him in some of the cases; in others we would not. A second difficulty is that the modern concept of authoritarianism is much narrower than that of Adorno *et al.* (see Altemeyer, 1981). This does not destroy the relationship between authoritarianism and military incompetence, but it is likely to be much weaker than Dixon seems to suppose.

Personality defects

Third, there is evidence to support the view that some of the most pervasive and dysfunctional aspects of behaviour in organizations may be a direct result of pathological elements in the personalities of top managers. It is, for example, quite possible to argue, as Dixon has done, that authoritarian personalities are attracted to military organizations because they promise 'gratification of certain neurotic needs'(Dixon, 1976, pp.318–9). He has presented a number of examples which show that the need to maintain such conceits has sometimes proved more compelling than the need to behave realistically, by taking account of contextual constraints.[18] More recently, very similar arguments have been put forward by Kets de Vries and Miller (1984).

They have suggested that five neurotic syndromes commonly found in clinical work may also be found in the top managers of some firms that are failing (albeit in a less severe form). The five syndromes, or neurotic styles, are labelled paranoid, compulsive, dramatic, depressive, and schizoid. Of course, the managers may be neurotic because the firms are failing, but Kets de Vries and Miller have raised the intriguing possibility that the firms may be failing because the managers are neurotic. They have argued that, in certain circumstances, top managers are able to shape their contexts in such powerful ways that 'Any elements of neurotic pathology in the executive's style are likely to be extensively mirrored in the way the firm is run' (p.22). In their view,

> Once the predominant neurotic style of the top executives has been identified, we feel that many aspects of the strategy and structure of the organization may be predicted, as well as its predominant culture and shared fantasies. We believe that these psychodynamic and organizational phenomena together form integral gestalts, or configurations. (Kets de Vries and Miller, 1984, p.43)

Thus, it will be possible to say that paranoid chief executives head paranoid organizations; that compulsive chief executives head compulsive organizations; that dramatic chief executives head dramatic organizations; and so on.

Kets de Vries and Miller have presented illustrations of each kind of case. We shall consider two of their examples to illustrate the style of their analysis, and to allow us to spell out some of the implications of their work. The first example is that of Paratech, Inc., a paranoid organization. Paratech manufacture semiconductors. There are two chief executives (who founded the firm). We do not know how paranoid the founders were at the start of the enterprise but it seems likely that they became paranoid because the firm was operating in an extremely hostile environment. To be specific, Paratech had suffered badly from industrial espionage. So had other firms. Some were going out of business. Not surprisingly, therefore, the founders took action to improve the position of their firm. To begin with, they made a number of changes designed to protect the security of the new product process. Next, they began to pay much more serious attention to the market, to see what their competitors were doing. Finally, they diversified, so that they were less dependent on any particular product line.

The three policies were perfectly sensible. However, they seem to have failed because, in each case, the executives failed to handle a major dilemma (perhaps because of their paranoia, perhaps for other reasons). The first policy failed because they failed to resolve what might be called the dilemma of confidentiality. The essence of the dilemma is that, whilst giving people confidential information risks a breach of confidence, it may be necessary for productive work. To improve security the founders fragmented the new product process. This meant that too few people in the company really understood what was required. The second policy failed because the founders failed to resolve what might be called the dilemma of commitment. This arises because there are obvious risks in making a decision too soon. Equally, there are obvious risks in leaving a decision too late. It seems that, although the firm began to pay more attention to its competitors' products the founders waited too long before making the decision to imitate those products. The third policy failed because the founders failed to solve the dilemma of diversification. If they did not diversify they were extremely vulnerable to any disruption in their main product line. However, if they diversified too much, they risked spreading their resources to the point where they were unable to compete. They seem to have made just this mistake. The net result of all this was that the firm became one of the least successful in the industry.

The second example is that of The Sealed Fresh Company, a depressive organization which made dairy products. The company was failing because the chief executive was content to operate at a low level of performance, making very few changes, and letting the business 'amble along . . . sustained mainly by momentum' (p.38). The net result was that the firm was trying to operate in a failing market with old equipment and an unimaginative product line. For some time the vice-president of marketing had been pressing the chief executive to make changes in the mix of existing products, to produce new products, and to chase contracts for wholesale sales. According to Kets de Vries and Miller the chief executive found reasons for keeping things as they were. However, his real motivation was not to make his job or his life any more complicated than it was already.

One important difference between the two examples is that the chief executives of Paratech were trying to lead the firm out of trouble. In contrast, the chief executive of The Sealed Fresh Company was doing little more than act as a caretaker. There was, therefore, a leadership vacuum. As a result leadership processes largely were absent from the firm's organizing activities. (These will be discussed in detail in the final chapter of the book.) In cases of this kind, it is very much harder to argue that the business strategy of the enterprise is a product of the chief executive's neurotic needs.[19] One possibility is that other top managers will get together and somehow manage to compensate for the deficiencies of the chief executive. Perhaps if the vice-president of marketing at Sealed Fresh had received substantial support the chief executive would have felt that it was easier to accept the proposals for change than to persist in his opposition. A second possibility is that the organization will become a political battlefield as other managers take advantage of the leadership vacuum to push their own pet projects.[20]

The example of the Sealed Fresh Company suggests that any dysfunctional elements in the performance style of the chief executive will only be mirrored in the performance style of the organization *if they receive social support*. The essential question to ask, therefore, is under what conditions the members of the dominant management coalition will share the world view of the chief executive officer. Part of the answer is that this is more likely to happen in small firms, with dominant chief executives, and centralized systems of control.[21] We may add that some groups, faced with tasks that are intellectually difficult and socially demanding, seem to control their anxieties by idealizing their leaders, leaving them to take all the initiatives. Kets de Vries and Miller refer to this as a culture of dependency.[22] This culture contrasts starkly with what we will call the 'culture of productivity' because it stifles independent thought and makes it impossible to do creative, collaborative work. It is not just that the chief executive is left to implement his or her own ideas, however bad they are. The members of the group are also highly motivated to discount warning signs that things are going wrong. Whatever benefits are to be gained from working in groups are therefore lost because, to quote de Board (1978), 'there is a sort of corporate madness in which every member colludes' (p.39).

The work of Kets de Vries and Miller provides a number of concrete examples which help us to explore the complexities of the relationships between persons and contexts. It is important, first, because it suggests that a diversity of personalities and a diversity of views is necessary, but not sufficient, for the health of a relational setting. Second, it shows that an understanding of leadership is central to an understanding of the dynamics of organizing. Third, it shows that skilful leadership requires a clear understanding of the nature of certain cognitive, social, and political dilemmas, as they characterize relational processes. Fourth, it suggests that certain dysfunctional aspects of the performance of individuals, groups, and organizations may be very resistant to change (because they are based on powerful unconscious motivations). Finally, it suggests that it may be possible to describe persons and contexts in the same kind of way (although it is not possible to move from the former to the latter in quite the way that Kets de Vries and Miller have supposed). This may help to provide theories which are compact, integrated, and easy to use.

Phenomenological approaches

Phenomenological approaches to personality form a very mixed bag. They are united in their opposition to 'entity-like' characteristics of personality which imply that human nature is fixed and unchanging. They also share an emphasis upon our own personal thoughts and feelings. It is, after all, what *we* believe that determines how *we* act. The best known theory is George Kelly's psychology of personal constructs.[23] It is one way of working out an approach to psychology known as constructive alternativism. We regard it as important because it starts from the assumption that social actions are inherently ambiguous and require interpretation. Indeed, Kelly himself has gone so far as to say that 'even the most obvious occurrences of everyday life might appear utterly transformed if we were inventive enough to construe them differently' (see Bannister and Mair, 1986, p.6). Thus, what I now perceive as a threat, I may later perceive as an opportunity. Furthermore, what I perceive now as a threat, someone else may now perceive as an opportunity. As Kelly put it himself, since our interpretations have 'no prior allegiance' they are 'always open to reconstruction' (Kelly, 1955, p.43). But it is not that 'anything goes'. Rather, we retain those concepts which allow us to maintain a coherent view of the world and discard others. We shall discuss this process in more detail in Chapter 4.

This is part of what Kelly meant when he said that constructs allow us to anticipate events. But he meant more than this. As Rychlak (1981) has put it so well:

> Too many psychologists have accepted the view that human evolution has ceased. For Kelly, what human nature 'is like' must still be seen as an open question, for we continue to alter, change and develop by *definition* . . . Human beings come at life with an active intellect, one that is not under control by events but that puts events under control by posing questions of experience and then seeking answers to them. As people find these answers and pose new questions, they constantly change their outlooks. That is, they do so spontaneously if they have not cut off such flexibility initially by freezing into a single outlook which is no longer open to such questions and answers. Human beings can *learn* or they can *avoid learning*. (p.712)

Kelly has used the image of people as scientists. This passage shows what he meant. It suggests that one of psychology's major concerns should be to show exactly when (and why) people are willing to learn, and when (and why) they are not. It also hints at Kelly's view that we do not need special theories of motivation (Fransella, 1981). All that is needed is to discover how people represent their contexts to themselves.[24] As we have already explained, we think that there is much to commend this point of view (see Preface).

Cognitive psychology

Modern cognitive psychology considers how people ask questions about the world, and organize the answers, so that they are able to act in, and on, those worlds. It is concerned with the nature of mind, considered as an information processing system (meaning a physical device capable of working with symbols). It has been dominated by three highly related themes. The first theme is that certain features of the system limit its ability to process information. Consequently, the mind is viewed as a limited capacity processing device. The second theme has recently been stated by Donald Norman. It is that 'The human mind is exquisitely tailored to make sense of the world. Give it the slightest clue and off it goes, providing explanation, rationalisation, understanding' (Norman, 1988, p.2). The third theme concerns the nature of human skills, abilities, intelligence, and expertise. We shall consider each of these themes in turn.

Limitations in capacity

Much of the early work in cognitive psychology was concerned to find out which features of the system limited its ability to process information. According to Simon (1981) the answer is that symbols must be processed serially; that the system can cope with only a few symbols at a time; that the symbols being processed must be held in special short-term stores; and that it takes a relatively long time to transfer information from short-term to long-term memory. Other writers have made the point that controlled information processing requires mental effort, and that the human mind has only a limited capacity to do mental work (Wood, 1983). Thus, if one task uses most of that capacity we will not be able to do another equally complicated task at the same time. A familiar example is that students find it extremely difficult simultaneously to listen to a lecture and to take adequate notes. One implication of all this work is that, if people are intelligently to adapt to the demands of an information processing task, they will have to find ways of working that allow them to work within their capacities. A second implication is that people who are socially skilled will send 'messages in ways compatible with the capabilities of those receiving them' (Welford, 1980, p.19). According to Welford, skill is the use of efficient strategies to match the capacities of the performers to the demands of the task. From this point of view a world which is well designed is one which helps those who work in it to find efficient strategies of just this kind. We will extend and develop these arguments in Chapters 4 and 5, to embrace the phenomenological position that people construct meanings in ways which reflect their relationships with their contexts.[25]

Some years ago Kenneth Craik made the extremely important point that human thought has 'a very definite function' to provide 'a convenient small-scale model' of the world (Craik, 1943, p.59). There is now abundant evidence to suggest that the mind operates according to principles of economy and principles of consistency (Steinbruner, 1974). The result is that, once formed, certain beliefs may be very resistant to change. To quote Steinbruner:

> The principle of stability asserts that cognitive inference mechanisms resist change in the core structure of beliefs. Because of extensive lateral and hierarchical relationships within a system of beliefs – each of which must be held to some level of consistency – a major restructuring of beliefs is likely to set off a chain reaction, imposing severe burdens upon the information processing system. Economy thus requires a bias against change in major components of belief structure once they have been established. (1974, p.102.)

There is a very large literature which shows some of the moves we make to keep our cognitions simple, stable, and consistent.[26] These include seeking self-serving analogies;[27] engaging in various forms of wishful thinking; the use of negative logic;[28] relying on a small number of highly salient cues; seeking out evidence to strengthen our beliefs; overweighting evidence which is consistent with our beliefs; underweighting evidence which is not; and polarizing judgements (especially if different alternatives are championed by members of competing groups). The net effect is that people see too much order and certainty in their social worlds; have too much confidence that their initial diagnoses are correct; form strong, categorical beliefs, even when evidence is mixed; and prefer explanations which are simple to explanations which are complex.

Evidence of this kind has some clear implications for the way we think about project work. The best known normative theory of decision making is subjectively expected utility (SEU) theory. It has been described as 'one of the impressive intellectual achievements of the twentieth century' by no less a person than Herbert Simon. However, as Simon went on to say, the theory is 'impossible to employ . . . in any literal way' because it assumes that people comprehend everything that lies before them 'in one comprehensive view' (see Simon, 1983, pp.12–14). In his view what is required is a theory which substitutes a vision of 'omniscient' rationality with one of 'bounded' rationality.[29]

Actually, there are two rather different kinds of bounded rationality. In the first case, the process is one which satisfies some of the assumptions of the original SEU model. It is still assumed that the person is trying to make the best possible choice, but the requirements of the process are scaled down so that it is possible to use the models as practical guides to action. This form of bounded rationality is called optimizing. Writers such as Steinbruner (1974) call the models 'analytic'.[30] In the second case, the process is one in which the person gives up any attempt to find the best possible choice. He or she is seeking only to find a choice that satisfies a small set of major constraints, so that it is acceptable, or at least good enough for now. This form of bounded rationality is called satisficing. It seems likely that the intellectual effort required by optimizing will mean that it is not always used, even when it seems clearly to be required (Janis and Mann, 1977).[31]

One reason may be that people feel severe stress when the demands of project work threaten to exceed their personal capabilities and/or their collective resources (McGrath, 1970). The central idea is that stress comes from the feeling that events are out of control. Such feelings may be particularly acute when people have to make important decisions, but have serious doubts about each and all of the options available (Janis and Mann, 1977). They may then feel that they will be damned whatever they do. Under such circumstances the likelihood that they will actively engage in open-minded thinking is much reduced.

Severe stress has a number of different kinds of effect. The first is to narrow the ways in which we diagnose issues and develop solutions. Wohl's (1981) review is one of many which shows that stress means people consider fewer alternatives, search less actively, and overreact to isolated pieces of information. Others go further and argue that stress means that individuals engage in information processing which is distorted, or even pathological. Janis and Mann, for example, identify a form of 'defensive avoidance' in which people produce 'flimsy rationalizations' which let them 'set aside their worries' (p.125). They refer to the cognitive mechanisms which produce these effects as cognitive defences (similar in some ways to Freudian mechanisms of defence, but different in others). It is also fairly well documented that, as stress increases, people in mixed-motive relationships see themselves as having less freedom of choice, and see their opponents as having more (Holsti, 1972).

The second kind of effect is that we may look for ways to leave the project. If we are forced to remain we may opt out psychologically in a number of ways. One method involves what Janis and Mann (1977) call evasion. Essentially, we allow ourselves to be distracted by other activities. We may take alcohol or drugs, or even develop 'fatalistic beliefs that support a precariously optimistic outlook' (Janis and Mann, 1977, p.58). A second method involves trying to 'pass the buck' to someone of higher status. We may then devote time and effort to find reasons to justify the conclusions we think they would like to reach . This is one reason why non-directive leadership processes are taken to be important in a wide variety of project groups.[32]

The third kind of effect is that we vacillate between alternatives, demonstrating a form of uncommitted thinking (Janis and Mann, 1977). In extreme cases we may even fail to act at all (Wohl, 1981).

Finally, when stress is intense and prolonged it sometimes produces a syndrome known as burnout (Paine, 1982). Those who suffer from it become physically exhausted and emotionally depressed. They develop negative attitudes about themselves and others, and about their projects. They feel that there is little they can do and that there isn't much that is worth doing. If the syndrome is recognized it may be reversed. According to Baron (1986) the people concerned have to admit there is a problem; change their priorities accordingly; establish a network of social support; and take actions which prevent them from becoming completely 'wrapped up' in their work.

Making sense of the world

Those outside psychology frequently view the discipline as dominated by behaviourism. For a while this approach dominated experimental psychology in America, but exerted much less influence in Europe, and elsewhere. Whatever its merits, it is now very widely agreed that behaviourism denied 'far too much of consequence in human behavior' and that, as a theoretical position, it is 'largely of historical interest' (Gardner, 1985, p.110). It has been replaced by a view in which the mind actively engages its environment so that information is selected, transformed, and enriched. These days, no psychologist would be surprised to learn that cognition involves a set of constructive processes.

Nowhere has this been demonstrated more clearly than in Bartlett's studies of remembering. Bartlett himself described the process as one of 'imaginative reconstruction, or construction, built out of the relation of our attitude towards a whole active mass of experience, and to a little outstanding detail which commonly appears in image or in language form' (Bartlett, 1932, p.213). He based this conclusion on a number of experiments, including some in which people were asked to read a version of a North American Folk tale, called 'The War of the Ghosts' (just over three hundred words long). They were then asked (repeatedly) to remember as much of the story as they could. Bartlett found that what emerged was an imaginative reconstruction involving condensation, elaboration, and invention. Most people remembered some dominant details and organized what they had to say around some main theme. However, they would regularly omit other details, supply their own causal links, and revise the plot, transforming the elements into a more familiar form. More recently, Neisser (1982) has described the testimony of John Dean, before the 'Watergate' Committee of the United States Senate, as constructed, staged and self-centred. He suggested that what Dean recalled as specific episodes were really 'screen memories' which accurately represented the theme of a series of conversations with Nixon, although the particular episodes described did not always occur. For these reasons, and for others, we may be quite clear that memory in particular, and cognitive processes in general, involve a good deal of inference (also see Steinbruner, 1974).

Exactly how we go about constructing our cognitions is a very complex business. Neisser has commented that:

> The circumstances and the man conspired to favor exaggeration. The events were important; his testimony was critical; its effect was historic. Dean was too intelligent not to know what he was doing, and too ambitious and too egocentric to remain unaffected by it. His ambitions reorganized his recollections: even when he tries to tell the truth, he can't help emphasizing his own role in every event. A different man in the same position might have reported more dispassionately, reflected on his experiences more thoughtfully, and reported them more accurately. Unfortunately such traits of character are rare. (1982, p.157)

To make a similar point in a rather different way, we might say that what is reported is a joint function of what is in the head and what is in the world. Indeed, we might say that all kinds of actions are determined by combining information in the head with information in the world.

Recently, Donald Norman has expressed this view in a quite striking form. He has been concerned with the design of everyday objects, such as telephones, switches, computers, and buildings. He has suggested that objects which are well-designed give us visible clues to their use which mean it is easy to see how they work. In contrast, objects which are badly designed give us too little help, so that obvious possibilities seem equally likely, or provide the wrong kind of help, so that what seems most likely turns out to 'trap the user'(Norman, 1988, p.2). We think that this design metaphor is important, but would like to restate it in relational terms. When everyday objects are well designed the designer works with the end user to find out how that object is likely to be used, and what that end user needs to know. When it has been established what the end user does know, it is then possible to design the object so that the operation of the object is visible to that user. To extend the metaphor we may say that social contexts are badly designed for a particular person when they fail to provide that person with visible clues which help him or her to understand that social context, considered as a setting for project work. Put simply, contexts which are well designed help people to make appropriate inferences about what is happening and why. They help people orient themselves to their social worlds.[33] We shall use this extended version of the design metaphor at several points in the arguments which follow later in the book.

Knowledge, expertise and skill

If modern psychology has shown anything it is that intelligent action is only possible because of all kinds of knowledge which, ordinarily, we take for granted. Some of this knowledge is task specific and some is of a more general kind. We shall consider the importance of each in turn.

Much of what we know about the importance of task specific knowledge has come from the study of those who are experts at games such as chess, or Gomoku (see Weisberg, 1980). A typical conclusion is that of De Groot. Apparently, 'a master is a master primarily by virtue of what he has been able to build up by experience; and this is: (a) a schooled and highly specific *way of perceiving*, and (b) a system of reproductively available methods, *in memory*' (De Groot, 1965, p.308). De Groot's research has shown that the difference between master and apprentice is that the master:

> quite literally 'sees' the position in a totally different (and much more adequate) way than a weaker player. The vast difference between the two in efficiency, particularly in the amount of time to find out what the core problem is (what's cooking really) and to discover highly specific, and adequate means of thought and board action, need not and must not be primarily ascribed to large differences in 'natural' power for abstraction. The difference is mainly due to differences in perception. (De Groot, 1965, p.306)

Because of an extensive and detailed study of the game of chess experts immediately see a position as similar to ones they have seen before, implying certain kinds of threat and certain kinds of opportunity. They can therefore go to work directly to handle the threats or exploit the opportunities.[34] The expert is an expert because he or she has learned to see relatively quickly what other people may never see at all. Thus, the skilled actor is a skilled perceiver.[35]

There is, however, no reason to believe that people who are skilled at chess will be skilled in other relational settings. Knowing whether someone has one set of abilities has not proven a reliable guide that they will have others. This is why faculty psychology has been coming back into fashion (see Gardner, 1983). A faculty is a set of abilities which is domain specific. There is little agreement about the number of faculties, partly because there is little agreement about the different domains.

Nevertheless, there seems good reason to suppose that executives who transfer from one industrial sector to another are unlikely to be effective until they learn the 'dominant competence' of their new enterprise (McKelvey, 1981). Part of the reason is that a major determinant of occupational success seems to be tacit knowledge of a kind which is rarely taught explicitly, but is learned with experience of particular relational settings (Wagner and Sternberg, 1986). It seems likely that those who will make the transfer most effectively will be those who have learned metacognitive skills which mean they have learned how to learn (Sternberg, 1985b). It also seems likely that they will build close relationships with those who are able to help them gain the right kind of experience with the right kind of projects. To judge from his memoirs, this is exactly what Ian MacGregor did when he first became Chairman of the National Coal Board (MacGregor, 1985).

This is not to say that people who are successful in different domains have nothing in common. Klemp and McClelland (1986) examined the characteristics that differentiated outstanding from average performers in a sample of senior managers from different kinds of organization. They found that outstanding performers paid more attention to *intellectual* tasks, such as seeking information to diagnose a problem; and to *influence* tasks, such as building ownership of controversial decisions. In addition, although they recognized difficulties, they 'never expressed any doubt that they would ultimately succeed' (Klemp and McClelland, 1986, p.42). The distinction between intellectual competencies and influence competencies, or something like it, is central to our account of the skills of organizing. However, we will stress the constructive nature of cognition and will stress the importance of social relationships in those constructions. This means, for example, that talk of the 'dominant competence' of an enterprise must involve talk of the culture that participants create. To develop this argument we must turn to the contributions of social psychology.

Social psychology

Social psychology is the study of how people think, feel, act and learn when they are with others, or when they have others in mind. Once again, to understand the central topics we need to explore the interaction between personal structure and social context (see Crano and Messé, 1982). However, to a social psychologist the most important aspect of our personal structure is that we give significance to social events by representing them symbolically in the form of evaluative beliefs. The most important aspect of the social context is that *it is made up of relationships with other people*. Once again, we shall see that people are both products of their social contexts and participants in the shaping of those contexts.

Kelly's work on personal construct theory shows quite clearly that the social context is not inherently orderly. Rather, it is *given an order* when people construe what is happening in terms of one set of constructs rather than another. That is to say, people make sense of their world by using more or less systematically organized systems of evaluative beliefs. The result is that people construct what Kelvin (1970) has called an *order of value*.

We shall use the term evaluative belief rather widely, to include opinions, attitudes, values and socially defined rules of conduct (called norms)(see Crano and Messé, 1982). One central message from social psychological research has been that our evaluative beliefs are very much more affected by the context in which they are to be expressed than we would ordinarily suppose. Thus, making sense of the world is social rather than solitary. What we learn, and how we express that learning, is very much affected by those we meet, where we meet them, and by our relationships with them.[36] Once again, we must reject any straightforward idea that people are fixed entities, so that we can describe what they bring to a situation in entirely straightforward ways. In a very real sense, who they are, what they are, and what they do, depends on who they are with and why.

The concept of an evaluative belief is one way to recognize that cognitions are value laden. When people are working on projects 'we find a high degree of ego involvement in prior commitments, persistent longing for gains they expect, and acute worry about the high costs and risks of intolerable losses' (Janis and Mann, 1977, p.45). Social psychologists say that their cognitions are 'hot' cognitions. Janis and Mann have used the metaphor of hot cognitions to remind us that people may be so beset by 'conflict, doubts, and worry' or struggling with such 'incongruous longings, antipathies, and loyalties' that they 'seek relief' by engaging in various forms of 'defensive avoidance', such as procrastination, rationalization, and 'passing the buck' (see Janis and Mann, 1977, Chapter 1 and Chapter 3). Consequently, people may be seen as 'reluctant' decision-makers. Janis and Mann have used the metaphor of the reluctant decision-maker to suggest that people may be capable of using either optimizing or satisficing strategies as they go about their project work. Which strategy they use will be a function of various aspects of their social contexts. Janis and Mann (1977) have made a thoroughgoing attempt to say just what these aspects are, and how they are related. We shall consider their work in more detail in Chapter 4.

The individual and the group

One of the central issues in the study of social psychology is 'how best to conceive of the initiative of individuals and the power of groups over them' (Asch, 1952, p.241). Asch's own text remains one of the best treatments of this topic. His main concern is to find some middle ground between those positions which we have called individualistic and those positions which we have called culturalistic. He argues that to do so we must 'take into account what both positions lack', namely 'an understanding of the fact of psychological interaction and the mutually shared field that it produces' (Asch, 1952, p.251). In his view, we must understand how it is that individuals and groups are both 'distinct' and 'inseparable'. We think that Asch has shown how this understanding is to be achieved. He has written elegantly and with precision. What he has to say is extremely important, and we shall quote him at some length.

> We need a way of understanding group processes that retains the prime reality of individual *and* group, the two permanent poles of all social processes. We need to see group forces arising out of the actions of individuals and individuals whose actions are a function of the group forces themselves (or others) have brought into existence. We must see group phenomena as both *the product and condition* of actions of individuals (1952, p.251)

It is the joint concern with both the social and the psychological that may be taken to distinguish psychology from some of the other social sciences. According to Asch, the way to retain an emphasis on the individual without committing the individualistic fallacy is to recognize that:

> there are group actions that are possible only when each participant has a representation that includes the actions of others and their relations. The respective actions converge relevantly, assist and supplement each other only when the joint situation is represented in each and when the representations are structurally similar. Only when these conditions are given can individuals subordinate themselves to the requirements of joint action. These representations and the actions they initiate bring group facts into existence and produce the phenomenal solidity of group processes. They are also the conditions necessary for the idea of a goal that can be achieved jointly.
>
> When these conditions are given we have a social system or a process of a definite form that embraces the actions of a number of individuals. Such a system does not reside in the individuals taken separately, though each individual contributes to it; nor does it reside outside them; *it is present in the interrelations between the activities of individuals* (emphasis added). (*ibid.*, 1952, pp.251–2)

People, we may say, represent contexts symbolically to themselves. That symbolic representation includes a view of how other people represent those contexts symbolically to themselves. According to Asch, this means that the relationship between the individual and the group is a part-whole relation 'unprecedented in nature' (p.257). In his view, the ability of people to represent relations within the group, both actual and possible, permits the mutual adjustment of different lines of action, to cooperate or to compete. It also means that, although people derive many of their thoughts and feelings from membership in groups, the group need not 'absorb' them completely. They may have thoughts and feelings which are idiosyncratic, or coincide with those of other members, or oppose those of other members. Consequently, Asch has concluded that people 'need not be, and indeed cannot completely be, a mere instrument of social forces. Each person is a centre of forces for the group' (p.258). As he has said, 'No account of group process can hope to make progress if it fails to find a place both for the initiative of individuals and for the power of groups over them' (p.258). We see in Asch's writing the beginnings of a model of social action similar to that subsequently set out by Harré (Harré and Secord, 1972; Harré, 1979).[37]

Harré's model of social action

Harré (1979) has attempted to articulate what he calls a 'performance theory of social action'. We shall select just three strands from this work. The first strand is a treatment of the relationship between people and environments which is very similar to that of Asch. Harré has argued strongly for a position which ultimately derives from the work of the philosopher Immanuel Kant. In his own words:

The Kantian position would treat the social and even the physical environment as a complex product of interaction between persons as active agents and the environment as a plastic construction that can be endowed with causal powers through the meaning-giving acts of agents. Environments do not exist in their fullness independently of the agents who enter them. They are in part created by the way the individuals who enter them assign meanings to the people, activities, settings, and social situations they find within them and even actively create. Then they are themselves affected by that which they have created. (Harré, 1979, p.143)

The second strand is to argue that we must shift away from trait approaches in which what a person does is merely a manifestation of those traits. We think that Harré has failed to appreciate the sophistication of some of the thinking about traits. Nevertheless, we are very much in agreement that we need to shift 'to the idea of a person as agent who uses or fails to use the cognitive equipment, social knowledge, and so on' that he, or she, 'has to hand' (Harré, 1979, p.267).

The third strand is about the importance of making public commitments and being held to account for them. When we make a public commitment to a project we are committing ourselves to certain lines of action. When we account for our actions publicly we describe what we have done so that people see this line of action rather than that. We may therefore be able to 'transform' our actions after the event. These points are important because:

if by accounting an actor can create and recreate actions and acts by use of publicly, socially intelligible speech to give specific meanings to human activity, *then it would be a serious error to look for the generative mechanisms of social activity only in the private and personal states and processes of individual human beings* . . . . By making a public commitment to a certain project an actor can generate actions prior to the over behaviour that realizes them concretely, just as he [or she] can create them posterior to that behaviour by accounting. Both activities play an important part in the genesis of human social life. (1979, p.273; emphasis added)

Evidently, we need a more detailed examination of the the role of commitment and of accounting in intelligent social action.

Conversations, commitments and intelligent social action

One way of looking at a project is to see it as a set of conversations, each committing someone to some future action, with the expectation that they will have to justify their actions, or their failures to act.[38] Much of this work has developed from the ideas of Winograd and Flores. They espouse a language-action perspective in which each manager has the job of generating and maintaining various networks of 'conversations for action' so that 'requests and communications lead to successful completion of work' (Winograd & Flores, 1986, p.144). One way of summarizing what this work has to offer is to note that communication has pragmatic, structuring and semantic aspects (De Cindio, De Michelis and Simone, 1988). We shall consider each of these in turn.

There is a *pragmatic* aspect to the communication because constructing a project means engaging in conversations about present actions and about possibilities for future actions. The conversations may be written or they may be spoken. But, if Winograd and Flores are correct, each speech act, whether written or spoken, commits the speaker to some sort of future action, developing a relationship with some other person.

There is a *structuring* aspect to the communication because the commitments function to coordinate project work. One aspect of this is that we may define roles in terms of commitments to produce or consume certain kinds of message in certain kinds of conversations. A second aspect is that those engaged in a project remember which commitments were made, and why, and with what effects. They use these memories to adapt, shape, or select new commitments so that the project is more likely to give them what they want. Since the future shape of the project is determined by what people remember of its past there is a clear sense in which those who control the past control the future (Middleton and Edwards, 1990). Consequently, people will be very anxious retrospectively to make sense of their actions, putting the best possible gloss on their contributions to the relationships of concern.

Finally, there is a *semantic* aspect to communication because members of a project group create a situationally determined 'world of words' in which words may have special meanings. It is this world of words which creates 'a linguistic consensual image of the domain of possible action of the group itself' (De Cindio, De Michelis, and De Simone, 1988, p.247). We shall return to this theme in Chapter 4 and Chapter 5.

Taken together, these dimensions of communication provide a history of shared experience which defines the *culture* of a group. Thus, talk about organizational culture is not a new and special topic. It arises immediately as soon as we examine the nature of conversations for action. What emerges from those conversations is a social order which reflects the values and commitments of the participants. It is a social order which is always emerging.

To explain the emergence of such order simply as a function of the personalities of the participants would be a mistake. It would miss the important point that the relationship between people and contexts is one of mutual creation. Furthermore, as we have already said, the social order is a negotiated social order. What is evident from studies of the creation of settings is that from the word 'go', 'conflicts arise about goals, tactics, and communication, and the resolution of these conflicts may be accomplished, postponed, or be of such strength that members leave to form their own setting' (Sarason, 1972, p.9). These arguments will be developed further in Chapter 3.

Of course, the process is one which may be influenced deliberately. Indeed, we shall argue that some people are obligated to take a major role in attempts to organize social processes so that the social order which emerges has certain desirable characteristics. In particular, we shall argue that skilful leadership is required to promote relationships in which people see the emerging processes as legible (meaning that actions are relatively unambiguous); coherent (meaning that they are able to see an integrated structure in the process); and open-ended (meaning that the social order is flexible, and may be renewed in response to events inside and outside the group). Relationships of this kind may be seen in highly productive groups. They define what has been called a 'culture of productivity' (Akin and Hopelain, 1986).

What we are saying, essentially, is that organizational structure comes from *structure in the process of projects*. And structure in process is generated by psychological factors such as our memories of what has happened in the past, and why. It is also worth noting that as soon as we shift to the analysis of conversations for action we have to talk about individual and collective processes *at the same time*. Thus, the individual and the collective become different sides of the same coin.

Summary

People use their intelligence in the service of projects which they hope will add value to their lives. The projects are constructed around collective decision-making tasks requiring conversations about present and future actions. The conversations commit people to future actions designed to satisfy both the practical and the expressive aspects of their social lives. Thus, people make personal investments in projects. However, the kinds of investments they will be willing to make in the future depends on how they understand the history of the setting. They use their understanding (intellectual competencies) to adapt, shape, or select new commitments (influence competencies) so that the project is more likely to add value to their lives. The concept of a person required for the study of organizing is that of someone with the kind of personal structure which makes intelligent social action possible.

Apparently, students of business often see little point in studying psychology. This is extremely unfortunate because psychology has a very great deal to say about the nature of the relationships between people and the contexts in which they live and work. There are two mistakes to avoid. One is to view people independently of contexts (leading to the individualistic fallacy). The other is to view contexts independently of people (leading to the culturalistic fallacy). It is essential, instead, to see the relationship between people and contexts as one of mutual creation. People are both products of their contexts and participants in the shaping of those contexts. They act *in* the contexts and act *on* the contexts.

The most important aspects of the context are other people. Attempts to progress work on a project may be welcomed, tolerated, or actively resisted, according to different conceptions of the threats and opportunities which lie ahead. What emerges is a negotiated social order which reflects both practical and expressive concerns. It is an order which continues to emerge. What we call organizational structure is essentially structure in the process of projects. It is not something to be defined independently of people and the way they work. It is something to be understood by talking about individual and collective processes at the same time. Such processes may be illuminated by contributions from personality theory, cognitive psychology, and social psychology.

Our review of personality theories identified various personality traits and types. These produced marked individual differences in the ways people approached the stages of project work (identification, development, selection, and implementation). We have suggested that each personal characteristic or trait may be a source of strength or a source of weakness, depending on the context. We have emphasized that people will attempt to seek out just those contexts (and just those projects) which mean they will be able to show their strengths rather than expose their weaknesses.

Our review of cognitive psychology has also helped us to build a model of our human minds. The main features of the model are that certain features of our minds limit our capacity to process information; that information from our senses is selected, transformed, and enriched; and that the mind is made up of a number of faculties. From an information processing point of view we may say that our worlds are well designed when they help us to find efficient strategies, matching our capacities to the demands of the task, and when they help us to see what is happening, and why. The idea that the mind is made up of a number of faculties reminds us that expertise is domain specific. Successful performers build up task specific knowledge which lets them see relatively quickly what other people may never see at all. In the case of management, there is evidence that successful performers pay more attention than other people to certain cognitive, social, and political problems which arise in project work.

Our review of social psychology shows that we may think of social contexts as relational settings. It is clear that what we learn, and how we express that learning, is very much affected by those we meet, where we meet them, and by our relationship with them. In other words, as relationships change so cognitions change. In particular, the same person may take quite different attitudes to the processing of information in different social settings. Unlike personality theory and cognitive psychology, social psychology takes as one of its central concerns the study of collective action. It is important to note that this is not just a matter of aggregating the contributions from different individuals. Rather, a social order emerges as people try to agree a set of shared descriptions to be used to monitor, control, interpret, and justify their actions. The social order which emerges reflects the values, interests, and commitments of the participants. But these change as circumstances change. Consequently, the social order is always emerging.

Notes

1. The terms assimilation and accommodation come from Piaget. Wood (1988) has provided an excellent introduction to Piaget's work. His own treatment of how children think and learn contains much that is valuable to a more general consideration of the nature of intelligent social action.
2. Intelligent social action may involve adapting to a project (accepting the current constraints); shaping the project (changing the constraints); or selecting a project (getting involved in this project rather than that).
3. Sarason (1972) would say that intelligent social action is needed to construct social settings. He has defined a setting as 'any instance in which two or more people come together in new relationships over a sustained period of time in order to achieve certain goals' (p.1). However, he has not made the mistake of assuming the goals are shared by all participants in the relationship. He has therefore attempted to illustrate some of the intellectual and interpersonal problems participants face in working out the terms on which they will continue to meet and work. He has shown that unless these problems are recognized, taken very seriously, and intelligently managed, it is all too easy to construct a social setting which fails to solve substantive problems. To quote Sarason, 'The problem is not how to have a live and functioning setting but how to have one which is true to its purposes' (p.43).
4. This is one way of saying that people want to preserve images of themselves as certain kinds of people (such as rational actors). It is one way of summarizing some of the central themes of a relatively new theory of decision-making called image theory (see Mitchell, Rediker, and Beach, 1986).
5. Our view of negotiation is thus very much wider that that espoused by writers such as Bernstein and Berbaum (1983), who treat it as only one element or 'routine' in the selection stage.
6. Friedman and Rosenman (1974) and Glass (1977) have identified a pattern of activity which is likely to increase the chance of someone having coronary heart disease. This pattern is called the type A pattern. The opposite pattern is called the type B pattern. Broadly speaking, type A people have extremely high needs for mastery and control of physical and social domains. They are characterized by competitive striving for achievement. They perceive time passing rapidly and, under certain conditions, may become extremely irritable, even hostile, when things are not going well. They are the classic 'workaholics', and work near their 'maximum' even without deadlines. As Baron says, 'they seem to develop a kind of tolerance for work, so that the more effort they expend, the more they feel the need for even greater challenge' (Baron, 1986, p.185). When they fail they tend to blame only themselves and become extremely pessimistic.

    Self monitoring refers to the difference between pragmatic and principled selves. The distinction is complex. Part of what is meant is this. When we are uncertain what to do there are two possible reactions. One is to look to other people, to see what clues they provide. The other is to look 'inside' and examine one's own values, attitudes, and beliefs. The first kind of person is called a pragmatic self and the second a principled self. For further information the reader is referred to Snyder (1979, 1987).

    Machiavellianism is a complex trait, linked to needs for esteem, and based on the work of Christie and Geis (1970). Like Machiavelli himself, those who score highly on the tests are seen as willing and able to manipulate others, often in very opportunistic ways. Baron (1986) presents a very unflattering picture of what this might mean, and advises how to guard against such people. However, at times Christie and Geis write as if the central core of the trait were the ability to handle others effectively. This has much less negative connotations. There is evidence that Machiavellians are sometimes effective leaders, able to structure problems for others, and to enlist their commitment and support (Geis, 1978).

7. London and Exner (1978, p.xiv) have noted 'the heterogeneity of concepts studied under the rubric of dimensions or personality or personality traits.' They have commented that 'There obviously has been no overarching plan...guiding the selection of topics for trait researchers'. This meant that they 'were forced to organize the book by means of the unsophisticated tactic of simply placing the chapters in alphabetical order'.

8. Hampson (1988) has argued that this requires coverage of five broad areas which identify what we really need to know about other people, namely: whether they will dominate us; whether we will like them; whether they can be trusted to do a good job; whether they are crazy; and whether they are smart. The implication is that we need five sets of traits: to do with extraversion; agreeableness; conscientiousness; emotional stability; and culture.

9. Aronoff and Wilson have used slightly different terminology. They have also included a separate stage to do with the planning and organization of work. We prefer to think that this is involved within and between each stage.

10. Axes of this kind are quite common in social psychology (see Leary, 1957; Carson, 1970; and Bales and Cohen, 1979). Aronoff and Wilson have defined the task dimension in terms of a contrast between initiation and concurrence. They have defined the social-emotional dimension in terms of a contrast between affiliation and disaffiliation. The axes are used to identify four performance styles: initiation plus affiliation; initiation plus disaffiliation; concurrence plus affiliation; and concurrence plus disaffiliation.

11. The four modes are defined in terms of two familiar contrasts. The first is that of co-operation versus competition. The second is that of information revealing versus information concealing. The adversarial mode is competitive and information revealing. The exploitative mode is competitive and information concealing. The ingratiating mode is cooperative and information concealing. Finally, the integrative mode is cooperative and information revealing.

12. This sort of emphasis is also evident in the work of Lawrence and Lorsch (1967b), Mason and Mitroff (1973), and Keen and Morton (1978).

13. Conventionalism means a rigid adherence to conventional middle-class values. Authoritarian submission means a submissive, uncritical attitude toward those given authority within the in-group. Authoritarian aggression means a tendency to seek out, condemn, reject, and punish people who violate the values of the in-group. See Adorno, Frenkel-Brunswik, Levinson and Sanford (1950).

14. There is some truth in this. For example, Billig (1978) found that some members of the National Front looked very like the classic authoritarian personalities described by Adorno *et al.* However, this was only part of the story. Billig has produced very powerful arguments to show that the analysis of ideology, social movements, etc. requires principles other than those derived from individual psychology (Billig, 1976; 1978).

15. Sanford (1973) has made this point very clearly. This sort of emphasis has also been evident in the wrings of R.D.Laing, whose work may be regarded as a contextual modification of traditional Freudian theory (see Collier, 1977).

16. Dixon has argued that each of the case studies shows what 'is essentially a human problem – a product of human behaviour, human intellect, human character, and

human error. No explanation in terms of geography, climate, broad political or military considerations can possibly do justice to the facts. At bottom (and at the top) we are confronted with issues that are primarily psychological and which only a reduction to psychological principles can possibly explain.'(Dixon, 1976, p.131).

17. Perhaps the most extreme example is provided by the case of Vice Admiral Markham, who did not question what seemed to be an impossible order from his Commander in Chief. The result was a collision in which H.M.S. Victoria sank with a very large loss of life. Here, Dixon relies on only one text, that of Hough (1959). Hough makes it clear that Markham lacked 'the ability to concentrate, to make quick decisions, and to anticipate situations in the rapidly changing circumstances of fleet evolutions' (p.60). But the reasons for this are much harder to find. There are only a dozen or so pages of biographical material in Hough's book, and much of this is not germane to the present concerns. Inevitably, there is a tendency to pick up on one or two of the nine traits identified by Adorno *et al.*, and to generalize from them. Certainly, Markham is described as being morally fastidious and puritanical. He is also described as helpless without the support of authorized and established practice. What little evidence there is is consistent with Markham having an authoritarian personality, but that is the best one could say.

18. Some writers (such as Zimbardo, 1969) have taken the view that, essentially, there are two sides to human nature. One is conscious, deliberate, calculating and rational. The other is unconscious, spontaneous, thoughtless and irrational. It is suggested that the latter may sometimes override the former so that, rather than doing what is required realistically, intelligent people may use their intelligence to sustain various kinds of neurotic dispositions and conceits. Dixon's research is very much in this latter tradition. He has expanded this theme in some of his later work (see Dixon, 1984, 1987).

19. Schizoid organizations also suffer from a leadership vacuum. In the case of schizoid organizations Kets de Vries and Miller have admitted that strategy is not usually a product of the intrapsychic fantasies of the chief executive. Evidently, 'The effective power for strategy making resides in a shifting coalition of careerist second-tier managers who try to influence the indecisive leader and simultaneously to advance their pet projects and their little empires . . . Strategy becomes more a product of individual goals, power, and politicking than any perceived key threats or opportunities in the external environment.' (Kets de Vries and Miller, 1984, p.39).

20. This is exactly what happened in the schizoid organization described by Kets de Vries and Miller. We see the similarities between depressive and schizoid interpersonal styles as more important than the differences, so we would expect similar responses to the leadership vacuum in some depressive organizations.

21. See Kets de Vries and Miller (1984) p.22. Also see Miller, Kets de Vries, and Toulouse (1982); Miller, Toulouse, and Belanger (1985); and Miller and Toulouse (1986).

22. The term culture of dependency comes from the work of Bion (1961). Bion argued that some groups developed shared fantasies which were founded in the unconscious motivations of their members. According to de Board (1978) such fantasies mean that the group acts 'as a closed system, ignoring external reality and defending itself from it' (p.42).

23. Useful introductions to Kelly's work are to be found in Fransella (1981), Rychlak (1981), and Sechrest (1983).

24. In Kelly's own words, 'If we reach an understanding of how a person behaves, we discover it in the manner in which he represents his circumstances to himself' (Kelly, 1955, p.16). Unlike other phenomenological theorists he was very much concerned to

provide methods to show just how people represented those circumstances to themselves. He described people's construct systems using a method which has become known as the Repertory Grid Technique. The use of this methodology has allowed psychologists to explore various formal properties of people's construct systems. Those who would like to explore the industrial applications of this technology are referred to Stewart and Stewart (1981).

25. Recently, the idea of limited capacity has been challenged by Neisser (1976). In his view what looks like a limit in capacity is really a matter of response compatibility. If we cannot do two things at once it is simply because we have learned the two things in ways which mean that it is difficult to put the two together. Given more time and effort who knows what could be achieved. Fortunately, however, we do not have to decide between these two positions. From a practical point of view, the result is the same. If we want people to do a number of difficult things at more or less the same time we will probably have to take special steps so that they are able to cope with the demands of the tasks. Welford (1980) has provided a very illuminating analysis of the kinds of moves which might be made.

26. Excellent reviews have been given by Jervis (1976); Kinder and Weiss (1978); Hogarth (1980); Nisbett and Ross (1980); Kruglanski and Ajzen (1983); Baron (1988) and Hogg and Abrams (1988).

27. As Baron (1988) has said: 'when supporters of United States intervention in Nicaragua search for historical analogies, they are likely to discover the Munich agreement with Hitler, and opponents, when they search for analogies, are likely to discover United States support of Batista in Cuba or the unsuccessful Bay of Pigs invasion' (p.258).

28. Foster (1986) has provided an extremely interesting discussion of the strengths and weaknesses of negative logic, with many practical examples. The topic is also discussed briefly in Steinbruner (1974).

29. SEU theory is designed to define rational choice in contexts where an actor is trying to choose between alternative policies. It is recognized that each policy may lead to a number of different states of the world, and that some states are more likely than others. Further, each state of the world is seen to have some advantages and some disadvantages. It is assumed that the actor is able to weight the advantages against the disadvantages in some consistent way (defining his or her utility function) so that a single cardinal number may be assigned to each state of the world, designating its net worth (or value). The utility of each possible state of the world is then weighted according to its likelihood (forming a product: probability times value). It is assumed that the environment is monitored and calculations updated as and when new information becomes available. Finally, the actor chooses that policy which maximizes his or her expected utility (computed by summing the products of probability and value across each possible state of the world). The theory has been heavily criticized because it represents an ideal of rationality which is quite impossible for people to attain. It has also been criticized because it says nothing at all about a number of important psychological processes. It has nothing to say about the construction of alternatives. It has nothing to say about the way values are organized and aggregated so that the actor is able consistently to apply a well defined utility function. It has nothing to say about the ways in which we ascertain what is happening now, and what is likely to happen in the future. Those who would like to read more about the theory and the various criticisms of it are referred to Steinbruner (1974).

30. According to Steinbruner (1974, pp.35–6) 'The quintessential analytic decision maker is one who strains toward as complete an understanding as possible of the causal forces

which determine outcomes. He [or she] seeks to predict the flow of events and, where he has leverage, to manipulate them to his advantage. The processing of information while making decisions is all done for the purpose of constructing and improving the blueprint from which the optimal choice emerges.'

31. The differences between the two forms of bounded rationality have been very well described by Steinbruner (1974) and by Janis and Mann (1977)

32. See Belbin (1981); Janis (1982a); Morley and Hosking (1984); Abetti (1986); Hosking and Morley (1988).

33. This is shown very clearly in Gombrich's (1979) analysis of the importance of global perception in decorative art. Consider his description of what might happen when we enter one of the courtyards of the halls of the Alhambra. To begin with, 'we react at first as we would react in any environment – we seek to orient ourselves. Such orientation takes time, but a very short time only because there is so much we feel entitled to take "as read". We do not have to focus on every pillar or window, for we rapidly and almost subliminally take in the continuities and the redundancies of the principal elements, their order and their position. . . . Our confidence in the orderly arrangement of the interior allows us to make use of peripheral and provisional inspection where there is no contrary evidence in sight. And perceiving the further orders of decorative enrichment we can continue in the same way, narrowing the visual span while still relying on the continuities vaguely perceived on its periphery' (p.116). Gombrich goes on to make the very important points that, 'We must resist the temptation to regard global perception as no more than careless perception. Thanks to the principle of progressive complication, we are able to absorb much more of the general character of a decoration than we can ever consciously analyse, let alone describe. . . .The skill and inventiveness of the master craftsman is not only aimed at our conscious awareness. It rests on the experience that we can sense the all-important distinction between confusion and profusion without piecemeal examination. We are confident that we are facing orders within orders which would respond to our probing for regularity without making us lose the feeling of infinite and inexhaustible variety' (p.116). The lesson to be learned is that we are more readily able to 'orient' ourselves to objects which have been properly designed because they provide us with helpful clues.

34. For further discussion of this point see Weisberg (1980) and Dreyfus and Dreyfus (1986).

35. Chess and Gomoku are examples of what Weisberg calls 'move' problems. They are well defined in the sense that the structure of the problem is given to the players. That is, their task is to move from an initial state to an end state, where the start, the finish, and the moves are all precisely defined. Other tasks used to study problem solving are much less well defined. Weisberg (1980) has made it clear that what counts as a solution, and what is available as a move, depends on the personal qualities of the person solving the problem. Thus, when we say a problem is well-defined or ill-defined we mean well-defined or ill-defined for that person. Practical problems in management are frequently extremely ill-defined in this sense (Mintzberg, 1973). That is to say, how the problem will be structured will depend on the qualities of the people involved in the project. Psychologists are beginning to pay much more attention to practical expertise of this kind.

36. See Asch (1952); Sherif and Sherif (1969); Steinbruner (1974); Abelson (1976); Crano and Messé (1982); Myers (1988); Hogg and Abrams (1988).

37. Harré and Secord have argued that social psychology has been dominated by a mechanistic model which 'has no literal employment in human social life' (p.17). In

their view traditional social psychology is quite inadequate to help us understand how we interpret the world and explain it. We see social psychology as having been more eclectic than they do. Harré's ideas have been extremely influential, however. At one time he was much concerned to argue that social psychology needed to adopt an 'ethogenic approach' in which social action was seen as governed by rules (Harré and Secord, 1972; Harré, 1977a, b; Schlenker, 1977). This led him to espouse a 'rule-role' model of social life based on a 'dramaturgical standpoint' in which life is seen as theatre. This standpoint is discussed in detail in Mangham and Overington (1987). There is also a very useful treatment in Billig (1989). Harré's more recent work recognizes, however, that rules do not 'have irresistible causal powers' (Harré, 1979, p.273). He has therefore attempted to flesh out the 'genesis of action' in more detail.

38. See Fikes (1982); Winograd and Flores (1986); De Cindio, De Michelis, and Simone (1988); Danielsen and Pankoke-Babatz (1988).

Chapter 2

People in organization

Introduction

In this chapter our focus shifts to the entitative concept of organization and its associated entitative concept of person. We present the culturalist fallacy and the individualistic fallacy at their most extreme. We do so in order to show what kind of concept of organization – what we shall call organizing – is required in order satisfactorily to theorize relations between persons and their contexts.

A case illustration

Qvortrup (1989) described the attempt, by Danish Television, to introduce a computerized filming, editing, and viewing system for the production of news and current affairs programmes. He did so to illustrate his argument that an entitative concept of organization dominates the design and implementation of computerized systems. Qvortrup suggested that the design of the computer-based system was premised on particular assumptions about the nature of the context (organization) within which the programme items were produced. One assumption was that production was organized as a continuous flow. Another was that programme units were produced through standardized procedures such that the method of their production was specified fully. Each item was seen as independent of all others; each was understood to be completed before a new one was begun. In these ways, production was understood to be routinized and formalized for all organizational members. Last, social relations analytically were reduced to flows of information – presumably concerning the production of individual items, and the flows of those items through the production system.

Taken together, these beliefs reflect a view of organization structures and production technologies as independent of the actors who were making the programmes. There was no recognition of the relationship between person and organization as one of mututal creation: a relationship in which, for example, a problem is seen as more or less structured depending on the actor(s) involved (see Chapter 1).

Attempts to implement the computerized system finally were abandoned – at great cost to the organization. The problem, argued Qvortrup, lay not with the hardware or the software. Rather, it lay with the designers' erroneous, entitative assumptions about the nature of organization. It seems that, in fact, programme items were not produced through routinized procedures which fully constrained the activities and interrelations of the operatives. Instead, the structure of the work process constantly was altered by the operatives on line, so to speak; steps in the specified procedures were ommitted, their ordering was changed, and so on. Further, it appears that programme items were not independent but were 'mutually interdependent' (Qvortrup, 1989, p.2). At any time, the actors' perceptions of external events could cause them to modify plans and processes. In other words, organization was, in fact, characterized by change. The structure in process (Chapter 1) reflected the participants' attempts to act intelligently sometimes by selecting, and sometimes by adapting to and shaping unforseen and perhaps unforseeable aspects of their context.

Last, by reducing social relations to information flows, the realities of what we have called conversations for action (Chapter 1) were ignored. In this way, the concept of organization excluded the processes in which social order constantly was sustained and created through processes of social influence, and in particular, through negotiation (see Qvortrup, 1989, and Chapter 1).

Entitative concepts in organization behaviour and organization studies

The entitative concept of organization dominates the literatures of Organizational Behaviour (OB) and Human Resource Management (HRM) (see Preface). An entitative approach to persons focuses on the characteristics and behaviour of individuals and groups 'in' organizations. Favourite topics include individual motivations and attitudes towards work, job design, leadership, and group dynamics. In these literatures we find a strangely mechanical, lifeless picture of persons, social relationships, and social action (see Chapter 1). In these literatures, *people* are the centre of interest, and person and organization are viewed as independent entities. For this reason, the concept of organization usually is implicit and undeveloped in the treatment of individuals and groups. In recent years it has become more usual explicitly to discuss organization. However, given that persons are theorized independently of their contexts, an entitative concept of organization inevitably follows (see, for example, Mitchell and Larson, 1987; Buchanan and Huczyinski, 1985).

The entitative concept of organization is more fully elaborated in parts of the Organization Studies (OS) literatures, broadly defined. These literatures consist of contributions from discipline-based subjects, particularly sociology and economics. They also reflect pragmatic interests in designing effective organizations and prescribing effective managerial styles. Contributions have come, for example, from practising managers (e.g. Fayol and Taylor), from sociologists (e.g. Weber), and from management consultants (e.g. Peters and Waterman). We will examine selected examples in which the entitative concept of organization is especially evident.

The elements of an entitative perspective

We have found only one explicit discussion of this perspective. This was by Meyer and his colleagues who suggested that the entitative approach has dominated studies of organizations (Meyer and associates, 1985). As they have said, '[We] have proceeded on the assumption that organizations were well defined units with identifiable, more or less permanent boundaries. We have assumed that since we knew what organizations were, entities called organizations were the appropriate units for research' (p.57). They went on to describe the essential, defining characteristic of the entitative approach as one in which the organization is viewed as a well defined unit or whole in its own right so to speak. We would add that organization is seen to require explanation as a whole, in its own right: this is where the assumption that person and organization are independent is most apparent. Meyer and his collegues suggested that the entitative perspective has five elements.

1. Membership and organizational boundaries. They noted that unlike informal groups, for example, an organization – in various ways – specifies who is and who is not a member. Membership specifications set the organization apart as an entity which is separate from other organizations or, more generally, separates an organization from its environment.

2. The whole has an identity of its own which is recognized by its members and by others.

3. The entity has a purpose or has purposes which are relatively well defined. This is a reference to what some have referred to as shared goals and/or shared values.

4. The entity has a structure which is formally prescribed, that is formalized, usually in some detail. So, for example, an organization chart will specify who is responsible for what, and to whom, will specify lines of communication, and will specify the hierarchy of authority. Structure is assumed to be a relatively stable characteristic of the organization as a whole, structures being seen as the means by which organizational purpose is translated into action.

5. The organization and its environment(s) are separate entities linked by relationships of exchange: the former takes inputs from the environment, converts, and exports them.

Meyer and his collegues went on to say that: 'the understanding of organizations as well defined entities has pervaded research, whether research has addressed closed-system, open system, or evolutionary theory'. If they are right about the entitative approach and where it is found, we should find the elements, summarized above, reflected in these literatures.

We shall continue by examining entitative treatments of organization. Our purpose, as noted earlier, is to show what we wish to reject in order to make our own position clear. Our reviews are highly selective and critical. They focus on arguments and assumptions concerning persons, organization, and their interrelations. For a more extended examination of these literatures, the interested reader is recommended to consult Rose (1975), Morgan (1986), and Pugh (1971).

Literatures will be reviewed under the following headings: early approaches to the design and management of organizations; the Human Relations approach; and organic systems approaches. Since all are characterized by entitative assumptions, the same criticisms – in varying degrees – apply in each case. For this reason, extended criticism is withheld until each literature has been examined. At that point, we will reconsider the elements of the entitative approach. Our criticisms of these elements identify major themes that we think especially important.

Early approaches to the design and management of organization

Here we will outline the early structural work of Max Weber. We also will examine the writings of two well known management theorists, Henri Fayol, and F.W. Taylor. They are, respectively, well known representatives of the so called classical, and scientific management schools.

Weber on bureaucracy
In his now famous work on bureaucratic organizations, Weber set out to identify the particular defining characteristics of this organizational form. He defined the pure, or 'ideal type' as characterized by hierarchical structures of authority; specialization of tasks and functions; and an impersonal, formalized (written) and explicit system of rules which specify obligations. These structures were argued to be grounded in, and to reflect, the 'rational-legal' authority of managers. Management's task was to administer rules in the rational pursuit of organizational goals.

Weber's interest in bureaucracy was not directed at persons or social relationships but focused on the organization as a unit of analysis. He argued that bureaucratic organization is effective because of 'technical knowledge'. For this reason, he argued it was crucial to exercise control through specialist techniques, knowledge, and skills. Weber reasoned that this was just as true in capitalist and socialist contexts and in large and small organizations, whatever their products or outputs.

Weber's arguments came increasingly to be questioned by critics such as Merton, Selznick, and Gouldner (see Pugh, 1971). Criticisms were drawn from research findings concerning the internal dynamics of the organization. Critics noted, for example, the many 'dysfunctional' consequences of specialization resulting in the division of labour, and the emphasis on formalized, impersonal rules. Attention was drawn to the ways in which persons, organized through specialization and hierarchy appeared to lack commitment to organizational goals, and to act in ways which implied disparity between organizational goals and work-group activities. Indeed, specialization was argued to create personal and sectional interests, and conflicts of interest, as actors sought to extend their power and control. Finally, the bureaucratic emphasis on impersonal control, and on predictable actions, was argued to lead to lost flexibility of action and therefore, to prejudice efficiency.

These are arguments about the interrelations between people and organization. They illustrate our earlier claim that the relationship between person and organization is one of mutual creation. In particular, such findings and arguments indicate that organizational structures influence the interests to which individuals and groups are committed and influence the processes through which they build and mobilize commitment. Research findings question the degree to which participants share organizational goals and, as a result, question the assumption of cooperative social relations. Critics question the degree to which bureaucratic structures direct and constrain activities in the mannner suggested by Weber; and also question the wholeness and identity of the bureaucratic organization. We will return to these themes when we describe contingency theories. Such theories reject the notion that a bureaucracy, or indeed any single organizational form, could constitute the one-best-way to organize.

Fayol and 'classical management' thought

Fayol described at length fourteen 'principles' of good practice (see Pugh, 1971). These included arguments about the desirable structural characteristics of organization. The principle of 'unity of command', for example, asserted that all employees should receive orders from only one superior. A further two structural principles concerned the division of work, and centralization of decisions concerning work standards, practices, and organization. The underlying arguments are very relevant to our present interests in an entitative perspective. For example, division of work, and centralization were noted to characterize organization in the animal world. These structural arrangements were believed to reflect natural principles of 'specialization' of function, and hierarchies of authority. In other words, Fayol implied that his principles necessarily were valid for social organization because they reflected nature's solution for organic systems.

In order efficiently to manage social organizations Fayol believed it was necessary to specialize functions; to separate doing from thinking; in a hierarchy of authority, to have 'unity of command', and to subordinate individual interests to the general interest. Fayol's arguments seldom are credited with the sophistication they deserve. Despite this, we will develop two broad lines of criticism which show something of what it is we wish to reject in an entitative perspective and which have important implications for any alternative.

The dualist treatment of competence. Fayol implied a sharp and natural distinction between two groups: managers and non-managers. This 'dualism' (Schein, 1980) suggests that only managers organize whilst non-managers do not; it depends on the explicit treatment of managers as a homogeneous group in the sense that all have certain personal competencies which non-managers do not. The former were assumed to have a natural right to manage through a hierarchy of authority – a natural form of organizing. Managers were seen as those who should make the decisions, for example, about organizational goals, means of payment, and discipline. Managers should see that human passions of employees (passions not possessed by managers?) do not prevail over the interests of the firm and the State. An *entitative concept of person* underlies this dualism: people in general are seen to have fixed, unchanging, qualities which set them apart from their contexts; managers are seen to have different competences from those possessed by non-managers.

The unitary treatment of interests. Fayol's perspective reflects the belief that the goals of management rightly are beyond question. These goals should provide the values (as standards) by which all organizing decisions and activities are judged. The goals of management were taken to be a matter of technical judgment, so to speak, to be value-free, and to be identical with the goals of the State. This assumption has been described as 'managerialist' (for example, Lee and Lawrence, 1985).

Fayol assumed that all managers share the *same goal*; he assumed that the goals of non-managers were compatible with those of management. The assumption that all individuals and groups share the same, or at least, compatible goals and interests sometimes is described as 'unitary' (e.g. Fox, 1966). Again, we find reflected here an entitative concept of person. However, whilst managers and non-managers are assumed to have different competencies (dualism), they are assumed to share the same or compatible goals. We first introduced evidence of differences in interest and commitment in our critique of Weber. This evidence presents a fundamental challenge to the unitary assumption that all actors necessarily share the same or compatible goals. This, in turn, raises the question of why managers' interests, assuming they have common interests amongst themselves, should be considered as any more legitimate than the interests of other identified groups. We will return to these issues to develop our arguments about political processes.

Taylor and 'scientific management'

Scientific management was emerging at around the same time as classical management. Taylor, an enginer, tried to build practical knowledge bases and techniques for organizing. The first of his 'principles' concerned the traditional practical knowledge of workers. He suggested that their rule of thumb methodology should be replaced with one which was scientific. By this he meant that the knowledge of workers should be made explicit, be brought together, be formalized, codified, and systematized. For Taylor, management would be scientific when managers practised:

1. The scientific measurement and organization of work through work study.

2. The scientific selection and development of employees through measurement of their personal characteristics and their work performance.

3. The organization of managers and workers through organization structures scientifically designed to separate thinking, particularly planning, from doing. This could best be done through a centralized and hierarchical decision-making structure, and through the grouping of tasks by function.

As is the case with Fayol, Taylor's work has been much misrepresented and it is worth consulting original texts. Taylor argued that one of the duties of management was deliberately to gather the 'great mass of traditional knowledge, which in the past has been in the heads of the workmen' (Taylor, in Pugh, 1971, p.125). Such knowledge could be gained through work study – through detailed observation and recording of the production process. Then this knowledge could be reduced to laws. The laws could be applied to increase financial surpluses for the good of all. It was supposed that 'The principles of scientific mangement when properly applied . . . must in all cases produce far larger and better results, both for the employer and the employees . . . ' (Pugh, 1971, p.124).

To begin with, let us make two general points. The first is that Taylor's concept of person was narrow, individualistic, and entitative. The second is that Taylor had little regard for social processes as a vehicle for the construction and performance of organization. Bearing this is mind, we shall consider how Taylor approached what we have called the political and cognitive aspects of social life. Much of what we have to say would apply equally to the work of Fayol, which has already been described.

Political aspects. Our reference to political aspects allows us to bring together and develop three lines of critique: the dualist treatment of competencies; unitary assumptions about goals and interests; and a physicalist separation of person and context which ignores sense-making processes.

As with Fayol, in Taylor we find an simple dualist distinction between management and worker. Each group was treated as internally homogeneous in their valuations and interests. All were seen to have a common, financial interest which could rationally be pursued. This being so, the interests of workers could be handed over to management for their protection and promotion. To elicit and to codify the knowledge of workers was seen simply as a technical, value-free device, that is, as a scientific method. However, as we have begun to show, interventions such as these cannot simply be technical as they are not value-free. Organizations cannot rightly be said to be characterized by shared goals. As we saw in our examination of Weber, actors differ in their relationships with their contexts such that they differ in the persons with whom they interact, differ in the tasks they perform, and may differ in the problems or issues with which they deal. Different contexts reflect and create differences in valuations. More generally, in their differing relations with other people and their projects, actors create relationships characterized by differing social constructions of reality (see Chapter 1). For these reasons, interventions such as those advocated by Taylor will be perceived by some as an opportunity to protect and promote efficiency. Others may view such interventions in relation to other valuations and see them instead as a threat to their autonomy and, for example, to their chances to have some slack time.

We need not assume that Taylor, or others like him, set out with strategic intent to disenfranchise workers. Conspiracy theories are not required. Nevertheless, Taylor's actions were *interested*, being grounded in particular valuations. His procedures and the resulting organizational structures constrain the possible relationships between actors and their contexts (remember, not anything goes).[1] As we shall see, relational processes are of significance, not least because of their influence qualities. When actors (persons and groups) differ in their relationships with their contexts, this has implications for the influence they can mobilize in relation to their own interests. So, for example, by having their knowledge collected and formalized by management, workers lost control over a valued informational resource. Studies have shown how information may constitute a significant potential power base and have shown that some actors at least may recognize this. For example, the computer programmers studied by Pettigrew (1973) did all that they could to avoid having their knowledge formalized and proceduralized, keeping control over the training of new programmers to protect and promote their own influence (see Chapter 5).

For us, Taylor's scientific principles highlight certain *political* aspects of organizing. First, actions, including attempts at technical and structural change, are grounded in more or less partisan valuations, that is, social constructions. Second, as they differ in their relations with their contexts, actors differ in their constructions of their contexts, that is, they differ in relation to particular valuations and interests. Third, and last, given that actors differ in their relations with their contexts, they also differ in the degree to which they are able to achieve influence in support of their own values and interests. These differences imply that organizing is, in part, a political process: a process performed by people, within and between groups, and by groups in relation to other groups.

Cognitive aspects. Our second area of comment focuses on Taylor's assumptions about cognitive and social processes. Taylor treated the actions of managers and workers as though they were goal directed, individual choices, arrived at out of a certain sort of systematic and exhaustive process. In other words, *decision-making processes* were asssumed necessarily to take a certain form – to be 'rational' (see Chapters 1 and 5). These processes were understood as *relatively solitary, comprehensive, analytical activities* of building understanding and taking action. Furthermore, financial interests were believed to play an exclusive and decisive role in determining processes of information search, interpretation, choice and implementation.

In Chapter 1, we laid out certain arguments and understandings concerning persons and relationships. Judged by what we understand today, Taylor greatly oversimplified and distorted what it is to be human. Cognitive processes do not take the form claimed by Taylor. They are not solitary. They are not characterized by 'omniscient' rationality but by 'bounded' rationality. They must be understood as 'in' and 'about' relational processes. They are individual and collective processes of social construction informed by, and performed in the context of social relations, past and present. As we saw in Chapter 1, actors adopt quite different approaches to sense-making depending on their context. Taylor analytically reduced social relations to flows of information and physical resources, as did the systems designers in the Danish Broadcasting Company. Taylor reduced social relations to formalized structures of *cooperation* in the rational pursuit of shared financial goals. As we have said, in these ways, Taylor failed to recognize that what actors believe is importantly affected by their social context: by who they are with and why they are there. Through what we have called 'conversations for action' actors influence, and are influenced by the valuations of others; they make more or less collective commitments to act in this or that way. Further, given their different relationships with their contexts, actors differ in their abilities to mobilize influence in relation to a particular issue. This means, for example, that social relations are not just relations of cooperation, but also are relations of competition and conflict to gain support for particular partisan valuations and interests.

Early approaches: Concepts of person and organization

What we have said so far may be brought together as a critique on the concepts of person and relational processes which flowed through early theories of managers, workers, and organization. The concept of person, particularly as it was elaborated in relation to workers, was individualistic, and therefore, what we have called entitative (see Chapter 1). Some have described it as a 'machine' concept of person (e.g. Morgan, 1986). However, when judged by today's standards, the machine looks very dated. The machine is simple, old, and lonely. The machine is simple in the sense that the worker, considered as a machine, was unable to learn, was unable to direct, control, or understand 'its' own performance, except in relation to financial incentives, and was unable to create something new. The machine is old in the sense that the 'smart' machines of the computer age can do much more than this. Last, but not least, the machine is lonely because it is treated as a closed system, open to its context, only through imports of money and exports of effort, regulated by management control. Non-managers were viewed as un-social entities, networked, so to speak, by other agents (managers and procedures), to other machines which they could not understand, and were equally un-social.

When non-managers are viewed as persons who have limited understanding and intelligence, and as isolated, a-social beings, it follows that managers, who are viewed as different kinds of persons, must provide the missing organization and control. Given these assumptions about non-managers, it follows that managers must specialize and fragment tasks; remove discretion from the point of production; routinize where possible; and structure activities and decisions through a stable hierarchy of authority. This is the dualism of which we spoke earlier. As we shall see in Chapter 3, a different concept of person implies a very different concept of organization.

The human relations approach

The label 'human relations' typically is applied to the themes which emerged from the Hawthorne Studies, conducted in America, in the Hawthorne Works of Western Electric.[2] The names of persons directly associated with these studies are Roethlisberger, Dickson, and Mayo (see e.g. Rose, 1975). The Hawthorne studies were conducted from the mid 1920s through to the the early 1940s. Their beginnings reflected the traditions of thought and practice already described, combined with the approach and interests of British 'human factors' psychology.[3] As far as the investigators were concerned, the studies consisted of the intentional variation of factors such as (i) physical aspects of the immediate work context (lighting levels), (ii) timing and length of rest pauses, and (iii) use of group bonus schemes. Dependent variables such as output levels were monitored and interviews conducted.

The conduct, reporting, and interpretation of the Hawthorne studies have been subject to considerable criticism. What is important for us here are the themes which have emerged from interpretations of their findings. First, the findings were taken to imply that the prevailing concept of person (or rather, non-managers) had to be revised to accommodate what otherwise could not be explained. A particularly important observation was the emergence, amongst production workers, of a social organization which was not planned, formalized, or legitimated by management, but rather, created, controlled, and legitimated by the workers themselves. The study of the Bank Wiring room, for example, is hailed as having demonstrated the emergence of informal but powerful norms – as shared standards (value) – specifying acceptable and unacceptable levels of production. 'Overproducers' and 'underproducers' were subjected to attempts to make the norms stick. Influence was attempted through relational processes in which social acceptance, satisfying social relationships, and a sense of belonging were manipulated by coworkers. Those who valued these relationships were amenable to the influence attempts of their coworkers. However, those who valued financial reward more than the acceptance of their peers, were more influenced by their relationships with management and the management systems of payment and work organization.

These findings were taken to imply that the concepts of person and organization should be revised to recognize that workers, to some extent, will organize themselves. It was recognized that, to some extent, non-managers will create, and be created by, their social relationships. Such findings were taken to imply that the concept of organization should be revised to recognize that individuals may act as members of groups, and therefore, organizing is done by and to groups, as well as by and to individuals.

For the full implications of these findings to be recognized, the entitative concept of person had to be rejected. It was not. Instead, the concept of a 'social need' was invented (see Schein, 1980). This is the second theme to emerge from the studies. It is one which constrained any more radical reformulation of the entitative perspective. Social needs simply replaced financial needs. It was assumed that social needs, such as needs for approval, support, acceptance, and belonging, constituted values which people would protect and promote through their actions in organizations. Why else would workers conform to informal norms restricting output and therefore reducing their earnings? By assuming workers had social needs, management was provided with new strategies for organizing workers. Their efforts now could be harnessed through the manipulation of social processes and social relationships. For example, group-based incentive schemes could be employed with groups of workers. Similarly, social relations between workers and supervisors could be manipulated through 'leadership' styles and through group-working.

A critique of the human relations approach to cognitive, social, and political processes

Perhaps the most important and most general conclusion is that the prevailing concept of person was not revised radically. The implicit dualist distinction between managers and non-managers was little questioned. The concept of person remained entitative. Social needs were seen to provide managers with instrumentalities which they could manipulate for the 'technical' purposes of regulation and control. Needs were taken to be what explained the direction and intensity of workers behaviour. Needs still were theorized as the properties of individuals stripped from their relational settings. Cognitive processes continued to abstracted from social and political processes; the relational and processual qualities of organizing had yet to be understood.

The dualist distinction between the competencies of managers and non-managers remained; along with the machine concept of the latter. No fundamental questions were asked about the organizing strategies of specialization, centralization of decision making, and hierarchical structures of authority. There were changes in work organization, a harnessing of social needs through group incentives, supportive supervisory styles, and so on. However, these changes were introduced and understood in the context of hierarchy. No fundamental challenge was felt to assumptions about effective organization structures, and therefore, to the sources of regulation and control; the values by which effectiveness should be judged were not shaken.

The non-manager still was seen as a lonely machine. Social processes, to the extent that they were considered at all, were theorized primarily as the expression of dynamics inside the individual – as 'spontaneous' phenomena serving intrapersonal needs. The entitative concept of person seems likely to account for the conservative interpretation of the findings. Many of those influenced by the human relations approach failed to recognize the significance of the emergent qualities of social processes. Equally, it was not appreciated that people created their own social order through relational processes (see Chapter 1).

It is crucial to recognize the significance that an entitative perspective has for the ways organization was understood. In an entitative perspective, persons are abstracted and sharply distinguished from their contexts. Like Russian dolls, persons and contexts are set apart from one another: persons are understood to be fitted into, or taken out of contexts; together or apart, each is seen to stay the same, and to retain a separate identity. The actions, evaluations, and interests of workers are believed to reflect their relatively fixed personal characteristics. In this view, persons can be selected and placed in organization. Since contexts are seen as independent of persons, contexts also can be manipulated. As a result, management is seen to have the technical task of manipulating structures in order better to harness the personal characteristics of workers; such a perspective is incapable of recognizing political processes. This is a model of inputs and outputs and of simple cause and effect. It is the model which today is reflected in much of what is called Human Resource Management.

Organic systems approaches

Eventually there came another shift in published works on organization. In this development, researchers came to supplant managers as writers on organization. They did so perhaps because of the methods they came increasingly to employ, and their perceived legitimacy as the methods of science. Increasingly sophisticated measures and statistical methods achieved prominence. Researchers became able to handle large samples of persons, organizations, and their possible interrelations. Attention came largely to focus on relationships between organization structures and technologies. These were viewed as features of the organizational context. They were understood to be independent of, and to affect, individual characteristics such as attitudes towards tasks, work performance (output measures), social interactions, values and conflict relations.

Much of this work followed naturally from Weber's arguments about bureaucracy. It includes the analysis of 'bureaucratic dysfunctions' described earlier, along with the well known 'contingency' studies by Woodward, Burns and Stalker, and the Aston group.[4] Organizations came explicitly to be viewed as systems, more or less *open* to their environments. Organic systems models, including contingency theories, became especially popular. Empirical studies examined relationships between variables which measured things which were seen to be characteristics of the organization, such as structure, technology, and size. Increasingly, attention was directed to relations between these characteristics and characteristics of the environment – especially environmental turbulence and change. The relations between organizational and environmental characteristics then were examined in relation to organizational performance. In sum, person and context each continued to be theorized as independent entities.

The 1960s and 1970s witnessed a blossoming of approaches which were described explicitly as open systems perspectives. Critics of existing approaches drew on research findings and on argument to suggest that social organizations cannot rightly be viewed as closed, mechanical systems, viable, regardless of the nature of their environment. Criticism rarely focused on the assumed status of an organization as a reality which exists independently of persons and their relational processes. Instead, researchers discussed what, from theory, made organizations open to their environments.

Researchers continued to focus on the structures and functions of the organizational whole, just as they always had done. Many set out an organic model of social organization in which it was assumed that the system functioned rather like a biological system. However, biological needs were replaced with the need of the system to survive or to achieve homeostasis. This is the conceptual equivalent of what Meyer and his colleagues referred to as the assumption of purpose (see earlier). The central, underlying assumption, usually left unstated, is the assumption of the functional unity of the system. The various parts of the system (the sub-systems) are understood to function in ways which service the needs of the entity which is the system as a whole.[5]

We will continue by describing a few particularly well-known examples of organic systems theories, focusing on empirical studies of organization characteristics.

Structures of organization and contingency theories

One element of the entitative approach, identified by Meyer and his colleagues, is the assumption that a stable structure characterizes the whole. The structure of an organization is often taken to comprise 'all the tangible and regularly occurring features which help to shape its member's behaviour' (Child, 1977, p.9). Earlier we described the structural characteristics which Weber identified in his definition of the bureaucratic type. This form now often is referred to as 'mechanistic' (Burns and Stalker, 1961) or is described as a 'machine bureaucracy' to distinguish it from other structural forms (Mintzberg, 1983). To recapitulate, Weber defined the bureaucratic structure as having the following characteristics:

1. A high degree of *specialization* such that different people perform different tasks. Tasks are grouped in different specialist departments, usually according to the functions they are understood to perform for the organization (system) as a whole.

2. A high degree of *formalization* to achieve precise definition and 'standardization' of those tasks. Duties, methods, and the discretion attatched to the position or job often are specified through written descriptions.

3. A managerial *hierarchy* of authority and command is created, with each level having delegated authority to control the level below. Authority is delegated down the hierarchy and information formally is regulated to flow upward. The hierarchy acts as a simple control system with the emphasis on vertical relations, and with horizontal relations relatively under-emphasized.

'Structural theorists' now take the view that any organization may be described in terms of varying degrees of these characteristics (see Pugh, 1971). This makes it possible, for example, to speak of the overall shape of the organizational whole. It has become usual to summarize the structural characteristics of an organization in terms of three principal components. These are 'complexity', 'formalization', and 'centralization' (see Child, 1984). Complexity refers to horizontal differentiation between units; to vertical differentiation between units; and to spatial differentiation between units. Formalization refers to the degree to which jobs are seen to be programmed and routinized so that they specify and limit the discretion of the job holder. Finally, centralization refers to the degree to which formal authority is seen to be focused in the positions of senior management.

Structures and their relations with other organizational characteristics. Structural characteristics of organizations have been examined for their relations with other organizational characteristics. Frequently, the *size* of the organization, usually measured by the number of employees, has been found to show systematic relations with structures when defined in this way. So, for example, complexity has been found to increase with size, and centralization to decrease with size (see Child, 1984).

The *technology* of the organization also has been related to structural characteristics and to organizational effectiveness. In this context, the term 'technology' refers to the way the organization transforms inputs into outputs. Woodward's (1965) research provides a well known illustration of the application of this approach to manufacturing enterprises. Woodward distinguished between 'small batch and unit', 'mass', and 'process' technologies for production. She investigated these in one hundred firms in the south-east of England. Her findings led her to conclude that each technology was associated with a different pattern of structural characteristics. Now it is clear that the relationships between technology and structure are systematic, but complex (Child, 1984). What is being debated is the extent to which technologies have simple causal effects on structural characteristics, and the extent to which management can fit technologies to structures, and vice versa.

Other studies have investigated the relations between organization structures and *environmental characteristics*. The most famous examples are the 'socio-technical systems' studies of Rice, Emery and Trist, and others at the Tavistock Institute in London (e.g. Trist *et al.* 1963); the work of Burns and Stalker (1961); and the work of Lawrence and Lorsch (1969). The environment, specified relative to the organization, tends to be defined in terms of other organizations and forces which affect the organization but over which it has little control. So, for example, Burns and Stalker identified 'mechanistic' (bureaucratic), and 'organismic' structural forms. Their research was conducted in the electronics industry. These firms had markets for their products which rapidly were changing; large-scale research and development activities were seen as sources of 'turbulence' and 'complexity'. Their research typically is taken to suggest that mechanistic structures are more appropriate in stable, simple environments (because they are static), whereas organismic structures are more appropriate in turbulent, complex environments (because they are dynamic).

A critique of organic models

The organic analogy, like many analogies, has certain strengths. However, analogies tend to get stretched to the point where similarities are over-emphasized and important differences are ignored. There are important differences between social and organic systems.[6] Here we wish only to continue the argument we have already begun and will, therefore, restrict our focus to three features of open systems research. These are the assumption that organizations are unitary rather than pluralistic (underplaying political processes); an overemphasis on relatively unchanging structures (at the expense of processes); and the distinction between person and context (which is too sharp because it ignores the relationship of mutual creation) (see Chapter 1).

Political aspects. Earlier we identified what we called a unitary assumption as characteristic of an entitative perspective. In organic systems perspectives we find it reflected in the treatment of the organization as though it has 'functional unity'. The problem with the biological metaphor is that it obscures the issue of functions by glossing the question of whose valuations set the standards by which functionality is judged. The significance of actors' different relationships with their contexts is ignored despite the fact that these differences are reflected in differences of interest, in activities of sense making, and in varying abilities to mobilize influence.

Structure and process. In an organic systems model, social structures are treated as comparable to biological structures. Again we see that an entitative perspective cannot handle the questions we want to ask. Here, the significance of the biological metaphor lies in the ways in which processes and change are understood. Biological species generally are seen to evolve slowly in relation to their environments. Change is developmental at the level of the individual member, and evolutionary, at the level of the species. Radical, disjunctive changes are rare in *organic systems*. They do not change their fundamental nature to become something different.[7]

Where social systems are concerned, the biological emphasis on stable structures understates those qualities of social relationships which are embodied, essentially, in social processes. An organic model, using the language of structures, distracts attention from the processes in which social order is reproduced, created, or sustained. Such models ignore what we have called 'structure in the process of projects' (Chapter 1). We take the view that social ordering is reproduced, created, and sustained in the social, cognitive, and political processes through which actors negotiate constraints, and mobilize influence in relation to projects. We shall go on to develop these arguments through the language of 'organizing'.

The independence of person, organization, and environment. Our third criticism is of the way research within the biological tradition sets people apart from their social contexts. We have already seen how entitative thinking sets people apart from their contexts. We need now to consider what happens when the context is divided into organization and environment.

Open systems theory has nothing distinctive to say about the relationships between people and organizations. It is often regarded as having something distinctive to say about the relationships between organizations and environments. At the level of theory this relationship is seen (correctly) as one of mutual creation. However, empirical studies usually treat the environment as a causal stimulus, to be characterized independently of the organization. Changes in the environment are understood to cause changes in the organization, and changes in organization are understood to cause changes in the person. To extend the metaphor of the Russian dolls, introduced earlier, we find that there are now three Russian dolls, rather than two, with people inside organizations, and organizations inside environments. People are characterized independently of organizations and organizations are characterized independently of environments.

A general critique of the entitative perspective

As we have seen, there are many who theorize organizations as objects which are independent of people and their relational processes. Employees are viewed as working in, and for the organization. By setting organization and person apart, organizations are treated as though they, themselves, are actors. As a result, the organization (as an entity) must be given its own motive force or goals. Like the actions of persons, the actions of organizations are invested with intentionality (see, for example, Allison, 1971).

We began this chapter by identifying the central characteristics of an entitative approach to organization. Most fundamental was the assumption that organization constitutes a well defined entity or whole which may be theorized as independent of person. Five further elements were identified, as follows. First, organizational boundaries and membership are well specified. Second, the whole has an identity of its own. Third, the entity is characterized by shared purposes, or values or goals. Fourth, the entity has a structure, which is usually formalized. Last, the organization is separate from its environment. These elements will be discussed, some separately, some together. The varying attention we give them reflects their varying importance for our own interests in organizing.

Organizational boundaries, membership, and identity

Meyer and his collegues observed that entitative approaches assume membership and organizational boundaries. This position is illustrated by Caplow's (1964) definition[8] of an organization as 'a social system that has an unequivocal collective identity, an exact roster of members, a programme of activity and procedures for replacing members' (Caplow, 1964, p.1). So, for example, membership and organizational boundaries may be expected to be identified through reference to legal specifications, such as Articles of Association, along with formalized administrative features which identify members, such as the organization chart, and the payroll.

Amongst the many criticisms which may be offered of this approach we may note that such definitions exclude, as organizations, what some would want to include, that is, enterprises which have no written charter, no written contract of employment, and no formal specification of members. Many voluntary enterprises and social movement groups would be excluded. These would have to be defined as informal groups and, presumably, be explained in other terms. Furthermore, to distinguish members from non-members is not as straightforward as it might, at first, appear. For example, it is not obvious whether descriptions of business organizations should include their share holders, Trades Unions, sub-contractors, and part-time labour.

Meyer and his colleagues took the view that organizations are 'nested' in larger organizations. They continued by saying that these 'are in turn nested in still larger . . . which of these units consists of the "real" organization . . . cannot easily be determined' (p.61). Here again we find the entitative separation of person and organization such that the former, like a Russian doll, is seen as 'nested' in the latter. Here we also see a very revealing assumption that there is one 'real' organization. However, our arguments about sense making, diverse interests, and varying influence question the assumption that any of the units to which Meyer and his colleagues refer is the real organization; there is not one, real organization. One advantage of abandoning entitative assumptions is that it becomes possible to investigate the plurality of participants' valuations, including, for example, their constructions of membership. As a result, it becomes possible to investigate the different identities constructed by individuals and groups as they reflect their different relations with their contexts.

The entitative approach may be abandoned by considering as members, those who define themselves as members. This has the advantage of directing attention to what being a participant means for the actors involved. In this way, person and organization are joined rather than set apart. Identities, and a sense of membership, then are seen as qualities which emerge out of relational processes as part of an emergent *'sense of social order'*. Of course, this is likely to mean that there will be multiple identities and social orders in any given enterprise as actors differ in their relationships with their contexts. This means, in turn, that the unitary qualities of an entitative perspective will need to be replaced by a pluralist perspective.

When person and organization are joined there is no need to depend on formalized procedures, charters, and records to locate the organization as an entity. It becomes possible also to study the activities and interactions of interdependent actors, organizing through their relations with one another, and in so doing, reproducing and creating patterns of social order within and between groups. In this way, it becomes possible to add to our understanding of organization through a conceptual framework which is not limited to formal organization, but rather, for example, allows us to investigate social movement groups (Brown and Hosking, 1986), and extended family networks (Grieco and Hosking, 1987) as they organize in relation to projects. In this way, it is possible to move towards a psychologically adequate model of relationships between persons and organization.

Purposes, goals, and values

Twenty years ago Gross (1969) observed that there seemed to be general agreement that organizations were distinguishable from other social groupings by their possession of goals. This is not often revealed in formal definitions since explicit definitions of organization seldom have been given. However, illustrations can be found. For example, Etzioni (1964) has said that 'organizations are social units (or human groupings) deliberately constructed and reconstructed to seek specific goals' (Etzioni, 1964 p.3).

We have seen the assumption of shared goals, in one form or another, in the approaches we have reviewed. The assumption is made necessary by the seperation of person and organization. When organization is conceptualized as an entity, independent of person, it is necessary to explain what holds 'it' together as a whole. We accept that there must be some minimum level of coordinated activity and coordinated understandings, that is, some degree of social order, before it is appropriate to speak of organization. However, what, more precisely, are these coordinated activities and understandings, how are they achieved, and by whom? It is the assumption of the organization as an entity which requires that all members share the same goals and/or make contributions which are functional for the whole.

Empirical studies have suggested that all members, as defined by the entitative concept, do not share the same degree of commitment to so called 'organizational goals'. Earlier we referred to critics of Weber and their claims that disparities are found between organizational goals and work group activities. Many since have argued that individuals and groups 'in organizations' have multiple values and interests, and these often conflict. This is the case, not just between management and workers, but also within the ranks of each (see e.g. Pfeffer, 1981). So, for example, within the ranks of management often there will be major differences between the interests of corporate and plant-level managers (see, for example, Parker *et al.* 1977), between production and sales, and between other managerial groups who perform different tasks. Similarly, non-managers differ in what they value, depending on their own skills, tasks, and Trades Union (see Chapter 5).

Such findings strike a mortal blow to the unitary assumption that all managers and non-managers share the same goals, values, and interests. When entitative distinctions between person and organization are abandoned, the focus shifts away from organizational goals to the valuations and to the interests of individuals and groups. These contribute to, and emerge from, their activities and interactions. They are part of what we earlier referred to as 'structure in the process of projects'. Valuations and interests are important to actors' identities and sense of membership: identities which are 'situated' (Chapter 1) in relation to their projects.

If the organization no longer is viewed as an entity, held together by, and acting in collective pursuit of shared goals, this leaves the question of how else organization should be conceptualized. A crucial part of the answer comes from what we already have said about persons and their need to gain the help of others to pursue their projects. We will develop this answer in the next chapter.

Formalized structures as stable organizational characteristics

We have taken the view that the entititative approach to organization examines people 'in organizations'. The treatment of persons, social relationships, and social action, is lifeless and mechanical.[9] When an entitative concept of organization is combined with an entitative concept of person, organization change can only be seen as change in the physical parts of the organization (structure, technology, people). The assumption is that change is designed by one class of person – managers – and not by others. Any change is seen as a technical problem and only as a technical problem (changing the shape of the organization to fit the environment).[10] There is no room for an account of culture as a history of shared experience, arising naturally from conversations and commitments (see Chapter 1). However, if organizations change it is because projects change and because relationships change. What is required is a new concept of person which gives people people the respect they are due as members of a species capable of constructing their own contexts (see Tajfel, 1981).[11] This means that we need a proper examination of the processes of organizing, as performed by managers and by non-managers. Change is endemic in the concept of organization as we understand it.

The entitative concept of organization does not define organization in terms of processes. As a result the (cognitive, social, and political) dynamics of organizing (and therefore change) are defined away. It is simply not enough to attribute agency to one class of persons, namely managers. Nor is it enough to invent the term informal organization to refer to those emergent processes which supplement the formal organization.[12] The formal organization itself emerges from the cognitive, social, and political processes central to our concept of organizing.

To illustrate this we can do no better than return to some of the findings of the Hawthorne Studies. There it was found that some actors restricted their production, resisted new methods of working, and fiddled control systems. To explain these findings, the term 'informal' organization had to be invented. The invention of this term made it clear that, in an entitative perspective, the term organization referred only to formalized goals, and to activities and relationships which were proceduralized and sanctioned in relation to those goals. Small wonder, therefore, that few have adopted a perspective similar to our own in which political processes are seen as endemic to organization (see Chapter 3). In rejecting the entitative aproach we will reject the unitary assumption of shared goals and values, and the overemphasis on relationships governed by standard operating procedures. As we saw in the case of the Danish Broadcasting Company, social relations cannot be reduced analytically to information flows and formalized procedures. Rather, actors are mutually interdependent. For them, communication is a constructive, relational, sense-making process which is cognitive, social, and political.

Structures as designed characteristics of organization

We have argued that when an enterprise is viewed as a fundamentally stable organization, attention is directed away from the ways in which social orders are created, actively sustained, and changed. Actors are given a very limited part to play in the dynamics of organization. In effect, the range of human action is restricted to executing (non-management) and designing (management) organizational forms for satisfying interests in organizational effectiveness.

This perspective has been associated with the growth of a literature on 'organization design'. In the design literatures, the explicit concern is prescription: to specify design alternatives and their implications for organizational effectiveness. In the design literatures, the dualist distinction between managers and non-managers reappears as a distinction between those who shape the organization, and those who do not. Often it is just the chief executive who is spoken of as the architect of the organization's characteristics – as the designer of strategy and structures (see Chapters 1 and 9). The argument that organization is designed recently has resurfaced in the newly fashionable treatment of leaders as the creators of cultures and organizations (e.g. Peters and Waterman, 1982; Bennis and Nanus, 1985). These literatures are characterized by a top-down view of organizations as designer goods – fashioned by chief executives. Similarly, the recent vogue for organization cultures has reflected the view that enterprise-wide cultures can be designed by a few for the many.

There is no need for a top-down logic for organizations as wholes, independent of the activities and relationships of participants. A psychologically adequate model of person accepts that actors, be they individuals or groups, differ in their valuing and differ in the projects they perform to add value to their lives (see Chapter 1). Attention must be directed to 'organizing': to cooperative and conflictual relational processes as they reflect, sustain, and influence valuations in the performance of projects. This view is consistent with some of the arguments for organizations as 'self designing systems'. The argument is that no one actor, no single design logic, and no predictable outcome of competing logics can be said intentionally to design an organizational whole (e.g. Weick, 1979). As we have seen the performance style of the chief executive will be reflected in the culture of the enterprise only to the extent that it receives social support (see Chapter 1). Social orders emerge, are reproduced, and change through relations of cooperation, competition, and conflict within and between groups.

In our account of organizing we shall give particular prominence to the processes of negotiation. Negotiation is a cognitive, social, and political process. Actors negotiate descriptions of social order with themselves, so to speak. More generally, actors negotiate in the course of their relational processes within and between groups. We shall combine descriptive and prescriptive arguments to focus on negotiation as a process in which actors build understandings and achieve influence in the performance of their projects. Negotiation is seen as a process of organizing through which actors create, protect, and promote certain sorts of social order. These may be 'cultures of dependence' or 'cultures of productivity', for example (see Chapter 1). Through their organizing, actors to some extent create their contexts, as well as being created by them. What emerges is not 'designed' by any single actor – though some may well achieve more influence than others.

The organization as a physical entity

Finally, we must draw attention to the one feature of an entitative approach which Meyer and his colleagues failed to observe. This concerns the ways in which the characteristics of entities (organization and environment) are measured, and the status they are given as a result. In an entitative perspective, the measuring of organizational characteristics has been viewed as a technical problem. The issue has been understood as a problem of designing procedures which will allow the accurate measurement of objective reality, that is, a reality which exists independently of actors' activities and sense making and about which all competant judges could agree. This is what Allport has called the 'physicalist' view of reality (e.g. Allport, 1955).

It is clear that the physicalist treatment of reality provides another major obstacle to the interests we wish to pursue. As we have seen, it is a feature of relational processes that actors construct their own more or less widely shared descriptions of social realities. A person's constructions are importantly affected by who they are with and why they are there (see Chapter 1). As we saw in our critique of Weber and in our review of contingency theories, different social constructions are associated with differences in tasks and/or projects, and with different social relationships. Actors' constructions differ in ways which reflect and create their relational histories and anticipated futures. This is part of what it means to say that perceptions are not just matters of 'fact', but also, matters of value (Vickers, 1968, p.122).

The implication of these arguments is that it is essential to appreciate that *relational processes – cognitive, social, and political – are at the heart of organizing*. Any concept of organization must reflect concepts of person and process which psychologically, are adequate. Organizing, properly understood, must be seen to be performed through a set of interrelated processes in which actors, to some degree, make their contexts whilst at the same time being made by them. These are processes in which realities are socially constructed to produce a 'sense of social order' which is narrowly or widely shared, and to produce social orders which may protect and promote particular valuations and interests at the expense of others.

Summary

In this chapter, we have detailed the elements of an entitative perspective. Such a perspective reflects the fundamental assumption that person and organization usefully can be theorized as independent of each other. In this way, organization is reified by being viewed as a context which exists independently of the actions and sense making of participants. An entitative approach cannot embrace an adequate theory of persons and processes. It is for this reason that the literatures of OB and HRM present such an impoverished and distorted view of persons and relational processes. As a result they fail to offer a convincing picture of the value of psychology to students of business and organization. We can do no better than quote the Sherifs who have pointed out that:

the part-whole relationship cannot be analysed satisfactorily by proposing one psychology for the individual when (they) are alone and another psychology for the individual in collective or group settings. Yet this is precisely what is implied in the attempt to analyse individual behaviour apart from its social context or, conversly, the attempt to treat behaviour in a social situation as though the principles governing the part (individual) were determined wholly by the character of the whole group. (Sherif and Sherif, 1969, p.89)

We will finish by identifying certain themes, begun in this chapter, which will recur throughout this text.

Organizing processes

We take the view that social organization is better understood in terms of relational processes. This requires attention to organizing as an activity which is achieved in and through cognitive, political, and social processes. Translated into systems terms: structures emerge through functioning, or rather, through the actions and constructions of participants. Structures emerge, not in relation to system needs, but in the process of projects. In systems terms, parts are interrelated, not through shared needs, but through the influential actions of persons past and present. Persons, through their social relations, create more or less widely shared constructions of their contexts. The significance of socially constructed realities cannot be overstated. Once they are recognized it becomes possible to theorize the interrelations between persons, processes, and organization.

Political processes
We reject 'managerialism' and the associated unitary view in favour of a pluralist argument. We do not take goals and organizational characteristics simply to be matters of technical interest, to be taken for granted as shared and similarly evaluated. Rather, actors, be they individuals or groups, are seen to differ in their valuing and in their interests, depending on their relationships with their contexts. Similarities and differences between actors (individuals and groups) are of considerable importance to their relationships. The political perspective emphasizes relationships of influence and the ways in which these affect, and are affected by the outcomes of decision-making processes. We theorize political processes as endemic to organizing, not – as most other theorists would have them – as aberrant, informal, self serving activities which mess-up formal organization.

Given these arguments, any attempt to understand some snapshot or vignette concerning an enterprise will need to identify: the actors, be they individuals or groups; their valuations in relation to identified projects; relationships between actors and between projects, including the extent to which they share understandings and influence one another.

Cognitive processes
We reject the emphasis on physicalist assumptions in favour of an emphasis on the processes by which realities are constructed. We use the term 'cognitive' as 'a generic term . . . to designate all processes in knowing' (Hilgard, 1980). Such processes are, necessarily, grounded in questions of value. Because of this they are 'affective, emotional, and normative' (Forgas, 1983, p.135). Interests are central to the processes of sense making (knowing), and the processes of sense making are interwoven with social and political processes. For these reasons, our approach to organization is best summarized as one which emphasizes social and political decision-making processes.

Social processes
Actors move around in social relationships with others. Their different valuations may converge that is, may overlap (see Chapter 1), they may differ, though be compatible, or they directly may conflict. Interacting actors may be pursuing converging, compatible, or conflicting projects. Actors will be more or less active in trying to produce and sustain or change a 'sense of social order' with actors with whom they are interdependent. It is through interrelated cognitive, political, and social processes that actors build diverse and possibly conflicting cultures. These may or may not be cultures of productivity. When they are participants are more likely effectively to protect and promote their projects.

Conclusions

In this chapter we have outlined the entitative concept of organization and its associated entitative concept of person. We described the former as having the following characteristics. First, the organization is seen as bounded, independent of the activities and sense making of participants and capable of being understood as separate from its environment. Second, the organizational whole is seen to be characterized by a single identity. Third, the whole has organization-wide purposes or goals. Fourth, the whole is held together by structures which translate its purposes into action. Finally, the interaction between the organization and the environment is described in terms of statistical interactions between characteristics of the organization and characteristics of the environment.

We argued that the literatures of organizational behaviour and human resource management are dominated by entitative concepts of person and organization; person and organization are theorized as entities, independent of each other. Both are seen as relatively bounded entities, characterized by relatively fixed characteristics such as identity, purpose, and structure.

For those who want to understand the relations between persons and organization, entitative concepts have serious deficiencies. Following the arguments of Chapter 1, we traced some of the implications of a perspective which views people as intelligent social actors. In so doing, we argued that, by virtue of their different relationships with their contexts, actors differ in their valuations, in their opportunities to develop and perform particular competencies, personalities and identities, and in their abilities to mobilize power in their performance of their projects. These differences imply that a political perspective must be taken of the mutual influence processes through which persons construct their contexts, whilst being constructed by them.

Finally, when persons and contexts are seen to be joined through processes of mutual creation, it is these processes which become the focus of interest in discussions of relations between person and organization. In Chapter 3, we will begin our account of the processes of organizing. As we shall see, the concept of process is reformulated. No longer will processes be seen as simple causal mechanisms which link inputs (from person and organization) to outputs (for person and organization). Rather, the processes of organizing will be seen to be complex processes of reciprocal influence, having emergent qualities which cannot be reduced to the independent contributions either of people or of contexts.

Notes

1. This is a crucial point. It was introduced in Chapter 1, and will be a continuing theme throughout the text.
2. It is important to note that the term *human relations* is variously applied to a more or less wide range of research findings and thoeries. This said, the Hawthorne Studies, and their many (mis-)interpretations, always are seen as central to the human relations perspective.
3. See, for example, Myers (1924) and Hearnshaw (1964).
4. See, for example, Child (1984). For a more detailed and critical review of contingency theories see Hosking (1981). For a recent defence of the contingency approach and its underlying assumptions see Donaldson (1985).)
5. For an excellent discussion of these issues see Burrell and Morgan (1979) and Morgan (1986).
6. Excellent and extended critiques may be found elsewhere. In our opinion the most useful of these is Buckley (1967).
7. As Hosking (1984) has remarked, it is only in Wonderland that human babies suddenly change into pigs. This raises the possibility of an important difference between social and biological systems. The former can change their fundamental nature and individual members (organizations) can achieve radical change. Researchers differ in their views concerning how typical and how difficult this is. However, the important point is that it is possible in ways which are not true of biological systems.
8. As we have noted elsewhere, few have offered formal definitions of their concept of organization. As a result, it has been necessary to infer an author's concept from his or

her narrative. Caplow provides an excellent illustration of the entitative treatment of organizational boundaries and membership.

9. See the Introduction to this chapter.

10. In earlier perspectives the organization was seen as a closed system. The view taken was that there was one best shape, such as Weber's rational-legal bureaucracy. From an open-systems perspective the issue is to match the shape of the organization to the characteristics of the environment.

11. We shall discuss this point in more detail in Chapter 4.

12. The evaluative significance of this distinction usually passes unnoticed.

Chapter 3

People organizing

Introduction

In Chapters 1 and 2 we described entitative perspectives of person and organization. In an entitative perspective, person and organization are set apart in ways which both seriously misrepresent what it is to be human and impossibly distort the relations between person and organization. We will continue by reconsidering elements of the entitative perspective in order further to develop our perspective on organizing.

Organization and organizing

Membership and identity

When critiquing the entitative perspective, we argued that identities are negotiated in the course of negotiating social realities and social order. Identities and social order 'arise in and through a process of ongoing negotiation about who shall be whom and what order shall obtain' (Gerson, 1976 p.796). When discussing organizational structures, for example, we produced arguments and evidence to indicate some of the ways in which actors differ from one another. We said that people differ in their relational networks, in their tasks, in the range of contexts to which they contribute, and in the social identities each constructs out of his or her participations. This means that being a member of a particular enterprise will mean different things to different actors, depending on their varying contributions and depending on the resources and constraints produced as a result of their participation. What is crucial for our arguments about organizing is that it cannot be performed by a single actor acting alone. Organizing is performed, not by a single actor, but by multiple actors (individuals and groups) producing and reproducing multiple identities through their relations with one another. Their social interactions may or may not reflect a shared sense of identity, may or may not be grounded in a formalized structure, and may or may not reflect formalized authority relationships. To take this view raises the question of how to explain interactions when an entitative perspective is abandoned. This we will now consider.

Goals, values and projects

Entitative perspectives were argued to be characterized by the assumption that the organization is held together by shared goals and/or values. We rejected this view, arguing that actors construct more or less widely shared, evaluative, descriptions or what Vickers called 'appreciations'. In their social relationships, actors *order value*. Through their social relations they construct descriptions (valuations) of social order including descriptions of the contributions that each actor will make, and the consequences of their participation. Actors differ in their relations with their contexts, partly as a consequence of their differing valuations, and partly because of those different valuations.

Social orderings are *orderings of power* as well as value. When actors are said to differ in their relations with their contexts, part of what this means is that they differ in their ability to achieve influence in support of their own valuations, in general, and their own projects in particular. These arguments led us to reject the managerialist and unitary aspects of the entitative perspective. In our emphasis on organizing, multiple actors – individuals and groups – are argued to be tied together by relationships of mutual interdependence such that each *needs the help of others* to construct their social order, and to pursue their projects. Social relations embrace co-operation, competition and conflict in that different actors seek to protect and promote different valuations and different projects.

Designed structures and emergent structures

The entitative perspective emphasizes formal structures and treats these as relatively fixed, stable qualities of the organizational whole, independent of the actions and constructions of participants. In our attention to organizing, the static emphasis on organization is replaced by a focus on relationships between actors and their contexts. It is these relationships which constitute organization and which produce the dynamic in organizing. Through structures in process, actors create more or less collective vehicles, in competition and conflict with others, to pursue their more or less collective projects.

The entitative perspective takes a top-down view of the structuring of organization. In arguing our contrary view, we suggested that a focus on organizing would have to recognize that no single design logic can be specified beforehand, and fully implemented, to produce a predicted social order. Instead, we shall argue that the inputs different actors make to their interactions with one another produce more or less consensual definitions of social order in the imaginations and joint actions of the participants. Through social interactions, new structures emerge in the process of projects: new orderings of influence and of value; social orders emerge, and what emerges is not predictable from the inputs of individual participants. Actors build relationships of cooperation, competition and conflict. In and through social processes, actors make it possible to merge their lines of action in relation to one another, and so organize their interdependencies. They may do so in ways which create what we shall call a 'culture of productivity'; we shall argue that a culture of this kind is more likely to enable participants to protect and promote their more or less widely shared interests.

Social realities

Earlier we suggested that a physicalist view of social realities is characteristic of an entitative perspective. It seems that this feature is not generally recognized, and yet it has profound and extensive consequences for any perspective on social organization. Fundamentally, it is this assumption which sets person and organization apart from one another and leads to reification of the latter. It is hard to overemphasize the importance we attach to our argument that social realities are socially constructed, imaginatively and in action. In and through their social interactions, actors construct social orders which to some degree protect and promote their own, more or less widely shared values and interests (projects). It is, in part, because social realities are socially constructed that organizing has an intrinsically emergent quality. It is because social realities are socially constructed that 'social orders' are described as 'systems of power and value' (Sherif and Sherif, 1969, Chapter 2). It is because social orderings are constructed that symbolic (see Chapter 4) and influence processes (see Chapter 5) are central to our understanding of social relations. Last, as will be seen, it is because of these qualities that an understanding of negotiation must be central to a theory of organizing.

Organizing

These points come together in the argument that organization is not well theorized when it is theorized independently of interdependent actors and their social relations, that is, when it is reified. Others, also interested in theorizing relations between persons and contexts, similarly have noted the significance of reification. For example, Cicourel (1973) has argued that 'so long as we continue to reify terms like "social structure", "culture", and "language", we shall miss the contextual and cognitive significance of everyday social organization' (p.9).

Arguments of this kind often are interpreted as reductionist in the sense that they are thought to suggest that social wholes can entirely be understood by being reduced to the lone thoughts and actions of individuals. However, those who entertain such suspicions usually do so in the context of what we called an 'individualistic' concept of person. Our perspective is one in which actors are firmly connected to their contexts in a relationship of mutual creation. As we have seen, the processes through which each creates the other are processes which have a fundamentally emergent quality. Social orders cannot be reduced to the acts of any one individual: they are the more or less continually produced in the processes of organizing.

What this means is that a theory of organizing will need to explain how joint action is made possible when actors differ in their relations with their contexts, in their valuations, and in their abilities to achieve influence. In other words, how are 'common social vehicles' (see Chapter 1) constructed to protect and promote a particular social order, and to pursue particular projects, in competition and conflict with other actors who have built their own social vehicle to promote other orderings and other projects? As we shall see, answers to this question show the importance of conversations, commitments, networking, and negotiation as interrelated processes which reflect and create relationships between persons and organization.

We again must emphasize that our particular interest is in the relationship between persons and contexts. We will focus on the processes through which organizing is performed, that is, on how organizing is achieved. For this reason, we are not interested, for its own sake, in the substantive content of what emerges. Rather, we concern ourselves with content only to the extent that it helps us to understand what, in Chapter 1, we called structure in process. Our interest is in 'patterns of interaction amongst people, patterns which both create individuals as individuals, and which stem from their activities' (Gerson, 1976, p.796). We shall focus on ongoing patterns of construction, especially as this is achieved through negotiation. We recognize that these processes are played-out in interrelation with larger scale, long-term patterns. The latter influence the contributions that different actors can make in a range of contexts, and influence the patterns of resources and constraints which are produced out of their participation in those settings.

Appreciation

In shifting attention to processes, we move away from an emphasis on outcomes as the end products of inputs from persons (e.g. traits) and organization (e.g. structural forms). Further, we move away from unitary interests in design and redesign, prediction and control. Instead we recognize that mattters of value and what some would call 'fact' are intermingled in descriptions of what is and should be (see Chapter 2). What one person or group takes as given, and the projects they pursue, inevitably is political in that their constructions will differ from the constructions of others with whom they are interdependent. And the differences cannot be decided in terms of right and wrong. So what then is our interest in organizing? For the reasons given we most identify with what Weick, and Vickers before him, have referred to as 'appreciative' theory. Such an approach recognizes that valuing (by ourselves and those we study) is inevitable. For this reason, we will endeavour to make our fundamental valuations explicit so that both you and we may critically examine them.

To pursue an interest in appreciation does not mean that traditional interests in the instrumental qualities of relationships will be ignored. Rather, as we have just said, issues of this sort will be addressed in relation to valuations which are exposed, rather than being left tacit and unquestioned. We shall locate the question of instrumentalities within the context of a very different set of understandings both about the definition of right and wrong and about the claiming of rights. 'Appreciation' is the first step to emancipation. So, for example, we have suggested that managerialism pervades entitative treatments of organization, the literatures of OB and HRM. Only when managerialism is recognized is it possible to ask whose values are likely to be added to by particular organizing activities and strategies. When the ubiquity of value-based processes is recognized it becomes possible fully to appreciate the degree to which organizing processes are cognitive, social, and political.

A language of processes

Shifting attention to organizing processes, rather than focusing on more stable qualities comes at a price. In particular, it is extremely difficult to develop a language which captures the complexities of social phenomena, whilst at the same time, being usable. Difficulties arise because it is *changing relationships*, rather than static entities, which are the focus of our processual account. So, for example, we emphasize relationships between the different projects of different actors, and between actors and their contexts. The relations are viewed as relations of interdependence, rather than one-way dependency relationships as is more usually the case. To deal with this we must move away from the relatively simple and narrow treatments of hierarchies of authority, top-down relationships, power and compliance. Further, to deal with this we must abandon entitative treatments of process as a mechanism which links inputs to outputs in a fashion which is, at least in principle, predictable. This point is extremely important. We will continue by developing our arguments about process to show what the term means when the entitative treatment is abandoned.

Reciprocal qualities and limits to relationships

First, process is not a simple, one-way, path between input and outcomes, persons and contexts. Rather, the relationships between actors and their contexts, that is, relational processes, have a reciprocal quality. In order better to understand what this means we can examine more closely what relational processes look like in an entitative perspective. In an entitative approach, simple, one-way causal relations are posited between person and context or, in the case of contingency theories, the simple relationships are modified by the action of moderator variables. In contrast, to recognize the reciprocal qualities of relational processes, it is necessary to bring out the extent to which actors simultaneously influence and are influenced by their contexts – particularly other actors. We saw many examples of how this is so in Chapter 1 – recall Dixon's argument with respect to authoritarians – selecting contexts which support their authoritarian traits and influencing those (and wider) contexts through the support they gain for their projects. We would add that theorizing the mutuality of influence is made more difficult by a second quality of relational processes. This is the quality of processes which arises through 'mutual creation' and perhaps is best described as the 'emergent' quality of relational processes. Given this quality it follows that the simple, one-way causal model of process cannot simply be revised by making more complicated the underlying statistical causal model (see Chapter 1).

It is necessary at this stage to say a little more about how we might 'bound' relational processes. Entitative perspectives make the issue manageable by assuming the boundaries we already have described between person and context and, in particular, by adopting a physicalist stance towards 'social facts'. Given our interests, we rejected this approach in favour of an emphasis on mutual creation and on the social construction of realities in and through social processes. However, we must emphasize that, in this relationship of mutual creation, not 'anything goes'. Again, we may return to the examples cited in Chapter 1. In the Sealed Fresh Company, the vice-president of marketing could not influence her Chief Executive – an important actor in her context – to change the marketing mix. On the other hand, the chief executive could influence the Vice-president's actions, but not the performance of his firm's products in relation to those of other firms (context). We may make aspects of our contexts by building good or poor working relationships with others. Similarly, we may describe our business situation as healthy, and persuade others in some sense to accept our description. Yet there are limits to what we can make of our contexts and they of us; not everything is possible. There are limits to the relationships we can build, to the activities we can perform, and to the social interactions in which we can engage. Similarly, there are limits to the sense of order we can construct, and limits to what others will accept as a valid description.

From what we have said in Chapters 1 and 2, it should be apparent that many of these limits are more mutable than they appear at first. One important reason is that where social contexts and social realities are concerned, the limits are not (relatively) simple matters of physical fact. Rather, they may best be described as conventional. Descriptions of social realities are constrained by what we take for granted in particular relational settings; by what is likely to be imagined in those settings; and by the emergent processes through which understandings are translated into action. In other words, the limits or constraints do not come from what is right or wrong, in the earlier described physicalist sense. That limits are conventional means that, potentially, they are open to change. If limits are recognized, then attempts may be made to change them. For example, an actor – such as a trades union – may attempt to renegotiate the terms and conditions of their relationship with a particular employer. As we shall see, it will be necessary to find ways to describe the reciprocal quality of relationships between actors and their contexts. Further, we will need to do so in ways which recognize their mutuality, in other words, which recognize that all actors always are dependent on other actors for supporting, reproducing and changing their constructions of order.

Ongoing and emergent qualities

In addition to the mutual and reciprocal qualities of relational processes, it also is necessary to capture their ongoing qualities. What is crucial is to do this in ways which recognize that, at one and the same time, some aspects are stable, whilst others are changing. Here again we find that to abandon the entitative approach is to open up to question issues which previously seemed settled. In an entitative perspective, stability is assumed and/or emphasized and change either ignored or framed as a predictable result of changes in the characteristics of the inputs. However, as we already have seen, relational processes have qualities which are 'emergent'. By this we mean that the outcomes always will represent something more than, and different from, the inputs: relational processes have a property which is inherently emergent (for example, Watzlawick *et al.*, 1974). As we saw in our discussion of the Danish Broadcasting Company (Chapter 2), this is true even when activities and relations are highly proceduralized as they are in some enterprises.

An appropriate language

Finally, we need to develop a language of processes which appropriately theorizes persons rather than trivializing and distorting their contributions (as we have emphasized throughout). This must be done in ways which allow person and organization to be joined. We have argued for a processual perspective, focusing on relational processes grounded in social relationships. As we have seen, this already means a lot in terms of what kind of concept of process is required. However, yet more must be said. In particular, it will be necessary to theorize persons and organization in terms which are commensurate. We shall build a language of 'organizing processes' to help us with this. We will continue by reviewing the central elements of our perspective on organizing.

We will argue that people and groups secure the help of others through influencing the ways those others describe and act on their context; these are social and symbolic processes and processes of influence. Actors also engage in the interrelated processes of negotiation and exchange; again, these are social and symbolic processes as well as processes of influence. We shall see that influence processes have important symbolic, social and political aspects. We shall argue that actors differ in the contributions they make to the processes of constructing particular social orders. Some actors attempt and achieve influence more than others. Actors' attempts to achieve influence depend on their constructions of their context in relation to other contexts. Actors will attempt influence, for example, depending on the extent to which they perceive a context as one in which they can mobilize sufficient resources to achieve influence. As we have seen, opportunities to influence a social order are constrained, for example, by the accepted rules and procedures of formal organization, and constrained by what interdependent participants find acceptable. Further, an actor may be more or less active in their attempts at influence, depending on the extent to which they see activities and relationships as supportive of their projects.

We will bring these arguments together in a description of organizing as political decision making, where decision making is defined just about as broadly as it is possible to imagine. More precisely, we will develop a view of organizing as a set of processes which are:

1. personal and collective processes in which social realities are created (cognitive or symbolic processes);

2. within and between groups of interdependent actors (social processes);

3. who differ in their projects and in the influence they can achieve (political processes).

Organizing interdependencies

For us to reject the entitative approach, we must find alternatives to shared goals, to relationships structured by the rules and regulations of formal organization – relationships treated as though they only existed between persons joined by formal definitions of authority and responsibility. As we have seen, these alternatives must, in a sense explain how and why interactions and relationships occur at all; must be able to explain the variety of relationships; and must provide explanations which allow person and organization to be joined in ways which psychologically are adequate. We need an approach which does not require that goals be shared, but accepts that they might be; an approach which does not assume that cooperation is the norm, but which is able to explain action in general, including conflict.

We have suggested that actions can be understood in relation to projects (Chapter 1) rather than in relation to shared goals or purposes (Chapter 2). We have suggested that to understand organizing, no special theories of individual motivation are required, and neither is the presumption of an organization characterized by shared goals. Rather, actors have been suggested to pursue their projects in social contexts. This means that an actor will pursue a project in interdependent relations with other actors who also are pursuing their projects.[1] As a result, a crucial aspect of organizing lies in the relationships between projects. Projects may differ, and may conflict; projects may differ but be congruent; projects may – through social interactions – come to be shared. Regardless of whether they are conflicting, congruent, or shared, all actors need the help of others to construct order and, in particular, to pursue their own project(s). This reveals what is crucial for the appreciation of social organization: actors are tied, one to another, in relations of interdependence.

Here we focus attention on interdependent relationships – regardless of whether or not goals are shared. We argue that social relationships, fundamentally, are about helping. In the context of our concepts of person and organizing, references to what is 'instrumental' must necessarily take on a much broader, and importantly different meaning than that which characterizes entitative perspectives (see Preface). Briefly, this is because of our emphasis on sense making, projects, and relational processes. In the most general and fundamental sense, social relationships are instrumental because they are the vehicle for constructing order, for making social judgments and constructing identities, and for making joint action possible. This said, given that 'not anything goes', relational processes may differ in the extent to which they contribute positively to the project(s) of an actor – individual or group. It is for this reason that we shall have much to say about skill: not as a personal property, but as a quality of relational processes. We shall argue that it is possible to produce general (content free) arguments about the instrumentalities of relational processes; we shall try to do so through the language of skilful processes.

It is important to note that our arguments imply that relationships are best viewed as characterized by interdependence, rather than one-way dependence. As we have argued, all actors need to construct order imaginatively to make social action possible. This emphasis is just one illustration of our earlier point about the mutuality of social relations. Actors are joined by their mutual dependence (Thibaut and Kelley, 1959). Each needs the help of others to construct their sense of identity, to act in relation to others, and to create and contribute to social contexts. So, for example, heads of department are dependent on their subordinates, just as those subordinates are dependent on them.[2] The dependency relationship probably is asymmetric, in the sense that a subordinate may be more dependent on her head that the other way around; however, it is two-way .

There are many reasons why actors must depend on one another to construct order. Not the least of these is that it is impossible fully to proceduralize the performances of others such that they are entirely predictable. It is not just that social orders continually are emerging but also that the social world is inherently equivocal . As we shall see in more detail in Chapter 4, any particular description is necessarily incomplete so that other descriptions always are possible.[3] What is possible is more constrained in some contexts than it is in others.[4] Given that actors depend on one another in the ways described, our departmental head *must* depend on his/her subordinates, to 'invent detail' around the 'general formula'.[5] It may be that managers who wish they could do everything themselves, may do so because they realize that they are, to some extent, dependent on others, and realize that this has implications for their power, and influence relations.

Some have chosen to make this general point more narrowly, emphasizing behavioural interlocks and shared means in relation to what we call projects (Allport, 1962; Weick, 1979). They argue that social relationships are grounded in the instrumentality that the behaviour of one person has for the particular projects of another. As an illustration of Weick's arguments about 'interlocking means', consider the projects of three academics. One has reached a certain point in his career and now actively is seeking promotion; another wishes to build a network of persons whose research interests are the same as hers; another wishes to get more favourable publicity for her subject. They join forces in organizing a conference; not one of them has resources sufficient for organizing the conference on their own; and each has different reasons (grounded in their different projects) for coordinating their actions in this way. We too will take this line. However, we do so in the context of our more general argument that relational processes, fundamentally, are to be understood as processes in which actors seek and help each other to create social order imaginatively and in action.

Interactions and the creation of order

The argument so far is that we engage in projects, succeeding or failing in adding value to our lives and the lives of others. In the most general sense, what this means is that we need the help of others in order to create order. More narrowly, we need the help of others to pursue our projects – whatever they might be. As a result, our relations with others are relations of mutual, though not necessarily equal interdependence: we are to some extent dependent on them and they on us. We also have discussed the possible specification of standards and procedures such that, were they to be specified fully, they would entirely initiate, direct and regulate activities, interactions, relationships, and constructions of reality. We have observed that a full specification of procedures, regulating activities and interdependencies, is not possible for reasons which are fundamentally psychological. The reasons follow from our earlier arguments about realities being socially constructed, constructions being grounded in value, and follow from our more general arguments about the emergent qualities of social processes. Regardless of the particular reasons why fully proceduralized performances are rare, one implication is clear. This is that the ways interdependent actors create order, and the ways in which these processes are constrained, represent major areas of interest for those interested in organizing.

If actors are made interdependent by their need for help from others, and cannot guarantee that help by proceduralizing performances, then they must find ways to influence their relations with others. As we shall see, this is why the processes of negotiation and exchange (symbolic, social, and cognitive processes) are central to our understanding of how organizing is performed. Actors will attempt influence to promote their constructions of social order through their relations with other actors who are attempting to do likewise. If the status quo appears to support and promote an actor's projects then the actor is likely to attempt influence to sustain the status quo. On the other hand, an actor's sense of the status quo may be such that it needs to be changed in order better to protect and promote their values and interests.

Social orders are not created *de novo* by actors; actors and relationships have their own histories, and actors contribute to patterns of social relations in which other actors already have built social orderings of power and value. In this sense, some of what will 'go' in any particular culture predates the particular performances of the present participants. So, for example, a new recruit may join an enterprise in which all recent graduates are thought to be a liability. A new recruit who is also a graduate is likely to find this labelling a more or less considerable constraint. However, it may be a constraint which, over time, they can influence and change.

The ease with which the status quo can be changed will reflect the relationship between the actor – individual or group – and their context.[6] For example, one of the chief executives we interviewed observed to us that she was constrained by certain aspects of the social performances of actors with whom she was interdependent. In particular, she noted that many did not understand why, how, and when to negotiate. In her view, this made it a lot more difficult for her skilfully to organize her interdependent relations with them.

The above example illustrates that not all aspects of the status quo are equally amenable to change. As we have said, the ease with which this can be achieved depends on both actors and their contexts or, more precisely, on the relationship between them. Not all actors are equally able to influence the status quo. However, since the limits often are matters of convention rather than fact, much more is open to influence than commonly is supposed. Often it is difficult, if not impossible, firmly to identify the boundaries between what can and what cannot be influenced.

We have said that actors will attempt influence better to protect and promote their projects and their sense of social order. In very broad terms, there are three interrelated elements in the ways actors may make active attempts of this sort. First, an actor may attempt to structure the ways in which others, with whom he or she perceives an interdependence, define their situation. The focus of the influence attempt could be the symbolic (constructive) processes of description. So, for example, I might try to persuade you that a change in your working practices will be in your long term interest. The second element, interrelated with the first, is found in an actor's more or less explicit attempts at exchange in their relationships with others. For example, as your employer, someone may persuade you to accept a changed job description in return for greater job security. The third element is interrelated with the symbolic and exchange processes described. It is found in processes of influence (particularly negotiation) in which actors, often tacitly, construct descriptions which can be said to embrace agreements concerning how they will help one another.

We shall review briefly what theorists have said about symbolic processes, exchange, and negotiation in relation to organization. We shall find that theorists usually have kept these processes apart. It is by bringing all three together that we develop further our arguments about the processes of organizing. We shall emphasize all three, focusing on negotiating as the fundamental process through which influence is achieved over symbolic processes (how things are valued and described) and the processes of exchange. It is through negotiating that actors, to some degree create their social order, making social action and joint action possible. It is through negotiating that actors may be more or less successful in achieving influence that will help them to protect their values and pursue their projects. In this way we will build both the descriptive argument of this chapter and lay the foundations for a more normative treatment of skilful organizing.

Symbolic aspects of interaction

There are substantial literatures in which theorists attempt to characterize social interactions, or more generally, to describe relations between persons and contexts (see, for example, McCall and Simmons, 1982). This said, there are major differences in the ways interactions are theorized, and different views of what is important. Many have chosen to stress the symbolic aspects of interactions – emphasizing that social interaction is mediated through language. One well known position called 'symbolic interactionism' emphasizes the meeting of minds and meanings.

As we noted in Chapter 1, this emphasis on symbolic activity and interpretation is not exclusive to symbolic interactionism. It is an emphasis shared, for example, by many social psychologists (e.g. Sherif and Sherif, 1969; Kelvin, 1970). However, to explain social interactions, much more needs to be said about what else might be going on. Symbolic interactionists address this issue by linking the activity of social construction to talk about selves, identities, characters, and roles. However, mostly they do so in order to say something about what it is to be a person. In contrast, our interest is more with the other side of the same coin. We are interested in the more or less collective social processes of organizing and with the symbolic qualities of these processes. The language of projects is intended to help us to situate organizing in relation to particular active interests. We combine arguments about negotiation, exchange, and social influence with arguments about symbolic processes to show how social orderings are created through cognitive (symbolic), social, and political processes.

Exchange aspects of interactions

Interactions often have been theorized as processes of social exchange; however, as we shall see, this means very different things to different theorists and few have articulated a perspective which is consistent with the arguments we so far have laid out. Some have focused on exchanges between two persons (dyadic exchange processes); some have tried to expand such arguments to the small group (e.g. Thibaut and Kelley, 1959; Homans, 1951). The exchange aspects of formal organizations also have been addressed explicitly (e.g. Blau, 1964). Where formal organizations are concerned, theorists have differed in the degree to which the exchange aspects have been made central, or left relatively untheorized as a basic condition. This difference is tied up with quite different treatments of persons and organization, sometimes entitative and sometimes processual. As a result, the exchange aspects of relations between person and organization have been theorized in quite different ways; few of these ways are congenial to our present interests.

Persons and organization have been tied, for example, by those who suggest that there is a more or less explicit, more or less formalized 'social' or 'psychological contract' between person and organization. Usually this has been done in the context of a broader, entitative perspective in which person and organization are set apart. Each entity is said to have expectations of the other, and each is argued to have understandings about the terms and conditions of their exchanges (for example, Barnard, 1948; Schein, 1965; March and Simon, 1958).

In contrast, there are *processual perspectives* in which persons and organization are more strongly and appropriately tied. The processes of exchange are theorized as the processes out of which complex social structures emerge. Perhaps the best known example of this approach is that of Blau (1964). Blau emphasized the dynamic qualities of relationships. He emphasized that aspects of relationships – like power and status – develop during the course of interactions. For Blau, it was because of these dynamic, developing qualities, and because of their feedback as new inputs to interactions, that social structures were seen to be described properly as emergent.

Exchange perspectives differ in their assumptions about the ways in which persons interact with their contexts. This takes us back to the theme of symbolic interaction. Some theorists reject the interpretive stance which emphasizes the social construction of realities and therefore symbolic processes. Instead, they treat the social context in a *physicalist* way (Chapter 2). In other words, they treat 'goods' and relationships as though their status were a matter of fact rather than a matter of (different) valuations. Blau took a physicalist view, making his otherwise attractive, processual approach, less relevant to our current interests.

Other exchange theorists have emphasized the symbolic aspects of exchange, and for this reason, are of more use to us. Such theorists view exchange relationships as matters of social judgement, that is, as relationships in which judgements of worth (value) are socially constructed. So, for example, individuals and groups are understood to differ in what they value as a resource, and to differ in their judgements of the rules of distribution (for example, as fair, or equitable). A further, and important consequence of this view, is that individuals and groups *value particular social relationships* (Homans, 1951). In our terms, an actor will attach greater value to those relationships which they see to be most helpful in their construction of order and their pursuit of their projects.

There are many good illustrations of the partial and parochial judgements actors form about the terms and conditions of their exchange relationships in a particular context, relative to those they experience in other social contexts and, in particular, relative to those enjoyed by others. For example, people tend to value their own 'inputs', 'outcomes' and 'input-outcome' ratios in ways which are systematically biased in favour of their own group (e.g. Adams, 1963; Patchen, 1961). Further, actors judge their own industrial action to be more justifiable than similar action undertaken by another group. In other words, we see again that social realities are socially constructed and different actors construct different descriptions of what people are doing, and why.

Homans (1951) is a good example of one who recognized that social judgements are intimately involved in exchange relationships. He did so through his references to 'psychic' rewards and costs. Unfortunately his penchant for formalism has tended to obscure his recognition of constructed realities. It is our intention, amongst others, to develop a more extensive treatment of the symbolic qualities of relational processes, not through an explicit emphasis on exchange, but rather, through emphasising the negotiation of order (Strauss, 1978).

We will develop arguments about the negotiation of social order to articulate further the processes through which actors negotiate between different valuations and different projects to settle on this description rather than that (imaginatively and in action). These processes are played out, in and through social interactions, to construct particular social orders and to protect and promote particular projects. In these ways, actors more or less collectively produce an ordering of value and influence the terms and conditions on which they will do business together. In any given context, some actors consistently may achieve more influence than others, and some projects may be better protected and promoted.

Negotiations and negotiating order

We have seen how theories of exchange differ and how few combine the arguments that we require. Theories of negotiation differ in comparable ways, and again, few combine an emphasis on symbolic, social, and political qualities satisfactorily to link person and context. For example, there are theories which focus on interpersonal or interparty relationships or both, with or without explicit links to formal organization. Many focus on negotiation as a certain sort of task (e.g. Morley and Stephenson, 1977). The task is seen to be performed by the representatives of counteracting groups[7] whose valuations and whose interests seem directly to conflict. The task, and therefore the social relations, may be more or less highly proceduralized through, for example, written agreements about who shall negotiate, when, and over what aspects of their relationship, and/or through the unwritten rules of custom and practice. We shall focus on 'negotiation' as a task, or rather 'project' in Chapter 6.

Other theorists have focused on negotiation as it might characterize certain relationships within formal organizations (e.g. Sayles, 1979). Such theorists departed from the more usual emphasis on vertical relations between formalized positions (superior–subordinate relations), and therefore moved away from a restrictive focus on the authority aspects of relations. Instead, attention was directed to lateral relations, often between those not formally tied by the organization chart. Here, the negotiated quality of relations was what was found interesting (Sayles, 1979; Dalton, 1959). However, negotiation was seen simply as the (informal) 'oil' which made the (formal) organization 'work'. It was not seen as a process by which organization was constructed because the authors remained confined by the assumptions of the entitative perspective.

Our general interest is in negotiation as a quality of relational processes, and therefore, as a quality of social interactions, and social constructions. More narrowly, we are interested in negotiations through which social orders are organized in relation to projects. With just a few exceptions, theorists seldom have made the processes of negotiation central to their analyses of organization. Part of the reason lies with the earlier noted dominance of entitative approaches. However, neither Weick (1979), who made much of processes leading to interlocking means, nor Pfeffer (1981), who emphasized the political aspects of decision making, pay any serious attention to processes of negotiation.

We say this not so much to criticize Weick or Pfeffer, but to suggest that the view of negotiating we are seeking only is possible when a number of key arguments are brought together. We must appreciate that cognitions are socially constructed through relational processes (as we shall show in Chapter 4). We must appreciate that actors differ in their valuations of particular activities, relationships, and social orders. Finally, we must appreciate that actors are interdependent because they need help from others to construct social orders and add value to their lives (see Preface).

In the literatures on negotiation, the arguments which come closest to what we seek are found in the negotiated order perspective. This perspective, potentially, is one of the most influential of interactionist arguments. Despite this, it has had little attention in the OB or HRM literatures. Negotiated order theorists argue that the social ordering of activities, values, and influence is, to an important degree, negotiated. They take the view that social rules emerge from social processes. They reflect, and are reflected in, orderings of activities, influence, and valuations (see Strauss, Schatzman, Bucher, Erlich, and Sabshin, 1963; Strauss, 1978; Cicourel, 1976; Gerson, 1976). People negotiate at least some aspects of what they do with, or for, other people. That is to say, they negotiate at least some of the conditions of their interdependence. In so doing they create a degree of predictability which makes future social interactions possible. In other words, they create a degree of order. Given our earlier arguments it should be plain that this is a perspective we value.

Arguments about negotiated social order were offered originally as a way to appreciate both stability and change as aspects of organization. There were two main reasons why writers such as Strauss, Cicourel, and Gerson placed such an emphasis upon processes of negotiation. First, negotiations are necessary when it is impossible fully to specify the rules by which actions should be regulated. Strauss and his colleagues argued that a 'generalized mandate', rather than a fully specified procedure is often all that exists.[8] Social interaction will not proceed smoothly unless the actors find the terms and conditions of their interdependence agreeable.[9] For this reason, order is something that has to be 'worked at' continually (Strauss et al., 1963). The work is the work of negotiation (Cicourel, 1973, 1976). Second, order was said to be negotiated because actors differed in their purposes (what we would call projects). It was further argued that popular references to organizational goals do not, in fact, describe shared goals, but rather serve a largely symbolic function. In other words, references to organizational goals represent attempts to legitimize the goals of particular actors. Although Strauss and his colleagues did not put it this way, their arguments imply that there is, inevitably, a political dimension to organization – one which arises from the psychology of persons and processes .

Strauss and his colleagues recognized that negotiating relations sometimes are explicit, sometimes are tacit, and are more or less constrained by the social context. So, for example, negotiations are temporally bounded in the sense that any major change in the status quo may allow some aspects of relationships to be renegotiated, or effectively may prevent renegotiation. Negotiations are recognized to be performed in social contexts which have an important historical dimension (see Chapter 4). This means that they are resourced and constrained by (relatively) longer standing relationships and agreements. So, for example, organization structures are viewed as a mixture of procedures which previously have been negotiated, and decisions which have not recently been tabled so to speak.

Others have found much to praise and much to criticize in the negotiated order perspective (e.g. Day and Day, 1977; Benson, 1977; Buckley, 1967). For our purposes, its attractions lie in the ways persons and contexts are joined. In contrast to an entitative perspective, the approach offers a much more realistic description of persons and processes as they relate to organization. We find the suggestion that a person's power depends on how he or she relates to their contexts particularly valuable, partly because it leads to the suggestion that power is situation specific (see Chapter 5). On the other hand, critics have objected that it is not clear what is negotiable and what is not. They have suggested, further, that it is not clear how negotiation differs from other kinds of social influence.

With respect to the first point, we agree with Strauss (1978) that what is negotiable and what is not is an empirical matter, 'to be discovered, not merely assumed' (p.131).[10] With respect to the second point, we have to agree. It *is* difficult to make simple, rigid, distinctions between negotiation and other types of influence, such as persuasion (see Chapter 5). However, the answer is not to do what so many have done and largely ignore negotiation. To do so is to fail to see the relationship between person and context as one of mutual creation.

Our own reasons for using the language of negotiation are as follows. First, we think it important to recognize that social orders are made – are socially constructed – imaginatively and in action. Social judgement and action, particularly joint action, simply would not be possible were this not so. Second, the language of negotiation draws attention to the mutuality of social relationships such that all parties must contribute something to allow the relationship to exist at all. Third, and following from the first two, skilful processes of negotiation facilitate the articulation of differences which could not long be ordered by fiat alone. When ordering is largely achieved through negotiation, rather than by other means of influence (particularly domination) relationships are more likely to assimilate, accommodate and shape changes in the status quo. In particular, negotiation is more likely to do so in ways which will better protect and promote the different values and relationships of interdependent individuals and groups, and better protect the collective project(s) of groups who achieve their ordering in this way.

Organizing processes

It is possible to join persons, processes, and organization by combining findings and arguments about symbolic processes and exchange, and to do so through an emphasis on negotiation and order. We shall do so by building on the arguments and findings already presented. At this stage, it will be particularly useful to provide a slightly more detailed account of social order; of the interrelations between constructed realities, negotiation, and influence; and of what we mean by political decision making. We shall consider each in turn.

Social ordering

Interdependent relations have a symbolic element in that the actors themselves define their interrelations and define resources in terms of their own valuations and in relation to their own projects. Actors often will differ in their valuations and therefore will differ in their descriptions of social order. Actors also will differ in their relations with their contexts such that some are more able than others to mobilize resources to support or 'discredit' particular valuations (Weick, 1979). This is one of the ways the processes of social ordering may be more or less skilful. Later we will argue that skilful processes are more likely to achieve agreements (about social order) which will 'stick', and are more likely to create social orders which can effectively assimilate, accommodate, and shape changes in ways which add value to the projects of the actor.

Ordering is reflected both in actions, and in descriptions, that is constructions of meaning, which comprise a sense of social order. So for example: some degree of ordering may be reflected in a particular set of influence relationships such that, over time, A influences B as often as B influences A. Examination of these actors' interactions, and in particular, their symbolic content, may indicate that they value 'distributed influence' or heterarchy. Women's groups, and other groups concerned with social movements[11] often attempt, more or less successfully, to achieve social orders in which values and influence are ordered in these ways (Brown and Hosking, 1986; Prince, 1988).

Given that descriptions of reality are descriptions from a particular point of view, any descriptions of ordering will be partial. If you are told that your department must accept a budget cut, whoever takes this view will have their own reasons for doing so. However, you may describe the situation differently. An actor's social constructions reflect particular valuations and interests, personal histories of relationships and interactions, and expectations and aspirations for their future relationships and projects.

We have argued that social order is created in relation to projects. It is the absence of projects, or some comparable concept of task, that makes negotiated order perspectives less useful than they otherwise might be, especially for theorizing organizing rather than person. This means that it is necessary to identify the projects of actors in order to situate their organizing activities. It is possible to do this by focusing on actors' descriptions of changes in the status quo – changes which they judge to have major significance, actual or potential, for their values. Actors may deem a change significant because it appears to threaten their values, or because it is judged to provide an opportunity to protect or promote them. When an actor succeeds in influencing others with whom he or she is interdependent to describe an issue in a particular way, that actor is able to focus attention and activity in relation to the issue as they see it. This is how an actor gains the help of others in relation to projects which are more or less widely shared. It is in this sense that organizing is all about change, actual and potential.

An illustration can be taken from our study of chief executives. Each was asked to provide accounts of major changes which, over a period of time, they came to understand and act on as either a *threat*, or an *opportunity*. Each was invited to describe: the ways in which they investigated the potential meanings of these changes; the ways in which they influenced others to pay attention to these changes; the ways they influenced descriptions of the significance of the change in relation to particular values; the ways they negotiated agreements concerning the course of action to be adopted, who should do what, and so on. In other words, though not using these terms, we asked questions designed to investigate the chief executives' views of how social ordering was achieved, in actions and meanings, in relation to their projects.

It is vital to appreciate that the processes of ordering described were performed by participants whose projects were interdependent. As we have seen, it is not necessary to assume that all shared the chief executive's project. Rather, the processes involved in organizing projects can be understood as a mixture of influence in the context of shared means, and influence in the context of shared ends. In the case of the former, interactions importantly will consist of negotiations about the distribution of help between the different projects of interdependent actors; these processes will include elements of distributive bargaining. Where social relations are grounded in a shared project, negotiations often will concern decisions about the patterning of contributions and the distribution of help within that project. These negotiations will involve questions of who will do what, and when, the values at stake, and the resources that can be mobilized. Through these processes, actors negotiate their identities and negotiate social orderings.

Negotiation, influence and exchange

Given our description of social ordering, more must be said to show how it is, to varying degrees, negotiated. It is negotiated through symbolic processes – in which an actor competes with others for acceptance of their descriptions, and for the translation of their descriptions into action. What this means, for example, is that a chief executive and his or her senior managers will try to negotiate agreeable descriptions of their interdependent contexts – as they are and might be – in relation to particular projects. In these ways, and to varying degrees, actors negotiate help, through processes which are more or less collective, and more or less skilful. In so doing, they negotiate a set of guidelines by which they may regulate their future interactions.

This is what we meant when we said that relationships are organized through influencing the symbolic processes of description. An actor must get others to adopt a view which they would not otherwise have formulated. An actor must convince others that his or her description is more valuable than other, competing descriptions. The processes of social cognition are central to everyday interactions, and to organizing. The recent vogue for organization cultures, and for leaders as manipulators of symbols makes sense only in the context of this sort of perspective. Unfortunately, the authors of these literatures take a top-down, entitative view of organizations; emphasize a mechanistic view of person; and therefore fail adequately to theorize the cognitive, social, and political processes of organizing (e.g. Peters and Waterman, 1982).

What emerges from this is that social action in general, and therefore, action in relation to projects, requires certain sorts of decisions to be made. The strategic aspects are particularly evident in the choices we make to begin (or abandon) this project rather than that; and whether or not we attempt to influence others to share our own projects or simply to give help which is instrumental to our projects. Either way, negotiation offers a way to create certain sorts of social orders. These are social orders which, over time, will better protect and promote the similar and different values of interdependent actors.

The following example, taken from our study of chief executives, illustrates the point that actors build and mobilize relationships as a way of gaining help for their projects. We asked the question 'What would someone need to know in order successfully to perform your job?'. In response to this, a number of our chief executives told us who they would need to know and the sorts of relationships they would need to have with them. Subsequently, they described the ways in which they built working relationships with some of those people. The relationships provided them with important intelligence (see Chapter 4) and allowed them to exert various kinds of influence (see Chapter 5). For example, the chief executives were able to try out[12] ideas about changes in the activities of their departments, and assess whether those changes were feasible. They were able to promote an image of their departments as positive, distinctive, and secure. They were able to influence the size of the budget they received.[13]

This account of organizing has described valuations, actions, and relationships: necessarily reflected in interlocking means; necessarily reflected in some (more or less) shared sense of social order. We have emphasized that relationships are to some extent chosen and made; involve symbolic processes of exchange, and are negotiated and renegotiated. The negotiations may be conducted more or less skilfully. As a result social relationships are the carriers of an emergent social order. We have yet to elaborate what we mean when we say that such processes are inherently political; it is this to which we turn next.

Political processes

Organizing processes are performed by interdependent individuals and groups who differ in their valuations and in their interdependent projects.

They also may differ in their views of the social order to which they contribute, and often will differ in the persons with whom they interact. Different individuals and groups also will differ in the help they can mobilize to achieve influence. This is part of what we meant when, in our discussion of negotiated order, we said that power was situational. We meant that resources, and therefore influence, are situated in relationships, and are not best understood as properties of individuals abstracted from their social context. As Stogdill (1974) has said, 'Social power implies a relationship in which participants are bound together by interdependency, influence, and exchange'(p.293).

It is for reasons such as these that we have emphasized interdependencies between actors and the mutuality of social relationships rather than hierarchy and one-way dependency relationships. The failure to recognize interdependence and mutuality as qualities of relationships may account for the lack of attention paid to negotiation and the over-emphasis on relationships of authority and dominance.

Relationships may be mobilized intentionally for the purposes of influence. Consider, for example, that A may have a strong relationship with B who, in turn, has a strong relationship with C. A may use his or her direct relationship with B indirectly to achieve influence over C. Many of our chief executives made reference to relationships which they mobilized in these ways. For example, one chief executive spoke of the relationships he had built with certain private contractors, and the ways in which he had occasionaly mobilized these relationships to achieve influence over particular Trade Union officials. He reported using these third parties to get over a message which he knew would not be believed (authenticated)[14] if he delivered it himself. In other words, he understood that the meaning of the message would be constructed in different ways depending on the relational context from which it was believed to originate; in the wider context of relationships, some are more influential than others.

The broad implication of our various arguments is that the static concept of organization needs to be replaced by the dynamic concept of organizing (see Chapter 2). Furthermore, both cognitive and political processes must be seen as intrinsic to the processes of organizing. Cognitive processes have been ignored almost entirely.[15] They will be discussed in detail in Chapter 4. Political processes have received more attention, particularly in recent years,[16] but little of this has found its way into into basic OB texts. Certainly, nothing has been done to change the entitative concept of organization which dominates the literature. When people have talked about politics is has been seen as something that happens *in* organizations[17] rather than something which is endemic to the activities of organizing (as we have seen in Chapter 2). As we have argued in Chapter 2, we think that this misses the point. The static concept of organization central to the entititative approach needs to be replaced with a dynamic concept in which organization is constituted and reconstituted through cognitive and political processes which emerge as people seek the help of others to add value to their lives.

Summary and conclusions

For those who are interested in the relations between person and organization, entitative concepts have serious deficiencies. Following the arguments of Chapters 1 and 2 we traced some of the implications of viewing people as intelligent actors who create their contexts, just as they are created by them. When persons and contexts are joined through processes of mutual creation these processes, processes of organizing, become the focus of interest. However, the concept of process is very different from that implied by entitative perspectives. No longer are processes seen as simple causal mechanisms which link 'inputs' (from person and organization) to 'outputs' (for person and organization). Rather, the processes of organizing are seen as complex processes of construction and reciprocal influence. These processes have emergent qualities which cannot be reduced to the independent contributions either of people or contexts. These qualities combine in complex ways 'what is in the head and in the world' (Chapter 1).

We joined persons and contexts through our arguments about interdependent relations and the implications these have for person's constructions of who they are (identities), and their more or less collective constructions of the social orders to which they contribute – in 'thought' and 'deed'. We argued that these processes can be contextualized further by locating them in relation to 'projects'. We argued that actors construct social orderings in relation to what they perceive to be 'issues' – major changes in the status quo; this is part of what it means to say that projects are set both by the person and their context. Actors do so through interrelated cognitive, social and political processes of organizing. These are processes in which actors negotiate their own descriptions of issues (social and cognitive) and seek to influence the descriptions and actions of others (social and political). They are symbolic processes, processes of influence, negotiation, and exchange; they are processes in which joint action is made possible; they are processes in which the valuations and interests of some actors are better protected and promoted than the valuations and interests of others.

Notes

1. Athay and Darlay (1981) are amongst the few who have attempted to develop the concept of projects. Their work is worth consulting in the original.
2. We do *not* intend to imply that participants are *equally* able to influence one another. Already, we have spoken of the importance of the historical dimension in social relations. Talk of ongoing social processes, negotiation, and influence, should not be taken to imply naiveté concerning power, dominance, and conflict.
3. Let us repeat, this is not to say that anything goes. We are not advocating relativism as a

replacement for realism. In any particular social context what is thinkable and 'doable' is constrained by the histories of the actors and their relationships.

4. See our earlier discussion of office work in Chapter 1, and the case of the Danish TV company described in Chapter 2.

5. This point was well understood by the so-called 'negotiated order' theorists. We shall make much of this general line of argument.

6. This issue often is discussed in terms of resources and constraints. We are unhappy with this language, both because a 'physicalist' stance often is taken (e.g. Stewart, 1976), and because the underlying picture of the instrumentalities of relationships is not one we share.

7. The term counteracting groups is taken from Fiedler (1967).

8. This makes it impossible entirely to rule by fiat, as we have suggested in Chapter 1 and Chapter 2.

9. For further discussion see Verba (1961) and Stogdill (1974).

10. Morley et al. (1988) have argued that one of the major tasks of research on relations between groups should be to explore the limits of the process of negotiation. Chalmers and Cormick (1971) have made the important point that issues which were once non-negotiable may become matters for negotiation when social contexts change. In their view, negotiation is part of a more general struggle for power, in which the agenda is controlled by the majority group. They have argued that, in some cases, minority groups must refuse to negotiate until they can negotiate the implementation of their own demands. For further discussion see Morley et al. (1988).

11. The Trades Union movement may, perhaps, be analysed in this way. Hartley et al. (1983) have argued that all trades unions face a democracy dilemma in which the need for leadership conflicts with the need for democracy.

12. For further discussion of the importance of trial arguments see Huff (1984).

13. By building strong relationships with those directly in the Treasury Department.

14. See Goldhaber et al. (1968). For further analysis see Chapter 4.

15. The reader who would like to see the state of the art is referred to Sims, Dennis, Gioia, and associates (1986).

16. The best examples are perhaps Olsen (1978), Pfeffer (1981); Mintzberg (1983), Kanter (1984), and Lee and Lawrence (1985).

17. See Bacharach and Lawler (1980), for example.

PART 2

Organizing processes

In Part 2, we bring together and develop further our arguments about organizing. In this way, we hope to show what it means to take seriously the concept of person which emerges from modern psychology. What it means, in a general sense, is that it is necessary to develop a picture of relational processes as qualities of organizing. Following the arguments of Part 1, we are in a position to build a more detailed picture of the various ways organizing is more or less collectively performed through interrelated processes which are cognitive, social, and political. Our central concern will be to paint a descriptive picture of organizing. However, we also develop further the skills argument begun in Part 1. This is to say that we try to make more familiar our normative argument that projects are performed skilfully through processes which participants find legible, coherent, and open-ended. So, for example, political processes are especially evident when the 'structure in process' of a project is incoherent, allowing particular actors to pursue their lines of action at the expense of others. This may be all very well for them in the short term. However in the longer term, their need for help, in the context of the interdependencies which characterize their relational setting, will mean that the 'agreements' which once seemed stable, will come 'unstuck'.

As we observed in the Preface, our distinctions between cognitive, social, and political processes are for analytical purposes. Without these distinctions, it would not be possible to make a manageable discussion – so much would have to be said at once. We have combined our discussion of social and cognitive processes in Chapter 4, and discuss social and political processes in Chapter 5. The discussion is organized in this way because, as we have shown, social processes are the vehicle both for the political, and for the cognitive processes of organizing. Both chapters emphasize relationships between the person and their context. Particular emphasis is given to *social relations* (relational processes) as they characterize contexts. Discussion is focused on persons and processes within and between groups, and on groups acting in relation to other groups. We stress that it is impossible to understand within-group processes if the group is abstracted from its social setting, that is, its relations with other groups.

When we refer to *cognitive processes*, we do so in order to focus on the attempts of actors *to build their own understandings*, descriptions, or what we earlier described as valuations. Given our focus on the constructive qualities of relationships between an actor and their context and – in particular – the significance of social relationships in the processes of construction, much of what we want to say about cognitive processes also requires talk about social processes. In Chapter 4 we discuss cognitive processes. These are the processes involved in knowing, that is, understanding – what we sometimes call making descriptions. We discuss the processes of mutual creation in which person makes their context whilst also being made by it. This means that we have two broad areas of concern. The first focuses on how persons make their context, for example, by striving for consistency, selecting and shaping and the like. The second focuses on the role of contexts as they shape a person's cognitions. Here is where we get into the argument that not 'anything goes'. So, when an actor constructs social order through the performance of their projects they interact with others who also are constructing their social order. When people act in relation to one another, especially when they expect their relationships to have a future, they influence and are influenced by the constructions of others. Joint action only is possible when there is a degree of agreement about those constructions such that two or more interdependent actors agree shared descriptions. At the level of action, actors sometimes agree to merge their lines of action, and sometimes the relationships between the actors is such that power and conformity preside, at least for a time.

In Chapter 5, we discuss political and social processes, this time emphasizing the political qualities of organizing. It is here that we pay most attention to social influence processes as they shape social constructions – in action – and 'inside peoples heads' so to speak. Remember, we see political processes as intrinsic to organizing. Unlike those who take an entitative perspective, we do not see 'politics' as something 'naughty' which happens 'outside' formal organization. Rather, we see organizing as political because persons and groups have quite different views about their contexts in general, and their projects in particular. In other words, they differ in how they wish to *'add value' to their lives and to the lives of others*. Another way to make this point is that *actors differ in their views about what kinds of help they, and others in their relational setting, will need* in order to act, to merge lines of action, and to agree a working and workable consensus about contexts and issues.

The significance of these differences becomes clear when it also is understood that social relations cannot be reduced to the qualities emphasized in an entitative perspective. So, for example, the political qualities of social relations cannot be understood when power and influence is seen only to flow from organization structures, legitimate authority, and the like. Equally, the political aspects of social relations cannot be understood when power and authority are viewed solely in relation to the more or less 'rational' pursuit of 'organizational goals' ('unitary perspective'). Last, the political aspects of social relations cannot be understood when human actors are seen as separate from their contexts such that cognitions their simply are 'right' or 'wrong'. Given that cognitions are socially constructed, actors always may influence the constructions and actions of others with whom they are interdependent. They may do so in ways which may be more or less helpful, to themselves and to others, both in the short-term and in the longer term. These arguments allow us then to shift our emphasis to organizing skills. We become more normative, suggesting that *skilful organizing processes are grounded in caring which takes seriously the future of relationships. If actors understand that they are connected by the help they need from each other, then this must be so.*

Chapter 4
Cognitive processes

Introduction

We have suggested that the activities of organizing have cognitive as well as political aspects, and that people need help to make sense of their social worlds (see Preface). The purpose of this chapter is to examine the cognitive aspects of organizing in more detail.

Cognition is a term used to refer to a large set of activities involved in knowing, learning, and thinking. Much of modern cognitive psychology is concerned to analyse these activities as cognitive skills, and to show how they form the basis for intelligent action. Some of this work has important implications for the study of the activities of organizing, as we have seen in Chapter 1. However, the attempt to study the mind as an information processing device has meant that most research on cognition has an intra-personal focus. It has been concerned with those individual processes which allow us to work with social or non-social 'objects'.

Relatively little attention has been paid to ways in which our cognitions are constructed socially. We have argued that one way of looking at a project is to see it as a set of conversations which commit people to some future action. Furthermore, we have made it clear that the people concerned will expect to have to justify their actions, or their failures to act. Such conversations provide the process, and constitute the context, in which our most important cognitions are formed. Consequently, if we are to illuminate the cognitive aspects of organizing we shall have to consider what has been learned about the social construction of cognition.

There are four major theoretical perspectives which have special significance for the study of cognitive aspects of organizing. We shall briefly describe them, and attempt to show what is distinctive about each approach.

Theoretical perspectives

Bartlett's social constructivism

Bartlett is widely regarded as one of the founding fathers of the current 'cognitive revolution' in psychology. His classic studies of remembering contain some vivid demonstrations of the constructive nature of cognition. We have already described some of this work in Chapter 1. Although that work was concerned with intra-personal rather than interpersonal factors Bartlett realized that social factors could not be ignored. He made it plain that many of the constructions were conventional (see Chapter 3), meaning they were current in some group to which the person belonged (see Bartlett, 1932, p.118). He also recognized that groups were important because they provided 'a persistent framework of institutions and customs' which acted 'as a schematic basis for constructive memory' (p.255). Later, he reached similar conclusions in his work on thinking (Bartlett, 1958).

Bartlett saw very clearly that the conventional elements in remembering and thinking had their roots in social interactions guided by social norms. Thus, he was concerned not only with the constructive nature of cognition, but with its *social* construction. This aspect of Bartlett's work has not always been appreciated,[1] although he was one of the first psychologists directly to study the social nature of cognition.

To study the social nature of remembering Bartlett (1932) examined the chains of recollection produced when memories of prose passages were transmitted from person to person.[2] His general conclusion was that people's memories were 'rationalizations' designed to reduce the material to 'any form which an ordinary member of a given social group will accept with a minimum of questioning'. He wrote that 'the actual manner of reduction to such a form may vary greatly from one type of material to another, although the underlying psychological tendency which is being satisfied remains the same' (p.175).

In his later work Bartlett (1958) examined the nature of 'adventurous' thinking using a combination of theoretical analysis, case studies, and laboratory experiment. To be specific, he was concerned with the kind of thinking done by experimental scientists, by artists, and by ordinary people, faced with problems of immediate communication. He took the view that each kind of thinking was 'an extension of evidence, in line with evidence and in such a manner as to fill up gaps in the evidence' (p.20). But how that evidence was *extended* depended on the same two factors identified as important in his work on memory, namely social interaction and social norms. This is nowhere more clear than in his account of the nature of scientific thinking. He wrote that this was 'fundamentally cooperative, social, and cannot proceed far without the stimulus of outside contacts' (p.123). He also examined the nature of the social conventions which gave each kind of thinking a certain distinctive character. As he put it, scientific thinking compels by proof, everyday thinking convinces by strong assertion, and artistic thinking satisfies by attainment.

Vygotsky's genetic psychology

At about the same time Bartlett was working on the social nature of remembering Vygotsky was working, quite independently, on problems of the cultural development of the child (Vygotsky, 1929). We have called his work 'genetic psychology' because it is based upon what he called the 'general genetic law of human development'. The term genetic does not mean that he was working within the discipline of molecular biology. Rather, 'genetic' is to be construed as 'genesis', demonstrating a focus on the origin and growth of knowledge. The law states that:

> Any function in the child's cultural development appears twice, or on two planes. First it appears on the social plane, and then on the psychological plane. First it appears between people as an interpsychological category, and then within the child as an intrapsychological category. This is equally true with regard to voluntary attention, logical memory, the formation of concepts, and the development of volition. (Vygotsky, 1981, p.163)

In other words, Vygotsky thought that the intra-personal processes which constitute higher mental functioning were social constructions embodied in the interpretive practices of particular social groups. This is why he thought that psychology required a socio-historical perspective (Bakhurst, 1990). It is why Bruner has said that the main implication of Vygotsky's work is that 'social transaction is the fundamental vehicle of education and not, so to speak, solo performance' (Bruner, 1985, p.25).

Some of those who have been influenced by Vygotsky have argued that children learn from adults rather in the way that apprentices learn from experts (Kaye, 1982). That is to say, the experience of the child is rather carefully constructed through a process of contingent instruction, so that the growing capacities of the child remain effectively coupled to the demands of the task (Wood, 1988). What happens is that the apprentice learns which problems the expert thinks are important, and why. He or she also learns strategies and tactics for handling just those kinds of task. A natural extension of this kind of metaphor is to say that what is true for children is also true for adults. This is one further reason why both children and adults may be expected to develop certain 'dominant competencies', involving 'local' rather than 'global' expertise (see Chapter 1).[3]

Part of this process involves learning various narratives, stories, sagas, or scripts about social life.[4] Whatever the language used, the general point is the same. Narratives, stories, sagas, and scripts 'make explicit the meanings inherent in the social dramas which they portray'(Orr, 1990, p.175). In terms of the design metaphor we introduced in the first chapter, they help us to 'go beneath the surface' because they help us to work out what is likely to happen, and why. Orr's own work has suggested that technical specialists diagnose faults in machines using stories in the 'community memory'. The stories are important because they

> combine facts about the machine with details of the context in which they are relevant, presenting both a fragment of theory about how the machine works with an illustrative example which both guides and constrains the application of the information about the machine... [The] technicians display a fine bricoleur's instinct in telling their stories, preserving the event in all its detail against the future chance to make something of it. (Orr, 1990, p.185)

Anyone with an old car will recognize the kind of community learning which is involved. What Orr has said of stories about machines we would say about relationships. As a reader you may like to pause and ponder the effect of changing 'machine' to 'relationship' and 'context' to 'social context' in the passage from Orr you have just read. From our point of view, stories are important because they situate general lessons about threats and opportunities in the context of particular project work.

We have argued that the social world is not inherently orderly because social actions and events cannot completely be described (see Part 1). Consequently, we have always to work out what actions mean on the basis of evidence which is fragmentary or incomplete. According to Bennett and Feldman (1981) stories help us to make unambiguous interpretations because they bring together and organize incomplete descriptions into structures which make sense because they link scene, act, agent, agency, and purpose in specific ways.

Symbolic interactionism

Vygotsky argued that cognitive processes were forms of mental activity mediated by systems of symbols, such as natural languages. In his view psychologists would only start to understand the nature of human consciousness when they began to apply the methods of semiotic analysis (see Bakhurst, 1990). Consequently, his views have much in common with those who work within the perspective of 'symbolic interactionism' (see Part 1)

Symbolic interactionism is one form of 'sociological social psychology' (McCall and Simmons, 1982). Like Vygotsky, those who work within this perspective take an approach to social cognition through interpretive understanding. However, in this case much of what they have to say has developed from the work of G.H.Mead. There are a variety of theories, but they share a concern with four main themes.[5]

First, it is argued that we we live in a world of artificial rather than natural objects. The objects are artificial in the sense that they are made by humans rather than given by nature. The objects are 'symbolized objects' known through a process of 'apperception'. To quote Weigert (1983), 'The prefix *ap* tells us that humans *actively* bring prior meanings to the events that are transformed into symbolized objects by the application of these meanings' (p.35). This is not controversial. We introduced some very similar ideas in Chapter 1. However, the symbolic interactionist treatment of interpretive understanding has done much more than other treatments to emphasize the *social characteristics* of symbols.[6] According to Weigert, for example, symbols have three important social characteristics. First, they are conventional, which means that they are part of a public rather than a private language.[7] Second, they are concomitant, which means that they may elicit the same reponse from different people. And finally, they are socially transmitted, which means that they are learned when the user internalizes the linguistic practices of a particular social group.

The second theme is that social action is only possible when symbols are shared. As we have seen in Part 1, if we are to coordinate our actions with those of other people we must be able to agree on the tasks that are to be performed, and negotiate commitments to certain lines of action. Without shared symbols we would be unable to communicate with each other to agree descriptions or to say what we intended to do. This does not mean that symbols will carry entirely the same meaning for different people. Rather, the symbols we use will 'point competent members in the direction of the relevant interpretations' (Weigert, 1983, p.81). What is required is sufficient consensus to permit the mutual adjustment of different lines of action. To quote Weigert:

> Through shared symbols, individuals are able to communicate with each other and to control, more or less, their own action and the action of others. The key characteristic of society . . . is a plurality of interactors who, more or less successfully, interpret, control, and predict their own and others' interaction.(p.55)

The third theme in the symbolic interactionist approach is the idea that some of the most important interpretive activity is to be construed as the negotiation of identities, or meanings for the self. It is said that we gain identities as social selves when there is a working consensus that we will attempt to pursue certain lines of action, in certain ways, because we are who we are. One of the most distinctive aspects of the symbolic interactionist approach is that the working consensus is seen as the outcome of a negotiation.[8] If this is correct, it is not possible entirely to separate persons from contexts. What we take to be individual personality is really a matter of the identities we attempt to develop or maintain in interaction with others who are attempting to develop or maintain identities of their own. Thus, the social context is much more than an environment in which people engage in various kinds of project work. To quote from Weigert once again, 'Self is a process but it is not contained within our skins... Even the most intimate experience of self is realized in relations with others and in the meanings they reflect back to self' (p.33).

Finally, symbolic interactionist approaches take a social psychological view of truth. They argue that truth is socially certified because it is socially shared. This means that for something to be 'true' it must be certified as free from the idiosyncracies of any particular person. However, there needs to be a further qualification since, as Weigert has pointed out, 'not all members of a community are equally recognized as competent to certify and validate the truth of a vital proposition' (p.63). Truth must be certified by those who are seen as competent by virtue of training, experience, or some other investment.[9]

Reference groups and social identities

The implication of Vygotsky's work is that we assign meanings to objects, people, and events when we learn the interpretive practices of a particular social group. We agree with this. We also agree with the symbolic interactionist point of view that some of the most important interpretive practices give meaning to the self. We now need to add that certain people and certain groups have special salience in that process of learning. Because of this they are called reference persons and reference groups. As Sherif and Sherif (1969) have put it, they provide 'anchors' for a person's 'relatedness'. This means that reference persons and reference groups are the source of a person's aspirations and evaluative beliefs.

Reference persons and reference groups are important because social actions are inherently ambiguous. As Bennett and Feldman (1981) have pointed out the same action may be described in a variety of different ways. We are able to work out what is going on, and why, because we have organized systems of evaluative beliefs derived from our interactions with reference persons and reference groups. Social psychologists have discussed such systems of beliefs under headings such as attitudes, images, outlooks, ideologies, or operational codes.[10] What is important about such systems of belief is that they all help to determine how we think about, feel about, and act with respect to particular projects. They are ways of codifying experience which first, direct our attention to factors which are important; second, let us 'amplify' new information by placing it in the context of what is already known; and finally, they help us to search for explanations of what is going on, and why. In this way, they help us to construct an order of value in our social worlds. They give us a distinctive point of view.[11]

Sherif and Sherif have described some of our attitudes as 'ego-involving' because they allow us to give some sort of integration to our feelings about ourselves. They have argued that the effect of making these attitudes salient is to 'generate modes of behaviour that are more consistent, more selective, and more characteristic of the person' (p.387). However, an alternative interpretation would be to say that attitudes are ego-involving to the extent that they focus our attention on the need to justify our actions, so that they appear reasonable to members of our reference groups. This would generate modes of behaviour that are more consistent, more selective, and more characteristic of the person considered as a member of that group .

Some writers have taken the view one person would act much like another to the extent that they act as members of groups. This is, for example, a central tenet of the Social Identity Theory elaborated by Tajfel, Turner, and their associates (Brown, 1988; Hogg and Abrams, 1988). According to this theory, having a social identity is a matter of belonging to a particular category or social class. Once people have been identified in this way we are able to think of ways in which class members are relatively similar, and distinctively different from members of other classes. The theory predicts that differences between people who belong to the same group are blurred. At the same time, differences between people who belong to different groups are sharpened. Apparently, we exaggerate the importance of comparisons which favour the in-group over the out-group; and we minimize the importance of com-parisons which favour the out-group over the in-group. It is suggested that cognitive biases of this kind allow us to establish, or maintain, social identities which are positive, distinctive, and secure.

This is a valuable suggestion, and it is now clear that Social Identity Theory may provide a systematic approach to a wide range of social phenomena. One of the reasons is that it is concerned with the ways in which relations between groups affect relations within groups, and vice versa. The mechanism is taken to be that of social comparison. Consequently, Social Identity Theory tries to explain how changes in relations within and between groups may affect the outcomes of the process of social comparison. It also explores the ways in which changes in those outcomes may lead to changes in relations within and between groups. There are, of course, other approaches to the study of intergroup relations, and there are critics of Social Identity Theory (including Morley, 1982a). Nevertheless, what Social Identity Theory does show is that we cannot understand what happens within in groups if we abstract those groups from the context of their relations within other groups. Consequently, when we spoke of the relationship between persons and contexts (Part 1) we should have made it clear that the context includes relations between groups. As Tajfel (1981) has said, 'the social setting of intergroup relations contributes to making... individuals what they are and they in turn produce this social setting; they and it develop and change symbiotically' (p.31).

According to Tajfel, the primary task of a theory of intergroup relations is to explain the nature of this symbiosis. One of his major achievements has been to show that certain kinds of theory are quite incapable of illuminating symbiotic relationships of this kind because they distort the nature of persons, processes and contexts (Tajfel, 1981). The theories are those we have called individualistic. They distort our concept of person because they fail to give people the respect that they deserve as participants in the creation of social settings; they distort our concept of a social process because they fail to appreciate the nature of collective social action; and they distort the nature of social contexts because they lack any sense of socio-historical perspective (see Morley, Webb, and Stephenson, 1988).

Constructing cognitions collectively

Putting the four perspectives together we are reminded, first, that cognitive processes select, transform, and enrich information, and allow us to make sense of our social worlds (see Chapter 1). We now see that how this happens depends on what we have learned of the interpretive practices of particular social groups. Some of these groups have such important effects that they are called reference groups. Even so, the process of constructing shared meanings is somewhat precarious because social actions are inherently ambiguous, and cannot completely be described. When we consider those processes by which collective cognitive images are created and changed it is important to realize that in many conversations what is said may be incomplete, ungrammatical, and hardly make any sense at all if taken out of context (see Weigert, 1983, p.103). What happens is that people construe events and pass their inferences on to others in summary form. Their summaries are not only partial but partisan, in the sense that they reflect different appreciations of what is important, and why. Consequently, different people may have very different ways of looking at the issues, alternatives, policies, and practices involved in project work. Two forces combine to produce a convergence of ideas. This first is the need for collective action. This requires a working consensus, sufficient to allow the coordination of different lines of action. The second is the need to use other people as 'reference points' or 'anchors' to test the validity of our ideas. Evidently, we validate our ideas when we find a working consensus amongst people similar to ourselves that this is how the world is, what we can do within it (Weigert, 1983).[12]

Contexts of learning and contexts of justification

When we join an organization we begin to learn a system of evaluative beliefs (valuations) which helps us represent relationships within that organization, and possibilities for action. Typically, we will be guided through the process by a small number of 'sponsors' (some people prefer the term 'mentor') with whom we form very close relationships (Baron, 1986). They help us to construct cognitions which are suitably elaborated, organized, and appropriate to a particular domain. Consequently, we learn to detect structure in that domain, and use that structure as a guide to action. This is why we have said that practical expertise requires organized knowledge of the world.

However, organized knowledge is a necessary but not sufficient condition for effective performance. As projects get larger it becomes more and more likely that important decisions will be made on the basis of abstracted, aggregated information (Steinbruner, 1974). Under such circumstances it becomes both more important and potentially more dangerous to rely on stable systems of belief about the world. Without such stable systems of belief it is almost impossible to make considered, consistent, judgements about issues, alternatives, policies, or practices. This is why certain high level officials who move from one sector to another sometimes show a 'syndrome of uncommitted thinking', in which they take over the beliefs first of one person, then another, without any higher order resolution of the two points of view.[13]

On the other hand, there are those with very general sets of beliefs, with components which are so tightly coupled and so ego-involving that they prevent actively open-minded thinking.[14] This may have two rather unfortunate consequences. First, it will always be possible to find evidence to confirm scripts derived from such beliefs, so that the beliefs will be extremely resistant to change.[15] Second, it may lead people to engage in a form of satisficing which involves an irrational search for cognitive consistency (Jervis, 1976). It seems that, when they make decisions, they begin by considering how well a particular policy seems likely to satisfy one or two of their most salient values. Let us say that they have good reasons for their choices, and their choices follow from those reasons. However, once they have identified the policy which is best in these respects they find reasons to believe that their chosen policy will be the best in many other respects. However, the reasons follow from their choices, rather than their choices from their reasons.[16] If Jervis is correct, one major motivation is to minimize cognitive strain by exaggerating the benefits of the chosen policy and minimizing the costs. He has also pointed out that the operation of cognitive dissonance may be involved.

The theory of cognitive dissonance was the original creation of Leon Festinger (1957). It started from the deceptively simple idea that people dislike inconsistency in their ideas. However, the inconsistency was not the inconsistency of the logician but the psycho-logic of the ordinary person. To mark the difference Festinger used the term 'dissonance'. He defined dissonance as a psychological state which existed when people thought that some of their cognitions followed from the obverse of others. He thought that people would find inconsistency of this kind uncomfortable and would try to reduce it.

One of the most striking implications of dissonance theory is that people will change their beliefs once they have made a decision, finding new reasons, or more powerful reasons, to support their choice. Such changes are not, however, the result of an open-minded reappraisal of the nature of the choice. Basically, it seems

> that people seek strong justification for their behavior. They are not content to believe merely that they behaved well and chose wisely – if this were the case they would only have to maintain the beliefs that produced their decisions.

> Instead, people want to minimize their internal conflict. This leads them to seek to believe that the reasons for acting or deciding as they did were overwhelming. (Jervis, 1976, p.382)

One way of looking at this is to say that people feel threatened when they focus on the costs of the policy they have chosen or when they focus on the benefits of the policies they have not. Consequently, they are motivated to find defensive rationalizations to bolster the choices they have made. The net result is that they see a greater difference between the policy they have chosen (more advantages, fewer disadvantages) and the policies they have rejected (fewer advantages, more disadvantages).[17] This is known as 'the spreading of the alternatives'. It may be observed both in laboratory and in naturalistic settings (see Janis and Mann, 1977).

What we have said so far involves talk about *self-justification* rather than talk about inconsistency between cognitive elements. It fits with more recent treatments of dissonance which have attempted to define dissonance in terms which clearly implicate the self. Many theorists now take the view that dissonance is only aroused when the relevant cognitions are ego-involving in some way, and when people commit themselves to choices for which they feel personally responsible.[18] However, once these moves have been made it is not clear that we need the concept of dissonance at all. Concepts such as self-defensiveness or self-justification do all the work. Furthermore, they allow us to take note of powerful emotional needs to avoid anticipatory fear, shame, and guilt.[19] Because of this we may expect to find that the spreading of alternatives may occur before people commit themselves to a particular choice. And there is some evidence that this does occur.[20] Janis and Mann (1977) have suggested that people very often engage in long periods of actively open-minded thinking, but begin to process information in a very biased way as they move towards a final choice (finding more and more reasons to support that choice).

More recently, Billig (1989) has argued that concepts such as dissonance need to be located in a 'rhetorical context'. He has shown convincingly that it 'is not inconsistency per se which is disruptive, but the criticisms of inconsistency, and it is the criticisms that raise the need for defensive justification' (p.162). This suggests that the intra-personal concept of dissonance needs to be replaced with inter-personal concepts such as criticism or justification. From this point of view, people will do whatever is necessary to minimize doubts that the policies they have chosen will be certified by competent members of their reference groups. In some rhetorical contexts this may increase the likelihood of biased information processing, such as that involved in the spreading of the alternatives. In other rhetorical contexts it may have the opposite effect, producing an increased commitment to interpretive practices based on systematic methods which promote actively open-minded thinking (see Chapter 7).[21] In some contexts, groups tend to 'insulate' themselves from other parts of an organization. They may seek out additional information in a one-sided way, looking only for reasons to support the choice that they would like to make, and ignoring other evidence. In contrast, there are other contexts in which people are highly motivated to build networks of organizational intelligence (see Goldhaber *et al.*, 1968). There is evidence that they

> have a strong incentive to increase, rather than decrease, their exposure to (and mastery of) the opposition's arguments when they are worried about inescapable encounters with powerful opponents who will attack their decision. They may go out of their way to change their social network by cultivating informal contacts with representatives of the opposition to learn how they think, which arguments they take most seriously, and how they can be won over or neutralized – all of which provides information for planning their defense in an impending dispute. (Janis and Mann, 1977, p.218)

Notice that it is not just the activity of building a network which is important. It is perfectly possible for people to spend a lot of time talking to other people and never find out anything of importance.[22] People need to understand the skills of questioning others. They must be aware that even those in the best position to listen, digest, and construe events, must fill up gaps in the evidence, and pass on their inferences in summary form (Dunsire, 1978). Furthermore, they must understand that what is said will depend on personal and collective aspects of the relationship between the speaker and the hearer. In general terms, we all have to piece together an understanding of social actions from people who are only able to tell part of the story, and who may tailor their presentations according to relationships and their settings.[23] This means that even when we believe information is authentic it is sensible to do what we can to contrast that information with information from other sources. What is needed is a proper appreciation of the contingency of human cognition (Schudson, 1990). It is this appreciation which makes us realize that any single perspective may be extremely misleading when social activity is informal or ill-structured. This is why Linstone and his associates have argued that intelligent social action requires the simultaneous application of multiple perspectives (Linstone *et al.*, 1984). Without such multiple perspectives it may be all too easy for people to jump to conclusions and see only what they expect to see (Jervis, 1976).

There are good theoretical reaons to believe that learning about the world requires people to use organized systems of beliefs to anticipate what is going to happen, and to explore what has happened. However, if they are not to see only what they expect to see they must also be sensitive to new information. Neisser (1976) has argued that there is a 'dialectical contradiction' between these two requirements. He has argued that the contradiction would prove fatal but for the fact that we are mobile organisms and live in a mobile world. If we want to learn about our social world the lesson is that we must move about that world (build social networks) or have the world come to us (engage multiple perspectives). Otherwise we will fail to look at the world from different points of view. We will fail to exploit the opportunity to learn from other people with views very different from our own.

Putting the core problems in a relational setting

There are some contexts which motivate people to pay a great deal of attention to problems of organizational intelligence. There are other contexts which do not. Janis and Mann (1977) have argued that whether or not people engage in actively open-minded thinking depends on the kinds of questions they ask themselves as they go through various stages of project work. Although they have used different labels, it is clear that Janis and Mann have in mind a series of stages similar to those we introduced in Chapter 1. The stages are stages in a process of decision making which is supposed to apply to individual and to collective work. Janis and Mann's general strategy has been to identify a number of questions a person might ask if he or she were making decisions on their own. They have then gone on to ask how that person might be affected by the collective setting if he or she were a member of a decision-making group.

From our point of view, this is too much of an abstraction of people from their social (relational) contexts. Even when people make decisions alone, if the decision is important, they will be concerned to justify both the process and the product of their activity to various members of their reference groups. Consequently, the questions they are likely to ask form part of the interpretive practices of those groups. Our own preference has been to consider project work as a combination of individual and collective work which takes place in social settings. The relationship between the people and the setting is one of mutual creation. The individual commits himself or herself to a collective frame of reference but is a participant in the creation of that collective frame. The process is one of negotiation.

As we have said, we see structure in the process of project work as one form of negotiated social order. This means that whether or not there is a clear sequence of stages is something to be negotiated within each social setting.[24] Furthermore, when we say that people negotiate the identification of issues, the development of solutions, the choice between alternatives, and the implementation of policies, we mean that the kinds of questions they ask are themselves the result of a collective process. To understand this collective process we need simultaneously to consider several aspects of the relational setting (see Morley, 1990).

Actively open-minded thinking and vigilant information processing

The term actively open-minded thinking is taken from Baron (1988). It refers to thinking which follows the rules of good thinking, defined by some prescriptive model, and which, therefore, is free from avoidable bias. One important principle is that people should not commit themselves to a particular interpretation of the evidence when they know new evidence may become available (and there is no special reason to believe that information coming in early will be more trustworthy than information coming in late). In other words, people should have fairly low confidence in their initial interpretation of what is going on. A second important principle is that neutral evidence should not be allowed to strengthen a belief. There is a great deal of evidence that people violate both these principles.

Janis and Mann (1977) have argued that, when people are involved in making decisions which have important consequences, for themselves or for others, good thinking may be defined in terms of a vigilant orientation to the processing of information. Those who take such an orientation strive towards the ideal of rational choice set out in SEU theory (see Chapter 1). However, demands of the task are scaled down so that people carry them out to the best of their ability, and within their information processing capabilities. In other words, Janis and Mann assume that when people adopt a vigilant orientation to the processing of information they strive to satisfy 'procedural criteria' which mean that they:

1. carefully collect information before, rather than after, a choice is made;

2. carefully establish the existence of a problem and the need to solve it;

3. carefully consider the full range of criteria any solution must meet;

4. carefully consider more than one policy (or possible line of action);

5. carefully consider the costs and benefits of each alternative policy;

6. strive for a comprehensive, coherent, and detailed analysis of the elements of the problem, and of systemic relationships between them;

7. intensively search for new information, process that information in an open-minded way;

8. carefully re-examine the consequences of each policy before making a final choice;

9. make some explicit attempt to work out how best to trade-off costs against benefits;

10. carefully consider how the policy chosen is to be put into practice, paying special attention to the contingency planning required to take account of known uncertainties and risks.[25]

Janis and Mann's analysis has the great advantage that it suggests that having a vigilant orientation is 'not an all-or-nothing affair', but something 'manifested to various degrees under different conditions' (Janis and Mann, 1977, p.12).

The different conditions are formed by various combinations of aspects of the relational setting. Some of the most important aspects are set out below.

Single perspectives versus multiple perspectives

Whenever people are at all unsure about how to think or how to act they are likely to turn to other people, to find out how they think or feel. Social psychologists have described this as a process of social comparison (Festinger, 1954). Initially, it seems that we look for people we trust and respect, and have similar values and beliefs. To the extent that our views are shared they become socially certified as free from personal bias. Consequently, we become much more confident that this is how the world is, and this is what we can do within it.

However, it is worth remembering that people typically see too much order and certainty in their social worlds (see Chapter 1). There is evidence that groups of relatively similar others build a working consensus that gives them confidence, even when such confidence is entirely misplaced.[26] This is why a number of writers have urged that the social comparison process needs to be opened up to include people with very different views. They have argued that what is needed is a 'many-in-one' approach (Morley, 1990) which 'considers ambiguities and differences between observers as essential aspects in the evaluative task' (Linstone, 1984, p.36). One example of this approach is the attempt to build cross-functional teams of specialists to work in engineering product design (see Chapter 7).

Morley (1990) has argued that building teams which engage multiple perspectives is a necessary but not sufficient condition for the long-term success of project work. The 'many-in-one approach' attempts to build collective strength into a team. However, all too often what we see is collective weakness because different kinds of people find it difficult to work together, and because the group fails to find ways of working which promote actively open-minded thinking or vigilant processing of information (see Part 3).

Cohesive versus non-cohesive groups

A group which contains people with very different backgrounds may still be cohesive because people very much want to belong to that group. Because there are many reasons why people want to belong to a group there may be many different types of cohesiveness. One kind of group cohesiveness, called interpersonal cohesiveness, is based on sentiments of mutual liking and respect. Another kind of cohesiveness, called task-based cohesiveness, is based on shared commitments to the task of the group. The first kind of cohesiveness may foster a group atmosphere in which people take too much on trust, and suppress their personal doubts about what is being said. They are likely to persuade themselves that their 'misgivings are not relevant' and that 'the benefit of any doubt should be given to the group consensus' (Janis, 1972, p.201). One effect of such self-censorship is to produce what Janis has called an 'illusion of unanimity' within the group. The second kind of cohesiveness may foster a feeling of commitment to the norms of the group. If these support actively open-minded thinking cohesive groups will be more likely to engage in actively open-minded thinking than non-cohesive groups. However, if the norms do not support actively open-minded thinking cohesive groups will be less likely to engage in actively open-minded thinking than non-cohesive groups. One possibility is that they will spend much more time paying attention to areas of convergence in their thinking, and paying much less attention to areas of divergence. The combination of high interpersonal cohesiveness, high task cohesiveness, and norms which encourage such one-sided thinking, is particularly unlikely to support effective project work (Janis, 1972).

The insulation of the group

As groups become more cohesive (whether in interpersonal or in task terms) they may become more inward looking, and increasingly isolated from other groups in the enterprise, even though members may be drawn from each of the main functional areas of the business.[27] Alternatively, the isolation may occur for other reasons. In any event, it is clear that some groups are composed of people who have lost touch with those networks of people who could provide them with organizational intelligence. The phenomenon is well known in the context of industrial and international relations.[28] It is one of the reasons why people say that those who are doing the negotiation develop different understandings from those who are more remote. It is one of the reasons why certain people are in a position to be persuasive. They are able to combine specific information with general expertise.

Winkler (1974) has made the particularly important point that when people lose touch in this way their images of out-groups are particularly likely to be based on stereotypes. Furthermore, his studies of boards of directors showed that quite inconsistent stereotypes may be accepted by the same person in the same conversation (e.g. 'It's all a few agitators' and 'There's a deep malaise in British industrial relations'). He thought, however, that deficiencies in information were only part of the story. Apparently, what happened was

> that directors activated those interpretations of workers' behaviour, which in varying concrete situations, best furthered their long-term interests. In some situations it suited them to see their workers as malleable (e.g. capable of responding positively to technical innovation and accepting job redefinition), in others as irremediably traditional (e.g. one cannot grant them staff status and equivalent fringe benefits because they would never work overtime).
> (Winkler, 1974, pp.207–8)

It seems that such 'instrumental inconsistency' in attitudes was fairly common, firstly, because of the isolation of the directors, and second, because the contradictions were unlikely to be pointed out in public debate.

Structure in the process of project work

Some time ago, in *The Human Side of Enterprise*, McGregor made the interesting observation that effective management teams were 'self-conscious' about their own operations. There is also evidence that effective groups are effective because they have carefully developed structures in the process of their project work which foster actively open-minded thinking (Morley, 1990). One possibility is to have a series of formal reviews of the progress being made, perhaps bringing in people who are not core-members of the project team. Effectively, this divides the project work into a series of stages and 'gates' (see Chapter 7). Furthermore, people may commit themselves to systematic methods of working within each stage, designed to support disciplined, creative work. It is a matter of considerable controversy which methods do support disciplined, creative work, on any particular task, and which do not, but it is clear that some methods are more likely than others to provide 'procedural safeguards against cursory and biased treatment of policy issues' (Janis and Mann, 1977, p.131).

Relations between groups

We always act towards people on the basis of information which is incomplete. We impute attributes to them, filling in missing information with a series of imaginative 'leaps' and 'jumps' (Cicourel, 1976). The result is that our actions are guided by a general image bearing what has been described as a 'probabilistic correspondence to the other person's themselves' (McCall and Simmons, 1966). There is considerable evidence that, when the other people are members of competing groups, it is all too easy for the image to be generated by various forms of 'black and white' thinking (White, 1970). For example, people often see proposals which are shared as coming only from their own side. The result is to make their own recommendations seem more comprehensive and compelling.[29] There is also evidence that people overestimate the achievements of members of their own groups (especially if they have high status), and underestimate the achievements of members of competing groups.[30] If competition turns into conflict there may even be 'stereotyped views of rivals and enemies as too evil to warrant genuine attempts to negotiate, or as too weak or stupid to counter whatever risky attempts are made to defeat their purposes' (Janis and Mann, 1977, p.130).[31]

Leadership

Janis has shown that, under certain conditions, cohesive groups try to avoid the emotional stress and cognitive strain of actively open-minded thinking (Janis, 1972). They do so, first, by directing their attention to whatever option seems to be preferred by the head, or by a coalition of high status members, or by a simple majority within the group. They then direct their efforts to justifying that choice, leading to the spreading of the alternatives which has been described above. It is clear that some groups who are supposed to be helping to make policy act as if it were their job to justify a policy which has already been made. This means that one of the main responsibilities of the person who heads the group is to avoid showing 'leadership bias' (see Chapter 7).

However, leaders have a much wider brief (as we shall see in Chapter 9). They have to take the lead in the attempt to organize structure in the social process so that the social order which emerges is visible, coherent, and understood by all. They have a special responsibility, for example, to ensure that groups use appropriate methods of work, and that the methods are supported by appropriate norms (Morley, 1990). If they wish to foster actively open-minded thinking they will have to show by their own example 'that the task of critical appraisal is to be given precedence over maintaining traditional forms of deference' (Janis, 1972, p.210).[32] They must also ensure that the group uses an effective communication system (Larson and LaFasto, 1989).

Conflict, commitment, and choice

The above considerations suggest that each of the core problems is least likely to appraised in an active open-minded way when the collective process engages only a single perspective; when the norms of the group discourage critical evaluation; when the group is insulated from other groups; when the structure in the process of project work does not support disciplined creative work; and when the head of the group shows 'leadership bias'. We suppose that the effect of these conditions is likely to be much larger when the group is highly cohesive (whatever the source) or when relations between groups involve competition or conflict (or both). Bearing this in mind, let us return to a consideration of the kinds of questions people ask as they examine the core problems involved in project work. We shall rely heavily on Janis and Mann's (1977) model of conflict, commitment, and choice (see above).

We have said elsewhere that the decision-making process begins when someone recognizes, and responds to, change, or the possibility of change in the existing social order.[33] In other words, decision making starts when someone sees that the change requires a reappraisal of existing policies, so that they, or others, are better able to defend themselves against new threats, or to take advantage of new opportunities. Janis and Mann have suggested that the key question is whether the reappraisal reveals that the threats and opportunities should be taken seriously (so that the decisions are consequential decisions). Typically, this means talking to people we trust, like, and respect, to see whether they agree that challenge deserves to be taken seriously. If they think the challenge is serious, and we ignore it, not only do we risk serious setbacks to our project work, but we also run the risk of losing their esteem.[34]

The discussions with other people help to diagnose the nature of the threat or opportunity a little more precisely. People 'amplify' their beliefs by telling some sort of story about the changes in the social order. This allows them to make preliminary assessments of the kinds of changes which may be required and what sorts of difficulties may be anticipated in putting them into effect. They will then decide whether to raise the issue more formally, bringing the 'issue' to the attention of the group as a whole.

Let us suppose that this decision has been made. According to Janis and Mann, what happens next is that people collectively examine what has happened in the past as a guide to what might happen in the future. From our perspective, this is part of what it means to act intelligently. It explains why, when people make decisions, individually or collectively, one of the outcomes of the decision process is a set of descriptions of the past designed to make sense of the future.[35] When aspects of the social setting foster vigilant information processing, people are likely actively to search for viable alternatives by interrogating those networks which provide them with organizational intelligence. Janis and Mann have said that the key problem is to identify those lines of action which seem to have a good chance of meeting the challenge 'without entailing intolerable costs or risks' (p.174). Consequently, they have described this stage as 'surveying the alternatives'. A vigilant orientation will not necessarily lead to more lines of action being considered, although this may happen. What is more important is that the lines of action which are considered are scrutinised with more care. If a satisfactory policy is identified it may sometimes be implemented without delay.

In other cases, however, people may have to think long and hard about whether to start a more formal examination of the alternatives. If there is no deadline, there may be quite long periods of 'conversations and speculations'[36] during which people try out various ways of 'framing' the issues.[37] Hickson *et al.* (1986) have referred to this as a period of gestation. They found gestation periods in just over half of the cases they analysed (N=150), mostly lasting one or two years. In one extreme case, people talked round the issues for approximately fifteen years before they were willing to set up a working party formally to examine what should be done. In contrast, the other cases proceeded fairly directly to a more formal examination of the pros and cons of the alternatives concerned.

Janis and Mann have described this more formal examination as 'weighing the alternatives'. The central questions are, of course, 'Which is the best available course of action?', and 'Does this course of action satisfy the essential requirements?' In some cases the best available course of action may not meet the essential requirements. What happens then depends on whether people think it realistic to hope to find a new policy which does meet those requirements. Essentially, they are likely to examine the resources available inside and outside the group to see what they might realistically hope to do in the available time. If they think there is a chance of finding a better policy in the time available, they are likely to keep thinking about the problem in an active open-minded way. Otherwise, they are likely to engage in various forms of 'defensive avoidance' (see Janis and Mann, 1977, Chapter 3).

When there is no deadline, people may procrastinate. This may be one reason for long gestation periods (although they may also reflect a vigilant appraisal of the difficulties likely to be involved). If there is a deadline, people will try to shift responsibility for the decision on to others, looking for someone who will tell them what to do. If they cannot find someone to tell them what to do, they will engage in a form of defensive avoidance known as bolstering. Under such conditions the members of a policy making group are likely to make a 'defective' or 'ill-considered' decision because they develop shared rationalizations based on selective exposure to information and on 'soft-headed' thinking. This leads to the classic 'spreading of the alternatives' and allows the members of the group to discount evidence that the policy they prefer will run into serious difficulties if it is put into effect. Janis (1972) was the first person to analyse this pattern of thinking in detail. He gave it the name 'groupthink'.[38] Finally, when people fear 'imminent entrapment' they may be so stressed emotionally that they impulsively implement any solution which seems to promise immediate relief. Wohl (1981) has described the process as one in which people fail to make the best use of their time because of 'emotional excitement, repetitive thinking, and cognitive constriction (manifested by reduction in immediate memory span and simplistic ideas)'.

The final stages of the decision-making sequence identified by Janis and Mann are concerned with the effects of commitment. The penultimate phase in concerned with the moves toward a final choice. The final phase is concerned with the effects of warning signs that the policy is going wrong. It may be no accident that most of the military fiascoes discussed by Janis (1972) were 'planned piecemeal over a long period of time, often with one small commitment growing out of another' (p.239). As we have already pointed out, even those who have engaged in long periods of actively open-minded thinking are likely to bolster their preferred choice as they move towards commitment, finding more and more reasons to justify their choice. Once decisions have been made the effects of commitment make it difficult for people to see that they have made mistakes, because they invent new arguments which convince themselves, and sometimes others, that they were right all along. Indeed, there seems sometimes to be a process of 'rhetorical escalation' which leads to further commitments along the same lines.[39] This seems to be what happened in the various decisions of the Johnson Administration to escalate the Vietnam War (see Janis, 1972). There is also experimental evidence that those who most need to justify their actions are most likely to persevere with a policy, despite signs that the policy is failing to have the desired effects (see Pfeffer, 1981).

Fortunately, the process is not inevitable. We will not always be able to convince others that we were right all along, and consequently, we will not always be able to convince ourselves. If a cohesive group has norms and working procedures which require a 'primary commitment to open-minded scrutiny of new evidence and a willingness to admit errors' the tendency to cling to unsuccessful policies may be replaced by 'a careful reappraisal of the wisdom of their past judgments' (Janis, 1972, p.118). On the other hand, when group members

> feel that loyalty to the group requires unwavering support of the group's past policy decisons, the usual psychological tendency to bolster past commitments is reinforced. Following a series of escalation decisions every member is likely to insist that the same old... drumbeat is the right one and that sooner or later everyone who matters will want to be in step with it. (Janis, 1972, p.118)

How people think collectively depends on how they talk collectively.[40] And how they talk collectively depends on the interpretive practices of the groups to which they belong. These may, or may not support actively open-minded thinking.

Summary

The activities of organizing are concerned with how people act in ways which make sense in particular contexts. Part of this process is cognitive and social. People build different descriptions of their world in different social contexts because their relationships with others provide different rhetorical contexts. People learn different things in different relational settings, and they justify their actions in rather different ways.

It is important to realize that social actions are inherently ambiguous, and cannot be described completely. People construe events in ways which select, transform, and enrich information, from a particular point of view. To use a famous phrase, they go beyond the evidence given, and pass on their inferences to others in a summary form. Consequently, the business of constructing shared meanings is somewhat precarious. We validate our ideas when we find that there is a working consensus amongst reference others that this is how the world is, and this is what we can do within it.

However, the process by which that consensus is constructed is very different in different social contexts. Our review of the literature suggests that the core problems are most likely to be appraised in an actively open-minded way when the collective process engages multiple perspectives; when the norms of the group encourage critical evaluation; when group members open up the process of social comparison by talking to reference others outside the group; when the structure in the process of the project work supports disciplined, creative work; and when the leader of the group shows by example that the rhetorical context is one in which actively open-minded thinking is required. To use the design metaphor introduced in Chapter 1, let us say that certain rhetorical contexts or relationship settings help people to think in actively open-minded ways. Others do not.

Notes ====

1. The social emphasis in Bartlett's work is only just beginning to receive the attention it deserves, and the interested reader will find very useful reviews in Clark and Stephenson (1989) and Shotter (1990).
2. The method is known as the method of serial reproduction. Bartlett used a variety of experimental materials, including folk-tales (such as 'The War of the Ghosts'), descriptive passages (from newspaper reports), and passages presenting arguments, logically arranged so that each point followed from one which came before (dealing, for example, with the modification of species).
3. Those who would like to learn more about Vygotsky's work will find much of value in Wertsch's (1985) *Vygotsky and the Social Formation of Mind*. Wertsch has also edited an extremely useful collection of papers, which place Vygotsky's work in contemporary perspective. For those who would like a concise commentary, we recommend Bakhurst (1990).
4. The term *narrative* has come to prominence fairly recently. Orr (1990) has given several interesting examples of the use of narratives in fault-finding. The term *story* has been used by Bennett and Feldman (1981) in their excellent treatment of *The Reconstruction of Reality in the Courtroom*. The term *saga* has been used by Clark (1972). The term *script* is prominent in cognitive science. Gioia and Poole (1984) and Sims and Gioia (1986) have argued that the term may also be used to illuminate certain aspects of behaviour in organizations.
5. Those who would like to explore the variations are referred to Meltzer, Petras, and Reynolds (1975). The particular summary given here has been much influenced by the work of McCall and Simmons (1966, 1982) and by Weigert (1983).
6. The social characteristics of symbols may be contrasted with their representational, or referential, characteristics.
7. Those who are interested in philosophy will see that the kinds of arguments used have much in common with those used by Wittgenstein in his *Philosophical Investigations*. Wittgenstein's arguments against the possibility of a private language are extremely well known.
8. This is shown very clearly in the work of McCall and Simmons (1966) and Cicourel (1976). Writers such as Goffman (1959) have alerted us to some of the effects which occur when the negotiations break down. Others have pointed out that there is a clear sense in which our social identities are 'situated identities' because they are negotiated with reference to speficic relationships and specific roles as members of specific groups (Hewitt, 1979). The implication is that in some respects we have as many identities as we have relationships or roles.
9. This conclusion has important implications for the study of creativity (which we will explore in Chapter 7). For example, Csikszentmihalyi (1988) has shown that what we count as discoveries depends on 'social processes of negotiation and legitimation' (p.328).
10. Much of social psychology may be construed as an attempt to explore how we relate to persons, projects, and other 'cultural obejcts' (Sherif and Sherif, 1969). The term *attitude* was long regarded as the indispensable concept because it helped to explain the magnitude and direction of these relationships. It has been used in various ways. Our preference is to follow Asch (1952) and treat attitudes as more or less well organized

systems of ideas, which are affect laden, and may have direct implications for action. The term *image* is taken from Holsti (1967). It refers to a set of beliefs about ourselves and others, and how, characteristically, we will think and act. The concept has been extensively used by political scientists interested in problems of perception and misperception in international politics (Jervis, 1970, 1976). The term *outlook* is taken from Davies (1980) and is used to describe various world views, each organized around a central 'project' or 'life-plan'. The term *ideology* is common in the social sciences. For a discussion of its various uses see Billig (1976) Chapter 7. The term operational code is taken from George (1969). It refers to an organized set of 'philosophical' and 'instrumental' beliefs which help people to identify threats and opportunities in project work, and provide guidelines for appropriate action. The concept of an operational code has been extremely useful in the analysis of the (evaluative) belief systems of political leaders such as John Foster Dulles.

11. Asch (1952) has argued that having a point of view

'marks something very significant about persons and the social process . . . To have a point of view means first that we orient ourselves to wide areas of social reality, that we assess complex situations conceptually, and that emotions, motives, and actions become organized around ideas . . . To be in society is to form views of social facts and relatively enduring concerns toward them. By means of these psychological operations we participate in the social process; they make possible the coherent interlocking of action between individuals and between groups; they define our position as members of the social body. Their stability and change seem closely connected with the stability and change of the social order.' (pp.521–2)

12. According to Festinger (1954) this process of social reality testing is one major source of pressure toward uniformity within a social group. Sherif (1936) has given the classic demonstration of this, using the autokinetic effect. This refers to the phenomenon that when we view a point source of light in a darkened room we see the light moving, even though we know it is really fixed. Sherif showed people the illusion a number of times and asked them, each time, to judge how far the light moved from its origin. Early responses were quite unstable, showing marked variation from trial to trial. Later responses were much more stable, however, and converged more and more closely towards a single value. Furthermore, the final value was quite characteristic of the particular individual, noticeably different from those of other people. Subsequently, Sherif placed pairs of individuals in the room, and had them make estimates publicly, one after the other. Once again, initial estimates were unstable, but the estimates of each member of the pair soon began to converge on the same value, characteristic of the pair, making this pair different from others. It seemed that each pair had come to an unspoken agreement about how best to describe what they each saw. To return to our earlier account of Vygotsky's work, we may say that each member of the pair internalized the social practices embodied in the process of mutual adjustment to the demands of their social task. Subsequent research has shown that, once formed, such internalized descriptions are extremely resistant to change (Sherif and Sherif, 1969; Crano and Messé, 1982).

13. The 'syndrome of uncommitted thinking' has been identified by Steinbruner (1974). He has noted instances of uncommitted thinking as people gain new responsibilities within the same sector. If he is correct, this form of thinking has been characteristic of certain Presidents of the United States of America, such as Theodore Roosevelt.

14. Steinbruner (1974) has called this the 'syndrome of theoretical thinking'. De Rivera (1968), Holsti (1967), Steinbruner (1974), and Jervis (1976) have provided a large

number of examples of theoretical thinking from the domain of international relations. There is no reason at all to suppose that the psychological factors they have identified will operate only in that domain. Those who would like to learn more about the nature of actively open-minded thinking will find a very instructive analysis in Baron (1988).

15. The classic example is that of John Foster Dulles, President Eisenhower's Secretary of State. De Rivera (1968) has argued that Dulles gave arms control treaties a low priority because he did not believe the Soviet Union could be trusted to keep its word. However, it seems there was nothing the Soviet Union could have done to convince Dulles that things had changed. It seems that Dulles 'would have interpreted the very acts that should have led him to change his belief, in such a way as to preserve his belief' (De Rivera, 1968, p.26). Apparently, some people become committed to such abstract and extensive patterns of belief that their images of others become virtually impossible to change. This may have unfortunate consequences in the context of in-group out-group relations, as Snyder and Diesing (1977) have shown.

16. Asch (1952) has described what happens with his usual elegance and precision. The person's 'attitude may decisively limit the mental field and resist contradictory facts. One may then tend to judge data and their relations in a way to justify a judgment one does not want to relinquish. Or, if we know the evaluation our group and party place on a given issue, we can solve the problem by seeing it in a way that enables us to arrive at the desired result . . . .The conclusion will come first, whereas judgment and discrimination will have the function of securing the conclusion.' (pp.441–2)

17. Jervis (1976) has described this as a form of 'irrational' consistency because he thinks that it is quite unreasonable to suppose the world is arranged in such neat, helpful, and benign ways.

18. There are excellent discussions of various points of view in Aronson (1969), Janis and Mann (1977), and in Petty and Cacioppo (1981).

19. The contrast between dissonance and defensiveness has been discussed by Deutsch, Krauss, and Rosenau (1962). There is an excellent treatment of self-justification in Aronson (1980). His own preference is to define dissonance in terms of the contrast between the actions expected and the actions performed by people who see themselves as competent, reliable, and trustworthy members of groups. The idea that the internal conflicts implicate anticipations of anxiety, shame, and guilt is central to Janis and Mann's (1977) conflict model of decision making. They do not reject dissonance as a concept, although they think that the motivation to reduce dissonance is often very weak. They also think, as we do, that talk about internal conflict raises different motivations to those considered by dissonance theory in its original form. In particular, they take the view that decisional conflicts induce high levels of stress which disturb our normal abilities to process information.

20. See Janis and Mann (1977) Chapter 4.

21. With due respect to Jervis, there will be occasions when people will be content to believe that they have behaved well and chosen wisely.

22. There are some excellent examples in Blake and Mouton's (1986) studies of executive achievement.

23. It is worth remembering Bartlett's experiments on serial reproduction. Similar pheonomena occur in organizations. It is not uncommon to find estimates that more than eighty percent of the content of a message may be lost as it passes from the top to the bottom of a five- or six-level hierarchy (e.g. Nichols, 1962). Many writers, such as Likert (1961), have taken the view that problems of upward communication are even more severe, largely because of the effects of status. This means that information is

passed from subordinate to superior in very selected forms. After a very measured review of the literature Katz and Kahn (1978) concluded that whilst people 'do want to get certain information up the line' they are often 'afraid of presenting it to the most relevant person or in the most objective form' (p.447). In general it is important to realize that people will tailor their presentations in ways which relate their own abilities, needs, and goals, to the abilities, needs, and goals of their audience, and to other aspects of their social settings (see Tedeschi, Lindskold, and Rosenfeld, 1985, p.69). Goldhaber et al. (1968) have presented a very useful review of some of the relational variables which may affect our abilities to obtain, digest, and use knowledge. In their view the 'extraction' of intelligence requires the selection of 'authentic' information. This means that to obtain intelligence we must be able to judge 'the loyalties, competencies, and motivations of members composing the intelligence network' (p.18). We must also appreciate that some people are able to tell more complete stories than others because they are located at nodes in the network which carry many communication links. This location means that they will also be better able than others to focus attention on their own summaries, and to generate commitments to actions based on those summaries. We shall consider such political aspects of building social networks in Chapter 5.

24. This is why writers have sometimes found a clear sequence of stages (Pugh and Morley, 1988b) and sometimes not (Hickson et al., 1986). When people talk about a clear, orderly progression through stages they usually have some sort of prescriptive model of decision-making in mind. The model is often contrasted with what happens in practice. We see the contrast in terms of the outcomes of negotiations. Attempts to implement any particular preseciptive model may be welcomed, or ignored, or actively resisted. The model will fail in practice if, either the prescriptions are not well-founded, or they are not accepted by the members of the groups concerned.

25. Janis and Mann (1977) only list seven criteria. Their list has been expanded along the lines set out by Pugh and Morley (1988a) to show the similarity between the criteria listed by Janis and Mann and the criteria listed by writers such as Steinbruner (1974).

26. The evidence is of various kinds. There are a number of studies of testimonial validity which have shown that groups are more confident about the accuracy of their testimony than individuals, even when that testimony is incorrect (see Clark and Stephenson, 1989). There are also a number of case studies which show that important decisions may be very badly made if a top executive is surrounded by like minded people who share his or her view of the world (see de Rivera, 1968; Janis, 1972).

27. This tendency is well known to those involved in the process of team development (Cummings and Huse, 1989). It has also beeen observed in Janis' (1972) studies of foreign policy-making groups, as one of the factors contributing to 'groupthink'.

28. See Walton and McKersie (1965); Winkler (1974); Mitchell (1981); and Morley (1982b, 1986, in press, b).

29. This is shown most clearly in the work of Blake and Mouton (see Blake and Mouton, 1961a, b, 1962; Blake, Sheperd and Mouton, 1964).

30. See Sherif, White and Harvey (1955); Bass and Dunteman (1963); Ferguson and Kelley (1964); Sherif (1966); Stephenson (1971).

31. For further examples of the way people think, feel, and act during periods of conflict between groups see Mitchell (1981) and White (1970).

32. Janis has argued very persuasively that unless group members commit themselves to this task almost all other recommendations for improving the quality of group decision-making are likely to fail, 'because each can easily be subverted by a group intent on pleasing the leader' (Janis, 1972, p210).

33. See Morley (1986); Hosking and Morley (1988).
34. Of course, what counts as a serious problem depends on what other problems are competing for a person's attention. When people are fully occupied they may be extremely tolerant of changes in the status quo. On other occasions they may actively monitor social settings, looking for opportunities to exploit. According to Burnstein and Berbaum (1981) this may be particularly likely when people who have been successful in the past gain significant new information, resources, or support. It may also mean that they see themselves as bound to succeed, whatever the risks. Janis (1972) refers to this as the illusion of invulnerability. He has suggested that it is one of the factors contributing to defective decision making in cross-functional teams of highly intelligent, experienced people, selected precisely because they have had a track record of success.
35. See Kanter (1984); Morley (1986); Morley, Webb, and Stephenson (1988).
36. See Hickson et al. (1986) p.106.
37. See Huff (1984).
38. Janis has argued that the groupthink syndrome is characterized by eight main symptoms. These are
   1. a shared illusion of invulnerability;
   2. collective efforts to find ways of discounting warning signs;
   3. a shared belief in the inherent morality of the in-group;
   4. stereotyped views of out-group leaders as evil, weak, or stupid;
   5. collective disapproval of those who question the group's stereotypes, illusions, or commitments;
   6. self-censorship of any doubts;
   7. a shared illusion of unanimity within the group; and
   8. the emergence of self-appointed 'mindguards' who take it upon themselves to 'protect' the group from evidence that runs counter to their current plans.
   See Janis (1972) pp.197–8.
39. See Janis (1972) p.117.
40. When Janis spoke of groupthink it might have been more illuminating if he had spoken of grouptalk, since the pattern of thinking he identified is only possible when the interpretive practices of the group discourage critical evaluation. It is quite clear that Janis is aware of this and, in this section, we have tried to show that his work is very much an examination of the effects of different contexts of justification. Regrettably, it has very rarely been described in this kind of way.

Chapter 5

Political processes

Introduction

We have argued that organizing processes have both cognitive and political qualities. In doing so, we have moved away from the entitative perspective, its unitary and managerialist qualities, and its 'physicalist' treatment of social realities. Our reference to 'political' embraces two broad lines of argument. The first starts with the view that actors, whether individuals or groups, *need the help of others to build understandings of self and social order, and to act in relation to other people, objects, and events*. For this fundamental reason, social relations are relations of interdependence. Second, *actors differ from one another in their relationships with their contexts*. As we saw in Chapter 3, this has major implications for relational processes. With cognitive processes we see that actors will differ in their understandings and commitments. With political processes we see that actors will differ in their opportunities to achieve influence and so differ in their opportunities to protect and promote their understandings and commitments.

In Chapter 4, we discussed the cognitive aspects of organizing. These are individual and collective processes in which the cultural setting influences constructions (knowing) and is influenced by them. So far, we have given emphasis to understanding rather than to influence. Now it is time to examine the 'other side of the coin' so to speak, namely, the political aspects of organizing. Here we are interested in the ways actors may structure the understandings and actions of others with whom they are interdependent and the implications this has for the projects and relationships that gain support.

Given our focus on organizing projects, we are especially interested in the influence processes which, first, make collective action possible and, second, may hinder or facilitate 'effective performance' (see Chapter 4). As we have seen, actors may create, reproduce, and sustain different kinds of cultures through the social processes of organizing. These may or may not be 'cultures of productivity' (see Akin and Hopelain, 1986). People identify issues, develop solutions, choose between alternatives, and implement policies through processes such as networking, negotiation, influence, and exchange.

The purpose of this chapter is to introduce findings and arguments which allow us to build a picture of how actors, whether individuals or groups, may influence others to adopt particular understandings and commitments. We shall do this in three main ways.

First, we shall examine literatures in which *organization and decision making* jointly have been discussed, paying particular attention to the more traditional ways in which decision processes are understood to be structured and why. There we discuss different assumptions about the context of such processes: the actors, the roles of goals and valuations, and whatever else might structure the processes of decision-making. Our arguments move in the direction of a pluralist perspective which emphasizes the significance of multiple actors who differ in their relationships with their contexts such that they differ in their definitions of core problems and in their opportunities to influence.

Second, and following on from the above, we shall return to and elaborate our earlier treatments of *actors* and interests, organizing relations within and between groups.

Third, we shall discuss *power and influence* and the ways these may be understood in relation to organization and organizing. There are substantial literatures which describe different 'power bases' and 'influence strategies'. We shall see that influence may be achieved through strategies which are more or less intentional, mobilizing power bases which are more or less acceptable to those who are influenced. As before, we will discuss the limitations of an entitative perspective in order to show what needs to be done in order adequately to join person and organization. An entitative perspective has limited the ways in which power and influence have been understood as qualities of social relations and organizing. So, for example, the emphasis on formal organization and hierarchy has been associated with attention to 'legitimate authority' as attatched to a role or position, and with attention to direction and control as proceduralized in the structures of formal organization.[1] Existing political perspectives of organization make a move in the right direction by recognizing multiple actors, mutiple interests, and a wider range of influence processes (see, e.g., Pfeffer, 1981). However, they fail fully to develop a process perspective of persons organizing. For this reason, we lack an account which discusses the social, cognitive, and political processes through which actors organize their projects with varying degrees of skill. This is the approach we will develop here.

How then do particular actors come to be more successful than others in their attempts to protect and promote their own valuations and projects? The reasons, broadly speaking, lie with relationships between actors and their contexts. In Part 1, we outlined the arguments we need in order to pursue this. There we outlined the nature of intelligent social action. We stressed that actors, be they individuals or groups, are more or less intelligent in their attempts to select and shape their contexts in ways which protect and promote their constructions. In the processes by which actors seek support for their own projects, in competition with other competing claims, structures of power and value emerge and are reproduced. In other words, structures of power and value are created in the more or less conflictual, relational processes, of networking, negotiation, influence, and exchange (Chapter 3). Some processes are more skilful than others. Skilful processes are more likely better to protect and promote the particular projects and valuations of participants, creating greater commitment to the understandings and actions involved.[2] In this chapter we continue to build this line of argument, here emphasizing political processes. In Chapter 9 we bring together our arguments about organizing to emphasize leadership as a more or less skilful process of structuring core problems in the process of projects.

Decision making, organization, and influence

Previously, we have outlined the so called classical management, scientific management, and human relations approaches as a way to illustrate the simplifying assumptions of the entitative perspective. The perspective reifies the organization by separating 'it' too sharply from the actions and constructions of participants. In this way, an organization is treated as though it were an actor in its own right. The organization is seen to pursue legitimate, organization-wide goals, through structures designed to direct and constrain activities in relation to those goals. The central assumptions are that organization is a unitary actor, engaged in *rational choice* processes of decision making, to pursue organization-wide goals. Contrary arguments suggest that organizations act, not as a single unit, but through multiple actors with multiple and often conflicting interests. For this reason, organization-wide rationality is hard to achieve and certainly cannot be guaranteed through formal structures.

Major problems arise to challenge 'rational choice' as a valid description of organizational decision processes. As we have seen in Chapter 1, it now is well accepted that decision-making processes are not characterized by 'omniscient' rationality in which information search, interpretation, influence and choice are shaped by 'perfect information'. What then does and can shape these processes? We have seen that rationality (in this special sense) is better described as 'bounded'. Important questions then arise as to what, exactly, this means and what factors make it likely that processes will be more or less rational in this bounded sense.

In Chapter 1, we outlined two kinds of answer: satisficing, and optimizing. In the case of optimizing, decision processes still are understood as shaped by the intention to make the best possible choice. What changes is that the process requirements are 'scaled down', although there is still explicit trading of the costs (for example of continuing search activity) and the benefits (for example, of getting a better picture). In contrast, a satisficing process is one in which actors will accept to search for a more or less local and partial knowledge of their contexts. Further, the process of search will be linear and sequential, guided by goals, but stopping at the first alternative that seems good enough ('satisficing'). A large number of alternatives could be considered, but often, only one or two are (see Janis and Mann, 1977).

Given our interests in organization and organizing, and how decision making is understood in these two concepts, it is important to separate two features of arguments about decision making. The first concerns the role of what, in the language of organization would be called the role of goals, and in the language of organizing valuations and, more narrowly, projects. We shall see that different 'models' of organizational decision making give these concepts more or less central roles in decision processes. For now, it is enough to say that goals do not necessarily constrain and direct choice processes. Goals also may emerge as rationalizations after the event, and as ways of legitimizing particular choices.

The second feature concerns what we already have said about cognitive processes, and the ways actors construct descriptions of social realities which are a mixture of value, and what some would call fact. These 'appreciations' are constructed out of the relationship between a person and their context (see Chapter 3). As we have said, to some extent actors create their contexts, and to some extent, are created by them. When organizing is understood as a process of political decision making it becomes important to consider what kinds of contexts support what kinds of political and cognitive processes. As we already have seen, contexts – viewed as cultures – may be more or less legible, coherent, and open-ended. A discussion of the political processes of organizing must show how an actor influences other persons and groups (part of their context) to agree one description of core problems rather than another, both in thought and action. Actors may create cultures of productivity or they may not. Later we shall argue that such cultures are most likely to be constructed through processes in which influence is achieved through negotiation and networking rather than, for example, through reliance on formalized procedures, hierarchical authority, or leaving the selection of policy to 'chance'.

Formalized procedures and decision processes

One particularly well known model of organizational decision making is the bureaucratic model. It argues that decision processes are structured by the effective influence of formalized 'standard operating procedures' and formalized decision rules. Actions are highly constrained. Actors do what they have always done. One way to describe this is that procedural rationality is substituted for substantive rationality (see Allison, 1971; Pfeffer, 1981). In other words, it is the requirements of the process (following formalized procedures) which influences decision processes. It is not optimizing or satisficing which is emphasized as the value which shapes the process and the choice of policy. Rather, the bureaucratic model argues that, for any particular issue – such as the size of this year's budget – the best predictor of policy will be knowledge of what happened before. Of course it could be that what is important is not so much adhering to procedures, but rather that the context is such that it is very difficult to depart from earlier policy. So, for example, in decisions about the size of this year's budget, the choice is most influenced by previous policy selections, that is, the size of last year's budget (see Wildavsky, 1979).

Multiple actors and the absence of consistent influence

In the bureaucratic model, 'organizational goals' lose much of their centrality in 'organizational' decision making. However, they still figure inasmuch as they are presumed to be reflected in appropriate and effective rules and procedures. There are other models which displace yet further, the influencing roles of goals and procedures. The 'garbage can' model provides a particularly stark contrast to the arguments of the bureaucratic model. In this model, decision processes are seen (descriptively) as unsystematic and un-orderly. In addition, the model states that there is no consistent control which constrains and guides (influences) decision processes. Choices are argued to emerge from decision processes. The model speaks of multiple actors who have different explicit intentions. However, a particular set of intentions is not seen systematically and consistently to influence decision processes. Indeed, intentions may not be apparent in the 'solutions' which, at some point, are adopted (see Cohen, March, and Olsen, 1972). In the garbage can model, like the bureaucratic model, it is suggested that goals may be attributed, after the solution was adopted, to rationalize and legitimize the choice which achieved commitment.

   To comment, the garbage can model moves in the direction of a political perspective of organizational decision making by emphasizing the multiplicity of actors who make contributions to the process. However, like the bureaucratic model, it leaves as peripheral the participants' differing valuations and projects and their differing influence. Yet these features are central to a political perspective. What we do find, in contrast to previous models, is a dual shift in emphasis. First, the unit of analysis ceases to be actors or structures or both, and becomes processes. In this way, the relationship between actors and their contexts can be recognized and this is to be welcomed. Second, the assumption of control and influence, as a feature of decision processes, is replaced by an emphasis on its lack. Goals and valuations are rejected as a source of ordering – as a source of structure in the process. Instead the process is, to use our terms, not coherent. No consistent set of core problems characterizes the process as a whole. There is no evidence that any of the actors attempt contributions to construct a culture of productivity.

When decision processes resemble a garbage can, they are processes structured by no simple, predictable, source of influence, such as a dominant coalition. Political influence processes, though within the scope of the model, are not the key to understanding. Rather, decision processes are argued to be characterized by 'chance collisions' of problems, solutions, actors, and choices to produce outcomes which are unpredictable, emergent and may, for all we know, constitute optimizing or satisficing for any or none of the participants.

Of course, the selection of a particular choice may result from chance collisions in the manner described by Cohen and his colleagues. However, this description is applied to a more or less arbitrarily bounded process, and refers to the choice which emerged in relation to what is known of the valuations of the actors. The varying degrees of influence of the different actors, and when in the process that was achieved, also may be relevant to the outcomes, but of this we know little. Yet the extent to which particular processes and outcomes appear to reflect chance depends on the extent to which a historical perspective is taken to consider how what has gone before constrains the range of present possiblities (see Lukes, 1974, for example). To be adequate, a political perspective must examine the history of relations between identified actors, and must investigate the differing influence they achieve in relation to particular issues. It is to relations between multiple actors, and difference of power and value, that we now turn.

Political processes, decision making and organization

We have seen that political models of organization, broadly defined, reject the presumption of the organization as a unitary actor, and reject the assumption of organization-wide goals. Attention is directed to relationships between the more or less partisan interests of different persons and groups, and to their differing ability to achieve influence in support of their (differing) interests. Interests typically are seen to be more or less emergent in, and played out through, processes of *conflict and influence*. Conflict and influence are emphasized in contrast to more traditional treatments of authority and co-operation. Theorists place more or less emphasis on organizational structures, and their historical development, to show how these are translated into resources and constraints for political action (for example, see Burns, 1961; Pettigrew, 1973).

To create an adequate political perspective, it is necessary to reject entitative assumptions concerning organization. Few seem fully to have recognized or achieved this. Typically, there is a shift of emphasis from the structural focus to favour less exclusive attention to formal and hierarchical relations. Emphasis is also given to differentiated social structures, whether formalized or not, and types of influence relations which are not grounded in hierarchy ('lateral' and 'informal'). Often, organization structures are rein-terpreted as resources and constraints which affect and reflect the ways in which actors are differentiated from each other. However, the full potential of a political perspective only is realized when the entitative concept of organization is rejected. It must be rejected in favour of a concept which makes relational processes central, recognizing that they are intrinsically political. So, for example, specialization of tasks/functions means that individuals and groups will differ from one another in what they do, who they are with, and why they are there (see Chapter 1). From this it follows, and for reasons already given, that they will differently describe their actions, their contexts, and changes to these (cognitive processes). Further, given their different relationships with their contexts, actors will differ in the influence they are able to achieve to protect and promote their own valuations and projects (political processes).

We shall make use of the lines of argument above to discuss political processes as they characterize organizing rather than organization. Further, we will do so in the context of our very particular understandings of actors and their social relations – grounded in the help that they need from one another in order to add value to their lives (see Preface and Part 1). This view of actors and relationships reveals major deficiencies in traditional treatments of power bases and influence strategies. The reasons for this will become clearer once we have said more about actors and interests.

Actors and interests

We have argued that a political perspective stands in contrast to the unitary treatment of organizations as wholes. The unitary view emphasizes one actor, one interest, and rationality in the pursuit of shared goals. A political perspective replaces this with an emphasis on multiple actors with a plurality of interests. Relationships and processes are characterized by networking, negotiation, influence, and exchange. Such processes produce more or less temporary commitments to particular descriptions or constructions of reality. Such processes produce more or less temporary commitments to particular actions as actors seek to implement *their* understandings, to protect and promote their values and interests.

To return to our concept of person as an intelligent social actor, we have said that actors construct their projects through individual and collective action within and between groups. Actors adapt, shape, and select their projects and, more generally, their contexts. These arguments may appear to emphasize a person's fundamental freedom of choice. However, as we have argued, choices are constrained by what can be imagined and by what can be done in any particular context. This said, given that social realities are constructed socially, the constraints are conventional and, potentially, open to negotiation. What is important for our present purposes is that actors must be able to make choices or intelligent social action would be impossible. And yet an actor must do so in the context of interdependent relations with other actors who also are attempting to act intelligently in relation to their own valuations and projects. This means that actors must achieve some degree of influence in their social relations. They must do so in order to achieve some sufficient working consensus about the kinds of help they need to sustain their relationships. Through the social processes of organizing such as networking and negotiation, actors contribute to the creation of their cultures.[3] They do so in relation to their own evaluative beliefs, that is, valuations. More narrowly, they do so in relation to their more or less collective projects.[4]

Actors' performances may be considered in terms of the extent to which they succeed in protecting and promoting their own valuations and projects, whatever they might be. Success will depend on the degree of skill effected in the processes of organizing. This means that an actor cannot be said to be skilled or unskilled, independently of their context (Hosking and Morley, 1988). It is skilful processes – social, cognitive, and political – which are critical. There is a very fundamental sense in which the descriptions and actions of interdependent actors make it more or less possible for a contributing actor, individual or group, skilfully to organize. One of our chief executives showed she understood this when we asked her what it would take for her to do her job better. She observed that few of those with whom she, as a chief executive, was interdependent had a practical understanding of negotiation as a quality of relational processes. She remarked that this was a major constraint because better relationships and agreements would result from practical knowledge of this kind. These arguments about skilful processes are of crucial importance for what we have to say about political processes and skilful organizing. They represent a radical departure from traditional ways of thinking about political skills. Further, with *this* kind of concept of person and relationships, much of the traditional literature on power and influence proves to be of little help to us.

In our view, the following four elements are central to the appreciation of organizing. First, it is necessary to identify the actors and their valuations in relation to an identified change, actual or potential. Second, it is necessary to understand to what extent, and in what ways, the change constitutes an 'issue' (project) for each actor, individual or group. Third, the relations must be examined, particularly those of interdependence, between actors and between projects. Last, it is essential to appreciate the political processes through which actors influence the structure in process and, in so doing, create and support certain sorts of setting (culture) and, to some degree, protect and promote particular projects (e.g. Pettigrew, 1977; Pfeffer, 1981; Lee and Lawrence, 1985).

Valuing, commitments, and culture

A focus on the political qualities of organizing requires attention to interdependent actors who, at any particular point in time, may broadly be understood to be pursuing particular projects to add value to their lives and the lives of others. We use the expression 'add value' very broadly to signify that all social action, and therefore social cognition, is a mixture of value and what some call fact (see Part 1). Our actions, and the actions of others with whom we are interdependent, have significance for us in that they may do more or less to protect and promote our valuations. In other words, our own actions, and the actions of others, are meaningful only in relation to value. In this sense, valuing represents commitments to particular descriptions, relationships, and activities or – more generally – commitments to a particular social order or culture. In this fundamental sense, valuing both reflects and creates social orders or cultures (see Chapter 3).

As we argued in Part 1, social orders, that is cultures, are constituted in and through systems of value and systems of power. Studies of culture reflect the expectation that valuations are organized in ways which differ between social collectivities such as groups, organizations, and nations. The language of culture again has become popular for the purpose of discussing values (usually in a very narrow sense) and their relationships with social actions and social relationships. Particular interest has been shown in what are called organization, or corporate cultures. Some have taken an analytical, social psychological approach (see Schein, 1985). Others have attended more to identifying 'cultural recipes' for success. In so doing, they have used the term value, not as we do here, but much more narrowly to refer to strategies and tactics. So, for example, 'excellence' has been argued to result from the creation of contexts characterized by values such as 'do what you do best', 'stick close to your customer', and the like (Peters and Waterman, 1982).

In our view, it is important not to confuse values – or what we prefer more broadly to describe as valuations – with strategies or tactics. Valuations embody *commitments to particular descriptions, activities, and relationships.* For this reason, they also act as injunctions in relation to other descriptions, activities, and relations (Emery and Trist, 1965, p.28). At their most fundamental, they exist as basic assumptions (Schein, 1985), not surface recipes. Valuing is both a cognitive process and a political process. Sherif and Sherif (1969) recognized that matters of value and matters of power both are central to the proper understanding of organization. By now it should be clear that we also take this view, but that we mean something very special when we use this language. Valuations are 'committed' in the making and maintenance of cultures in general, and projects in particular. Shortly, we will describe the different ways in which commitments, in this sense, are created, mobilized, maintained, and changed.

As we noted earlier, given this approach to valuing, we are forced to recognize that when interdependent actors are committed to different descriptions ('let the market decide' or 'we make the markets'), the 'same' action (removal of exchange controls) will mean very different things to them (cognitive processes). For example, from the point of view of a university personnel department, the proposed introduction of performance appraisal may be described as a move towards more efficient human resource management. However, the academics who will be appraised may describe the proposed action as an attempt to increase managerial control; both parties may be committed to their very different and conflicting descriptions. As we have said many times, these descriptions are not matters of fact, either right or wrong; each is more or less accepted and acceptable depending on the relationship between the actor and their context. Depending on how committed they are to maintaining or changing the status quo, depending on the influence they believe they can achieve and support, both Personnel and Academics will attempt to structure the issue. Each will attempt to protect and promote their own valuations. This perspective on valuing makes clear that a key quality of political processes is to influence the descriptions and actions of interdependent others who are committed to different descriptions and actions.

Last, it is perhaps helpful to note that these arguments do not imply that actors have conscious or salient valuations with regard to every conceivable task, action, relationship, or context. Further, it is not necessary to assume that organizing is driven by valuations in the way implied by the language of goals, or the language of values as preferences. Given our interests in this text, what is particularly important is the argument that consideration of actual and potential changes in the status quo highlight for interested actors:

1. The valuations to which they are committed in their activities and relationships.

2. The implications of those changes for the kinds of help they might need in their relationships and, in particular, the implications of those changes for the projects to which they presently are committed.

3. What may be required in order to sustain and to change their commitments.

The processes of political decision making are processes in which persons and groups more or less collectively create and mobilize value' to achieve influence. More narrowly, we describe organizing as a process in which interdependent persons and groups mobilize value to influence actual or potential changes in the status quo. Actors may give or withhold help; actors may be more or less successful in adding value to their lives and the lives of others.

Actors and action, people and groups

In a political perspective people and groups often are referred to as 'stakeholders'.[6] Actors are seen to stand to lose a stake or gain a prize. It is in this sense that their actions and descriptions are interested. The state of their interests, so to speak, will depend on what valuations are supported by the status quo, and on the help that they and interdependent actors can mobilize to create or resist changes. At the same time, organizations typically are viewed as more or less shifting coalitions. In a political perspective, coalitions are understood to continue until there is a change in the status quo which affects, in different ways, the relationships between the actors and their contexts. Such a change may promote new coalitions or alignments to reflect changes in the systems of value and influence.

In a political perspective, analysis often is focused on identified actors – individuals or groups – acting in relation to identified interests as summarized above. The unit of analysis, so to speak, may be the individual and their behaviour in relation to other individuals. Alternatively, analysis focuses on a group, theorized in some way, and their relations with other groups. Whichever is the case, there is a more or less explicit concept of person and context. As we shall see, this is usually entitative.

Our own approach is rather different in that we focus our analysis of organizing on projects and relations between projects. Persons and groups provide the actions, constructions and relations which allow us to appreciate how projects may be organized more or less skilfully. Of course just like everyone else, we have our own concepts of actors. Unlike everyone else, we try to make them explicit, although, in fact, our primary interest is in relational processes in the performance of projects. At this point it may be helpful to say that we differ from other political theorists in our dislike of the term 'stakeholder'. To speak of stakeholders invokes the perspective we have rejected, that is, of people as related through the manipulation of instrumentalities, pragmatically exploiting relative advantage, investing stakes and winning prizes. We shall say something more about our concepts of person and group in the context of our present interest in political processes.

In Chapter 1, we rejected as fallacies the individualistic and culturalist approaches which make a hard and fast separation between the person and their context. An adequate concept of person does not treat the person's biological entity as the boundary of some functional unit, and does not treat the person as a relatively fixed unit having particular, stable, design characteristics such as personality. A more adequate concept of person was outlined – a concept in which person is recognized both to make their contexts, and to be made by them (e.g. Gerson, 1976). An important way in which they do so is in organizing projects.

Organizing is made difficult to appreciate because persons simultaneously are differentiated from one another in many ways: by task, ethnic origin, gender, skill, job and departmental title, and the like. A person's actions reflect the history of their activities and relationships, and the futures they anticipate with particular groups (Morley, Webb and Stephenson, 1988). People are, at one and the same time, members of many groups. Any action may reflect a person's membership of a particular group; that action may be performed in interaction with other members of that same group (within group), with more or less reference to the intergroup context (between group).

Without knowledge of a persons' group memberships it is difficult to appreciate what meanings to attach to a particular performance. Consider a person's contributions in a particular group setting. These might reflect the actors' membership either of the present social group, or of another: past, present, or anticipated. For example, a corporate board may include directors from different divisions or strategic business units (SBUs). In any board meeting, there will be interactions which are meaningful, not as an expression of board membership, but as an expression of the director's identification with their own SBU. For example, a director may argue for an increase in the total funds made available for investment because she wants more for her own unit and believes this is the only way she might get what she wants. Similarly, in a board meeting, that same director may argue in support of what she believes to be emerging view of the board. Later, she may make a public statement on behalf of the board, or argue the board's point of view with her own managers.

It has proved very difficult satisfactorily to theorize groups as actors. Many of the problems we met in relation to the concept of organization also arise in relation to the concept of group. So, for example, what sense does it make to treat a group as an entity? What is it that people may be said to share which makes them a group? What does it mean to share, and what does it mean to speak of a group acting, as in, for example, the concept of collective action?

Our concept of person has major implications for the ways in which we theorize the group as an actor. Having argued that persons to some extent make their contexts, and vice versa, we have rejected the view that a group or organization may entirely be understood by being reduced to the actions of individuals. An important part of our argument was that organizing processes have emergent qualities which are not predictable solely on the basis of knowledge of individuals.[7] By arguing in this way, we have rejected what others have called 'methodological individualism' (e.g., Szmatka, 1989); by arguing in this way we have favoured attention to relational processes. This implies that we need a concept of group which avoids the usual entitative assumptions.

Given the above, it is unfortunate that those who analyse the politics of organizations typically take an entitative perspective on groups. Take, for example, what Bacharach and Lawler (1980) had to say about the literatures. They argued that three different types of group are critical in the political analysis of organizations: work groups, interest groups, and coalitions. They theorized organizations as collections of interest groups. Unfortunately, relatively little attention was devoted to theorizing the different kinds of groups, as groups, or to theorizing the differences between them. Yet constantly we meet terms such as clique, coalition, and cabal – terms invented variously to describe different kinds of group actors. Distinctions are imprecise; different terms are not used systematically in particular ways; often it is unclear why a particular distinction is thought useful.

Other approaches to groups and organizations are found in the OB and HRM literatures; they do little better. Especially common distinctions between groups of different kinds include task and social, formal and informal, vertical and horizontal, and so on. These distinctions have the drawback that they often reflect tacit 'managerialist' assumptions (see Chapters 2 and 3). Such taxonomies tend to overemphasize groups as entities, defined independently of their contexts – particularly their relations with other groups. Further, groups are treated as being 'in' organization. In other words, both groups and organizations are treated as entities, independent of the relational activities and valuations of persons.

For these reasons, it is perhaps not suprising that there are those who doubt that an understanding of groups might facilitate the appreciation of organization. Such doubts have been expressed, for example, in the argument that groups do not necessarily form 'in' organizations, and that when they do (in some undefined sense) they do not necessarily develop shared norms (Lee and Lawrence, 1985). Such arguments reflect an entitative view of groups and fail to appreciate the range of social-psychological theories and findings. Any concept of group must recognize that groups must not naively be treated as bounded entities; there are *degrees* of groupness. A process perspective makes it possible to speak of cognitive, social, and political processes within and between groups. The emphasis is on processes – including participants' own constructions of their identity in a particular context. Our concept of group does not assume fixed boundaries; groups may or may not be relatively stable across contexts. Instead, we emphasize relational processes as they affect, and are affected by, major changes in the status quo (what we call issues). Finally, since theorists want to use the term to cover a wide range of social phenomena a process perspective has the advantage that it can accommodate changes in the content of the setting.[8]

Different definitions of group serve different purposes. Examination of the social psychological literatures shows that, broadly speaking, there are two kinds of definition: groups as social categories, and groups as social orders. We will describe these in order to show what kind of work the concept of group can and must do for the analysis of organizing processes.

Groups as social categories

A group may be defined as a *set of people who share a social identity because they share a social category* (Tajfel, 1981) such as administrators, academics, marketing, financial strategists, or production. Tajfel and his colleagues have done most to develop this line of thinking. They argue that self identity merges into social identity as people see themselves as a member of a particular social category. A person is said to strive to create social identities which are positive, distinctive, and secure (see Chapter 4).

The concept of a group as a social category, and Tajfel's arguments about social identity, have very particular implications for the ways competition is theorized within and between groups. In the case of within group competition, Tajfel and his collegues argue that persons attempt to construct a certain image or definition of themselves in the social cognitions of others. Persons compete to become the most prototypical member of their social category. Such processes, for example, often may characterize groups of religious zealots, where persons achieve greater influence by being more zealous than other members of the social category. They seek to demonstrate that they best exemplify those values which determine membership of the category. It seems that this might have been one of the processes going on in President Nixon's advisory team. Each member accepted Nixon's core values: 'the Nixon way'. Each tried to stand apart from, and be better than, the others in embodying and implementing Nixon's values. Each tried to conform more and more closely to his value for hard driving methods, and for showing contempt for his enemies (see Morley and Hosking, 1984).[9]

Given Tajfel's arguments about groups as social categories, competition between groups is competition in which actors are seeking to construct a definition of their group as superior in terms of values which they and others hold. A group is seen as more or less able to gain commitment to particular descriptions of their value depending on the scarcity and importance of the resources they contribute to their wider setting. Following these arguments, it is possible to understand why, for example, in the 1960s and early 1970s, those with skills in computing achieved greater influence (status) in the larger system of relationships of which they were a part. However, in the late 1980s, the rhetoric of 'excellence' emphasized marketing skills, with consequent shifts in the status and influence of marketing departments and personnel. Given our present focus on organizing projects, it is clear that a person's projects may reflect their identification with a particular social category – Greenpeace, IBM, Islamic – and so on.

Groups as social orders

The second kind of definition emphasizes groups as *structured patterns of social relationships which are created out of collective activity*. Definitions of this type emphasize social action and social order as a feature of social actions and understandings. Social order therefore, is grounded in systems of power and value. This is the position developed by Sherif and Sherif (1969). Essentially, they argued that groups are built through the construction of more or less stable relationships (social order) involving patterns of reciprocal activities (roles), and power (status). Part of this consists of an ordering of value which, for example, defines standards of acceptable and unacceptable member contributions. For the Sherifs, competition within groups is competition to achieve influence over the creation of social order, to create a particular kind of order. Competition between groups was seen as competition for resources, and therefore power, and largely has been theorized in terms of its significance for social ordering within the group.

We have spoken of different kinds of social groups being actors: groups as social categories, and groups as social orders. We also said that these different definitions serve different purposes. For this reason, we do not need to choose between them. However, since talk about organizing requires talk about processes of action and social interaction we will more obviously draw on the social order traditions reflected in the work of the Sherifs.

However, we *do* need to choose between entitative and relational treatments of groups. Not suprisingly, we reject the former. Like entitative treatments of organization, they emphasize shared values, goals, or common interests. In an entitative view, persons are argued to act collectively to protect and promote the *same values* – security – democracy, or whatever. In this sense, a group of actors, by definition, acts as a group to protect and promote one and the same goal or interest. Each group member could, in principle, describe their actions in this way.[10] Interestingly, close examination reveals that, even in a political perspective, authors may retain the conceptual equivalent of a shared goal as an explanation of collective action at the level of the group. Some speak of joint interest (Morgan, 1986) and some of a 'common goal' (Bacharach and Lawler, 1980).[11]

To speak of shared values as a defining characteristic of groups has three major drawbacks. First, it is unhelpful simply to speak of shared values without specifying what values a group is thought to share. Groups don't just share any and all values. Second, to speak of groups in terms of shared values invites the inference that a managerialist perspective is what motivates the description. The assumption that organizations are characterized by shared goals earlier was shown to be associated with the belief that sub-units of the formal organization – departments and groups – also shared these goals.[12] As we have argued, this managerialist perspective is grounded in unconsidered values – the values of those who made the attributions. A third and related point is that the expression 'shared values' seems to encourage the misapprehension that consensus and cooperation are being emphasized at the expense of conflict and competition.[13] This misapprehension is serious. The point is that those who merge their lines of action must share some values or they could not act in relation to one another. However, there will be many values which participants will not share, and often they will not know that they do not share them.

Relational processes and groups

At this point we can dismiss the entitative perspective and draw upon other arguments to develop a view of groups which fits with our interests in the cognitive, social, and political processes of organizing. First, we need to comment on collective activity as a possible indicator of group action. The term 'collective activity' may be used broadly to refer to recurring patterns of 'social acts' in which 'two or more actors merge their lines of action with reference to one another' (Becker, 1987). As we have seen from Tajfel's definition of a group as a social category, the term group can be theorized without the necessity for collective activity in the sense described. Further, even when collective activity is observed, many would not take this as sufficient evidence of a group actor. From the point of view of our interest in organizing, collective activity is of considerable importance. However, its presence does not necessarily signal the presence of a group. To us, what is crucial are the *relational processes* which connect participants, and the *range of issues* (changes in the status quo) which they construct in the context of those relationships.

What this means is that stronger degrees of 'groupness' are found in recurrent interactions and continuing relationships between persons. Such relationships are characterized by more or less continual relationship building and support, including the negotiation of value and influence. Participants may not share an extensive range of central values (sense of social order), though they will share some. The more they share, broadly speaking, the more likely it is that the same group will act as a group in relation to a wide range of issues.

When we consider organizing as a political decision process our analysis does not proceed in the usual way, focusing on formal organization structures and individuals as position holders. Rather the analysis proceeds by identifying relational processes and collective activities in relation to issues. Of particular importance are the valuations that connect people and groups, and the influence they consistently achieve in relation to issues. The social order, or culture, which emerges will protect and promote some valuations whilst disadvantaging others. It is not that formal structures, positions, and titles are irrelevant, rather that their potential significance lies in their implications for relationships between the actors.

In the relational perspective we are developing here, we have laid emphasis on the actor (individual or group) as an agent – as an active (part) creator and (part) selector of contexts.[14] Actors and contexts are seen to be 'connected' so to speak, through more or less collective social processes: through the more or less collective and conflictual processes in which commitments are sought for competing constructions of reality. What this means is that, for any particular project, the analyst will need to identify the competing descriptions which actors make happen.

If interdependent actors attempt to support different cultures or, more narrowly, different projects, there will be competition, and there may be conflict. As we saw in Chapter 4, conflict within an interacting group is likely to have major implications for relationships between the actors and for the continuing status of the group as a group. So, for example, one or more members of a political party may seek to discredit unilateral disarmament and credit a value for multilateralism. They are likely to confront competing descriptions. In the processes through which the differences are played out, relationships will change. Some actors will achieve greater influence than others; some may leave the group. As we said earlier, competition within groups of this sort is competition to influence descriptions – the valuations – which characterize the group's culture. As a result, of these 'within-group' activities, the group may achieve greater or less influence over other groups; relations within groups have important implications for relations between groups, and vice versa (see Chapter 4).

It often is difficult to determine whether a contributor to collective activity is seeking to protect and promote their own, partisan values, or those which are more widely shared. The recent vogue for 'vision' (e.g. Bennis and Nanus, 1985) and 'beautiful values' (e.g. Peters and Waterman, 1982) gets it right, as it were, by emphasizing the importance of value articulation and implementation. However, given our arguments, it seems astonishing that the political[15] qualities of these processes are ignored. Literatures which emphasize leadership as the creation of 'strong cultures' of excellence ignore the question of whose values are being promoted, how widely shared they are, how they came to be so, and how they will continue to be so. As we have seen, systems of value are created, sustained, and changed through processes of power and influence. Our approach requires that the analyst explore how and why *these* descriptions were 'made' by actors past and present. This will require attention to processes of influence. As we shall see, to theorize these, we will have to go beyond conventional treatments of power and politics to discuss the political aspects of the social processes of networking, negotiation and exchange.

Political processes, power and influence

The focus of our interest this chapter is on the processes through which actors may attempt to influence others so as better to protect and promote their own values, active interests or 'projects'; these are what we call political processes. We have suggested that, to achieve influence, actors may attempt to manipulate commitments to particular descriptions of reality, and/or to manipulate particular activities and relationships. More generally, what this means is that actors attempt to manipulate commitments to particular contexts. Individuals and groups attempt to mobilize power so as to influence other individuals and groups with whom they are interdependent. They attempt to direct and constrain the ways in which those others define particular aspects of their contexts. They intend, as a consequence, to direct and constrain or facilitate their activities (e.g., Kapferer, 1972, p.206).

Our discussion will continue with a more detailed description and illustration of political processes. First, we will review the various ways in which the term 'political' has been used in the literatures in order to show what's distinctive about our approach, and why we have taken it. Second, we will outline arguments and findings concerning the sources and qualities of power. We will continue with a more processual emphasis on influence strategies, presenting research which illustrates some of the ways in which influence is achieved. We will finish by linking arguments about influence, networking, and negotiation. We will show how it is possible to create and mobilize commitments to particular descriptions of core problems and to particular ways of translating these descriptions into practice.

Definitions of political activity

As we noted in Chapter 3, writers on organizations seldom have theorized political processes as endemic to organization.[16] Until recently, politics received very little attention at all.[17] The reason for this lies partly with the underlying entitative concept of person. Particularly important was the physicalist treatment of perception as a matter of fact rather than a process of social construction. Treatments of organization also were entitative, the unitary and structural emphasis leading to politics being ignored. The entitative treatments of actor and context has led to politics being treated as a by-product of individualistic strivings and psychodynamics (e.g. Zaleznik, 1980). From an entitative perspective it is not possible to understand influence as intrinsic to relational processes – processes through which participants legitimately may attempt to build commitments to their own constructions of their core problems. Strangely, even when power has been emphasized as both a cause and a consequence of social organization, few have recognized that when combined with differences of value, the implications are necessarily political (e.g. Olsen, 1978).

Organization structures and political behaviour

Recently there has been a resurgence of interest in what has become known as 'organizational politics'. A common theme is the emphasis on power and influence. Also common is the emphasis on *political structures* rather than processes. So, for example, Zaleznik (1980) observed that organizations, whatever else they might be, are political structures (Zaleznik, 1980, p.315). He meant that organizations are intrinsically political in the sense that there is a differential distribution of authority through the formalized administrative hierarchy. In this way, the 'legitimized' procedures and relationships provide a differential distribution of a power. The argument is that this creates the conditions for social comparisons in which inequalities are perceived, so creating conflicts of interest. This, in turn, produces social competition to achieve influence.

Another approach has emphasized *political behaviour*. Farrell and Peterson (1982) identified three 'key dimensions' of political behaviour. The first they described as the internal–external dimension – referring to the focus of resources which actors attempt to build and mobilize. External resources included use of the media, forming alliances with others in other organizations, lawsuits, and the like. Internal resources include exchange of favours, blocking, management information systems, positional status, and the like (see also Pfeffer, 1981).

Farrell and Peterson's second dimension was vertical–lateral. Already we have seen what some regard to be the political significance of hierarchy (e.g. Zaleznik, 1980) – here referred to as the vertical dimension. We should add that attention to hierarchy is not confined to downward influence. There is a small but important literature on upward influence (e.g. Mechanic, 1962; Cheng, 1983). Farrell and Peterson also drew attention to lateral relations and the ways they might be mobilized to achieve influence. A well known illustration of the potential use of lateral relations is found in Strauss's study of purchasing agents. Strauss showed how purchasing agents used their boundary-spanning position, and their knowledge of suppliers ('external' and 'lateral' resource) to achieve influence in their internal, lateral relations. Similarly, Sayles (1964, 1979) did much to document the lateral relationships which managers may build to manage interdependencies between specialized tasks. By building relationships with those over whom they had no formal authority, managers were able to mobilize those relationships to influence interdependencies which they could not influence in other ways.

Last, Farrell and Peterson noted that the legitimate–illegitimate dimension is a key dimension of political behaviour. As we have seen, politics usually is defined as illegitimate activity. Writers have taken for granted the legitimate quality of hierarchical authority as a characteristic of organization, and have contrasted this with what they describe as the illegitimate or political use of power (e.g. Mintzberg, 1983). In other words, politics typically is seen as behaviour which is not sanctioned in relation to organization goals. Such behaviour implicitly is defined as beyond the bounds of formal organization and therefore illegitimate. A representative example of this perspective is found in Farrell and Peterson's claim that 'political behaviour resides in informal structures and relates to the promotion of self and group interests' (Farrell and Peterson, 1982).

The distinction between legitimate and illegitimate is very much a part of the managerialist tradition. When this view is taken, political processes often are of interest, broadly speaking, because they 'mess-up' organizational decision-making: politics is what interferes with what otherwise would be a 'rational' process.[18] We reject this view. More generally, we reject the roles we have seen given to formal organization, hierarchy, and legitimate authority for the reason that they reflect entitative assumptions about organization. Instead, we take the view that organizing is intrinsically political[19] because interdependent actors differ in what they value, and differ in the influence they are able to achieve. We prefer to discuss political processes by focusing on social relationships rather than authority structures. We will do so by considering the various ways actors may build and mobilize relationships in relation to what they perceive to be major changes in the status quo. We will use the language of networking, negotiation, and influence to do so.

Resources, power, and politics

We already have commented on our dislike of the language of resources for the reason that it reflects a view of relationships and their instrumentalities which we do not share. Olsen is one of many who emphasize resources as the basis for power. He observed that 'social power is generated through the use of resources' (Olsen, 1978, p.37). Before organizational politics became the fashionable topic they are today, Burns described organizations as 'alliances of resources', and as 'systems in which people compete for advancement; in so doing they make use of others. Behaviour is ... political when others are made use of as resources in competitive situations' (Burns, 1961, p.257). He described resources as 'voluntary' and 'extorted commitments' which are used to maintain the status quo or to achieve change. He argued an exchange perspective in which actors are seen to surrender resources (information, persuasive powers, skill, etc.) in return for advancement of their own more or less material and 'transcendental' interests.

Whilst some have emphasized exchange as the link between resources and power, others have emphasized negotiation and conflict as processes in which differential distributions of resources are produced (e.g. Wildavsky, 1979; Pettigrew, 1977). So, for example, Pettigrew argued that individuals and groups engage in 'political behaviour' in the course of organizational strategy formulation. They do so by mobilizing power in support of demands that particular strategic 'dilemmas' receive attention, whilst others are suppressed. He defined political behaviour as that which 'makes a claim against the resource-sharing system of the organization' (Pettigrew, 1977, p.81).

We already have discussed theories of negotiation and exchange, noting that few combine the arguments we require (Chapter 3). We argued that negotiation must be seen as a quality of relational processes, that is, of the social, cognitive and political processes of organizing. We advocated that negotiation be understood as a process through which cultures are created in relation to projects. In this way, participants create systems of power and value. To follow this line of argument, power must be theorized in a rather special way. In particular, it must be understood as a quality of relationships. Whether or not it is theorized using the language of resources, it will be crucial to recognize the role of understandings and commitments, and crucial to recognize the significance of differences between actors in their relationships with their contexts. For these reasons, actors will: differ in how they describe their contexts; differ in the ways they can be influenced and in the influence they find acceptable, and; differ in the ways they will attempt influence. It is to the concept of power that we turn next.

The concept of power

A number of fundamental points need to be emphasized about the concepts of power and influence. First, power is not a fixed, structural characteristic or property of persons, groups, or organizations. Rather, it is better understood as relational and contextual. To say that it is relational is to say that it is produced and reproduced in relationships (see, for example, Walsh, Hinings, Greenwood, and Ranson, 1981). To say that it is contextual is to say that power may be mobilized in some relationships, and not others.

Second, power is situated in difference. Actors may attempt to mobilize particular resources such as money, information, influential allies, and the like. This is illustrated by the work of those who have focused on 'uncertainty' as a crucial factor in the achievement, maintenance, and mobilization of power.[20] The general line of argument is that a potential resource comes from the ability to control important sources of uncertainty, such as when a machine will be repaired, or the ability to stop and start production. When the resource is central, for example, when the costs of lost production are considerable, and when no substitute is readily available, the actor who has this control may achieve a considerable degree of influence. However, what counts as a resource is, in large part, a matter of social construction; anything can be a resource if it is valued by others (e.g. Olsen, 1978). It seems that this is not well recognized in the literatures. So, for example, actor A may or may not be convinced by actor B that B's skills are scarce, vital, and not easily replaced (see above). If A is not convinced of this description, then B may falsely construe their power in their relationship with A. Perhaps another way of making this point is to say that 'power bases' are potential sources of influence. Whether or not they are mobilized depends on the relationships between the actors and between the actors and their contexts.

Third, the above arguments show that the 'source' and 'target' are joined, so to speak, by interdependent relations. We have seen that actors are interdependent to the extent that they need the help of others to add value to their lives. We have seen the significance of this in relation to cognitive processes. When power and influence are brought into the picture, we see that interdependence characterizes relationships in that someone who attempts to mobilize power needs to know something of the 'targets' valuations in order to be able to influence them. For influence to be achieved, the attempt must fall within the target's 'latitude of acceptance' (Barnard, 1948; Sherif and Sherif, 1969). Some influence strategies are more acceptable than others. For example, chief executives may attempt to achieve acceptable influence through negotiation, even when they have a relationship of formal authority with the target. Later we shall take the view that persons may be identified as making leadership contributions when they consistently achieve acceptable influence and are perceived and expected to do so.

We use the language of interdependence to emphasize the two-way nature of the relationship. In so doing, we mean to recognize that the dependency may be biased strongly to favour one of the parties, and also, to emphasize that some greater or lesser degree of choice can be exercised to judge the acceptability of attempted influence. The choice may be highly constrained, but should not be ignored; it is choice in the context of conflict, negotiation, and exchange: choice to be committed to particular descriptions and actions, at least for a time.

Our fourth point draws from the first two: understandings of power relations, or in our terms, political processes, must recognize the ways in which they are intimately connected with cognitive–social processes. Given our immediate interests in this chapter, what we most wish to emphasize is that, fundamentally, political processes are processes in which social realities are constructed in 'thought and deed'. As we have said before, some actors – individuals and groups – achieve greater influence than others in the manipulation of symbolic processes: in the 'management of meaning', or what we have described as the process of negotiating descriptions (see Kapferer, above; also Pondy, 1978). What is important are the processes through which particular combinations of actors and contexts, past and present, 'credit' some descriptions (competition, excellence, etc.) whilst 'discrediting' others (communism, liberalism, etc.)(Weick, 1979). In any relational setting, the realities which can be constructed may be highly constrained by the patterns of dominance which previously have been created. For this reason, certain values, and therefore, potential issues, relationships, and resources are kept off the agenda (see earlier). However, actors also may attempt intentionally to mobilize bias (Schattschneider, 1960) – to structure the ways in which those with whom they are interdependent define their social reality. In this way, they can influence social orders, descriptions of core problems, activities and relationships.

The above points are quite general. However, often they are not given much prominence, or their significance fully explored. So, for example, discussions of power bases such as expertise often understate the extent to which these are cultural (contextual), reflecting the valuations of the target and the agent. Similarly, it seems all too easy to be carried away with the everyday talk that treats power as something a person 'has', regardless of contexts.

Power bases

Earlier we argued that, to analyse political processes, it is necessary to identify actors, their interdependencies, the social order to which each actor is committed, and the processes by which each attempts to influence others. The processes of influence have been characterized as processes in which two or more actors attempt to create and mobilize resources or 'power bases' to structure their social order. Discussions of power and social action have tended to assume or to emphasize individuals pursuing their own individual ends; human actors are seen as manipulators and manipulated, joined by the differing instrumentalities of their relationships. Power bases and influence strategies are seen as the means employed by one person to manipulate their relationships so as to make them more or less instrumental to themselves. Given this view of relationships, the same perspective can be generalized to the group (as an entity or aggregate of individuals) with no fundamental change being required. This view also is reflected in traditional conceptions of managerial leadership. We shall continue by outlining the taxonomies of power bases because coercive power could be mobilized by withholding and/or OB and HRM. We discuss the ways in which these are lacking, given our interest in organizing. We finish by shifting emphasis to the social processes of networking and negotiation: processes which are major vehicles for political processes.

French and Raven identified five 'especially common' types or 'bases' of power in terms of 'the relationship between (the actors) which is the source of that power' (French and Raven, 1968, p.262). These are reward power, coercive, legitimate, referent, and expert power.

Reward and coercive power

By reward power, French and Raven meant A's power to mobilize any good, broadly defined, to which B attaches positive value, for example, money, or social acceptance. Coercive power was defined in terms of the power to manipulate negatively valued goods such as punishment or dismissal. They further argued that it was, at times, hard to distinguish between these two power bases because coercive power could be mobilized by witholding and/or withdrawing rewards.

There are problems in circumscribing the meaning of reward power. This is because it must be grounded in the actor's definitions of what they find rewarding, that is, what they value. And yet, since the time at which French and Raven generated this set of categories, it has become clear that no simple list will capture the range and complexities of what actors might value. So, for example, theories of motivation have shifted away from attempts to specify the content of motives, and instead have attempted to specify the processes of motivation, leaving open the specification of what a particular actor might value. The problem for French and Raven is that, in this more general sense, all power is reward power, open to being theorized as a resource in the broader theoretical context of exchange relationships. This means that reward power must, to some extent, be defined in relation to the other categories from which it is distinguished.

We have said that actors differ in their valuations such that they will find different power bases and influence strategies more or less acceptable. Depending on the context, reward power often is seen as more acceptable than coercive power. Further, coercive and reward power differ in their consequences for the relationships in which they are mobilized, again, depending on the wider relational setting. Last, we may say that the kinds of rewards which typically are considered reflect entitative ways of thinking about persons and organization.

Little has been said of the sorts of rewards that might be emphasized in a relational perspective when helping is seen as what is fundamental to relationships and when helping constitutes the revised notion of instrumentalities. Given the particular emphasis we place on social processes, particularly networking and negotiation, rewards often will be best understood as grounded in social relationships. They may include the following: relational messages of support; helping others to enjoy supportive, egalitarian relations; in various ways helping others to perform their tasks despite their 'limited capacities', desire to see too much order and the like (see Chapter 1); helping others to a practical understanding of their context, for example, by facilitating a legible, coherent structure in the process of projects, or; more generally, helping others to learn and to make sense of change (see Chapter 1). Networking is a social process of building helping relationships. For this reason, networking is fundamental to the mobilization of *any* power base (not just reward), and fundamental to the achievement of influence. We shall have more to say about this process as a feature of project work and in particular, as a way of building a culture of productivity.

Legitimate power

This was defined by French and Raven in relation to the cultural values of particular social contexts. In other words, legitimate power is contextualized by the valuations of a particular social order. As we have seen, this argument can be developed to have very wide implications. They suggested that, through processes such as socialization, actors internalize particular norms of appropriate and expected behaviour. These are experienced as 'oughts', such that actor B believes they should act in certain ways towards actor A whom they see to have the right to that conformity. So, for example, traditional arguments about rights to manage have been grounded in more or less tacit beliefs that those who own the capital, equities, machinery, materials and the like, have a legitimate power base on which they can draw to influence their employees.

When the view is taken that social order is negotiated, references to legitimacy are understood as reference to agreements which which have been negotiated in relationships of interdependence. Such agreements have been referred to as 'custom and practice' (e.g. Brown, 1973). This language brings to the fore the cultural qualities of social practices. Through their interactions with others – as we would argue – through networking and negotiation, actors construct and internalize valuations concerning, for example, the definition of equity and social justice. Such valuations have important implications for the influence aspects of relationships. Constructions of legitimate power are, in important ways, implicated in all relationships, however exchange is conceptualized. For example, actors can feel committed to honouring the terms and conditions of their agreement because they have internalized values for equity or social justice. This can result in a situation where they will go to enormous lengths to honour an obligation (see Homans, 1954). More generally, valuations will include constructions of who are the actors are who are connected in a relationship, along with descriptions of resources and descriptions of the responsibilities of contributors.[21]

Referent power

Referent power was defined by French and Raven as the power which A derives from B's identification with A. In the case of A being a group, for example, attraction to the group, one indicator of group cohesion, refers to the power of the group to achieve conformity to group norms (ssee Chapter 4). In the case of A being an individual, it may be that B wishes to become like A in some respect(s). Whether the actor be a person or group, if a context is seen as highly uncertain,[22] or rather equivocal, B may attempt to create a sufficient sense of social order by identifying with A's descriptions of social reality. In this way, B 'gives' A referent power. In times of crisis, a chief executive may be given more referent power by those who perceive him or her to have the right descriptions of what is 'going on', what to do, and how (what we call core problems).

Expert power

Expert power also was identified by French and Raven. Other, related concepts since have been developed. In respect of expert power, B's construction (evaluative) of their context may be that certain knowledge and skills are required. B also may perceive that, in relation to this context, A has the relevant expertise. When this is the case, A is said to have 'expert power' in relation to B in this context. However, again it is important to note that it is not A who possesses expert power. Rather, the power lies in the relationship between A and B, in relation to aspects of the wider setting – the task to be performed or the issue to be dealt with.

One concept closely related to expert power is informational power. Here, for example, an actor may be in the position of a 'gatekeeper': able, as it were, to open and close the gate – overtly or covertly – selectively to pass information (e.g. Pettigrew, 1973). Views about informational power connect with arguments about 'position power' to which we will turn next.

Position power

Position power has been identified as power which comes from an actor's position in a particular network of relationships, and the power this can give them to manipulate and mobilize resources of many kinds. Position power has been theorized in relation to the power leaders have in small groups (e.g. Fiedler, 1967). Similarly, it clearly represents an important feature of power in larger networks of relationships, including those captured in the concept of formal organization structure.

It is important to note that position power often is narrowly understood in the context of formalized organization structures, and more generally, within an entitative perspective. In our political perspective, the term is not restricted to formalized organization structures but is located in the context of networks of relationships, formalized or not. Position power can be mobilized by actors whether or not they are in a position of formal authority, relative to a subordinate. For example, Mechanic (1962) focused on the upward influence of subordinates in formal organizations. His research suggested that subordinates can achieve influence when they have information that others value, and have relationships with those others they wish to influence. Again we see why networking is such an important social process. When considered for its political aspects we can see that those who are active in networking are able better to build relationships of influence; this is partly for the reasons captured by the concept of position power. However, what is crucial to appreciate is that, through their networking, actors may attempt to facilitate either their own influence, relative to others, or may attempt to build 'distributed influence'. In the case of the latter, they can try to enable others. In this latter sense, networking can reflect a fundamental valuing of the helping nature of relationships . In this latter sense, networking is all about connection rather than separation, and about caring and support, not dominance and exploitation. We shall return to these arguments when we discuss networking and skilful organizing.

Finally, we must note that position power also is implicated in an actor's ability, covertly to manipulate the agenda for decision-making, so that certain issues never get tabled so to speak. What has been called 'non-decision-making' can be effected by making sure that particular actors never get the opportunity fully to participate in organizing decisions, or only are able to participate after commitments have already been made. It is important to distinguish non decision making from other aspects of position power. This is because, unlike the other power bases we have discussed, its success does not depend, in quite the same way, on the social constructions of those affected. What is crucial here is not B's perceptions of A, but rather A's ability to prevent B from constructing particular understandings and mobilizing particular relationships. Again, networking can be used as a means to keep others out of a particular decision. However, as we shall see, cultures of productivity are not achieved in this way, but through networking which reflects a valuing for helping relationships.

Influence strategies

By understanding the sources of power, we are better able to understand the strategies that actors might employ to build and mobilize their influence. A number of writers have considered influence strategies as the more or less skilful development and mobilization of resources. Lee and Lawrence (1985), drawing on Handy's analysis of the literatures (1976), identified five influence strategies: push, pull, persuasion, preparatory, and persuasive. Kipnis and his colleagues solicited self reports from managers concerning their influence strategies, and from these reports identified seven strategies and three types of managers (Kipnis et al., 1980,1984).

Push and pull strategies

These we have met before. The former mobilizes coercive power and the latter, reward power. Push involves what Handy described as force, or the threat of force. The force may be physical, or may constitute the withholding or withdrawal of resources. Whatever the resource that 'A' manipulates, 'B' feels pressure to comply. The 'power-coercive' strategy, identified in the literatures on organizational change is a push strategy. It has been suggested to be the one most frequently employed by management in attempts at organization wide change (Chin and Benne, 1976). Kipnis et al. (1980) have identified three push strategies used by individual managers. These are: 'blocking', as for example, in threats to withdraw cooperation and support; 'sanctions', including threatened loss of promotion, perks, and/or employment; and 'assertiveness', as found in close supervision and monitoring of performance, setting deadlines, and rule enforcement.

Push strategies have no place in skilful organizing. Admittedly, they will be more acceptable in some cultural settings than others. However, actors are reliant on other actors to act intelligently. This means that they must create cultures in which participants are willing and able to negotiate and renegotiate descriptions of tasks and commitments to action (see Chapter 1). For this reason skilful organizing is achieved through influence which is acceptable to participants. Pull strategies, and influence achieved through networking and negotiation, are more likely to achieve and sustain cultures of this kind.

Persuasion strategies

These involve what Kipnis and his colleagues described as the use of reason. Argument, evidence, and facts are what here are emphasized. Lee and Lawrence (see above) include in this category the use of induction training, socialization, management development programmes, propaganda, and other activities which influence values, and therefore actors' descriptions of their contexts. Handy (1976) suggested that persuasion is the preferred influence strategy, and the one most likely to be used, where possible. Certainly, Kipnis and his colleagues found 'reason' to be reported as the most frequently deployed strategy. However, this is not entirely consistent with what is reported in the organization change literatures where the power-coercive strategy is suggested as the most often employed (see Guest, 1984). Further, it seems likely that views about the desirability of persuasion, and its frequency of use, must be evaluated in relation to the wider perspective (evaluative) from which such descriptions are made.

There are problems in distinguishing the use of persuasion from other strategies; often rules and authority may be perceived as the power bases which actually are being mobilized. Similarly, those over whom influence is being attempted may construct the attempt as one which is grounded in the offer of exchange; Handy identifies exchange as a strategy in its own right; Kipnis et al. identify 'bargaining' as a strategy of this kind.

In our arguments about organizing processes persuasion effectively is treated as part of a wider process of networking and negotiation for influence. In our arguments about organizing, persuasion, like pull and reward, is understood as a feature of the relational processes involved in project work.

Preventative strategies

These involve what we previously described in terms of non decision making and gatekeeping. They are mobilized to keep people out of the process of decision making, to prevent particular issues from being raised, and to prevent disagreement over the description and handling of core problems. Here, Lee and Lawrence refer primarily to Bachrach and Baratz's arguments about the less visible aspects of power, as when actors mobilize their influence to keep things off the agenda for decision-making. Such activity may help to organize knowledge (Chapter 4). However, given our arguments about the importance of multiple perspectives and actively open-minded thinking, such activity is unlikely to facilitate collective project work and cultures of productivity. Skilful organizing is more likely when participants negotiate (rather than prevent) differences, recognizing that their mutual need for help constitutes the basis of social relationships. This too is why enabling, linking the capacities of actors with the demands of their tasks, is an influence strategy which characterizes skilful organizing; we shall have more to say about this in Part 3.

Preparatory strategies

These are 'specifically concerned with creating the right environment for other strategies to be more successful' (Lee and Lawrence, 1985, p.158). They include what Kipnis et al. (1980) identified as 'ingratiation' – which they later described as 'friendliness' (Kipnis et al., 1984). Coalition building can offer this potential. Attention to external image may help a corporation or department to gain the help and support of others when needed. Some instances of a preparatory strategy may be more visible than others and some may be more acceptable in particular cultures. Networking may embrace the building of friendships, not as a manipulative strategy in the way implied by the terms friendliness and ingratiation, but in the context of a helping perspective.

Influence processes and skill

Different influence strategies have different negative side-effects so to speak; this varies with the cultural setting. So, for example, push strategies need a lot of resources to maintain the influence, once achieved: close supervision may achieve 'satisfactory' standards of production, but only when it is present. The issue is recognized through distinctions between compliance, identification, and internalization (e.g. Handy, 1976). In addition, Kipnis et al. (1980) suggest that the skilled actor, like other actors, uses a range of tactics, but uses them more selectively and flexibly. Kipnis suggests that those who are attempting influence should consider what they are trying to achieve, and who they wish to influence, and the status of those they are hoping to influence: peer, subordinate, or boss. By now it should be clear that such arguments reflect an individualistic concept of person. Such arguments reflect a view of social relationships as more or less instrumental for the individual to protect and promote their own 'beautiful values', regardless of the interests of others. The underlying perspective reflects what some refer to as a 'masculine culture' (Dachler, 1990). It is a skilful actor, rather than skilful action which is the focus. The skilful actor is one who is more effective in manipulating differences to achieve and support their own (superior) separation from others. As we have said, this is not a view we share.

We have argued that skilled performances can only be understood by attending to the relationship between actors and contexts. We shall develop the skills argument in relation to political decision-processes. Central to these arguments is our emphasis on networking and negotiation as processes through which political and cognitive problems are handled in the construction of order. How they are handled is captured in our arguments about skilful processes.

Negotiating commitments

We have argued that actors must be viewed as fundamentally active – as agents competent to pursue their own projects – and doing so more or less intelligently. We have argued that they do so through collective and collaborative relations which, in turn, are conducted in the context of conflict relations, actual and potential. The opportunities for conflict arise both within and between groups as actors struggle to gain commitment for their own descriptions and activities. Given our own interests in the 'how' (rather than what) of organizing, we are interested to pursue the question of how commitments are created.

First, it is useful to recall that we have rejected as specious the independent theorizing of person and context, arguing that neither is logically prior or causally superior to the other. When speaking of people, we observed that in a very real sense, who they are, and what they are, depends on where they are, and why they are there (see Chapter 1). The processes through which actors make contexts and contexts make actors is, in a very fundamental sense, a matter of negotiation: 'both social order, and individuals, arise in and through a process of ongoing negotiation about who shall be whom, and what order shall pertain' (Gerson, 1976).

As we have already remarked, negotiations are not conducted *de novo*, but are temporally located in relation to constructions of the past and the future. From past activities and interactions, emerge patternings of resources, value, and commitments. These are reflected, and to some extent are reproduced, through ongoing negotiations. Further, contemporary negotiations are performed in anticipation of future negotiations, so that, for example, relationships between the actors are preserved, thus enabling future negotiations.

Both persons and contexts are negotiated. More precisely, this can be understood in terms of the contributions of the actors and the consequences of these contributions. Contributions simultaneously represent both resources and constraints: contributions provide resources, for example, in the form of rich and convincing descriptions of the context, and what needs to be done; contributions are, simultaneously, constraining in that actors must make them, and will be bound by their limits (Gerson, 1976).[23] Through their contributions to different contexts, actors create patterns of resources, constraints, and commitments in different relational settings. Depending on the number and variety of contexts in which actors participate (directly, or through others), they will be more or less able to mobilize resources across contexts[24] (see Part 3). We have argued that organizing creates and reflects commitments to particular contexts and therefore, commitments to particular activities and relationships, and to particular descriptions of social order.[25] This means that to understand any context, we must attend to: the patterns of resources, constraints, and commitments; the ways these are renegotiated into new patterns of commitment; and the relationships between contexts, for example, as created through networking, which means that actors differ in their patterns of commitment across contexts.

Summary

We have taken the view that organizing is intrinsically political. We have done so out of our argument that actors differ in their relations with their contexts such that they differ in their understandings and commitments, and differ in their ability to achieve influence. We are especially interested in the individual and collective processes through which actors organize structure in the process of their projects. The focus here has been on the influence processes which make collective action possible, and which may promote or prevent a culture of productivity.

We take a perspective on organizing which views the processes as those of political decision making, broadly defined. For this reason, we examined literatures in which are discussed the relationships between organization and decision making. This allowed us to lay out arguments in favour of a pluralist perspective on organization, or rather, organizing. In other words, to be adequate, a political perspective must make central the relationships between multiple actors, valuations, and projects. We also advocated shifting attention from structures and formal authority to relational processes and social influence.

It became necessary to elaborate our earlier discussion of persons and groups in order to situate organizing as a quality of relational processes within and between groups. The processes of political decision making were shown to be processes in which persons and groups more or less collectively construct commitments to particular descriptions, relationships, and activities or – more generally – commitments to a particular social order or culture. Traditional treatments of power and influence were argued to be limited by more or less tacit assumptions about the goals, structures, and perceived legitimacy of formal organization. We argue for attention to the relational processes of networking and negotiation as processes of power and influence. These processes may be performed more or less skilfully in the context of interdependent relations between actors who need help from one another in order to add value to their lives.

Notes

1. See our earlier discussion of the Danish TV company, plus what we have already said about the impossibility of creating and sustaining social setting by fiat.
2. Of course, it does not follow that actors whose values are better promoted are necessarily more skilled than actors for whom this is not true.
3. What we refer to elsewhere as contexts, settings, or social order.
4. As we have seen, these arguments should not be taken to imply that actors merge their lines of action and agree descriptions only when they rightly can be considered to share projects (or goals or whatever). What is crucial here are our arguments about social relations, instrumentalities – in the sense of helping – and interdependencies arising out of these qualities of relations. As we saw in Chapter 3, arguments about interlocking means (such as those of Weick, 1979) also avoid limiting and distorting assumptions about shared goals.
5. At this point many writers would use the language of resources. Indeed, in the literature on power, resource-dependency perspectives are popular (see Pfeffer and Salancik, 1978; Hickson *et al*, 1986).
6. We dislike this language because it reflects a separation of person from context (other persons). Relationships are understood as more or less *instrumental* in the ways implied by most traditional treatments of negotiation, exchange, and influence.
7. We would add that part of the reason this is so also derives from a historical perspective. For us, this would require attention to earlier decision processes in which particular patterns of advantage and disadvantage were created and reproduced. Such processes removed particular issues – and therefore, opportunities for commitment – from the agenda for decision making, and sustained, or changed, patterns of power and value.
8. See, for example, Chapter 8 on the projects of chief executives. The content of the projects, processes, and relationships varied enormously. However, a process framework makes it possible to handle such variations.
9. We would add that Tajfel's general arguments, and this illustration of their possible appearances, seem to reflect the valuations of a masculine culture. This contrasts with feminine cultures which value connection (rather than separation), caring and responsibility. See Dachler (1990) and Dachler and Hosking (1991).

10. Political theorists sometimes use the term *clique* to refer to groups of this kind.
11. We have shown (see Chapter 3) that the assumption of interlocking means is sufficient. We most prefer the more general and abstract argument that actors are joined by the *help* they need from one another.
12. To speak of groups in terms of shared values should not necessarily be taken to imply managerialism. There are groups of this sort and definitions of groups must allow for this.
13. Later we shall develop this point to argue that for actors skilfully to organize, they must have a practical knowledge of the values they must protect and promote (private or collective), and a practical knowledge of the interdependent values (private and collective) of other actors.
14. Some have argued that this emphasis understates the degree to which contexts make actors. However, this criticism seems to incorporate a tacit individualistic model of person. These are difficult arguments. Suffice it to say that we accept (a) that actions are constrained and (b) that actors do not achieve perfect control in relation to their contexts. We prefer to emphasize actors as agents.
15. Not just political, but, given our arguments, also the social and cognitive processes through which this is more or less effectively achieved.
16. For a rare exception see Mangham (1979).
17. Notable exceptions are to be found in the work of Dalton, Sayles, and Burns.
18. See e.g. Drory and Romm (1988); Farrell and Peterson (1982); and Robbins (1984).
19. Others explicitly have taken a contrary view. Studies of perceptions of organizational politics are cited as evidence in support of this. It appears that actors do not describe all behaviour as political. However, such findings are of little relevance to us here in that 'political' was defined in the context of the managerialist perspective (see Drory and Romm, 1988).
20. E.g. Hickson *et al.* (1971); Salancik and Pfeffer (1977); Crozier (1964); and Pettigrew, (1973).
21. More usually, these issues would be discussed in the language of the terms and conditions of exchange, stakes and prizes, who stands to gain, who to lose, and so on. In other words, the entitative emphasis is reflected in an emphasis on instrumentalities and manipulation. In this context, it is interesting to note that British students find it hard to believe the research on equity theory concerning overpayment. Is this because they are so used to thinking of relationships in terms of their instrumentalities and opportunities to exploit? This also may be one reason why, in the literatures on OB and HRM, we find so little consideration of negotiation as a basic relational process.
22. We prefer to say equivocal in order to register that alternative descriptions of social reality always will be possible (see Part 1). The language of uncertainty tends to be taken to imply that certainty could be found by identifying the 'right' description in the physicalist sense.
23. These, he argued, could not be fully proceduralized. We have made much of the importance of this argument. It has considerable significance for our arguments about skilled performance. We shall develop it later in relation to particular contexts.
24. Again, we will draw a great deal of significance from this point – arguing that skilled performance involves 'moving around' – thereby creating more transferable resources.
25. Hardly surprising then that there is 'resistance' to change.

PART 3

Structure in the process of projects

We have argued for an emphasis on social action in the performance of projects. Projects are set partly by actors and partly by their contexts. Actors create cultures characterized by differences of value and influence, through interrelated social, cognitive, and political processes. Cultures reflect and support *some* valuations and not others. Whether we are speaking of thought or action not 'anything goes'. This brings us to the question of how organizing is performed in ways which are more helpful to participants. We discuss this through focusing on skilful processes in the performance of projects.

In developing our argument about processes we have emphasized both the *historical* and the *emergent* aspects. An historical perspective may range from a relatively short-term focus on personal reports of past projects to accounts of long-term developments in industrial concentration, and changing relations between Capital and Labour. It recognizes that actors do not create cultures *de novo*. To recognize that processes have emergent qualities is to recognize that no actor, whether individual or group, has perfect control over the creation of a particular social order. As we shall see there are literatures which imply, for example, that chief executives do achieve this. We do not agree. We use the language of skill to emphasize that skills are not properties of actors, abstracted from their contexts, but are best understood as a quality of the relationship between actors and their contexts. We seek to provide an appreciation of skilful performances. Our interest is in process knowledge. This is knowledge of *how* rather than knowledge of *what*. It is knowledge of relational processes. Relational processes must be central to a social actor perspective.

Regrettably, there are few studies in which social processes are tracked over time in ways which make it possible to analyse the different contributions and influence of participants. Instead, the literatures tend to focus on the qualities and actions of individuals. There are three reasons for this. The first is pragmatic. It is relatively easy to take individuals as the unit of analysis and follow them around. It is much more difficult to take processes or a project as the unit of analysis. The second reason is theoretical. Many take the view that the individual must be the centre of social inquiry, and go on to commit the individualistic fallacy. Finally, physicalist treatments of social reality mean that few show any interest in a particular, identified actor's own descriptions. Fewer still show an interest in *how* actors arrive at the descriptions they do – how particular descriptions emerge in a particular sense of social order and in particular relationships and activities. Writers often fail to make clear from whose point of view a particular account is given. These features reflect a failure to take seriously the social processes through which actors construct social order, and the general significance of the processes through which actors, more or less collectively, construct realities. This makes the literatures particularly hard to interpret. If all actors construct more or less partial descriptions, grounded in their own values, then a description can only be meaningful when interpreted in relation to the values, projects, and contexts of the actors who generated it.

The chapters in Part 3 have a more obviously applied focus than those which have gone before. They represent an attempt to show how it is possible to provide useful practical advice based on the results of psychological theory and research. Our general strategy has been to analyse particular projects in some detail. Thus, our treatment of formal negotiation begins with an analysis of collective bargaining in the context of industrial relations; our treatment of teamwork is concerned with teamwork in the context of engineering product design; and our treatment of top management is concerned with the work of the heads of departments at the level of Australian State Governments. In each case, we have tried to make the most of the limited data available by placing it in a wider context. To some extent this has meant considering wider domains of activity. So the study of formal negotiation has been broadened to include data from international negotiations; the study of teamwork has been broadened to include various kinds of management team; and the study of top management has been broadened to include a wider consideration of the nature of managerial work.

From a theoretical perspective the approach we have taken is social constructivist, broadly speaking. Our major concern has been to articulate some of the skills of organizing. This means that we have tried to show how social processes are structured collectively so that people are able to make sense of change, and decide how to act. We rely heavily on the idea that high performance systems are characterized by cultures of productivity in which certain social orders are valued in themselves but remain sufficiently flexible to adapt to change. We analyse the development of such cultures through an examination of the processes of networking, negotiation, and enabling.

This examination is brought to its conclusion in the final chapter, where we examine the skills of leadership in some detail. We argue that traditional treatments of leadership have given only very partial and distorted treatments of the cognitive and political problems we wish to bring centre stage. We argue that the essence of leadership lies in the dialogues in which processes of networking, negotiation, and enabling come together, to create cultures in which differences between people are recognized, respected, and form the foundation for creative, collective work.

Chapter 6
Formal negotiation

Introduction

Processes of organizing function to create a social order. That order is a negotiated order. Accordingly we shall now consider the process of negotiation in more detail. As we have seen in Part 2 negotiation is a form of collective decision-making which is used to manage change. Formal negotiation is a process whereby representatives of groups meet explicitly to discuss the nature of the relationship between those groups. They meet to discuss whether certain changes in the relationship are possible, and at what cost. The outcome of their deliberations is a set of rules, defining the terms on which members of the parties will do business in the future. Essentially, the rules defined the terms on which members of the various groups will commit themselves to certain kinds of project work.

Typically, the negotiations are conducted in the context of existing rules. The effect of the negotiation is to change the rules (by adding new ones, or amending the old ones). This is why negotiators have been described as writing social history.[1] However, they do not write the history on their own. The changes have to be explained to other people, and accepted by them. This is why one important outcome of a negotiation is an agreed *story* about what has happened and why. The story provides a *rationale*, linking what is happening now to what has happened in the past, and to what will happen in the future (Morley, in press, b). It shows that the negotiators have learned their lessons from the past, and are using that experience in appropriate ways (Sarason, 1972). Without such a rationale negotiation is likely to be prolonged, or to break down. Unless the rationale is accepted by principals outside the immediate negotiation the rules will be broken when attempts are made to implement the agreements which have been made.

When we speak of formal negotiation it is important to realize that we are talking about a process which cycles through stages involving discussion within the parties (internal negotiation) and discussion between the parties (external negotiation). What happens in the internal negotiation affects what happens in the external negotiation, and vice versa, because each forms part of a collective process whereby participants make sense of change, and decide collectively how to manage it.[2] For this reason, amongst others, we shall emphasize the similarities between internal and external negotiations.

We consider negotiation as a form of intelligent social action, which may be understood from the language-action perspective set out in Chapter 1. To apply this perspective we must decide, first, when a negotiation begins. This means following each issue back to the point where someone first saw change, or the possibility of change, in the existing social order, and decided to describe that change to others. The language-action perspective suggests that negotiators have two central tasks. The first is to describe the change and reach some sort of internal consensus that the changes are of a certain kind, implying certain kinds of threats,[3] or certain kinds of opportunities. The second is to forge commitments to collective action based on those descriptions, either to stay with existing policies, or to change those policies in various ways. The two tasks correspond to what we have called the cognitive and political[4] problems of social life.

Success in negotiation

Consider the following description of the negotiations conducted at the Potsdam Conference (held at the end of the Second World War).[5] Apparently

> The solution was the worst form of compromise. It solved nothing and left too many gaps and loopholes which could cause misunderstanding in the future. It gave neither side what it regarded as even minimum requirements. The eventual decision was incompatible with the political realities of the post-war world. (Morris, 1973, p.49)

This implies that there are two sides to the activity in negotiation, and two related criteria for negotiation success (Morley, 1986).[6] Both criteria need to be satisfied. The first is *cognitive*. In general, it is important not to leave too many gaps and loopholes because these mean that participants take away very different ideas of which commitments have been made, and which have not. The second is *political*. It is also important that each party is willing to commit itself to the collective agreement because each thinks that it will provide practical solutions to important problems. This implies a multi-partisan criterion, since if any one of the parties is extremely dissatisfied about the terms of the agreement, the agreement is likely to fail when implemented.[7]

Broadly speaking, we take the view that a successful negotiation is one which satisfies the parties' competing interests as well as possible, and as quickly as possible, in ways that are seen to make sense, so that the settlement is viable, and 'sticks' when put into effect.[8] To quote Davey (1972), 'The mutual purpose of negotiation should be achievement of a collective agreement that will work' (p.128).

This means that negotiators must understand what has been agreed, and why. They must also appreciate that, in the long run, it may be better to break-off negotiations than to reach agreements prematurely, before the consequences of the agreement have been considered in detail. There is evidence that effective negotiators understand this very well. Those who are less effective are too anxious to reach an agreement.[9] They would 'prefer to leave ambiguous points to be cleared later, fearing that making things explicit might cause the other party to disagree' (Rackham and Carlisle, 1978a). However, there are times when not to disagree means not to solve the problem.[10]

If we are to understand what makes negotiation successful we shall have to explore those collective processes by which negotiators handle their cognitive and political tasks. As a first step, we shall summarize certain aspects of Warr's (1973) description of company wide pay and productivity negotiations at a firm in the North of England.[11] This will allow us to set down our own account of the skills of negotiation, in outline form.

A case study

The pay and productivity negotiations were largely 'domestic', although the union side consulted outside officials from time to time. There was a management team, of five people, and a union team, of nineteen people. Each team engaged multiple perspectives (see Chapter 4). The management team consisted of two plant managers, the company administration manager, the industrial relations manager, and the personnel officer. The union team was drawn from the thirty-two members of the Joint Shop Stewards Committee (JSSC). The idea of a company wide agreement was quite an innovation, and most of the negotiators were quite unused to dealing with proposals (from management) which covered sixty-five typewritten sides of A4 paper.

The cognitive tasks

Some cognitive problems derived from the scope and complexity of management's proposals. Consequently, whilst management began external negotiations with a fairly clear idea of what they regarded as an acceptable agreement, the union side did not.[12] The union negotiators faced problems of information overload. We may surmise that they also faced problems of interpretation because social actions are ambiguous, and because they cannot be completely described.

The management team recognized the complexity of their proposals. Their initial strategy was to stand firm and not make any concessions until they were sure the unions understood the proposals. Whilst this strategy was not without its problems (Morley, 1979a) it did mean that at the end of the first stage of negotiations the union side had a fairly clear understanding of the company's proposals, and had identified those issues which were of most immediate concern.

Most members of the union side – at least a simple majority – were probably generally sympathetic to the idea of a company wide agreement. They seemed to have accepted the proposals in principle, but because so much remained to be sorted out in practice, they were very unwilling to assert positively that they were willing to come round to management's points of view. The team lacked a clear, impartial leader, able to organize structure in the process of negotiation. Consequently, those who were in the majority probably failed to realize that there were many others of like mind to themselves. A minority of stewards, with positions which were easier to articulate and to defend, were able, therefore, to persuade the JSSC to press for new negotiations 'quite unrelated to national agreements for the engineering industry' (Warr, 1973, p.117).[13]

This was a mistake because it violated agreed procedures, negotiated at national level. The members of the JSSC appear not to have known of this agreement. Consequently, when management announced that they would have to register a failure to agree, and enlist outside help as required by that procedure, the union team 'dispersed in some confusion' (Warr, 1973, p.117). Negotiations were temporarily suspended.

The political tasks

At the end of the first stage of negotiations the union side had succeeded in identifying the issues they needed to argue about. The second stage was one in which the unions faced major problems of internal adjustment[14] as they attempted further to articulate the nature of the threats and opportunities they faced, and as they began to work through the other core problems (see Chapter 4). Many harsh words were spoken as the union team attempted to negotiate solutions and select a line of action from the alternatives proposed.

Evidently, the union side failed to organize a satisfactory political process because they failed to resolve two of the most central dilemmas of political life. The first dilemma was whether decisions required unanimity or whether they could be made by majority rule. The second dilemma was whether Stewards should take a leader or a delegate role in relations with their constituents.[15] The combination of the inexperience of the Stewards and the lack of leadership within the union team meant that the dilemmas 'ground the negotiating team into indecision' (Warr, 1973, p.113).

When negotiations were suspended the union team were able to take advice from District Officials. As a result, the size of the union team was reduced from nineteen to eleven. The union side decided that the way to handle the first dilemma was by the judicious application of a majority voting rule.[16] They also realized that in negotiations of this scope and complexity it was quite undesirable that they simply took a passive delegate role.

When negotiations resumed the main concern of the two sides was to keep talks going so that each could gain a better understanding of what the other thought was important, and why. Management's actions were designed help the union team solve its problems of internal adjustment. They gave the union access to financial information and did everything possible to help union negotiators convince their constituents that the external negotiations were proceeding along the right lines. This helped those Stewards who favoured management's new approach to problems of pay and productivity to establish a dominant frame of reference within the union side.

In the final stage of negotiation there was considerable debate about the details of the agreement, both within and between the sides. However, by this stage the union side had evolved a much more effective process to handle political problems within the negotiating team. Their major problem was 'specific group resistances' from some of the sections affected by the agreement. District union officials were called in to help overcome some of those resistances and, with the help of some final concessions from management,[17] the union team felt able to go ahead and sign the agreement.

Effective negotiation

The purpose of this chapter is to examine the kind of process which leads to success in negotiation. That is, it is concerned with the skills of negotiation. We shall use the case study above to illustrate some of the main components of our analysis.

The core problems

The core problems are those of identifying issues, developing solutions, selecting an alternative, and implementing a policy (see Part 2). From management's point of view the internal process began when someone began to consider the advantages of negotiating a pay and productivity agreement company wide. From the union's point of view the internal process began when they first learned of those plans. The first formal stage of the external negotiations began when management presented their proposals to the JSSC in written form. The union's task was to organize internal and external negotiations to identify the main issues; to consider possible responses; to agree with management what changes in their relationship were possible, and at what cost. They had also to agree a procedure for putting those changes into practice.

Successful negotiation is not something that just happens. The process has to be organized properly, so that the participants are able effectively to cope with the cognitive and political aspects of negotiation task (whether internal or external).

Working out what is happening, and why

As negotiations become more complex and wider in scope negotiators have increasing difficulty coping with the intellectual demands of their task. There seem to be two problems of comprehension (Winham, 1977). The first arises because negotiators have only limited capacities to process information (see Chapter 1). There is no doubt that inexperienced negotiators would find it extremely difficult to cope with the size and variety of the data base they had been given. To the extent that the proposals were ambiguous and were not completely described they would introduce problems of uncertainty and discretionary content.[18] Problems of this kind make it difficult for negotiators to work out the implications of a particular policy. They also make it difficult to structure the internal process so that deliberations converge on to policies which are understood by all and accepted by all.[19]

Some problems of comprehension are likely to arise simply because of the size of the union team. Essentially, the union side was a coalition of people representing different groups (see Chapter 5). At the beginning of the external negotiations the union side was nineteen strong. This is likely to have been a major source of difficulty, since there is evidence that, as the number of parties to a negotiation is increased, debate becomes less lucid, and therefore harder to follow (Midgaard and Underdal, 1977).

In Chapter 1 we argued that effective social action requires a suitable knowledge base, encoded in the form of suitably organized evaluative beliefs. We argued that expertise in a particular domain meant that people were quickly able to see a position as similar to ones they had seen before, so that they were able to see certain kinds of threat and certain kinds of opportunity, which others did not. We argued that, in this sense, the skilled performer was a skilled perceiver. We argued, later, that organized knowledge of this kind was a necessary, but not a sufficient condition, for effective performance (see Chapter 4). The negotiators described by Warr lacked the relevant experience of complex negotiations. Consequently, negotiations were much longer, and much more difficult than they might otherwise have been.

The importance of such a knowledge base is hardly ever discussed in writings on the psychological aspects of negotiation. Nevertheless, it is important that members of a negotiating team have sufficient expertise collectively to cover whatever commercial, technical, contractual, or social issues arise in the course of a particular negotiation. According to Marsh (1974) the leader must be able to make a serious contribution to each of the items to be discussed, and have sufficient knowledge intelligently to direct and coordinate the activities of others. It is evident that there was no one on the trade union side with that kind of expertise.

Building a working consensus

In the negotiations described by Warr the trade union side faced major problems of internal adjustment. The size of the group meant that a large number of values and interests had to be accommodated. In itself, this makes consensus more difficult to attain. Furthermore, different people are likely to focus on different aspects of the agreement. This may mean that they are each too confident that they have understood the others' positions (Jervis, 1976). In some relational settings misunderstandings of this kind may to lead to increased antagonism, increasing the likelihood that any agreements reached will be the worst form of compromise (see Bonham, 1971).

Warr's major contribution has been to appreciate that consensus within a team isn't something which just happens. To be effective, the political process needs to be properly organized. In particular, the negotiators need to cope with certain *dilemmas* inherent in the process of decision making (also see Chapter 1). Warr himself regards the two dilemmas identified above, namely unanimity *versus* majority rule and leader *versus* delegate role, as 'the central ones of any negotiating group' (p.113).

From our own perspective the central dilemma is one of how to achieve a social order which will provide the basis for coordinated social action without closing the minds of the participants to the possibilities of change (see Part 2). Nevertheless, the dilemmas identified by Warr are extremely important because they involve conflicts between ends and means. On the one hand there is the need to achieve sufficient internal consensus to prevent others from exploiting internal divisions within one's own side.[20] On the other hand there are the values attached to a participative process. This leads to a series of dilemmas which may perhaps be called 'democracy dilemmas'.[21]

Networking

Although Warr does not describe the process in detail, it is quite clear that both management and union engaged in a good deal of networking. This serves two functions: that of collecting organizational intelligence (see Chapter 4); and that of building commitment to particular lines of action (see Chapter 5). This dual function is seen very clearly in the role of the district officers who became involved in the problems of internal adjustment on the union side.[22]

Leadership

We have argued elsewhere that leadership is central to the dynamics of organizational groups[23] (and we shall repeat some of those arguments in Chapter 9). For the moment, however, perhaps it will suffice to note that Warr's case study shows very clearly just why leadership is important. The problems of internal adjustment within the union team were made very much more difficult because the team lacked anyone capable of taking the lead in handling what Kanter has called the 'creative' and 'political' aspects of change. The creative aspects of change arise because people need help to make sense of their social worlds (see Chapter 4). The political aspects of change arise because people value possible lines of action in different ways. Effective leadership is a process in which leaders collaborate with others to generate commitments based on a shared sense of social order. Without such a sense of order it is all too easy for groups to be ground into indecision, as Warr has shown.

Strategy and tactics versus messages and meanings

Most of the current social psychological approaches to the study of negotiation treat negotiation as a game of strategy. This metaphor comes from work on the theory of games, which was introduced as an attempt to define rational action in contexts where the outcomes for each actor depended partly on their own actions and partly on the actions of others.[24] There is now a voluminous literature dealing with empirical investigations of interaction in matrix games, such as the Prisoner's Dilemma.[25] Studies of this kind do not provide direct models of the kind of communication involved in negotiation (Morley, 1979b), although they help to characterize some of the dilemmas inherent in the process (Walton and McKersie, 1966). It is clear that the outcome of a long series of games cannot be predicted in advance. It depends on the interaction in the game.[26] It is also clear that the hope of finding one best strategy to follow regardless of context is doomed to failure.[27]

Nevertheless, Axelrod's (1984) analysis of the evolution of cooperation shows that certain classes of strategy seem fairly robust, meaning they are successful in a variety of contexts. Broadly speaking, it seems that robust strategies exhibit the following qualities. Those who use such strategies might be described as 'nice', 'provocable', 'forgiving', and 'clear'. Being nice means that they will be cooperative as often as possible, and will never be the initial cause of a breakdown of trust. Being provocable means that they will retaliate against breakdowns of trust. Being forgiving means that the retaliation will be restrained. Being clear means following a policy which is easy to recognize and to understand. Without wishing to overstate the case it is tempting to say that those strategies which are robust are legible, coherent, open-ended, and elicit reponses from the other which allow them both to do well.[28]

A second class of games of strategy derives from economic statements of what is called 'the bargaining problem'.[29] Such models more or less ignore the effects of social contexts. They attempt abstract analyses based on the assumptions that the bargaining relationship is one of bilateral monopoly and that the issues involve the distribution of some quantitative resource which has already been defined. From this perspective, problems of internal adjustment are ignored. The parties to the bargaining relationship are treated as individual actors, whose main task is to plan a cooperative or a competitive strategy. The process of negotiation is reduced to a sequence of bid and counterbid, halting at the point where concessions converge. This is the 'solution' to the bargaining problem.[30]

Research within this tradition has used what have been called 'games of economic exchange'.[31] Empirical research has not, in our opinion, provided a useful model of the processes of communication in negotiation because there is usually much more to negotiation than a sequence of bid and counterbid (Webb, 1982). Part of the problem is that communication has been treated simply as a series of strategic moves rather than a series of messages and meanings (Putnam, 1985). There is no room for a process in which collective cognitive images are created and changed until the participants find a solution which makes collective sense.

Other experimental research has used role-playing games or simulations which bring real life disputes into the laboratory (see Morley and Stephenson, 1977; Morley, 1979b). Such paradigms introduce new possibilities for communication because there is something to argue about. In such cases questions of strategy (how to outwit an opponent) may be subordinated to questions of structure (how to find a dominant definition of the problem), as Winham has shown in his reports of State Department Training Simulations (Winham, 1977; Winham and Bovis, 1978).[32]

Case studies of negotiation,[33] including those which use systematic observational methods,[34] and studies of the rhetoric of conflict[35] show the importance of both cognitive and political aspects of the process of negotiation. However, whilst the political process is one of struggle, it is not concerned simply with winning. Rather, it is concerned with what has been called ideology in action (Breakwell, 1983). This means that people attempt to find arguments which embody the interpretive practices of particular groups in particular contexts and actively disseminate them to others (see Chapter 5).

The skills of negotiation

The process of internal adjustment has the objectives of preserving flexibility of response;[36] finding integrative solutions if they exist;[37] identifying essential, important, and less important interests;[38] preventing premature commitment to descriptions which are plausible, but misleading or incomplete;[39] maximizing the ability of team members to learn from the process of external negotiation;[40] and finding a collective rationale, linking the present to the past and to the future.[41] The process of external negotiation has the objectives of reaching agreements which all parties understand and which all parties can accept, because they see the agreements make sense.

Cognitive aspects

Cognitive problems arise in negotiation for two reasons, essentially. The first reason is that the participants need collectively to understand the issues and understand why the policies they propose are practical solutions to the political problems (Morley, in press, b). The second reason is that negotiators may find that their capacities to process information are insufficient to cope with the demands of their tasks (Welford, 1980). We have already considered each of these issues in a general form (see Chapter 1 and Chapter 4). We shall consider them now as they relate to formal negotiation in particular.

Generating shared meanings
We have suggested, in Chapter 1, that there is good evidence that people form strong categorical beliefs, even when evidence is mixed, and that, for various reasons, they generate too much order and certainty in their social worlds (see Kinder and Weiss, 1978). Essentially, they are able to go beyond the evidence given because they have relatively stable systems of evaluative beliefs, and

because they have access to community memory in the form of various kinds of stories (which situate general lessons about conflict in the context of particular disputes). Because of this, the participants are able to look at existing policies in the light of the threats and opportunities afforded by change, or the prospect of change, in the existing social order (see Chapter 4).

How threats and opportunities are defined depends on the person in the context (see Chapter 1). The person is important because some negotiators may be described as rational, and some as irrational, in an information processing sense. According to Snyder and Diesing (1977) 'rational' bargainers are those who appreciate the contingency of human cognition (see Chapter 4); 'irrational' bargainers are those who do not. Whereas the rational bargainer has low confidence in his or her diagnosis of what has happened, and why (because he or she understands that social actions are inherently ambiguous, and that social actions cannot completely be described), the irrational bargainer relies on forms of theoretical thinking which render descriptions and actions virtually immune to change.[42] If the process of internal and external negotiation is organized properly so that the person is forced to argue with others who take different points of view, he or she will be able to test hypotheses, and identify arguments which are invalid, or misleading, or incomplete (see Chapter 4). Otherwise, he or she may participate in various pathological forms of collective action, such as groupthink.[43] If we are correct, it is particularly important that people understand why certain proposals are particularly attractive to members of the other side, so that they focus on the interests of the other side, rather than the positions they are advocating at any particular time.[44] Unless a negotiator understands the appeal of the others' arguments from their point of view he or she is unlikely to be able elicit responses which let them both do well.

According to Kennedy et al. (1987) preparation for negotiation should be regarded as something which happens all the year round. As they say, 'Gathering intelligence about the other party ought to be elementary no matter what it is you are negotiating about' (p. 33). Skilled negotiators will take care to build intelligence networks which include members of the other team. In this respect it is germane to consider evidence that some negotiators develop 'strong', or 'close', or 'high' bargaining relationships with members of other sides.[45] Such relationships have both affective and cognitive components. As Brown and Terry have said,

> We shall define the bargaining relationship that exists between two opposing negotiators as the extent to which they are able to make each other aware of the constraints under which they operate and the likely reactions by one organization to actions by the other. We thus see the concept primarily in terms of information flows . . . we would describe a bargaining relationship as 'high' when the two protagonists are able to communicate changes in their bargaining positions rapidly and thus have a high degree of certainty about likely outcomes from fresh developments. (Brown and Terry, 1975, p.8)

Such relationships are frequently collusive, since the participants help each other by exchanging confidential information about the problems of internal adjustment with their own sides. They are valued by the participants since they help each to get what he or she wants (Batstone et al., 1977).[46]

It is also important that negotiators build strong, or close, or high bargaining relationships with members of their own sides. The exchange of information within a party helps party members to learn the same strategic vocabulary, and helps them to see issues in the same kind of way.

Matching capacities to demands

Welford (1980) has set out the elements of a general model of social skill which may be applied to various groups and to various collective tasks (see Morley, 1986).[47] The central idea is that, if one part of the task takes a lot of mental effort, people may not be able to do another part of the task at the same time (because they run out of mental resources). Research and theory combine to suggest that the way to handle this kind of problem is to take steps to reduce ambiguity, to clarify communications, and to slow negotiation down (Snyder and Diesing, 1977; Rackham and Carlisle, 1978a, b; Fisher and Ury, 1983). This helps Party and Opponent to work through the core problems (of interpretation, development, selection, and implementation). Some examples may help to show how this is done.

First, skilled negotiators activate their social networks to get their messages through by sending them through different people. Second, they keep repeating the same theme so that people have time to work out the consequences of what has been said. Third, they label their actions, presumably because they recognize that it is all too easy for others to interpret those actions in different ways.[48] Fourth, they test their understanding of what others have said, and communicate that understanding to them by restating content, reflecting feelings, and summarizing what has been said.[49] Fifth, they recognize that others may not always be listening to them because they are working out what to say in reply.[50] Sixth, they resist the temptation immediately to respond to a proposal with a counter-proposal of their own, because they realize that their protagonists are not ready to listen to what they have to say. Seventh, they ask where people would like to go, rather than ask them to justify where they have been. Finally, they take pains to convey new information in the light of what has gone before.[51]

The purpose of this activity is to remove unnecessary conflict between the sides. Some idea of the scope of the problem may be gained from the observation that negotiators very frequently fail to realize their interests are compatible, as Blake and Mouton, and others, have shown (see Chapter 4). This is why some authors have suggested that one member of a negotiating team specifically be given the role of observing the members of the opposing team, and listening carefully to what they have to say (Walton and McKersie, 1965; Kennedy et al., 1987).[52]

Political aspects

The political process of negotiation is concerned with the organization of disagreement within and between groups. It is important to determine just how strongly each of the parties feel about the issues, because one test of an agreement is whether it is viable in the context of the power relations between the sides. In this respect is is important that negotiators are not afraid to disagree. However, it is also important that the disagreement is seen as a natural part of a business relationship rather than something which requires a defensive response. Finally, a political process is needed to build a working consensus within each of the sides.

Differentiation and integration in external negotiation

The most obvious dilemmas in negotiation concern changes in position. They concern where to open, when to move, how far to move, and when to settle.[53] According to Snyder and Diesing (1977) the mixed-motive relationship between the parties sets up tensions between the major goal of reaching a settlement and the constraint that the settlement needs to be a settlement of a certain kind. From one perspective the purpose of external negotiation is to find a formula which lets each party reach the major goal whilst satisfying its most important constraints (Zartman, 1977). Once a formula has been found the rest is detail (which is sometimes easy to sort out, and sometimes not).[54]

To find a formula, each side will have to change its position, or at least indicate its willingness to change. One dilemma is whether to make the change explicit or whether to leave it implicit. If it is made explicit it may expedite the process of reaching agreement. On the other hand, such gains have to be balanced against the costs of position loss and image loss (Pruitt, 1971). A second dilemma is when to indicate a willingness to change in position, early or late? Those who indicate that they are willing to move early in negotiation may encourage the other side to take a constructive approach. But they may give the impression that there is more to come. Those who stand firm protect their reputations for resolve, but they run the risk of being seen as totally intransigent. There seem to be various ways of dealing with the first dilemma (Morley, 1981a). However, the negotiator who moves before establishing 'a convincing image of firmness' runs a serious risk that his or her position will be seen as one which can be exploited (Snyder and Diesing, 1977, p.248).

This is one of the reasons why some writers have characterized the first stage of negotiation as one which functions to assess the strength of each side's resolve.[55] Morley and Stephenson (1977) have used a metaphor from horse racing to point out that, in this first stage, the negotiators 'are assessing the form of the parties with respect to the particular course on which the present contest will take place' (p.288).[56] It seems that the more clearly and firmly negotiators articulate differences between their positions at this stage the more likely they are to find agreements which make sense (Douglas, 1962).

There are several reasons for this. First, negotiators face conflicting demands from three sets of forces. McGrath (1966) has described these as a force, R, toward Party's position; a force, A, toward reaching agreement; and a force, C, toward satisfying the interests of the parties in constructive and creative ways. We see the conflict between these forces as posing dilemmas for the negotiators.[57] The conflict between R and A forces means that those who move too soon may be seen failing to discharge their obligations as representatives of groups. Similarly, the conflict between R and C forces means that negotiators may feel unable to look beyond the obvious options until they have articulated their party positions as fully and as firmly as possible.[58]

Douglas (1962) has described the first stage of negotiation as one in which there is a great show of muscle. Her studies of mediation in American industrial relations show that

> There are vehement demands and counter-demands, arguments and counter-arguments. Each side shows prodigious zeal for exposing and discrediting its opposite, and sooner or later there almost invariably comes from each side a conscious, studied, hard-hitting critique of the other. These attacks are typically vigorous and spirited; not infrequently, they are also derisive and venemous. (Douglas, 1962, p.15)

However, whilst it is important clearly to articulate the differences between the sides it is important to do so in a constructive, businesslike way, lest what is said provokes defensive reactions. Destructive argument of the kind described by Douglas is common in various kinds of negotiation but leads to spirals of 'attack-defence' or 'blame' (Kennedy et al., 1987). It is probably one of the reasons why the negotiatiors described by Douglas were needing help from third parties to manage their disputes. There is evidence that negotiators with a track record of success avoid antagonizing their opponents (Rackham and Carlisle, 1978a).[59] They are not afraid to disagree.[60] But when they disagree they do so in ways which avoid provocative language.[61] They take steps to ensure that disagreement between the parties is not perceived as antagonism between the persons.

In this respect it is interesting to note that negotiations which end in success go through a process in which it is relatively easy to see when negotiators are acting officially, as representatives of groups, and when they are acting unoficially, as actors in their own right (see Chapter 5).[62] In the first case, it is easy to identify negotiators from unlabelled transcripts, simply by examining the content of what has been said; in the second case, it is not. When negotiators are obviously operating as representatives, disagreement is clearly located at the party level. When they are obviously acting unofficially they are free to explore alternatives without prejudice, so to speak.

The process of internal adjustment
The process of internal adjustment is sometimes called intra-organizational bargaining. It is rarely discussed explicitly, but the interested reader will find

useful treatments in Walton and McKersie (1965) and Morley (in press, b). The central problem is one of achieving consensus within the party organization.

One aspect of the problem is that representatives may find that those they represent have quite unrealistic expectations of what can be achieved. This is why so much of Walton and McKersie's analysis has been concerned with the power of the chief negotiator to modify or ignore the expectations of his or her reference groups. If they are correct, that power is based on a combination of specific information,[63] general expertise,[64] and careful choice of tactics.[65] One tactic is for the chief negotiator to take the lead in preparing objectives, or to do so in collaboration with other members of the team. A second is to prevent ideas from 'crystallizing' into demands by asking 'suggestive questions'.[66]

The importance of being able to ask suggestive questions is shown by examples of the problems faced by teams who are unable to consult with their principals. Some of the clearest examples come from the arena of international relations. For example, the American delegation to the Paris Peace Conference of 1919 found it extremely difficult to consult with President Wilson. Because they were unable to ask suggestive questions,[67] and because Wilson was 'shockingly ignorant of the European situation', the American delegation was unable to work out a coherent point of view (Elcock, 1972). Consequently, the President found that negotiations began from positions which were defined by the British or by the French. This meant that he 'had to take up, therefore, a persistent attitude of obstruction, criticism, and negation if the draft was to become at all in line with his own ideas and purpose' (Keynes, 1961, p.24). Such an attitude made it impossible for the negotiators to handle issues which were technically complex, and also emotionally laden, in any sort of constructive way. Not surprisingly, perhaps, the Treaty of Versailles, which included a Covenant for the League of Nations, and dealt with issues of German war guilt, reparation, and disarmament, was roundly condemned after the event. We doubt that problems of this kind are confined to the domain of international relations.

A second aspect of the process of internal adjustment concerns the need for an effective political process to build consensus within a team. In the case of the negotiations studied by Warr the union side were only able to make progress when they recognized that, if all else failed, collective decisions would have to be made through the use of a majority rule. Other decision schemes are possible but what is important, from our perspective, is that the process is one which the participants all understand and all accept (otherwise they will not commit themselves to the decisions which follow from it).

Unnecessary conflict and realistic conflict

What is evident in what we have written is a contrast between processes which remove unnecessary obstacles to agreement and processes which bring realistic conflict to the fore (Morley, 1986). Cognitive processes make negotiation no harder than it needs to be in so far as they help negotiators to match their intellectual capacities to the demands of the task (Welford, 1980; Morley, 1986). Skilful negotiators use tactics which reduce ambiguity, clarify communications, test understanding, and generally slow negotiation down. Political processes remove unnnecessary obstacles to agreement in so far as they help negotiators to organize disagreement so that it is seen as a natural part of a business relationship. Skilful negotiators use tactics which mean that disagreement is seen as disagreement between the parties rather than something which requires a defensive response.

Cognitive processes help negotiators to organize their intellectual activity, so that they are able to think clearly about the issues. This helps to remove unnecessary obstacles to agreement. It may or may not diminish conflict between the groups. This is an empirical question to be answered afresh in each particular case. The important point is that the conflict is more likely to be realistic because the participants have a better understanding of the issues.

Political processes are concerned with the organization of disagreement within and between groups, so that decisions made will be accepted by the participants, and viable within the wider context of relations between the groups they represent. The skilful negotiator is not afraid to disagree because he or she is aware that some kinds of compromise are worse than useless in the long run. He or she is not afraid to challenge others' positions nor to ask others to explain what they are trying to do, [68] because not to disagree may be not to solve the problem. Consequently, he or she will make negotiation as hard as they think it needs to be to negotiate agreements which make sense.

There are some tensions between the two kinds of process. It is important that tactics which remove unnecessary obstacles to agreement are integrated with tactics which bring realistic conflict to the fore. It is possible, for example, to slow negotiation down to the point where one is not seen to be negotiating at all. As a matter of fact this seems to have happened in the early stages of the pay and productivity agreement described above. According to Warr, management's initial strategy was to stand firm, to note down what the union said, and to assert that certain aspects of the documents had not been understood. Not surprisingly, this soon 'irritated' the union side. The Shop Stewards had expected to be able to settle several of the items and then report back to the JSSC. Apparently, the Stewards were 'quite thirsting for a fight' and were infuriated that 'management would not even leave their corner' (Warr, 1973, p.97).

By a judicious combination of tactics the skilful negotiator makes negotiation no harder than it needs to be, but is aware that agreements are validated in the struggle between the sides. Because of this he or she is more likely to negotiate agreements which provide practical solutions to problems of change.

Summary and conclusions

Formal negotiation is a process by which participants, who are representatives of groups, openly meet to discuss whether certain changes are possible in the business relationship between the groups, and at what cost. The output from their deliberations is a formal document which legitimates certain changes and adds to the set of rules which formally define the terms of that business relationship. It is important that the rules have to be explained to people outside the immediate negotiation, and accepted by them. Because of this, one important outcome of a negotiation is an agreed story about what has happened, and why.

Negotiations, whether internal or external, are part of a collective process whereby participants make sense of change, and decide collectively how to manage it. A language-action perspective suggests that negotiators have two central tasks. One is to describe the relevant changes in the social order (the cognitive task). The other is to forge commitments based on those descriptions (the political task). This means that there are two aspects to negotiation – a cognitive aspect and a political aspect – and two related criteria for negotiation success. From our point of view a successful negotiation is one in which all sides understand that their interests have been satisfied as well as possible and therefore commit themselves wholeheartedly to the agreements they have made.

From a *cognitive* point of view, negotiators must be able to work out what changes are being proposed, and why. They must also be able to work out the effects of those changes. This requires an effective knowledge base, encoded in the form of various kinds of evaluative belief. It also requires regular input from a network of people who provide help in the form of organizational intelligence. Skilful negotiators will recognize the dangers of information overload and take various steps to test understanding, clarify communication, and slow negotiation down.

From a *political* point of view, negotiators must organize disagreement within and between groups. One main objective is to find agreements which will be viable in the context of historical relationships within and between the sides. If negotiators are to build commitments to particular lines of action they will have to handle various dilemmas inherent in the process of negotiation. The most obvious dilemmas in internal negotiation are concerned with conflicts between means and ends. The most obvious dilemmas in external negotiations are concerned with changes in position. The way these dilemmas is handled is a major determinant of negotiation success.

There is also a contrast between processes which remove unnecessary obstacles to agreement and processes which bring realistic conflict to the fore. The skilful negotiator is someone who helps others so that negotiation is no harder than it need be. However, the skilful negotiator is also aware that it is important fully to explore the differences between the sides. This may force opponents to look beyond the obvious options and search for alternatives which maximise joint gain. It may also help to convince party members that those who represent them have done full justice to party's case.

Notes

1. See Morley (1986); Morley *et al.* (1988).
2. For further discussion see Morley (1982b, 1986, in press, b). This is why we would agree with Tajfel (1981) that the relationships between persons and groups are symbiotic. In the case of formal negotiation what happens within groups and what happens between groups are what might be described as the 'planning' and 'action' stages of a single process (see Marsh, 1974).
3. This is why Morley (1981a) has written that 'Conflict begins when some change in existing circumstances (whether deliberate or inadvertent) creates a situation in which one actor (person or party) must confront another' (p.89). The conflict may begin with a coercive act or with a negotiation phase, but however it begins, the participants' first job is to work out what has happened, and why. Until they have done this they will not be able to plan a suitable response.
4. Organizing is political in the broadest sense because actors differ in their relationships with their contexts so that they differ in their valuations and in their abilities to mobilize influence (see Chapter 5).
5. It has been suggested that the shortcomings of the negotiations at Potsdam started a process which led eventually to the Berlin blockade and the Cold War (Morris, 1973).
6. Although Morris' description is of an international negotiation there seems no reason to suppose that other arenas are any different in these respects. For further disucssion see Walton and McKersie (1965).
7. McGrath and his associates have measured overall success in terms of the product of ratings obtained from officials of each of the parties (see McGrath, 1966). They also included ratings from judges who rated agreements from the point of view of the community at large. This is because they have argued that negotiators are 'ex officio' agents of the wider community to which both Party and Opponent belong. There is little doubt that settlements are sometimes judged from this wider point of view, and that adopting this view may lead to negotiations which are cooperative rather than competitive in orientation. However, such cooperative negotiations are rare. For further discussion see Morley (1982b).
8. Similar views have been expressed by Fisher and Brown (1989). For an alternative perspective see Kochan (1980). Our own feeling is that negotiators would do well to remember Scott's (1988) injunctions that all parties need to do a good job for their own side. Consequently, each needs to find ways which will enable the others to take home a deal they can sell to their principals and gain their approval (see Scott, 1988, p.108).

9. Strictly speaking, all talk about effectiveness or skill is talk about processes which relate actors to their contexts.

10. This has been one of the main exphases in Morley's work (Morley, 1981a, 1981b, 1986). It is also an important part of Drucker's (1970) analysis of executive effectiveness.

11. For other examples see Morley (in press, b); Meredeen (1988); and Walton and McKersie (1965). Warr's own treatment of negotiation has not received the attention it has deserved, perhaps because he set out deliberately to write an introductory text. Nevertheless, he has much to say which will repay further study (see Morley, in press, b).

12. Asymmetries of this kind seem fairly common in British industrial relations. They are likely whenever complex proposals are introduced at the bargaining table. This is one reason why there is an irreducibly psychological component to negotiation. As Winham (1977) has pointed out, 'Negotiation is an enduring art form. Its essence is artifice, the creation of expedients through the application of human ingenuity' (p.87). Furthermore, even when all parties spend a great deal of time preparing for negotiation they will still not be sure exactly what the other side wants this time, and why. They will not be sure of the others' resolve to stand firm on particular issues (Snyder and Diesing, 1977). According to Chamberlain negotiators are only able to estimate exactly what can be achieved and at what cost through the process of negotiation itself (see Chamberlain, 1951; Morley, 1979a).

13. This is a good example of the way in which cognitive and political problems interact.

14. The term *internal adjustment* is taken from Anthony's extremely useful text on the conduct of industrial relations (Anthony, 1977).

15. Hartley *et al.* (1983) have argued that this may be called the democracy dilemma, because the need for strong leadership has to be set against the need for very wide participation in decision-making. They have shown that unless this dilemma is resolved union members may face considerable uncertainty about how to act. For further discussion see Morley (in press, b).

16. Voting rules of this kind are sometimes called decision schemes. The effects of applying various decision schemes has been the subject of much investigation, notably by Davis and his associates (Davis, 1969, 1982).

17. Warr has described the concessions as 'marginal in cost but considerable in emotional value' (p.145). The importance of this kind of move has also been highlighted by writers dealing with problems of social exchange, as in Homans' studies of status amongst clerical workers (see Homans, 1961).

18. The importance of discretionary content has been stressed in analyses of strategic choice in local government. For further information the reader is recommended to read Friend and Jessop (1971).

19. For further discussion see Morley (1982b).

20. This does happen (Meredeen, 1988), although perhaps not as often as one might suppose. As Warr's example shows, it is not always to one side's advantage to exploit differences within the other side. What is important is that the agreements reached are viable in terms of the power in use possessed by each of the sides (Kanter, 1984; Morley, 1986). For further discussion see Morley (in press, b).

21. For further discussion see Hartley *et al.* (1983) and Morley (in press, b).

22. For further analysis of the importance of networking in industrial negotiations see Batstone, Boraston, and Frenkel (1977, 1978) and Morley (in press, b).

23. See Morley and Hosking (1984); Hosking (1988b); Hosking and Morley (1988).

24. See Morgenstern (1949). This turns out to be possible within the context of zero-sum

games where it makes sense for each to maximize the payoff he or she can *guarantee* however the opponent plays the game. Such a strategy does not seem rational, however, in the context of non-zero sum games (Peston and Coddington, 1967).

25. The term prisoner's dilemma derives from an anecdote about a particular form of plea bargaining between a prosecutor and two defendants. The logic of the situation has been encapsulated in the form of a two-person two-choice mixed motive (variable sum) game in which each of two players (P1, P2) is required independently to choose a response (C or D) from a set {C, D} of alternatives. Each person's payoff is determined by the combination of responses which are made. When the two people make the same choice they are given the same payoffs. When they make different choices the person who chooses D gains at the expense of the person who chooses C. To take just one example of a Prisoner's Dilemma matrix, let us suppose that the CC *combination* gives each person £3; that the DD combination gives each £1; and that the CD combination gives £5 to the person who chose D and £0 to the person who chose C. When the game is played under laboratory conditions it is iterated for a number of trials.

    The C response is meant to stand for cooperation since the CC combination gives both people higher payoffs than the DD combination. However, to choose C without knowing the choice the other is going to make requires each to trust the other, for when one person alone chooses D he or she gains relative to the CC combination and the other loses. The D response stands for defection. The dilemma is that it can be argued each player should choose D whatever the other is going to do. If they do this each will gain only £1 when each might have gained £5.

    It has been argued that games of this kind may provide abstract formulations of the concession dilemma identified by Walton and McKersie (1965) and by Pruitt (1969). To understand what is happening all the reader has to do is to identify the C choice with concede and the D choice with stand firm.

26. This is an example of what we have described as the emergent quality of organizing processes.

27. Indeed, to quote Hofstadter (1985) the concept 'is incoherent, since all depends on environment' (p.728).

28. Hofstadter (1985) has provided a very concise and extremely accessible account of Axelrod's work (see Chapter 29).

29. See Walton and McKersie (1965); Rubin and Brown (1975); Bacharach and Lawler (1981); Pruitt (1981).

30. Strictly speaking there are many solutions to the bargaining problem since different theories give different solutions. Bacharach and Lawler (1981) have provided a very clear and very useful summary of the main theories, making clear the assumptions used by each.

31. See Morley and Stephenson (1977) and Morley (1979b). For a review of this research by one of those most closely associated with it see Pruitt (1981). For a more critical treatment see Gulliver (1979).

32. These simulate complex trade negotiations.

33. See Warr (1973); Snyder and Diesing (1977); Friedman and Meredeen (1980); Morley (1982b, in press, b); and Meredeen (1988).

34. See Landsberger (1955); Douglas (1962); Morley and Stephenson (1977); Rackham and Carlisle (1978a, b); Stephenson, Kniveton and Morley (1977); Webb (1982).

35. See Marengo (1979); Breakwell (1983).

36. Rackham and Carlisle (1978b) have shown that negotiators with a track record of negotiation success are less likely to plan detailed sequences of activity. Consequently,

they are less likely to be surprised by the others' responses. Scott (1988) has suggested that negotiators plan for external negotiation by canvassing their main objectives (on a single sheet of A4 paper), arranging the most important points under four headings (on a single sheet of A5 paper); and taking the headings into negotiation as aids to memory (on a single sheet of A6 paper).

37. See Morley (1979a).

38. Kennedy *et al.* (1987) argued in favour of what they call the L-I-M approach. L is a list of the objectives someone would *like* to achieve; I is a list of the objectives he or she *intends* to achieve; M is a list of the objectives he or she *must* achieve. Winkler (1988) has put forward a similar scheme, suggesting that negotiators plan for external negotiation by establishing what they would *like* to have, what they *must* have, and what they *do* not want. This may make it easier for each side to identify actions they might take which would give most value to their opponents at least cost to themselves. This sort of approach is an important component of constructive negotiation or integrative bargaining.

39. See Chapter 4.

40. See Snyder and Diesing (1977). Fisher and Ury (1983) have argued that this means that negotiators should not attempt to identify a 'bottom line'. The reason is that whilst this may avoid agreements which are disastrous, it is too defensive. Negotiators who focus on their best alternative to a negotiated agreement at any given time are more likely to learn from the process of external negotiation.

41. See Morley (in press, b).

42. Also see De Rivera (1968); Jervis (1970, 1976); Kinder and Weiss (1978); Lockhart (1979); and Morley (1986).

43. See Smart and Vertinsky (1977) and Waddington (1987).

44. It is important to realize that there are political reasons why issues are raised in certain forms rather than others (Morley, Webb, and Stephenson, 1989; Morley, in press, b). Diagnosing the concerns which lie behind those demands is an important element in the process of 'integrative bargaining' described by Walton and McKersie (1965). Without such diagnostic activity it may be all too easy to set up objectives and see only one way of getting there, so that opportunities are missed to upgrade common interests, and achieve long term goals (Morley, 1981a).

45. See Batstone *et al.* (1977, 1978)

46. As Morley and Stephenson (1977) have pointed out, 'The understandable fear is created that negotiators by virtue of their personal relationships with their opponents may somehow neglect their duties, by putting the preservation of their personal relationship before the interests of their constituents' (p287). Such fears are an inevitable part of the process of collective bargaining.

47. Also see Chapter 8.

48. This means that they are careful explicitly to point out that they are asking questions, stating proposals, and so on. There are good reasons to believe that effective negotiators take special steps to separate the people from the problem, to use Fisher and Ury's phrase.

49. See Rackham and Carlisle (1978a); Miron and Goldstein (1979); and Dickson (1986).

50. This is why Fisher and Ury (1983) have suggested it is sensible, first, to state a problem, and then to suggest a solution. If this seems counterintuitive it is worth remembering that once a solution has been stated the other participants may start thinking how to present their objections rather than listening to what you have to say. Kennedy *et al.* (1987) reverse this advice. However, their main motivation seems to be to insist that

proposals and reasons need to be presented in a clear, orderly sequence They give a very useful example of the difficulties of handling proposals when they are presented in what they call a 'shambolic ramble' style (p.93). Those who would like to read the full text of an industrial negotiation are referred to Morley and Stephenson (1977).

51. There is good evidence that this is important with respect to internal negotiations (Winham and Bovis, 1978; also see Morley, 1981a). We see no reason, however, why the principle should not be equally important in external negotiations.

52. As Kennedy et al. have pointed out it is important that the observer's limited capacity is not overloaded. In their view the observer must be freed from the obligation of thinking what he or she might say, if asked. Their own recommendation is to ban them from speaking during the external negotiation.

53. See Walton and McKersie (1965); Snyder and Diesing (1977); Pruitt (1971, 1981); Morley (1986); and Kennedy et al. (1987).

54. For example, the union negotiators described by Warr (1973) were ready for a major struggle about the details of an incentive scheme which formed part of the general pay and productivity framework.

55. See Douglas (1962); Morley and Stephenson (1977); Snyder and Diesing (1977).

56. In their view the first stage of negotiation serves to establish the parties' strength of case and strength of feeling about the issues.

57. We do not wish to accept McGrath's model in its entirety, but we do think it provides a useful way of thinking about some of the important dilemmas inherent in the process of external negotiation. For further discussion see Morley (1982b).

58. See Morley (1981a) and Carnevale and Keenan (in press). Broadly speaking, negotiators should be aware of premature agreement. First, they cannot be sure they would not have done better if they had stood firm for longer. Second, they may not have understood what the issues really are (see Fisher and Ury, 1983). We suspect that, as in other areas of social life, there are no short cuts to effective performance.

59. They also avoid irritating phrases in which they say 'gratuitously favourable' things about themselves.

60. According to Rackham and Carlisle (1978a) negotiators with a track record which is only average are afraid to disagree, especially in the final stages of negotiation. Apparently, they are more willing to leave ambiguous points to be sorted out later, 'fearing that making things explicit might cause the other party to disagree' (Rackham and Carlisle, 1978a, p.9). Effective negotiators are more willing to disagree because they are more aware that their job is to reach an agreement which will 'stick' (because it makes sense).

61. One way of putting this is to say that they try to separate the people from the problem (see Fisher and Ury, 1983). One way of doing so is to speak more about themselves (and Party) rather than about others (and Opponents).

It is quite certain that personal antagonism is detrimental to the process of negotiation. Antagonism arises when people feel threatened personally, and become defensive. Disagreement has to be expressed, but the same point can be made in a number of different ways. Consider the difference between saying 'We feel discriminated against' versus 'You are discriminating against us'. According to Fisher and Ury, effective negotiators often emphasize disagreement by commenting on their feelings in the following kind of way: 'You know, the people on our side feel we have been mistreated and very upset. We're afraid an agreement will not be kept even if one is reached. Rational or not, that is our concern. Personally, I think we may be wrong in fearing this, but that's a feeling others have. Do the people on your side feel the same way?' (p.31)

62. When negotiation is unsuccessful, the separation between official and unofficial action is much less clear. The distinction between stages in which negotiators act officially as representatives of groups and stages in which they act unofficially as actors in their own right is made most clearly in Morley and Stephenson (1970). For further discussion of interpersonal and interparty stages in negotiation see Douglas (1962); Stephenson, Kniveton, and Morley (1977); Morley and Stephenson (1977); and Stephenson (1981).

63. Usually denied to those remote from the external negotiations.

64. Especially on certain technical aspects of relations between the groups, 'such as seniority and welfare arrangements, in which the programs are rather complicated' (Walton and McKersie, 1965, p.317).

65. The most thorough discussion of tactics is still that of Walton and McKersie (1965) Chapter IX.

66. See Walton and McKersie (1965).

67. The American Secretary of State was advised, in writing, that 'The Allies . . . know exactly what they are going to ask in the ways of territorial concessions. Their demands will be immediately accompanied by their reasons and their arguments. Are we agreed that the Alsace-Lorraine of 1871 shall be conceded? Or the Alsace-Lorraine of 1814? . . . Are we agreed on a principle with which we will meet a demand for the cession of the entire left bank [of the Rhine]? How are we going to get the President's views or instructions on such questions?' (Elcock, 1972, p.58).

68. This tactic is especially important if the negotiator adopts the 'principled' posture advocated by Fisher and Ury (1983).

Chapter 7
Teamwork

Introduction

This chapter is about the task tuned organization of groups.[1] It is about teamwork. This means more than just team building, although this may be one of the 'tracks' (Kilmann, 1989). We take the view that a theory of teamwork is part of a more general theory of group performance. It is that part of the theory of group performance which considers the collective performance of people who come together to work on projects as members of a team. In this chapter we shall attempt to set out some of the elements of a general theory of group perfomance and show how they may be used to articulate a theory of teamwork in engineering product design.

Cognitive and political problems in teams

Teams are often defined as groups of people working together to achieve objectives which are shared (e.g. Pearson and Gunz, 1981; Nolan, 1987). Furthermore, enterprises are often viewed as networks of teams, some temporary and some permanent (Likert, 1961; Nolan, 1987). This leads frequently to a unitary view in which organizations are characterized in terms of shared goals (see Part 1).

However, all groups face cognitive and political problems of the kind we have outlined in Chapter 4 and Chapter 5, and teams are no exception. Put simply, the cognitive problems arise because team members have to organize their intellectual activity so that they think clearly about the issues and develop a shared understanding of what is happening, and why. The political problems arise because team members have to accept direction and give up some of their autonomy. The political process needs to be organized so that team members develop shared commitments and work collectively to achieve them.

Teams are examples of social units which are deliberately designed (McGrath, 1984). A theory of teamwork should show, in general terms, how to organize the collective process to produce high quality products with minimum 'process loss'.[2] What we will get from the theory will be a set of general guidelines. We shall have to work out how the guidelines are to be used in any particular case. In the case of engineering design the ideal process is one which converges efficiently towards solutions which everyone understands and everyone accepts.[3] It is a process which is 'purposed' in Vaill's sense (Vaill, 1982).

Group effectiveness

Consideration of what makes a group effective raises questions of value from the word go. We shall rely heavily on literature which begins with a focus on performance and accomplishment in work. That is to say, we shall be concerned with groups as productive, high performance systems (Vaill, 1982; Akin and Hopelain, 1986).

We face two main problems in this enterprise. First, there are a variety of performance standards which may be used. Consequently, when we speak of a high performance system we should speak of a system which performs well in certain respects. It is by no means obvious that a system which performs well in one respect will perform well in others (Might, 1984; Pugh and Morley, 1988a). Second, the final outcome may be the result of a project which lasts months or even years. This is often the case in design, whether we are concerned with engineering product design, or with some other form of design (e.g. the design of software). The final outcomes are a result of a number of different processes, occurring at different stages of the design.

The core elements or stages in design
In Chapter 6 we argued that project work involves collective activity in which decision making should proceed through stages of identification, development, selection, and implementation, in that order. We argued that some iteration was both inevitable and desirable. However, what is important is that, at any particular time, the members of the team know what they are each doing, and why. We presumed that an ordered sequence of stages might help to promote a 'workscape' which was 'legible' and 'coherent' (Akin and Hopelain, 1986). To proceed further we need to examine how these general ideas may be used to describe the process of engineering product design.

Fortunately, there are a number of detailed models of the activities which occur in various areas of design. These are usually called design activity models and have been described by Pugh (Pugh, 1986; Pugh and Morley, 1988a). According to Pugh they show that there are six stages which are common to all kinds of design, forming a 'core' of design activity. The stages are investigation of the market; development of a product design specification; concept design; detail design; manufacture; and sale (the reason the product was made). Essentially, what he has described is a sequence of decision areas, each involving its own problems of identification, development, selection, and implementation. The output from each stage is a set of documents to be used as input by the next. Consequently, design may be described as a planning process (Morley, in press, a). It is characterized by the growth of commitment to ideas which become more and more specific as we move through the design core (Morley, in press, a; Levin, 1976).

The general idea is that investigation of the market should provide as output a detailed product design specification, accepted by all members of the design team. The specification should be consulted regularly and used to guide, regulate, and control the design activity which follows. It provides input to the stages of conceptual design, detail design, and manufacture, because the object of the exercise is to produce a design which 'equates to' or is 'completely in balance' with the specification. This is shown graphically in Figure 7.1. The product design specification is shown as a cylindrical 'boundary' which encloses (and therefore limits, constrains, or directs) the activity of the design core. In the ideal case we might say that the activity of the design core functions to provide an increasingly detailed product design specification, which leads to a test specification for the factory at the end of the day (Pugh and Morley, 1988b).

The stage of conceptual design has the function of making a decision to go about satisfying the specification in this general kind of way rather than that. The output may be a fully working model, with detailed drawings, stringently tested to demonstrate the functionality of the product.[4] The stage of detailed design develops the product to the point where there is a full technical specification which may be used to guide the first models for production tooling (Pugh and Morley, 1988b).

Our general view of design is that it is a multidisciplinary activity which requires the collective effort of specialists with different kinds of expertise (Pugh and Morley, 1988a). Consequently, it is inevitable that things will go wrong. As Jones and Overton (1988) have said:

> Despite the best endeavours of competent, creative, experienced designers the design process is far from perfect. Faults, flaws and errors creep into the most accomplished of designs. Correcting faults at an early stage is simple and unconstrained. At later stages it becomes more expensive, more difficult and more constrained. Unfortunately, the Design Team is often too close to any fault to recognize it as such.

Similarly, Petroski (1985) has argued that

> the process of successive revision is as common to both writing and engineering as it is to music composition and science, and it is a fair representation of the creative process in writing and engineering to see the evolution of a book or a design as involving the successive elimination of faults and error. (p.79)

This is true. But unless the process is organized properly the final product will contain errors which could and should have been avoided. The labour may

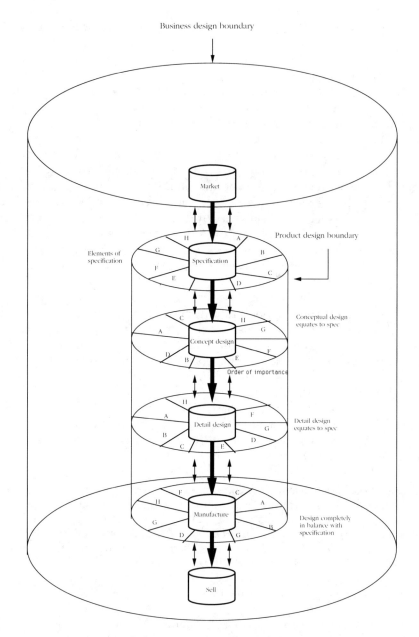

Figure 7.1 *Structure in the design core: dynamic concepts.*
Adapted from Pugh (1986).

take longer than it need. Some lines of development may be ruled out without proper consideration. Others may be followed for much too long, despite clear warning signs that things are going wrong. Consequently, the process of design becomes much harder than it needs be. Unnecessary obstacles are put

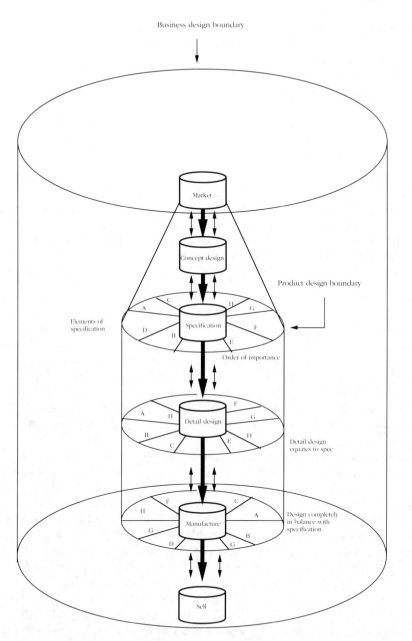

Figure 7.2 *Structure in the design core: static concepts.*
Adapted from Pugh (1986).

in the way. We shall try to explain why this happens, and suggest some ways of improving the quality of current practice.

We shall rely heavily on social psychological research which shows that the advantages of working together in groups are often lost because of faulty group processes which degrade the cognitive and political activity of the group (Morley and Pugh, 1987; Pugh and Morley, 1988a). There are three main strands to this research.

The first strand comes from attempts to classify tasks and to produce models of group productivity for each type of task. We have found the work of Steiner (1972) and McGrath (1984) of particular relevance. Steiner's formulation that the actual productivity of a group equals its potential productivity minus losses due to faulty process has been particularly influential. In his opinion:

> How well a group can perform a task depends upon the adequacy with which members' resources meet task demands. How well the group actually performs depends, in addition, upon the willingness of members to contribute their resources to the collective effort, and upon the success with which members coordinate their individual activities. Actual productivity equals potential productivity when there are no losses due to nonoptimal motivation or coordination. (Steiner, 1972, p.131)

Steiner referred to a large body of experimental evidence which showed that group performance was hardly ever at the level of the best member, and sometimes fell below the performance of the average member. Essentially, his theoretical framework is an attempt to explain why this is so often the case. More recent work has been concerned to investigate the conditions under which groups might produce what used to be called an 'assemby effect bonus' (Collins and Guetzkow, 1964). The general idea is to invent interventions that will enhance interaction within and between groups (Hackman and Morris, 1975, 1978; Hoffman, 1982; McGrath, 1984). It is hoped that people will come together in ways which mean they develop new motivations, find more effective ways of working, and develop new kinds of competence.[5]

The second strand comes from Belbin's (1981) study of over two hundred senior management teams, formed from practising managers in England and Australia. The central idea is that successful teams and unsuccessful teams contain individuals with different resources, and organize themselves in different ways. Belbin shows very clearly that we cannot just take a group of highly creative individuals, put them together, and expect them to do better than other teams. They will sometimes perform extremely well and sometimes extremely badly, depending on a variety of factors, such as the activity of the leader. We shall examine Belbin's ideas in some detail. A useful summary of Belbin's work is given in Chell (1987). Pugh and Morley (1988b) have also discussed some of the strengths and weaknesses of this work as applied in the context of engineering design.

The third strand relies heavily on Janis' analyses of 'groupthink' in policy making groups, which we discussed in Chapter 4. Janis (1972) studied the behaviour of cohesive groups making fundamental decisions under crisis conditions. Later he produced a general model of emergency decision making (Janis and Mann, 1977). His work has been extremely influential because it explores the dynamics of making important decisions in organizational groups. It shows how, under certain conditions, groups mobilize their collective resources to do the wrong kind of thing. They engage collectively in defensive forms of information processing which mean they no are no longer capable of confronting difficulties head on, in an active, open-minded way (Morley and Hosking, 1984). They fail to process information vigilantly, even when vigilant information processing is clearly required. Consequently, they make decisions which go wrong, and which deserve to go wrong.

It is extremely important, however, to note that Janis does not think that the way to counteract these tendencies (which he calls 'groupthink') is to change the composition of the group. His analysis shows that those responsible for one fiasco[6] were quite capable of critical evaluation once the President changed the mode of operation of the group (Janis, 1972; Morley and Hosking, 1984). Morley and Pugh have shown how some of Janis' ideas may be extended to cover teams working on engineering product design (Morley and Pugh, 1987; Morley, 1988; Pugh and Morley, 1988a).

Design as disciplined creativity

The design activity models summarized by Pugh make it clear that when we talk about design we are talking about a broadly based business activity. Pugh and Morley call this activity 'total design'. It is activity in which specialists collaborate in the investigation of a market, the selection of a project, the conception and manufacture of a product, and in the provision of various kinds of user support (Pugh and Morley, 1988a). It is activity which may be described, usefully, as 'disciplined creativity' (Bailey, 1978; Morley, 1988).

Morley has written that he intended the term 'disciplined creativity' to carry four main implications:

> that we are concerned with designs that add value to those which have gone before (hence with creativity rather than innovation); that we are concerned with doing creative work rather than having creative ideas; that we should view design as a social activity, rather than a solitary one, requiring the collective effort of specialists with different kinds of expertise; and that the collective effort must be disciplined or organized so that the process is systematic, coherent, and understood by all. (Morley, 1988)

An extended justification for this stance is set out in Pugh and Morley (1988a).

Creativity versus innovation

When Morley says that design is concerned with creativity rather than innovation he is simply making the point that 'too frequently that which is new is only different, not better' (Bensinger, 1965, p142). Like Morley, we are concerned with the design of products that are better than (and therefore add value to) those which have gone before. Design is 'getting from here to there'

(Petroski, 1985). The means 'may be limited only by our imaginations', as Petroski says. But the important point is that we are trying to go somewhere which satisfies certain constraints, not just anywhere. In the case of engineering design the constraints are built into the product design specification.

Doing creative work versus having creative ideas

Guildford (1956, 1967, 1986) has proposed that abilities may involve one of five kinds of basic intellectual processes. These are cognition, memory, divergent production, convergent production, and evaluation. He concluded that creativity involved much more than divergent production, but that divergent production was one important element. This led to an emphasis upon variety of output through fluency, flexibility, originality and elaboration. Guildford's own views were fairly balanced, but others have come to see the key problem as one of producing many unusual ideas. Weisberg (1986) has characterized this as part of 'the myth of divergent thinking'. He suggests that a distinction is frequently drawn between 'logically applying one's past experience to a problem' and some other sort of thinking which leads to 'leaps of insight'. It is supposed that this second kind of thinking is more spontaneous, requires us to withhold judgement, and may only emerge when various blocks or inhibitions are removed. Weisberg's own work directly contradicts this view (Weisberg, 1980, 1986, 1988).

First, he argues that examples of creativity in science, technology, and the arts may be regarded as examples of creative problem-solving.[7] Second, he argues that when we examine paradigm cases what we see is not sudden leaps of insight based on divergent thinking, but straightforward, incremental modifications of earlier work.[8] What we see in these examples, and others like them, is not divergent thinking but creative failures, perseverance, determination, resourcefulness, extended revisions, and incremental gains.[9] Third, he reviews experimental evidence and argues that, once again, there is no need to postulate a special process called 'insight'. Some of this evidence concerns the effectivness of techniques such as brainstorming. Weisberg draws the very clear conclusion that:

> the more one knows about the criteria a solution must meet, and the greater role these criteria play in the actual generation of solutions, the better the solution will be. Thus, if one wishes to solve a problem effectively, one should try to determine as precisely as possible what criteria the solution must meet before starting work on the problem, try to keep these criteria in mind as one works, and work alone. (1986, p.66)

Putting all of this together provides a strong case for shifting the image of the creative person away from that of someone who has creative ideas to that of someone who does creative work.

Design as social rather than solitary
We shall have to qualify that part of Weisberg's conclusion which says 'and work alone' (as does Weisberg himself). When Weisberg wrote that better solutions are generated when people work alone he had in mind the literature on 'brainstorming' (see Stein, 1975; McGrath, 1984). Much of this compares the performance of 'real' and 'nominal' groups. The nominal groups are formed by taking the output from a number of individuals working alone and combining it to form a single product. The evidence is clear that nominal groups outperform real groups. To quote McGrath (1984) the differences are 'large, robust, and general' (p.131). It is probably sensible, therefore, to look for design methods in which individuals generate ideas alone before joining decision-making groups. This is what happens, for example, in Pugh's method of concept generation and selection (Pugh, 1981, 1991), and is probably one reason for its success (Morley, in press, a).

Weisberg's view of creativity in scientific research is very similar to the view we take of creativity in design. When we say that design is social rather than solitary (Foster, 1986) we are recognizing that

> a certain social milieu naturally leads to an interest in certain kinds of problems, in certain kinds of methods, and may provide specific starting points for further research. Furthermore, when research seems to be getting nowhere, information, suggestions, and criticisms from other people may be crucial if further progress is to be made. (Pugh and Morley, 1988a)

Further elaboration of this point of view is given in Weisberg (1988).

The view of creativity most appropriate to the study of engineering design is, we think, the systems view of Csikszentmihalyi (1988). Actually, there are three systems, providing three sets of forces: the person, the field, and the domain. These are shown in Figure 7.2. What is important is the conclusion that

> We cannot study creativity by isolating individuals and their works from the social and historical milieu in which their actions are carried out. This is because what we call creative is never the result of individual action alone; it is the product of three main shaping forces: a set of social institutions, or *field*, that selects from the variations produced by individuals those that are worth preserving; a stable cultural *domain* that will preserve and transmit the selected new ideas or forms to the following generations; and finally the *individual*, who brings about some change in the domain, a change the field will consider to be creative . . . Creativity is a phenomenon that results from the interaction between these three systems. Without a culturally defined domain of action in which innovation is possible, the person cannot even get started. And without a group of peers to evaluate and confirm the adaptiveness of the innovation, it is impossible to differentiate what is creative from what is simply statistically improbable or bizarre. (Csikszentmihalyi, 1988, pp.325–6)

In the case of engineering design Morley and Pugh have described the social organization of the field in terms of the 'triple synthesis' of a 'product design boundary', a 'business design boundary', and an 'interpersonal design boundary' (Morley and Pugh, 1987; Pugh and Morley, 1988a, b; Morley, in press, a). The product design boundary has already been described. The business design boundary exists because creative activity doesn't just happen. It needs to be managed so that the activities of the design core are given a structure and provided with appropriate support. The interpersonal design boundary exists because different people bring different resources to bear on the activity of the design core. Morley and Pugh speak of an interpersonal design boundary because this affects the structure of the design team (Golembiewski, 1962b). We would add that it affects the creative process because our outlooks, attitudes, and the arguments we produce are very much affected by those we meet, those we expect to meet, and those we hope to meet, particularly if they have high status, or stand in strong relationships to us.

Structure in the design core

We take the view that process losses will be minimized when the design core is structured in ways that make the activity 'legible, coherent, and open-ended' (Akin and Hopelain, 1986; Pugh and Morley, 1988a). An activity is legible when its elements are easy to understand. It is coherent when the elements are integrated, and 'work together to give the same overall message' (p.27). It is open-ended when the activity is responsive to change, and when it may be 'enriched' by the activity of new members. We suppose that just such a 'culture of productivity' is necessary if design activity is to converge productively on to solutions team members understand and team members will accept. It gives the activity of the design core a certain internal 'logic'.

However, it is also important to distinguish two kinds of design: one in which concepts are dynamic (shown in Figure 7.1) and one in which concepts are static (shown in Figure 7.2). When concepts are static new designs are based very firmly on what has gone before. As Pugh puts it, the expansion of options is constrained by precedent and practice, as in the case of the differential gear (Pugh, 1983, 1991). The point of the new diagram is to show that, in such cases, it is possible to take a market need, and an overall concept as fixed. The product design specification may then be drawn up around a concept and a market context which is well understood. Hence, much conceptual design may occur before the full product design specification is known. This becomes impossible when concepts are truly dynamic, and design starts with a 'clean sheet', so to speak. The design is innovative in the sense that the expansion of options is constrained neither by precedent nor practice. A good example is the design of TEMAKI loudspeakers by Mitsubishi Petrochemical and Yonmarugo (see Matsumura, 1987, pp.40–41). They are 'paper thin' and fold into shapes which disguise their function. They will also accept printing so that they may be used for advertising or publicity. This sort of design requires a design core structured as in Figure 7.1.[10]

Faulty performance and faulty process ≡≡≡≡≡≡

Studies of why things go wrong may be very illuminating. They reveal the importance of things we take for granted when things go right. Consequently, there is much to be learned from studies of planning disasters (Hall, 1980; Janis, 1982a), systems failures (Bignell and Fortune, 1984; Petroski, 1985), and failures in the design of everyday objects (Norman, 1988). For example, both Hall and Janis have much to say about the reasons poor plans are sometimes very convincing. Both Bignell and Fortune and Petroski present case studies which underline the importance of managing various kinds of risk (also see Bergwerk, 1989). Bignell and Fortune show that when something goes wrong it is made worse if the system is overloaded, or if the 'system' lacks 'organized connectedness' and 'internal coherence' (see p.155). Petroski is concerned with failures in structural engineering. He argues that failures show we have gone too far too soon in responding to pressures to be competitive. He also reminds us that many successful designs evolve as people learn from their early mistakes. This is true, but there are also forces working against evolutionary design, as Norman (1988) has shown. He has also provided a brief and provocative analysis of why it is so easy to fault the design of everyday objects. If he is correct there are five main reasons.

The first is that in the 'design community' the elements of the product design specification are out of balance. In particular, considerations of aesthetics dominate considerations of what the end users want (see Sommer, 1983).

The second reason is that designers often think of themselves as typical users. Frequently, however, they are not.[11] Norman argues that 'the designer's interaction with potential users must take place from the very beginning of the design process, for it soon becomes too late to make fundamental changes' (p.156). He goes on to quote the comments of one designer, working for a telephone company:

> It's really interesting to watch engineers and computer scientists go about designing a product. They argue and argue about how to do things, generally with a sincere desire to do the right thing for the user. But when it comes to assessing the tradeoffs between the user interface and internal resources in a product, they almost always tend to simplify their own lives. They will have to do the work, they try to make the internal machine architecture as simple as possible. Internal design elegance sometimes maps to user interface elegance, but not always. *Design teams need really vocal advocates for the people who will ultimately use the interface.* (emphasis added)

Pugh goes further. In his view it is a basic principle of total design that all facets of the business have to interact with the design core (Pugh and Morley, 1988a; Pugh, 1991).

The third reason is that the designers' clients are often not the end users themselves. They are often purchasing departments who are 'interested primarily in price, perhaps in size or appearance, almost certainly not in usability' (p.157).

The fourth reason is that most designers work in teams. Consequently, they may 'share common modes of thinking and common sets of approaches, and thereby fall prey simultaneously to the same problems' (p.230). A theory of teamwork in design will have to show how to prevent group effects of this kind.

Finally, Norman makes a set of comments which are so important that we will quote them in full. They refer to what Pugh and Morley call the business design boundary.

> Designers face a tough task. They answer to their clients, and it may be hard to find out who the actual users are. Sometimes they are even prohibited from contacting the users for fear they will accidentally reveal company plans for new products or mislead users into believing that new products are about to be developed. *The design process is a captive of corporate bureaucracy*, with each stage in the process adding its own assessment and dictating the changes it believes essential for its concerns. The design is almost certainly altered as it leaves the designers and proceeds through manufacture and marketing. All participants are well intentioned, and their particular concerns are legitimate. *The factors should be considered simultaneously*, however, and not subject to the accidents of time sequence or the realities of corporate rank and clout. (p.158; emphasis added)

This is part of the reason it is important to consider design as 'total design' (Pugh and Morley, 1988a).

As we have said, Pugh and Morley have attempted to describe the activity of total design in terms of a triple synthesis of forces arising from the product design boundary, the business design boundary, and the interpersonal design boundary. We shall use this classification as a way of examining errors in design. The account we give relies heavily on the work of Pugh and Morley (1988a, b, 1989) and Morley (in press, a).

Faults in the product design boundary

The product design boundary derives from the product design specification. Ideally, it should establish a set of interrelated constraints which the product has to satisfy as a whole. It should feed back to constrain the activity of marketing because it should be the output from an investigation of product status and user needs. It should feed forward to show what counts as doing creative work (namely, designing a product which meets the product design specification).

Pugh and Morley (1988a) have reviewed a number of studies of new product development which show that:

1. Design often proceeds without a thorough and systematic investigation of the market for which it is intended (see e.g. Cooper, 1988).

2. When the needs of the user are well understood the information may not be written into a comprehensive product design specification. Hollins and Pugh (1989), for example, have described the typical product design specification as 'woefully inadequate'.[12]

3. When there is a comprehensive product design specification it may not be used to guide, regulate, and control the design activity that follows (Pugh and Morley, 1988b). This does not mean that changes cannot be negotiated, but it does mean that when changes are negotiated they should be reflected by changes in the specification.

What is required is a document which follows from a comprehensive review of the users' needs and translates those needs into a form which can be used efficiently to structure the activity which follows. Unless there is such a document, and unless it is properly used, it is very likely that products fail to sell, either because they leave too much out (they are under-designed) or because they put too much in (they are over-designed). Pugh and Morley take it as axiomatic that without an adequate product design specification it will not be possible to see how different requirements conflict, nor fully to examine whether they may be reconciled . Consequently, what happens will be more a matter of good luck than good design.

Faults in the business design boundary

Let us return to Norman's view that design is the captive of corporate bureaucracy. We have said that total design requires that all facets of the business (including end users) interact with the activities of the design core. Frequently, this interaction is arranged so that control passes sequentially from one department to another. However, the mechanisms which link the donor department to the recipient are frequently inadequate. It is extremely difficult to achieve high differentiation and high integration in the activities of the design core,[13] despite the use of formal linking mechanisms such as coordinating departments, cross-functional committees, task forces, formal liaison roles, and the like.[14] The documentation which goes with the design is often seriously deficient (Rzevski, 1984): perhaps because people underestimate the difficulty of problems they pass on to others;[15] perhaps because they can pass problems 'over the wall'[16] and forget about them.[17] Whatever the reason, there is very little documentation which matches Pugh's (1981) criterion that documentation should record all design decisions and why they were made.

There are, of course, strong political pressures which sometimes prevent the design core from being 'well formed' (Dill and Pearson, 1984). Some of these have been discussed in Bergwerk's recent analysis of the role of prototypes[18] in managing product innovation risks (Bergwerk, 1989). His central argument is that prototyping brings out differences between groups in the perception of risk.[19] As he says:

> Marketing departments for instance will be required to make an assessment of the sales prospects of the proposed new product. According to the agreed programme they are expected to base their judgement on the customer reactions during the field trials of the prototype. From their point of view, however, the details of the performance achieved by the prototype are not very relevant to the dominant risk. They are more likely to worry that the product specification is the real gamble in the market-place and although they may have had a major voice in the specification chosen, they still require reassurance. They will therefore be tempted to use the prototype to explore the specification with prospective customers rather than evaluate its performance, much to the chagrin of the designers who regarded the specification as a decision which had been agreed long ago. (1989, p.117)

Changes in the product design specification made late in the day may occur for other reasons. They often exemplify faulty coordination and lead to loss of motivation (Pugh and Morley, 1988b; Evans, 1989).

We take a view of the management of design which is similar to that of Cooper (1988). The first job is to identify key activities in the design core. The second job is to set in place a 'formal and systematic approach' which coordinates those activities, and makes sure that each is properly performed.[20]

The stage-gate process

Cooper (1988) has argued product development should be organized as a 'stage-gate' process. He argues that marketing activities and technical activities should proceed in parallel through stages of assessment, definition, development, testing, trial, and commercialization. Between stages there should be 'gates' which may only be opened after projects have been reviewed, and an explicit decision made to 'go through'. This leads to a list of thirteen key activities, arranged on a time-line. A number of studies of the new product process (the 'NewProd' research) have shown how performance of these key activities relates to measures of financial success. According to Cooper (1988) 'deficiencies and holes are glaring and pervasive, and sadly, they impact strongly and negatively on performance' (p.230). As he says, 'The message is clear: more complete projects are more successful; and the best way to increase the odds of failure is to skip over or delete two, three or more of the . . . activities' (Cooper, 1988, p.241). This is particularly true if the activities skipped over or deleted are those 'up-front' or early in the process.[21]

The stage-gate organization, or something like it, serves a number of important functions (Cooper, 1988. p.254). First, it disciplines the creative activity of the design core by building in key activities (making it more complete). This has been shown empirically to improve the likelihood that a project will be a success. In particular, the members of the project team are forced to address key issues early on, before the project enters the development stage. Consequently, they are able to avoid premature commitments to designs which have not been sufficiently well appraised (Morley, 1988). Second, the stage-gate organization is 'visible and relatively simple . . . and provides a road map which facilitates (rather than impedes) the project'. These are important characteristics of the culture of productivity identified by Akin and Hopelain (1986). They are also made central in the treatments of Morley (Morley and Pugh, 1987; Morley, in press, a) and Pugh (Pugh and Morley, 1988a; Pugh, 1991). Third, the job of the day-to-day leader of the project is better defined. Finally, process losses are minimized, because the firm is much more likely to get it right the first time (Cooper, 1988, p.249). Similar arguments are to be found in Pugh and Morley (1988b), with some additional evidence to support a position of this general kind.

Mechanistic versus organic systems

The distinction between mechanistic and organic forms of social organization is central to contingency theories of management (Morgan, 1986). It comes from Burns and Stalker's now classic work on the management of design (Burns and Stalker, 1961). It is based on classifying the organization of work, the nature of authority, the system of communications, and the nature of employee commitment (see Morgan, 1986, pp.52–3).

The most mechanistic form of social organization is that of the 'machine bureaucracy' described by Weber, Taylor, and others (see Part 1). Jobs come with clearly defined responsibilities. There is a clear hierarchy of control with formal channels of communication. In Burns and Stalker's study the net effect was that 'People in the organization thus knew precisely what was expected of them and attended to their job responsibilities in a narrow, yet efficient way, to create a competitively priced product' (Morgan, 1986, p.50). In other cases the outcomes have not been so benign. Bertodo (1989), for example, has argued that most machine bureaucracies are overmanaged, producing employees who are unresponsive to the real demands of their task. They are able only to adapt to their environments (see Chapter 2), which are rigidly controlled.

Organic structures, on the other hand, encourage people to shape their environments (see Chapter 2). Jobs are negotiated. Authority is informal. Power is expert power. Communication is completely free and informal. Consequently, people commit themselves to central tasks. According to Morgan (1986):

> In successful organizations in . . . areas of the electronics field, where the need to innovate was an essential condition for survival, . . . jobs were allowed to shape themselves, people being appointed to the organization for their general ability and expertise and allowed and encouraged to find their own place and to define the contribution that they could make . . . Thus in the firms observed by Burns and Stalker the process of finding out what one should be doing in one's job proved unending, defining a mode of organization linking inquiry

and action. Successful electronics firms avoided organizational hierarchies and avoided narrow departmentation, defining and redefining roles in a collaborative manner in connection with the tasks facing the organization as a whole. They created a form of organization having more in common with an amoeba than a machine. (p.51)

A brief, but useful, discussion of the organization of product design units is also given in Oakley (1984).

There is clear evidence that many firms are moving from mechanistic to organic forms of organization. A good example is that of Austin Rover at Coventry (Bertodo, 1989). A number of changes are involved. One is a move to lean, flat structures, with decentralized controls. Another is toward 'an environment of fluid relationships based on expertise, rather than rank or status'. This seems to be especially important if professional people are not be 'demotivated' (Badawy, 1975; Zachary and Krone, 1984; Abetti, 1986; Kolodny and Dresner, 1986). The literature suggests disciplined creativity will only flourish when people share norms which emphasize individual expertise, collective achievement, open communication, and interpersonal trust (Bensinger, 1965; Bower, 1965; Cherns, 1976; Katz and Kahn, 1978; Bass and Barrett, 1981; Zachary and Krone, 1984; Barko and Passmore, 1986; Kolodny and Dresner, 1986; Pugh and Morley, 1988a).

A shift to a more decentralized structure will not, *in itself*, guarantee a culture of productivity (Might and Fisher, 1985; Pugh and Morley, 1988a). Control procedures need to be integrated with the activities of the design core. They will be regarded as an additional burden unless they help solve the cognitive and political problems inherent in the activities of the design core (Might, 1984; Pugh and Morley, 1988a). This requires leadership, at global and local levels (Morley, in press, a). What is needed is a system of control which all participants understand and all participants accept. They should see that the process helps to identify and control various technical and political risks (Pugh and Morley, 1988b; Evans, 1989; Morley, in press, a).

Furthermore, it is entirely possible that different structures are appropriate in different contexts. Recently, Slusher, Ebert, and Ragsdell (1989) have produced a contingency theory of design, based on the work of Perrow (1967), and Daft and Lengel (1986). They locate different designs in four cells, which they label creative design (cell 1), intensive design (cell 2), incremental design (cell 3), and complex design (cell 4). They argue that incremental designs involve static concepts and that intensive designs involve dynamic concepts (in the sense of Pugh and Morley, 1988a). They then detail the different processes of design management which are required as shown in Figure 7.3. Their main argument is that mechanistic structures are appropriate when design is incremental and that organic structures are appropriate when design is intensive.

We would rephrase this argument. The distinction between static and dynamic contexts is not quite as Slusher, Ebert and Ragsdell suppose. Both creative design (cell 1) and intensive design (cell 2) involve dynamic concepts.

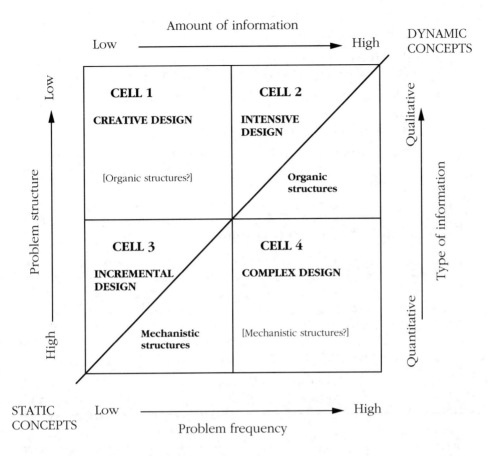

Figure 7.3   *A contingency model of design management.*
Adapted from Slusher et al. (1989).

Both incremental design (cell 3) and complex design (cell 4) involve static concepts. The shift from creative design (cell 1) to intensive design (cell 2) and the shift from incremental design (cell 3) to complex design (cell 4) may be described as a shift from simple designs to complex designs. The increased complexity means three things: first, that people will have to seek out new information; second, that they will have to pay more attention to the module structure of the design;[22] and third, that they will have to pay more attention to the coordination of work done by different people in different places. The conclusion that Slusher, Ebert and Ragsdell ought to draw is that mechanistic structures are most appropriate when concepts are static and designs are relatively simple. They are least appropriate when concepts are dynamic and designs are relatively complex.

Morley (in press) has taken a rather different approach. He has argued that, whether we use mechanistic or organic forms of organization effective design requires control processes which:

1. bring together inputs from different functional specialists at each stage (Levin, 1976; Pugh and Morley, 1988a);

2. audit the process at key points, paying particular attention to inconsistencies within the design team (Jones and Overton, 1988);

3. ensure that the process of design is guided, regulated, and controlled by a full product design specification (Cooper, 1988; Pugh and Morley, 1988a; Hollins and Pugh, 1989; Evans, 1989);

4. ensure that design activity within and between stages is systematic, legible, and coherent so that there is a 'culture of productivity'(Akin and Hopelain, 1986).

Faults in the personal design boundary

However it is organized, engineering product design is a collective enterprise involving many functions and many disciplines. Let us repeat that it is activity in which specialists collaborate in the activities of the design core. It is activity which requires disciplined creativity. It is activity which is social rather than solitary. This means that the personal design boundary described by Morley and Pugh (Morley and Pugh, 1987; Pugh and Morley, 1988a) is really an interpersonal design boundary (Morley, 1988, in press, a).

The personal characteristics of designers

Most writing on the psychology of design deals almost exclusively with individual psychology, in an effort to identify personal characteristics which lead to successful design.[23] Some of these accounts provide useful reminders of how design may go wrong (Papanek, 1984). However, they face two main problems (in general). First, the list of personal characteristics needs to be clearly linked to the activities of the design core. Otherwise the lists lack theoretical integration, become arbitrarily long, and fail to advance our understanding of the process of successful design. We are simply left feeling that what is required is some magical combination of personal qualities and individual skills. Second, most lists of personal qualities entirely fail to appreciate the ways in which individual action is constrained, guided, regulated, and supported by the social contexts in which it occurs (see Parts 1 and 2). This is why we so often find that people expected to do well actually do badly, particularly if they are working in groups (Belbin, 1981; Janis, 1982a; Steiner, 1972; Hackman and Morris, 1983).

One natural outcome of the individual approach is to select people on the basis of their creativity (Bailey, 1978; Broadbent, 1988). However, it is clear that some kind of contingency theory is required, since different kinds of creativity are required when concepts are static and when they are dynamic. Here, it is useful to consider Kirton's (1976) distinction between high adaptors and high innovators. As shown in Figure 7.4 high adaptors are likely to work

High adaptors	High innovators
1. Accept problems as defined.	Redefine problems: 'move goalposts'.
2. Creative within context of well-established problems and procedures.	Creative in unstructured contexts. Prefer to do things differently.
3. More cautious.	More adventurous.
4. Seen as wedded to existing system. Find it difficult to handle change.	Seen as essential in times of change. Find it difficult to stay in established role.
5. High adaptors find it difficult to work with high innovators.	

Figure 7.4   *Characteristics of high adaptors and high innovators Source: Kirton Adaptation Inventory.*

most effectively when concepts are static and high innovators are likely to work most effectively when concepts are dynamic. Kirton has designed a psychometric test to measure adaptation and innovation, the Kirton Adaptation Inventory. It is widely used by management consultants. However, whilst the distinction between high adaptors and high innovators is intuitively appealing we know of no evidence which validates the distinction in the context of design.

Morley (1989) has set out some of the implications of the psychological literature on creativity for the selection of members of design teams.[24] We may extend these ideas to take account of the contingency theory of Slusher, Ebert and Ragsdell (1989). Thus, as we move from concepts which are static to concepts which are dynamic, and from problems which are simple to problems which are complex, we require:

1. People who are widely informed, with wide ranging interests, willing and able to get to grips with 'foreign' disciplines. This means that they will probably have to be able to read quickly, scan for essentials, and know when they have to read something in depth.

2. People who are willing and able to deal with several unstructured problems at more or less the same time.

3. People who are happy to combine qualitative and quantitative information.

4. People who are willing to question the fundamentals of design practice, including ideas of their own which they now see as 'dead ends'.

5. People who have the ability successfully to communicate with people in all walks of life.

6. People who are able constructively to work as members of cross-functional teams.[25] This means that they must be low authoritarians, neither overly conscious of status, nor unduly worried about fear of failure. They must expect disagreement, and realize that disagreement is different from dislike.[26] They must be sympathetic to the views of other people, so that they see warning signs that things are going wrong. On the other hand they must not be so sympathetic that they show a tendency toward uncommitted thinking.[27]

There are very definite limits to the individual approach, however. For example, Weisberg's (1986) analysis of 'the myth of genius' shows that we should be very suspicious of the idea that there is a consistent set of personality characteristics which will allow us to identify creative people. If he is correct, and we think he is, which personal characteristics are important depend on exactly which problem a person is trying to solve. His analysis[28] implies that there may be wide variation in the performance of a particular individual within each of the four cells identifed by Slusher, Ebert and Ragsdell (1989). We should also note that some creative people are fairly introverted, particularly in the field of software design. The solution is not to keep them out of design teams, but to recognize that if they are to be useful members of a team they will need a good deal of social support. In such cases it is the responsibility of the leader to establish norms in which the group is oriented towards helping rather than towards achievement as individuals (Zander, 1982; Chell, 1987). Finally, it is worth noting that some selection policies would lead to homogeneous or 'pure' teams. There is evidence that these develop characteristic strengths and weaknesses (Belbin, 1981; also see Chell, 1987). They may excel from time to time. However, they are not likely to perform at a consistently high level because they lack the resources to meet 'a full range of problems and situations' (Belbin, 1981, p.29).[29]

Broadbent has argued that 'what we really need . . . is some means of transcending personality'. His own analysis relies heavily on the contrast between convergence and divergence. In his view, the process of design requires architects to be convergent and divergent. He considers that one way of achieving this is to combine convergers and divergers in a single team. We are suspicious of the value of the concepts of convergence and divergence, but Broadbent's general point is well taken. We shall therefore examine research which is concerned to specify the combination of personal resources required in successful teams.

Top team planning

Ramsden (1973) has written a book on 'top team planning'. It begins with an attempt to characterize individual decision styles in terms of the strength of the motivation to perform twelve 'essential functions'. The method is to use a detailed analysis of posture and gesture to infer each of the basic 'action motivations' set out in Figure 7.5. They are grouped into four sets. Sets 1, 2, and 3 describe distinctive strengths in a decision-making sequence which moves from attention to intention to commitment.[30] Each contains two basic action motivations, plus an 'interaction motivation' which reveals the extent to which each person is able 'to benefit from another's contribution and build on it, so that the net result is greater' (p.38). Finally, set 4 deals with two more general personal characteristics: dynamism, dealing with 'total energy or drive', and adaptability, meaning 'the readiness to change even one's most basic attitudes to fit in with a changed situation' (p.40). It also includes a measure of identification, although 'identification' is probably the wrong word. What is measured is something more like a form of cohesiveness (p.194). It makes for an easy, spontaneous, informal atmosphere. It is assumed that in team with 'a thin spread of identifying . . . less will occur spontaneously and hence perhaps less altogether' (p.195). Taken together the twelve scores form an 'action profile' which identifies those strengths spontaneously available for an individual to use. The action profile is supposed to remain the same[31] from time to time and from situation to situation. The decision style revealed is therefore characteristic of the person.

Subsequent analysis proceeds in two ways. First, the team is treated simply as a collection of individuals. Here, the key question is how many people have strengths adequate to perform each of the twelve essential functions. Second, the team is considered as a rather more complex unit. Here, Ramsden points out, quite correctly, that 'The areas of action covered by the team members acting singly may be different from the kind of action produced as a function of team interaction' (p.194). To explore this possibility the strengths of the interaction motivations concerned with communicating, presenting, or operating are considered as a 'mix'. A team whose members are individually biased towards, say, investigating and exploring, would be strong in the first stage of decision making in which participants monitor the environment (to identify issues). If the members were also strong in communicating and, in general, identified highly with the group:

> this would result in a very homogeneous and complete style of team interaction. Singly the team members would tend to promote the activities of investigating and exploring and collectively there would be a joint sparking off of these activities. It would be a uniformly research minded team in fact. (Ramsden, 1973, p.194)

Ramsden's work has the advantage that it tries to look at groups as groups, with a range of collective strengths and weaknesses. It provides a basis for putting people together. However, it has the disadvantage that its data is extremely time consuming to collect, and has not been adequately validated. We do not mean this as a criticism, although we are suspicious of the claim that the action profile cannot be changed (see Chapter 1). The work is complex

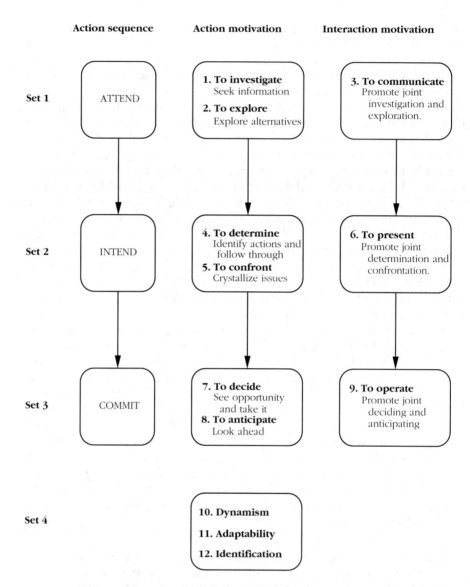

Figure 7.5   *Twelve basic motivations in top team planning.*
Adapted from Ramsden (1973).

and research is at an early stage. A series of mini case studies suggest that the work has promise, but more needs to be done to show that interventions lead to systematic improvements in 'top team' performance.

Strategy sets in architectural design

Powell has used Kolb's Learning Style Inventory[32] to analyse the nature of decision styles in design (Newland, Powell and Creed, 1987; Powell, 1988).

He has shown that architects have preferred action styles which are similar to the action motivations described by Ramsden. That is, they have the effect of directing effort to some parts of the decision process rather than others. However, whereas the managers studied by Ramsden sometimes showed a wide range of strengths, the architects studied by Powell tended to think and design using one of four 'strategy sets'. Powell labels the four types dynamic architects, focused architects, rigorous architects, and contemplative architects. He has argued that 'to achieve an effective "well rounded" design solution, all strategies should be utilised' (Powell, 1988, p.145). However, he has also provided evidence that architects who attempt to use all four strategies 'become ineffectual' (Powell, 1988). He believes that the solution is to build multi-disciplinary teams. In his view, 'No one individual may possess all the skills required but a team acting as a unified entity certainly can, wielding its joint abilities with strength and acumen' (Powell, 1988, p.145).

Diversity of roles within a team
We have already noted the tendency for 'pure' teams to perform erratically: sometimes well and sometimes badly. Belbin (1981) has argued that

> The useful people to have in teams are those who possess strengths or characteristics which serve a need without duplicating those already there. Teams are a question of balance. What is needed is not well-balanced individuals but individuals who balance well with one another. In that way, human frailties can be underpinned and strengths used to full advantage.
> (p.77)

Belbin has based his analysis on data obtained from training courses run for senior management. This has the advantage that it is fairly easy to relate measures of balance to measures of effective performance. However, it has the disadvantage that the performance is the performance of a group detached from its normal organizational context.

Effective groups seemed to be well balanced in the sense that, between them, the individual members of the team were willing and able to carry out the eight roles shown in Figure 7.6. In groups of less than eight people some of the members would, of course, have to take more than one role. Fortunately, this is possible because Belbin argues that we each have a preferred role, but we may also be able to take at least one other 'back-up' role should the need arise. Those of you who would like to find your own preferences may find it instructive to complete the self-perception inventory given on pp.153–8 of Belbin's (1981) book. The two highest scores indicate your first and second preferences.

There are several lessons to be learned from Belbin's work.

1. Most teams have particular strengths and weaknesses. However, some teams seem never to do well. There are three reasons for this. First, there is

Company worker	Resource investigator
Personality – disciplined, conscientious, tough-minded, practical, trusting, tolerant, and conservative.	**Personality** – enthusiastic, extroverted, and open. Develops ideas or fragments of ideas originated by other people.
Role – turns concepts and plans into practical working procedures. Carries out agreed plans systematically and effectively	**Role** – liaison. Looks for help inside and outside the group.
Chairman	**Monitor Evaluator**
Personality – realistic, calm, disciplined. Strong commitment to basic goals and objectives. Extrovert capacity for enthusiasm, but otherwise prone to detachment in social relations.	**Personality** – strives to follow paradigm of rational actor and make deliberate, considered, calculated choices. Critical analytical thinker.
Role – presides, coordinates, facilitates. Willing to listen to others but quite capable of rejecting their advice. Knows how to use and organize resources within the team, and brings the best out of other people. Imparts a sense of direction and purpose.	**Role** – specialises in analysing and evaluating ideas. Will raise critical issues, however uncomfortable. May help to deal with lack of consensus when crucial decisions are to be made.
Shaper	**Team worker**
Personality – tough, anxious extrovert, impatient for achievement. May overreact to disappointments. Prone to challenge, to argue, and to disagree.	**Personality** – trusting, sensitive. Sociable without being dominant. Wants to meet people and talk to them.
Role – classic dominant task leader. Motivates slow moving systems. Negotiator who is a major force for change.	**Role** – social specialist who smooths potentially disruptice conflicts. Skills in listening and managing awkward people.
Plant	**Completer-finisher**
Personality – introverted but nevertheless forthright.	**Personality** – introverted perfectionist who pays great attention to detail.
Role – originator of ideas on strategy and other major issues. Expected to be the most creative member of the group.	**Role** – shows how ideas work out in detail and ensures that nothing is overlooked. Worries about schedules and specialises in administrative staff work.

Figure 7.6 *Roles within management teams. Source: Belbin (1981)*

no one who is obviously highly creative or highly analytical. That is, the team needs to have at least one person who is either a plant, or a resource investigator or a monitor-evaluator. Second, various obstacles may prevent people from taking their preferred team role. Finally, the group may contain too many people who have no clear preference for one role rather than another. This seems to mean that members of the team work more or less alone, taking responsibility for individual decisions, but with very little planning or coordination.

2. Successful groups organized themselves in different ways to unsuccessful ones. In particular, they made sure that no-one worked in isolation and that team members were well informed about what was happening, and why.

3. The role of the leader was 'vital' in the development of an appropriate form of organization (Belbin, 1981, p.50). Here it is particularly instructive to consider the performance of those teams composed exclusively of clever and creative people. Although such teams, known as 'Apollo' teams were sometimes very effective, their average level of performance was extremely poor.[33] The few teams that were successful seemed to have leaders who were able to combine certain aspects of the chairman and shaper roles. That is, they were able to hold their ground without dominating others, and without imposing an obvious structure on the interaction within the group.

Pugh and Morley have asked members of five design teams to fill in Belbin's self perception inventory. It was not always possible to interview all the members of a team, so that much of the data was speculative. Nevertheless, the data from one of the firms showed some of the dangers of relying on a model of group performance which is concerned with only one set of constraints: those which form the interpersonal design boundary. The firm was probably the most successful in the sample. Yet no-one had a first or second choice for the resource investigator, or monitor-evaluator, or completer-finisher roles. This may mean that the preferences were no longer important because the firm had well established procedures which, in some sense, provided substitutes for the roles (Morley, 1988), just as some procedures may provide substitutes for some kinds of leadership (Kerr, 1983). Or, to put the point another way, we may say, perhaps, that Belbin's theory is most useful when firms lack systematic working procedures and rely too heavily on informal methods of communication (Morley, 1988).

Other writers have identified other roles. Clutterbuck's (1979) scheme is, for example, simpler than Belbin's. There are four roles: generating, integrating, developing, and perfecting. In some respects these seem similar to Belbin's roles of plant, team worker, resource investigator, and completer-finisher, although the corrrespondence is by no means perfect. At this stage it seems safe to say that effective groups require diversity of roles within the team. Whether four roles are needed, or eight, will require further research.

		Vigilant information processing
	1.	Adequately documents the existence of a problem and the need to solve it. Thus, the PDS follows from a thorough investigation of the market.
	2.	Actively open-minded search for information before design choices are made, so that the PDS controls the design.
	3.	Careful consideration of the full range of goals, constraints, and values implicated by each element in the PDS.
	4.	Careful consideration of more than one policy (design strategy, product strategy, conceptual design, etc.).
	5.	Careful consideration of the costs and benefits of each policy (e.g. many concepts and many criteria in a concept selection matrix).
	6.	Strives for a comprehensive, coherent, and detailed analysis of the elements of the problem, and of systemic relationships between them (as in VDI 2221, for example).
	7.	Intensively searches for new information. Remains sensitive to messages from other people (even when the messages are unpalatable). This allows for evolution of PDS, changes in concepts as process iterates through the design core, etc.
	8.	Re-examines consequences of all known alternatives before making a final choice, including any which had been discounted initially (e.g. re-examine concept selection matrix).
	9.	Attempts to optimize. Some explicit attempt to recognize costs and benefits and to trade-off benefits against costs (using any one of a number of technical methods).
	10.	Considers in detail how the policy chosen is to be put into effect (e.g. design for manufacture). Pays special attention to contingency planning to counter known uncertainties and risk (e.g. check dual sources of supply).

Figure 7.7   *Vigilant information processing in engineering product design. Adapted from Pugh and Morley (1988a)*

Vigilant and non-vigilant processing of information

We have described the activities of the design core as a series of collective decision-making tasks, located in a particular business environment. Let us now add that within each stage people may adopt a vigilant or non-vigilant attitude to the processing of information (see Chapter 4). Pugh and Morley (1988a) have suggested that when members of a design team share a vigilant

	Non-vigilant information processing
1.	Fails adequately to document the existence of a problem and the need to solve it, increasing the chance of producing a product which will not sell.
2.	Collects information to justify choices which have already been made without explicit analysis, so that the design controls the PDS.
3.	Careful consideration of a very restricted range of goals, constraints, and values implicated by the elements of the PDS.
4.	Serious consideration of only a restricted sample of policies, sometimes only one (so that design is based on one concept).
5.	Careful consideration of a restricted sample of costs and benefits, more or less ignoring a formal PDS and its implied constraints.
6.	Relies on intuition to avoid a detached, deliberate, detailed analysis of the elements of the problem, and so may rapidly discount one or more concepts without serious analysis.
7.	Fails intensively to search for new information. Is insensitive to messages from other people (especially when the messages are unpalatable). Consequently, ignores early warning signs that design is going wrong.
8.	Evaluates alternatives only once, taking them one at a time (e.g. fails to re-examine the consequences of an idea which is plausible, but false or incomplete; 'staccato' design).
9.	No attempt systematically to balance the pros and cons of a particular design. Regards design as acceptable if it satisfies a few major constraints and is easy to justify in ordinary language.
10.	Fails adequately to integrate the problems of manufacturing, marketing, sales, etc. into the activities of the design core, so that major modifications in design may be required at the production stage.

Figure 7.8 *Non-vigilant information processing in engineering product design. Adapted from Pugh and Morley (1988a)*

orientation the design core is more likely to have the general characteristics shown in Figure 7.7. When they share a non-vigilant orientation it is more likely to have the general characteristics shown in Figure 7.8.

As we pointed out in Chapter 4 people will often not bother to process information vigilantly. This is sensible when decisions can be reversed easily without incurring serious costs. Some design decisions are like that. However, we assume that, in general, the activities of the design core will involve important decisions which become increasingly difficult to change. The decisions are what Janis and Mann (1977) have called 'consequential decisions'. Thus, we assume that the design activity described in Figure 7.8 will, in general, lead to poor design. For example, one immediate result is that the group fails adequately to document the existence of design problems and the need to solve them (Rzevski, 1984; Pugh and Morley, 1988a; Morley, in press, a).[34]

Towards a theory of group performance

We are now able to say a great deal about the social conditions which make vigilant or non-vigilant information processing more or less likely. We believe that statements of this kind form an important part of any general theory of group effectiveness. The most important sources for our ideas have been Janis (1982a), Janis and Mann (1977), and Pugh and Morley (1988a, b).

Broadly speaking, it seems that non-vigilant information processing may arise for two main reasons. We shall consider each in turn. First, members of design teams may use intuitive processes which, unless checked, will produce biases in information interpretation, information search, influence, and choice. Some of the relevant literature has been discussed in Chapter 1. General reviews are given in Nisbett and Ross (1980), Hogarth (1980), Sage (1981), and Myers (1988). Sage's review is particularly useful in the present context because he suggests that one way of avoiding cognitive bias is to use systematic methods which 'assist in processing information updates', and which collect both quantitative and qualitative data (Sage, 1981, p.649). Second, non-vigilant information processing may arise from social processes which occur when the design team is a cohesive group; when the organization has structural faults; and when decision makers are stressed by 'provocative situational contexts' (Janis, 1982a; Janis and Mann, 1977; Morley and Hosking, 1984).

Group cohesiveness

Cohesiveness is a complex concept, as we have seen in Chapter 4, and its role in decision making is often misunderstood. It may be defined in various ways, but there seems broad consensus that it measures the net force attracting members to a group (Golembiewski, 1965) or the net force acting on members to remain in a group (Shaw, 1976). There will be times when it is important to distinguish different kinds of group cohesiveness, because they may have rather different effects.[35] In general, however, it seems safe to describe cohesiveness as a 'strategic group property' (Golembiewski, 1962a, p.110) because members of highly cohesive groups are more likely to agree on the norms of the group (Rasmussen and Zander, 1954), and to act upon them (Festinger, Schachter and Back, 1950). They are more likely to pay serious attention to the positions espoused by other group members and more likely to be influenced by their arguments (Back, 1951).

Given all of this it is not surprising that Janis (1972, p.13) has argued that: 'a group whose members have properly defined roles, with traditions and standard operating procedures that facilitate critical inquiry, is probably capable of making better decisions than any individual in the group who works on the problem alone.' However, Janis was quite clear that groups, like individuals, would sometimes perform extremely well and sometimes extremely badly. Thus, he went on to say that

> the advantages of having decisions made by groups are often lost because of psychological pressures that arise when members work closely together, share the same values, and *above all* face a crisis situation in which everyone is subjected to stresses that generate a strong need for affiliation. In these circumstances, as conformity pressures begin to dominate, groupthink and the attendant deterioration of decision-making set in. (p.13; emphasis added)

'Groupthink' is one form of non-vigilant information processing produced as a collective response to the effects of stress (Janis and Mann, 1977).

Three related mechanisms seem to be involved. First, stress generates strong needs for affiliation within the group. This means that group members want 'to match their opinions with each other and to conduct themselves in accordance with each other's wishes' (Janis, 1972, p.201). Not surprisingly, Janis calls this 'concurrence seeking'. One direct consequence is that people who have misgivings keep silent and increasingly give the benefit of the doubt to the emerging group consensus. Second, 'groupthink' may be seen as a form of 'defensive avoidance' in which individuals avoid the stress of actively open minded thinking.[36] It is most likely when people see a decision as lose-lose, because each of the obvious options carries serious risks, and because they see the obvious options are the only realistic options (Janis and Mann, 1977; Janis, 1982a). Under such circumstances group members are likely to focus on whatever option seems to be preferred by the leader, or by a coalition of high status members, or by a simple majority within the group. They will then use mechanisms of selective attention and distorted information processing, pooling their collective resources to minimize the risks associated with that option. Third, strong needs for affiliation generate strong pressures to conform to the norms of the group. These may facilitate critical inquiry or they may 'evoke conformity with the leader's views' (Janis, 1972, p.211). Thus, 'groupthink' becomes more or less likely, depending on the norms of the group.[37] Indeed, 'groupthink' is sometimes described as the result of a norm of concurrence seeking, adopted by the entire group (Janis, 1972, p.213).

Janis has argued that 'when appropriate precautions are taken, a group that has become moderately or highly cohesive will probably do a much better job on its decision making tasks than if it had remained non-cohesive' (Janis, 1972, p.199). We agree. Indeed, we have found it helpful to think of cohesiveness, in general, as something which amplifies the effects of other variables. Thus, when other factors promote vigilant information processing, vigilant information processing will be more likely in cohesive than in non-cohesive groups. Equally, when other factors promote non-vigilant information processing, that will be more likely in cohesive than in non-cohesive groups. So vigilant information processing is sometimes more likely in cohesive groups, and sometimes not.[38]

Networking within and between groups

According to Janis and Mann (1977) non-vigilant information processing is more likely in individuals and groups when the group is insulated from others within the enterprise; when the group lacks methodical procedures for making decisions; and when the group lacks impartial leadership. We shall consider each in turn.

Insulation of the group

The groups studied by Janis (1972) were cross-functional teams of advisors engaged in high level planning of various aspects of American foreign policy. Nevertheless, in some cases, the entire group seems to have developed a norm of concurrence seeking, leading to 'groupthink'. This finding is of particular interest in the context of engineering design because more and more enterprises are attempting to integrate the activities of the design core by building multi-disciplinary or cross-functional teams.[39] Janis' work shows that this is not enough. In his view, it is necessary for each member of the team to go back to his or her part of the enterprise and discuss current thinking with trusted associates (Janis, 1972, p.213). He suggests, also, that well qualified associates may be invited to participate in team meetings from time to time.[40] What he is trying to avoid is 'insulation of the decision making group from the judgments of qualified associates who, as outsiders, are not permitted to know about the new policies under discussion until after a final decision has been made' (Janis, 1972, p.197). To use the metaphor introduced in Chapter 4, he is trying to ensure that participants gain the advantages of being mobile organisms and 'move around' their social world. In other words, he is trying to ensure that participants engage in appropriate forms of networking. However, such attempts to integrate different specialists into a process of design may be welcomed, tolerated, or actively resisted, depending on circumstances.[41]

Lack of methodical procedures for search and appraisal

Systematic ways of working are important for three main reasons. First, they may encourage vigilant rather than non-vigilant modes of processing information (Janis, 1972). Second, they may help people to work together effectively, so that disagreement converges productively on to solutions which all can understand and all can accept (Morley and Pugh, 1987; Morley, 1988, in press, a). That is, they may produce a process of 'controlled convergence' which helps to deal with those cognitive and political problems endemic in project work. Finally, they may keep in check those aspects of individual personality which would otherwise inhibit the workings of the group (Broadbent, 1988).[42]

The interested reader will find a review of some of the available methods in Broadbent (1988). Broadbent's treatment is geared to architectural design but it is fairly comprehensive, and interesting to read. We do not intend to review these methods in detail, but we do wish to make a number of rather general remarks.

To begin with let us note that methodical procedures do not guarantee success. Pugh (1991) has suggested that it may be particularly dangerous to use formal methods of choice[43] unless a comprehensive product design specification has been drawn up and agreed by all relevant parties. Without this firm foundation he argues that designers 'go wrong with confidence'. What is required is some combination of methods which foster vigilant information processing at each stage of design. It is also important that, at each stage, qualitative and quantitative concerns are given due weight (Sage, 1981).

Attempts should be made to identify those parts of the task that are better performed by individuals working alone and those parts of the task that are better performed by groups (McGrath, 1984). In the case of engineering design it may, for example, be better to begin the process of concept selection by having individuals begin working on their own. Once each individual has generated a number of ideas of his or her own they may be listed, evaluated, and developed collectively. McGrath (1984, p.128) refers to this as the 'nominal group technique'. This sort of procedure has been used with some success by Pugh (1981, 1991).

Finally, the methods should support cooperative group work in a variety of ways. Robinson (1989) has provided an excellent discussion of some of the issues which are involved. We believe that two of his ideas are of particular importance. They are that methods should satisfy the criterion of 'mutual influence' and that they should satisfy the criterion of 'double level language'. The first criterion says that people should feel free to retract their views, restate them, or move to completely new positions when they learn what other people think and feel. The second criterion says that methods should support 'formal' and 'cultural' levels of language. The formal level comes from the formalism of the method. The cultural level comes from the conversations that go on as the method is used. Robinson argues that applications will not be successful unless they support both levels of language.[44]

Leadership in design teams
Janis (1972) has argued that leaders have a special responsibility to structure the process of decision making so that information is more or less vigilant, depending upon the demands of the task. He has set out five prescriptions

designed to offset what he calls 'leadership bias'.[45] They are designed to prevent the group turning away from active open-minded thinking towards bolstering a policy choice they think the leader wants to make (Morley and Hosking, 1984). To give just one example, Janis recommends that:

> The leaders in an organization's hierarchy, when assigning a policy-planning mission to a group, should be impartial instead of stating preferences and expectations at the outset. This practice requires each leader to limit his briefings to unbiased statements about the scope of the problem and the limitations of available resources, without advocating specific proposals he would like to see adopted. This allows the conferees the opportunity to develop an atmosphere of open inquiry and to explore impartially a wide range of policy alternatives. (Janis, 1972, pp.210–11)

Recommendations of this kind are well worth taking seriously, but it is also important to realize that leaders have a much wider brief. Leaders do have a special responsibility to structure the activities of the 'design core' so that information processing is vigilant rather than non-vigilant. But this is just one example of a more general responsibility to structure social process so that we get the right kind of social order. They must ensure that the collective effort in design is disciplined or organized so that the process is visible, coherent, and understood by all (Akin and Hopelain, 1986; Morley, in press, a). This means that they have a responsibility to ensure that the team uses appropriate methods, amongst other things, and that the methods are supported by appropriate norms. They may also take a major role in sorting out political problems inside and outside the group.[46]

A basic principle of 'total design' (Pugh and Morley, 1988a, b) is that all facets of the business be represented in the 'design core'. Given the political problems identified by Dill and Pearson (1984) we believe that this may only be possible when there is a design director on the board, and when he or she builds close personal relationships at the top level, particularly with the directors of marketing and production. We regard this as a special case of networking. The importance of such activity is vividly illustrated in the 'mini' case history of Firm A set out in Pugh and Morley (1988b).

Interviews conducted with the Director of Research and Development at this firm (let us call him Director A) also revealed the importance of some of the other elements in our general model of social skill. Director A had made changes in Firm A which had led to quite dramatic improvements in the performance of design teams within the firm. Pugh and Morley (1988b) identified four main reasons for this success. First, Director A had initiated attempts to structure the activities of the design core so that they were visible, coherent, and legible, forming a 'culture of productivity'. Second, he was concerned with success in a business sense, rather than with technical excellence for its own sake. Third, the result of the activity of networking was greater balance in the activities of the design core. That is to say, he was able to use his own relationship with the Director of Marketing to facilitate the 'front end' of the process of design. He was also able to cross functional barriers by bringing functional specialists into the main design team, as and when required. Finally, Director A was particularly cognisant of certain dilemmas inherent in the activity of total design.

The first may be called the dilemma of succession. The issue is whether to keep the same team throughout the project (with the same leader) or whether to have different leaders and different members at different stages of the project. Firm A were attempting to follow the latter strategy. The design process was divided into a number of formal stages, with formal design reviews at the end of each stage: namely, strategic planning; conceptual design; feasibility; design; development; pre-production; and production. This is shown in Figure 7.9. Initially, the team was 'market led' with Director A leading the team through the first three stages (strategic planning, conceptual design, feasibility). Subsequently, leadership passed to a Design Manager who led the team through design, development, and pre-production. Finally, leadership passed to Manufacturing proper.

There may be circumstances in which it is advisable to keep one leader throughout a project. Pugh and Morley (1988b) mention three possibilities, for example: 'where projects are much larger; where many more people are involved in the design; [and] where there are fewer major projects on the go at one time' (p.12). However, Director A was trying to maximize the use of his limited resources by changing the leaders of the design teams, freeing them to work on new projects. His own view was that

> it can be a soft option in a company this size to try and get a product leader to go through concept [conceptual design] right to the end. Because it does limit what that person is capable of achieving in the design sense, so by going back and getting new products following through, we ensure a continuous roll out. (Pugh and Morley, 1988b, p.12)

If this process is to work there probably has to be considerable overlap in membership between one stage of design and the next. This means that people are committed to the project because they 'own' it, in a sense. It also helps to optimize the interface between different departments.

Director A was also much concerned with a second dilemma. This involved the flow of information within the design team and involved questions of confidentiality, trust, security, and creativity. Giving people confidential information risks breach of confidence, but it may be necessary for creative work. To quote Director A:

> communications is part of the process for making it all happen. I mentioned a quarterly meeting amongst section heads at departmental level. We have strategic planning meetings of the department with one or two managers, and all the section heads get copies of the confidential minutes of those meetings. Because how can you expect to operate with people who are working for you as part of the team if they don't know what's between the covers. My first

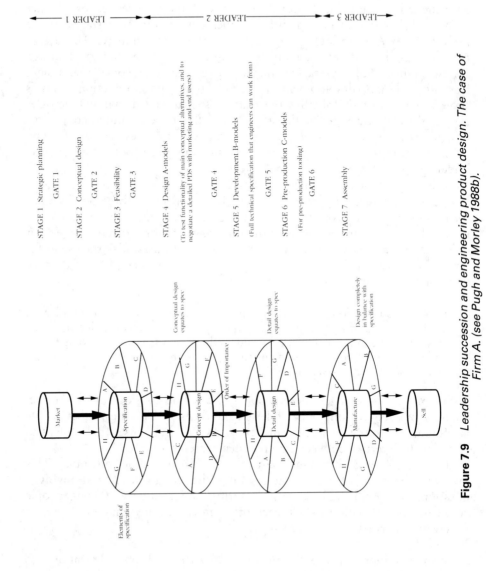

LEADER 1 ← → LEADER 2 ← → LEADER 3

STAGE 1 Strategic planning
  GATE 1

STAGE 2 Conceptual design
  GATE 2

STAGE 3 Feasibility
  GATE 3

STAGE 4 Design A-models
  (To test functionality of main conceptual alternatives, and to
  negotiate a detailed PDS with marketing and end users)

  GATE 4

STAGE 5 Development B-models
  (Full technical specification that engineers can work from)

  GATE 5

STAGE 6 Pre-production C-models
  (For pre-production tooling)

  GATE 6

STAGE 7 Assembly

Elements of specification

Conceptual design equates to spec

Order of Importance

Detail design equates to spec

Design completely in balance with specification

Market — Specification — Concept design — Detail design — Manufacture — Sell

Figure 7.9 *Leadership succession and engineering product design. The case of Firm A. (see Pugh and Morley 1988b).*

objective was to build a team that I could have confidence in and trust and work with, and it was a two-way trust. Then you could open up the communications as such so that when people saw something that was confidential they could use it in a positive sense.[47]

The principles of total design

Morley and Pugh have set out some of the social psychological principles which underly the process of 'total design' (Morley and Pugh, 1987; Pugh and Morley, 1988a; Morley, in press, a). The main implications of what they say are set out below.

To begin with, let us agree that, other things being equal, effective performance is more likely when we have cohesive groups, particularly when they have sentiments of mutual liking, and respect for each other's expertise. Conventional wisdom suggests that, where possible, project teams are chosen to be cohesive in just this way. We might say, therefore, that the interpersonal design boundary is designed to minimize the likelihood of antagonism within the group. This is very sensible. But the clear message from the social sciences is that groups of this kind will sometimes perform extremely well and sometimes extremely badly.

If we are to realize the full potential of such a group:

1. We need a social process which is organized to provide a 'recurring contribution of information and reasoning from the widest possible range of sources' (Levin, 1976, p.226). Perhaps the fundamental principle of 'total design' is that which says all facets of the business should interact with the activities of the design core (Pugh and Morley, 1988a).

2. There must be sufficient expertise within the group, and sufficient diversity of expertise (Friedlander and Schott, 1981).

3. Group members need to have clear ideas about the nature of their task and their place within in (Pearson and Gunz, 1981). In particular, the process of design needs to be organized into stages which are visible, coherent, and legible. The object of the exercise is to generate a culture of productivity (Akin and Hopelain, 1986) in which there is controlled convergence onto solutions all can understand and all can accept (Morley and Pugh, 1987; Pugh and Morley, 1988a).

4. The group must have norms and standard operating procedures which facilitate actively open-minded thinking (Janis, 1972; Morley and Hosking, 1984). This means that there must be periodic reviews in which team members repeatedly scrutinize and test the assumptions they have made and the information they have obtained (Janis, 1972; Levin, 1976; Jones and Overton, 1988). The general idea is to control the process of commitment

so that there is a 'growth of commitment to plans at successively higher levels of specificity' (Levin, 1976, p.34). It is particularly important that teams do not become committed prematurely to ideas which may be false or incomplete.

5. The group networks with other parts of the enterprise rather than being 'insulated' from them (Janis, 1972; 1982b; George, 1974; Pugh and Morley, 1988b).

6. The group is organized so that, between them, group members take a variety of 'primary' roles (Clutterbuck, 1979; Belbin, 1981). It is possible that, in some cases, the roles may be performed by procedures rather than people (Pugh and Morley, 1988b). That is to say, which roles are most important will depend upon which operating procedures are in place.

7. The leader of the group takes special responsibility for ensuring that the emergent group process has certain desirable properties. This means ensuring that activity within and between the stages of the design core is visible, coherent, and legible (Akin and Hopelain, 1986; Pugh and Morley, 1988b). It means using methods and procedures which support actively open minded thinking, and enhance creative work. It means building a set of appropriate norms. It means clearly separating individual from collective work (McGrath, 1984). It means organizing design activity so that we see a social process of disciplined creativity in which participants converge on to solutions they all understand and they all accept (Pugh and Morley, 1988a; Morley, 1988, in press, a).

Hopefully, this will minimize unnecessary losses from faulty group process and maximize the chance of process gains (Hackman and Morris, 1978; Hoffman, 1982; McGrath, 1984).

Notes

1. The phrase the 'task tuned organization of groups' is taken from Cohen (1969).
2. See Steiner (1972); Hackman and Morris (1978); Hoffman (1982); McGrath (1984); Pugh and Morley (1988a).
3. See Morley and Pugh (1987); Pugh and Morley (1988a); Morley (in press, a).
4. At this stage it may not look like the finished product at all. To quote one Director of Research and Development interviewed by Pugh and Morley (1988b) 'it may be made of different materials, different processes to the final production item'.
5. See Stewart and Chadwick (1987).
6. The invasion of Cuba, at the Bay of Pigs, in April 1961. Janis has written that: 'The Kennedy administration's Bay of Pigs decision ranks amongst the worst fiascoes ever perpetrated by responsible government. Planned by an over-ambitious, eager group of American intelligence officers who had little background or experience in military matters, the attempt to place a small brigade of Cuban exiles secretly on a beachhead in

Cuba with the ultimate aim of overthrowing the government of Fidel Castro proved to be a "perfect failure." The group that made the basic decision to approve the invasion plan included some of the most intelligent men ever to participate in the councils of government. Yet all the major assumptions supporting the plan were so completely wrong that the venture began to founder at the outset and failed at its earliest stages' (Janis, 1972, p.14). However, many of the same people advised Kennedy during the Cuban Missile Crisis of October 1962. Janis points out that 'this time they functioned in a much more effective way and showed few, if any, symptoms of groupthink' (Janis, 1972, p.138).

7. Examples include Watson and Crick's discovery of the structure of DNA (see Watson, 1968); Darwin's theory of evolution (see Gruber, 1981); Edison's invention of the kinetoscope (see Jenkins, 1983; Jenkins and Jeffrey, 1984); and the development of works of art (see Arnheim, 1962; Blunt, 1969).

8. Weisberg (1988) describes the work of Watson and Crick in the following terms: 'we have here one of the great discoveries of modern science, and it seems to have come about in manner very different from the romantic view of the scientist working alone in the laboratory until a sudden insight leads to the creative solution to the problem. In the case of Watson and Crick, their initial work grew directly out of the work of others, and when it was shown to be wrong, they modified it in straightforward ways, until a satisfactory solution was arrived at.' (p.162). Darwin's reaction to the work of Malthus, which was very important in the development of the theory of evolution, is placed in its historical context thus: 'when Darwin read Malthus, his ideas had been changing for over a year, to the point that Malthus could make a crucial impression on him. Malthus triggered no great leap of insight, but rather provided the capstone on a reasoning process that had moved in small steps from a theory that was a rather simple variation on already known themes to a theory that would change the world' (Weisberg, 1988, p.164). With respect to Edison, Weisberg comments that 'there is little doubt that the kinetoscope evolved directly out of the phonograph, as Edison took the idea of the horizontal rotating cyclinder and tried to use it in a different domain.' (Weisberg, 1988, p.165). The development of Picasso's large mural Guernica proceeded from sketches:

> 'The first few sketches contain some of the main characters . . . but their organization changes greatly from one sketch to another, and some of them . . . are not present in all the sketches . . . In addition, there are elements that are introduced in the middle of the work, but are then removed before completion . . . Picasso was making revisions even after the mural was hung in the Spanish pavilion in the Paris exposition . . . Picasso developed Guernica out of themes that had appeared in his earlier works. Furthermore, Blunt has traced some of the specific gestures and configurations used in Guernica to specific sources in the works of earlier artists with which Picasso was familiar.' (Weisberg, 1988, p.167)

9. Also see Bensinger (1965); Shockley (1976); Petroski (1987); Atherton (1988); Pugh and Morley (1988a).

10. Further discussion of the difference between static and dynamic concepts is given in Pugh (1983, 1984, 1991), Pugh and Morley (1988a, b), and Hollins and Pugh (1989).

11. In some cases 'There is a big difference between the expertise required to be a designer and that required to be a user. In their work, designers often become expert with the *device* they are designing. Users are often expert at the *task* they are trying to perform with the device.' (Norman, 1988, p.156).

12. Also see Evans (1989).

13. See Lawrence and Lorsch (1967a, b); Tushman and Nadler (1986); Oakley (1984).

14. See Lorsch and Lawrence (1970); Tushman and Nadler (1986).

15. We are indebted to David Miller of the City of Birmingham Polytechnic for this suggestion.

16. The phrase 'over the wall' design is borrowed from Professor Stuart Pugh, Design Division, University of Strathclyde.

17. This is one reason why design audits are so important (Jones and Overton, 1988).

18. He is concerned with those prototypes which occur after it has been established that the project is feasible. These are what Pugh and Morley (1988b) have described as development models ('B-models') and pre-production models ('C-models').

19. In our terms this is because they have different values and different social constructions of reality.

20. See Cooper (1988); Pugh and Morley (1988a); Morley (in press, a).

21. Here it is worth noting that a substantial majority of the projects included in the study (and there were just over two hundred) failed to include 'market study or detailed market research' (Cooper, 1988, p.240).

22. As Rzevski (1984) has pointed out, when subsystems do not fit together things may go from bad to worse. Then everyone is working under intense pressure, and more mistakes may be made.

23. See Matousek (1963); Bailey (1978); Papanek (1984); Broadbent (1988).

24. For further reading see Stein (1974); Bailey (1978); Weisberg (1986); Sternberg (1988); Broadbent (1988).

25. This would imply selecting people with scores in the middle range of the Kirton Adaptation Inventory.

26. There is evidence that skilled negotiators learn skills which mean that their personal relationships survive hard hitting attempts at influence and control (Douglas, 1962; Morley and Stephenson, 1977; Morley, 1981a). These skills are also characteristic of members of many effective groups (McGregor, 1960; Chell, 1987).

27. See Chapter 4. Also see Broadbent (1988).

28. Weisberg (1986) Chapter 5.

29. As Belbin says, 'Whether a team with a certain type of member achieves good or poor results depends on the characteristic opportunity setting in which the team finds itself. That is why the attributes of teams always have to be assessed against the demands and possibilities of the situation' (Belbin, 1981, p.24). We agree entirely. 'Pure teams develop a style and quality of their own. If the situation matches the style the pure company can excel' (Belbin, 1981, p.29). Otherwise it may fail badly.

30. These stages are similar, but not identical, to the stages of identification, development, and choice considered in Chapter 4.

31. Within the limits of the errors of measurement.

32. See Kolb (1976).

33. However, it is not true to say, as Chell does, that Apollo teams 'invariably came last' (Chell, 1987). Apart from this, Chell has provided a very useful introductory review of work on team building.

34. Other possible consequences are set out in Wohl (1981); Sage (1981, 1984); Morley and Pugh (1987); and Pugh and Morley (1988b).

35. See Chapter 4. Also see Back (1951) and Golembiewski (1962b).

36. Whyte (1989) has argued that Kahneman and Tversky's (1979) prospect theory may be used as the basis for a simpler explanation of phenomena such as groupthink. Prospect theory is a descriptive theory of decision making under risk. It predicts that people will

be risk aversive when decisions are framed in terms of gains and risk seeking when decisions are framed in terms of losses. Whyte (1989) has argued that, in the cases studied by Janis (1972, 1982a) most people would be likely to prefer the risky option (holding out the hope of limiting the damage). He treats groupthink as a special case of group polarization, in which the group makes the risky choice initially preferred by a majority of its members. He argues that 'groups will amplify the behavioral tendencies on which prospect theory is founded' (p.51).

37. Janis has argued that: 'In the policy-appraising committee responsible for approving the Bay of Pigs invasion, the leader, probably without realizing it, induced the group members to give the highest priority to preserving group unity by avoiding harsh criticism of the CIA's plans. In each of the other fiascoes we have examined the same type of norm can be detected. But in the Executive Committee that dealt with the Cuban Missile Crisis, no such norm developed; instead, the norm was to discuss openly all doubts about each alternative course of action . . . Adherence to this norm requires a delicate balance of mutual suspicion and mutual trust – suspicion about the soundness of each other's arguments, combined with a basic attitude of trust that criticizing each other's ideas will not be taken as an insult or lead to retaliation' (Janis, 1972, pp.178–9).

38. This aspect of Janis' work is commonly misunderstood. Janis does not say that group cohesiveness will, in general, be negatively correlated with the quality of group decision (see Brown, 1988).

39. See Peyronnin (1987); Pugh and Morley (1988a, b); Coplin (1989); Bertodo (1989).

40. According to Janis (1972) 'the visitors would have to be trustworthy associates carefully selected because of their capacity to grasp new ideas quickly, perspicacity in spotting hidden catches, sensitivity to moral issues, and verbal skills in transmitting criticism' (p.214).

41. See Pugh and Morley (1988a). For further discussion of political processes see Dill and Pearson (1984) and Whipp and Clark (1986).

42. Broadbent was thinking about design in architecture; specifically about the need to bring convergers and divergers together in some form of group. He added that 'we need some mechanism to ensure that the worst features of convergence and divergence do not inhibit the workings of the group. A great deal of thought, in the last few years, has been devoted to devices which will help us do this, under the general heading of systematic design method' (Broadbent, 1988, p.24).

43. Rating and weighting methods which represent an attempt to find the best possible design.

44. He was concerned with computer supported cooperative work. We have extended his ideas to cover any way of providing decision support.

45. See presciptions 1 and 2 (Janis, 1972, pp.209–11) and prescriptions 7, 8, and 9 (Janis, 1972, pp.214–19).

46. One project leader, working within a matrix management structure, described his role as that of a 'facilitator', meaning that his main job was to act as a 'resource investigator', so that when the team 'got bogged down' he went 'outside' to examine the nature of the constraints, and remove unnecessary obstacles getting in the way of their work (Morley, personal communication).

47. From the transcript of an interview of Director A conducted by Pugh and Morley. This part of the transcript is not reported in Pugh and Morley (1988b).

Chapter 8

Top management and its projects

Introduction

Studies of top management often are reported as studies of top managers: chief executives, general managers, American Presidents, military officials, and the like. The individual manager usually is the unit of analysis. Typically, an entitative, individualistic concept of person is adopted, where, for example, a chief executive, General, or President, is attributed personal properties, for example of personality, which set them apart from their contexts. As we shall see, chief executives often are theorized as 'heroic actors'. In other words, they are treated as though they were the sufficient, efficient cause of organization design (see Part 1), of their own actions, and of the valuations and actions of others. All too rarely do we find a social action perspective in which persons and contexts are argued to be joined through relationships where each to some extent selects and produces the other (but see, for example, Biggart, 1981). More rare still are studies which abandon entitative concepts of person and organization to join and theorize each through an emphasis on organizing.

Throughout the text, we have been developing a view of organizing as a process of political decision making performed within and between various kinds of groups. Organizations, or – as we prefer to call them – enterprises, are in this sense viewed as more or less loose coalitions of many groups, groups which have overlapping membership because, for example, each member of the top executive team is also a member of other groupings – business, functional, and so on. It will be clear that there is no agreed view of the task of top management, or how otherwise to conceptualize the relationship between top management and organization.

We will begin by examining what, in Chapter 2, we called a natural systems perspective. We use this perspective, in all its variants, as an illustration of the degree to which an entitative perspective limits and distorts the view of top management. We continue by examining the diverse literatures which contribute to our understanding of the social, political, and cognitive processes in which top management more or less collectively engage. We will draw upon treatments of top management as those who, amongst others, and by various means, create and mobilize social orderings of power (see Chapter 2; e.g. Mangham, 1986) and social orderings of value (e.g. Selznick, 1957; Peters and Waterman, 1982). We also will draw upon our own research with chief executives (Hosking, in press, a).

The functions of top management: Integrating system needs

In Chapter 2, we reviewed various examples of an organic, natural systems perspective. Natural systems theorists include those such as Burns and Stalker, Lawrence and Lorsch, the 'socio-technical' systems researchers from the Tavistock Institute, along with population ecologists (see Morgan, 1986). At its most general, a natural systems perspective focuses on: intra-system relations between sub-systems, identified in various ways; relations between the organization (= system) and 'its' immediate task environment; and the survival of the system whole, often theorized in terms of system needs.

Discussions of *intra-system relationships* focus on the importance of integrating the needs of individuals and organizations. So, for example, a major system function, often attributed to top management, is that of integration of these different needs (e.g. Argyris, 1964). The particular content of the argument varies, depending on the needs that are emphasized. So, for example, sociotechnical systems theorists drew from psychodynamic traditions, arguing that particular modes of organizing were better than others at satisfying social and psychological needs (Rice, 1958; Trist *et al.*,1963). These needs included meaningful activities which actors themselves controlled, which allowed them satisfactory relationships with others, and so on. This general line of argument developed into the claim that social and technical systems must jointly be optimized for a system to be fit and healthy.[1]

Other discussions focus on relations between the organization (= system) and its environment. The managerial function is not just to match or integrate the needs of subsystems internal to the organization. What is crucial is that top management designs, so to speak, a best fit between the organization and its context (see Chapter 2).[2] This may be achieved through successful adaptation of the organization, and/or by selecting an environmental niche in which there is relatively little competition. So, for example, senior management is understood to have the strategic function of 'fashioning the longer-term future' (Jaques, 1976) – initiating policy for others to implement (see also Katz and Kahn, 1978). More generally, the task of top management is argued to be that of strategic choice: integrating the relations between strategy, structures, technology, the needs of the subsystems (including individuals), and the external environment (see Child, 1972).

Top management has a very different task when theorized from another natural systems perspective – that of 'population ecology'. Those who argue this line take a long term, historical, perspective. When judged from this viewpoint, they argue, it doesn't really matter what top management does. The strategic choices of top managers are played down, relative to much more important effects of environmental changes. The perspective is drawn from Darwinian arguments about evolution. The environment, and the resources it provides, constitutes the central actor; organizations compete for resources; some organizational forms are fitter than others (see e.g. Morgan, 1986).

Comment: Entitative treatments

Arguments from a natural systems perspective theorize persons, organizations, and environments independently of each other. Each is treated as an entity, that is, as having functional unity (see Chapters 1 and 2). This characteristic is a weakness for those who are interested seriously to consider the relations between person and organization. This is because, as we have argued, each to some extent, makes the other – constructing social realities in thought and action. So, for example, social actors – individuals and groups – to some extent make their environments hostile or munificent, 'paranoiagenic' or 'requisite' (see Jaques, 1976). Actors may, through more or less collective social processes: create what they expect to find, and then attribute that creation to their contexts, rather than to their own actions (e.g. Weick, 1979), and structure the uncertainties of social order, obtaining the collusion of others to enact relations of dominance and submission (e.g. Moch and Huff, 1989); these are processes of what Weick calls enactment (Weick, 1979).

Our interest is in theorizing the relationships between persons, process, and organization. From this point of view, the natural systems perspective over-emphasizes needs as fixed qualities of systems and subsystems. As a result, it is impossible fully to recognize persons and groups as agents more or less actively constructing their social orders in the pursuit of their more or less collective projects. We shall continue by examining the social, political, and cognitive processes of top management and the projects they may pursue. Note that our emphasis, as always, is on organizing processes, that is, on how organizing is performed.

Looking ahead

We will begin by reviewing literatures in which are described the activity patterns and relationships through which senior managers carry out their projects – whatever those projects might be. Much of the available data are low inference observations of how individual managers spend their time; however, higher inference interpretations of relationships also are reported. These studies give a picture of the social processes through which top managers, rather than top management as a group, attempt to perform their projects. The studies indicate that management conduct their organizing through 'live action', moving around in networks of social relationships and often, in relationships where they have no formal authority. We continue by giving our own account of these social processes. We do so by taking a decision-making perspective, emphasizing networking as a process of social interaction through which is performed the cognitive and political processes of organizing. We end with a picture of the reciprocal qualities of relations between actors and their contexts, and relationships of negotiation, exchange, and influence through which some projects, rather than others, come to be translated into action.

Social processes

Surface activities

There has been a long tradition of research into 'managerial behaviour' and 'managerial work' (see Hales, 1986). Studies typically have focused on 'concrete, empirical reality' (Davis and Luthans, 1980). Researchers have collected surface data concerning observable activities to produce objective descriptions, that is, descriptions which different observers find it relatively easy to agree. Research methods have included: following managers around for days at a time; various techniques of activity sampling; questionnaires; and getting managers to keep diaries of how they spend their time, and who they spend it with.

Observations are made of: the proportion of work time spent in various categories of activity; and of the number and types of personal 'contact' – subordinates, boss, and peers. *Activities* are classified, for example, as: working alone; in pre-arranged or chance meetings; on the phone; on paperwork; and by the duration and location of the activity. *Contacts* typically are classified as vertical and as lateral. The former refer to contacts with a boss or subordinate in the context of the formalized hierarchy within which the managerial role is defined. The latter refer to the contacts managers may have with other actors over whom they have no formal authority. Contacts of this sort can be internal or external to the manager's own enterprise (see Chapter 5).

Studies of this sort have been conducted to examine the activities and contacts of managers from different specialisms and hierarchical 'levels'; from the public and private sectors; and from manufacturing, the police, education, and so on. Few studies have focused exclusively on chief executives, exceptions being found in the work of Carlson (1951), a study of nine managing directors, and in Mintzberg's (1973) structured observations of five chief executives. Most studies have focused exclusively on male managers, without recognizing that this might be important: very few have focused entirely on women.[3]

A clear picture seems to emerge from these studies, regardless of whether or not the manager is a chief executive (Mintzberg, 1973, 1989). In general, managerial work is performed at a hectic pace. Activities are varied, typically of short duration – less than half an hour – and often interrupted. For these reasons, Mintzberg described managerial work as 'fragmented'. Managerial work also tends to be performed in interaction with others, particularly with those over whom the manager has no formal authority. Social interactions often occur in meetings; little time is spent reading, or in solitary activity. For these reasons, Mintzberg characterized managerial work as 'live action'. We shall offer our own interpretation of the significance of social interactions.

Interpreting activities and interactions

Interpretations of managerial work may start from theory . For example, we have seen already what natural systems perspectives imply about the what of managerial work: integrating the needs of subsystems; initiating policies and structures; 'fashioning the longer term'; and 'strategic choice' of relations between the organization and its environment. Others start with descriptions of activities – attempting then to interpret the content, the what, or purposes of those activities. However, as both Mintzberg and Stewart have remarked, descriptions of activities largely are silent as to their content (Stewart 1976; Mintzberg, 1973). One approach is to apply content analysis to behavioural acts to categorize behaviour as 'politicking', 'exchanging routine information', and so on (Luthans and Lockwood, 1984). Another is to take the broad range of managerial activities and attempt to infer what roles these might serve (e.g. Mintzberg, 1973).

In neither the natural systems perspective nor the empirical approach, is there explicit recognition of the point of view from which is made the judgements as to content. Neither approach is able to contemplate the possibility that multiple interpretations of the same descriptive account could be produced, each of which might be equally reasonable when located in the wider context of the actors' cognitive frameworks. When Luthans and Lockwood speak of time on the phone as 'time wasting', this is their interpretation; they know nothing of the agendas that managers might have for that activity. To attribute particular activities to particular roles requires judgement, and different judges may not agree. This may be because particular activities may contribute to more than one role, or because it may not be possible to describe the content of an activity until it has produced an effect (see Weick, 1979). Further, as we have argued already, descriptions of social realities are constructed in ways which reflect the evaluative beliefs of those making the judgments (see Part 1). So, for example, a chief executive attending a public function and making a speech may describe this as 'building the reputation of her department', 'creating a sense of indebtedness', 'building relationships', and so on. All may be equally reasonable descriptions. On the other hand, subordinates may describe such activities as unnecessary, or as evidence that the executive is always away. A contextualist perspective is required which recognizes and respects different constructions of reality.

We shall go on to develop our own interpretation of managerial activities. We shall make much of the significance of 'live action', of the significance of social relationships, and of the roles that social interactions might play in managements' attempts to add values to their lives. We shall begin this by looking more closely at studies of managers' 'contact networks'.

Networks and relationships

Studies of the 'contact networks' of managers[4] suggest that they may have very large social networks indeed – often 'hundreds or thousands of individuals' (Kotter, 1982, p.67).[5] Landsberger reported that over 40 per cent of the communications of six British middle managers were with peers (Landsberger, 1962). Carlson's (1951) study of nine managing directors also showed that they spent much of their time in *lateral* relationships.[6] Kotter suggested that the general managers he studied 'developed relationships with . . . any and all people upon whom they felt dependent because of their jobs' (p.67).[7] In other words, contacts are not simply down the line between managers and the subordinates to whom they are joined by a formalized hierarchy of authority. Rather, a manager's contacts often are lateral. These could include others to whom they are joined by formal structures of organization, that is, other members of the same enterprise, and external actors, such as suppliers and government officials.[8]

As with descriptions of activities, the general picture seems clear: managers not only spend a lot of their time with others, but much of the time the 'others' are 'lateral contacts'. These findings raise doubts about the traditional weight of emphasis upon hierarchy and top-down relations; on relationships of power and authority; and on relations within the enterprise.

Lateral relations also were much spoken of in our own interviews of chief executives. We shall have more to say about these findings later. For now we wish to show the importance our chief executives attached to relationships, particularly to lateral ones. In the interviews we 'floated' the observation that 'some take the view that good relationships help a manager to do their work, what do you think?'. All agreed – usually with some fervour. We then asked them to identify those relationships which they saw as especially helpful. We have examined five transcripts in detail. Two of the five chief executives referred exclusively to relationships with others outside their department. All five chief executives named more external than internal relationships. These included elected officials in Government, 'external' stakeholders, and 'other networks' and 'hierarchies'. They described such people as actors from whom they could get information to find out what was going on, and actors who could help them to achieve influence. Further, one chief executive specifically made reference to relationships which gave her opportunity to connect: that is, to enjoy union and interdependence with others, through making contact, cooperating, and being open to other points of view and to change.[9]

Taken together, these findings suggest that any attempt to theorize managerial work, or – given our present interest – to theorize the projects of top management – must take seriously the many networks of social relationships through which managers appear to 'do their work' . In particular, there is need to appreciate the extent of non-authority relations, and relations with actors 'outside' the chief executives' own enterprise (lateral relations).

Entitative interpretations of networks

Network analysis has a long tradition in subjects such as social psychology, micro-sociology, and anthropology but is less common in the literatures of organization studies. A focus on networks provides one way to describe social relations between actors in terms of similarities and differences in valuations and in status. As a few have remarked, the network concept can provide a useful way to theorize the structures and performance of organizations. A focus on networks provides a way to link micro and macro 'levels' of analysis (e.g. Crozier, 1972; Pearce and David, 1983) or, to use our own terms, to link person and organization (see Chapter 3). Perhaps most important, a focus on networks makes it possible to 'de-centre' the formal structures of enterprises, blending the formal and informal in a focus on relationships. In this way, it is possible to avoid the managerialist distinction between formal and informal organization.

Networks of social relations are characterized by social orderings grounded in patternings of *influence* and *value* (Chapter 3). Finding that managers spend much of their time in social interactions raises certain obvious questions. These include: who initiated the contact? In relation to what issues? How is the relationship sustained, and why? How does each achieve influence, and in relation to what? What valuations do the actors share? And what interests is each seeking to protect and promote through their relations?

Perhaps the broadest way to approach these questions is to attempt to understand why managers are so active in contact networks, and especially, in lateral relations. One common suggestion is that they do so to obtain *information*. For example, Wrapp (1984), referring to managers as makers of policy, suggested that hierarchy and specialization cause information to be 'filtered', and create structures of power such that some actors would be indifferent to the managers' policies, whilst others would oppose them (see Part 1). For these reasons, Wrapp (1984) argued that 'good' managers 'keep open channels of information' – they develop a network of information sources in many different departments. In this way, the good manager is able to 'keep his [her] information live and accurate' and is able 'to seek more than one version of the situation' (Wrapp, 1984, p.8).[10] We shall return to this argument, emphasizing that 'information' is socially constructed.

Kotter (1982) claimed that his research showed that general managers tended to approach their jobs in similar ways. So, for example, they built networks of relationships and used those networks to 'receive' and 'gather' information (p.63). This helped them to compose an 'agenda' of 'loosely connected goals and plans'. More successful general managers appeared to seek information 'more aggressively', ask more questions, and find projects that would achieve multiple objectives. Networks were described as 'incredible information-processing systems' (p.78). Furthermore, networks were used, directly and indirectly, to achieve influence. General managers shaped their networks in various ways – through selection, by trying to manipulate norms and values – so that others in the networks helped them to implement their agendas.

It is not uncommon to find arguments that managers' contacts can constitute a useful source of live information, to facilitate understanding for the purposes of strategic decision making. In principle, such arguments could be espoused in relation to all functional phases of decision making: identification, development, selection and implementation (see Chapter 4). In practice, most emphasis has been devoted to 'search' or 'scanning' – to identify what are variously referred to as 'issues', 'policies', or 'problems' (e.g. Anguilar, 1967; Wildavsky, 1983), or for 'decision recognition' and 'diagnosis' (Mintzberg, Raisinghani, and Theoret, 1976).

Similar interests and arguments are found in the literatures which view chief executives as 'leaders'. Chief executives, either by appointment, or by what they actually do, are viewed as those who are active in leadership. The general line of argument is that chief executives 'shape values' (Selznick, 1957). Apparently, chief executives 'wander around' to 'listen' (say, to what the customers want), and signal 'primary concerns', that is, their valuations[11] by 'reaching the vision'. They communicate the vision 'consistently and with fervour' (Peters and Austin, 1985, p.284).[12]

Influencing the valuations of others also is emphasized by Bennis and Nanus (1985) in their descriptions of the 'strategies' a leader may 'opt for'. These include 'attention through vision', 'getting the right vision' and 'personifying it'. The chief executive, as a leader, should 'manage meanings' to create commitment to a 'clear vision', and so on. This general line of argument has become very popular of late.[13] Using our own language, the argument is that chief executives do and should influence the valuations of others to manipulate their definition of the situation, including their constructions of what is important and what to do about it (see Hosking and Morley, 1988).

Finally, influence is emphasized by those who focus on the *exchange* aspects of relationships. We have seen that Kotter developed arguments in this area. So too, did Kaplan (1989), emphasizing that networks provide managers with opportunities to exchange: to 'trade' with others in order to gain resources and cooperation. Sayles (1964;1979) also linked managerial performances, exchange, and influence. As with the arguments about networks and information, we shall return to the links between networks and exchange to develop a very different perspective.

A constructivist perspective on networks

The above arguments about information and influence rest upon unstated physicalist and unitary assumptions about social realities (see Part 1). The language is revealing: environments are 'scanned'; information is 'given' or 'sent' through 'channels' (we would say relationships); values are 'instilled'; power is effectively treated as a zero-sum game in which actors attempt control, and exploit inequalities of exchange, to influence decisions and manipulate relationships in ways which will add value to their own lives, regardless of how this affects the lives of others.

We already have argued for a perspective which sees social realities as socially constructed. Actors have been shown to be active agents (some more active than others), pursuing projects which they hope will add value to their lives, and organizing them through cognitive, social, and political processes. Persons are seen as agents who, to some extent, select and make their contexts, whilst also being made by them. Given this concept of person, moving around in different social relationships must be understood as understanding, influencing, and being influenced by, other actors' definitions of the situation. An adequate treatment of networking will recognize and examine 'conversations for action' (Chapter 1).

An adequate treatment of networking will recognize the reciprocal processes of influence – including negotiation – through which actors build more or less shared descriptions of what is important, and what to do about it. Furthermore, a broader treatment of power becomes possible: situating influence in relationships; recognizing that power can be created through relationships; locating strategies such as enabling; and recognizing that activity of this sort may be done in the context of collaborative rather than competitive relations.[14]

A small number of writers have taken seriously the processes of social construction;[15] very few have done so in the context of interests in management and organization. Weick is perhaps best known for arguments of this kind (see Chapter 3). He argues that 'reality is selectively perceived, rearranged cognitively, and negotiated interpersonally' (1979, p.164). When meanings – for example of actual and potential events – are equivocal, then networking is likely to mean 'moving around'[16] many different constructions of what is, what is important, and so on. This is one reason why networking is so important to an actor who needs the help of others.

These arguments can be linked to our earlier arguments about specialization and the division of labour;[17] when actors move around in relation to their projects, they move around other individuals' and groups' definitions of their situation (e.g. Sayles, 1979; Smith, 1989). What this means, amongst other things, is that an actor who networks has a more complete understanding of: who has or might demand an involvement in their project; how such actors might or do define their interest, as helped or hindered; and how each actor might attempt to mobilize influence. These are the understandings of which we speak when we link networking and influence. Networking facilitates understanding, not just of what may constitute an issue, but also, of how to 'develop', 'select', and 'implement' policy. When Sayles remarked on the importance of a manager 'knowing the structure of the problem' and 'knowing the structure of human relations around the problem' we think this is something of what he meant.

So, the chief executive who networks can negotiate multiple meanings 'inside his or her own head', so to speak. A chief executive also may negotiate socially – with those who may or may not claim an involvement. In these ways, they may help themselves to develop a coherent view of the issue, the valuations, and the actors who could be involved. A chief executive who networks develops a 'high variety' language which accommodates multiple meanings (Daft and Wiginton, 1979). Such an actor understands how equivocal is the potential meaning of their project for the future activities, relationships, resources, and projects of those with whom their project makes them interdependent. When meanings are equivocal, the contextualists who move around to build their understandings of different perspectives can appreciate the significance of others' judgements and preferences, and are more likely, therefore, to achieve effective influence.[18] This may be especially important with respect to the influence that women chief executives are likely to achieve.

Chief executives may network to achieve influence, and may do so in many ways (e.g. Sayles, 1979). They may attempt to influence the constructions of those who could help or hinder their projects. They may negotiate descriptions with those they need to influence. By moving around in different relationships a chief executive may build relationships which, at some time, may be mobilized to gain understanding and influence. Two points need to be emphasized.

First, when realities are recognized as socially constructed, arguments about influence cannot be reduced to physicalist arguments about the exchange of goods and services. Kotter and Kaplan were right to emphasize exchange processes as important aspects of social relationships. They were wrong to ignore the symbolic and political qualities of these processes.

Second, when social realities are recognized as socially constructed, it follows that a major way in which influence is achieved is through political processes in which language is used as a strategic tool for influencing what others count as knowledge. Language constitutes the symbolic medium through which a chief executive, and other actors, may influence the valuations – the descriptions – of those with whom they are interdependent.[19] Those who argue that chief executives 'shape values' (see earlier) are right to do so; but they are wrong to ignore the valuations of other actors, and wrong to ignore the political processes through which issues are contested, negotiated, or kept 'off the agenda' for decision making (Chapter 5).

We have seen that, usually, networks are thought of as sources of information and as media for exchange and influence. Underlying these arguments we found a physicalist treatment of information, with the result that social relations were reduced to information flows, flows of resources, and influence grounded in exchange.[20] From this perspective, two sorts of argument have been offered as to why managers network. We shall outline them and interpret them in the context of our own perspective (which emphasizes social constructions).

The first argument is one that we have met before in Part 1. It is that managers network because 'they cannot escape being dependent' (Kaplan, 1984). As far as this arguement goes, we have to agree, although we would rather speak of interdependencies to recognize the reciprocal qualities of relationships. However, we agree not because we take an entitative view of organization – seeing goals and/or values as shared. Rather, we agree because the means by which actors pursue their projects (common, congruent, and conflicting) are interlocked – actors need the help of others to add value to their lives (see Part 1). Interdependent relationships are interdependencies of valuations and interdependencies of influence.

The second argument is also one we have met before. It is that the significance of networking follows from the fact that it is impossible fully to proceduralize organizing processes. As a result, managers must 'fashion an organization' (Sayles, 1964, p.27). Again we agree – but for the reason that social realities – and therefore social orders – are socially constructed. Fundamentally, it is because realities are socially constructed that actors must 'invent detail'(Part 1), building relationships and so building social orders, 'stabilizing and patterning work processes' (Sayles, 1964). This is why organizing is characterized by uncertainty, or rather, 'equivocality'.[21] It may be why Sayles argues that 'the individual manager does not have a clearly bounded job with neatly defined authorities and responsibilities. Rather, he [or she] is placed in the middle of a system of relationships out of which he [or she] must fashion an organization that will accomplish his [or her] objectives' (Sayles, 1964, p.27). To conclude, networking is *what happens because people are social actors* (Chapter 1) and social realities are socially constructed. This is why it never is possible fully to proceduralize descriptions (cognitive processes), activities, and interactions; this is why influence will 'stick' only when it is acceptable (see Chapter 3).

Top management organizing their projects

Our present interest is to provide an appreciation of the projects of top management. In our view, it is profitable to take seriously the implications of abandoning entitative perspectives of person and organization. This means, for example, that organizing is understood to be effected through the social, cognitive, and political processes through which top management pursue their projects. Some of these processes will be effected through formalized, hierarchical authority relationships. However, as we have seen, much is missed by restricting attention to vertical relationships and by restricting attention to one-way influence, grounded in legitimate power. As we have intimated, much is missed by focusing on the individual manager, failing to take seriously relationships as the vehicles through which organizing is achieved. Further, the projects and organizing of top management and those with whom they interact, must be recognized as grounded in social contructions of realities.

Applying our earlier arguments about persons and organizing, the activities of top management may be seen to reflect structures in the process of projects. These structures reflect the many 'conversations for action' (see Chapter 1) through which are produced social orders which favour some projects and not others. Whilst in varying ways constrained, top managers, like everybody else, to some extent select and negotiate constraints; much of the time they do so with, and through others. Given that activities and relationships never are proceduralized in full, top management builds understandings, that is 'appreciations', of social orders 'for themselves' so to speak: these are cognitive processes; and attempts, more or less strategically, to influence the understandings and activities of others with whom they perceive an interdependence: these are political processes.

Another way of making the above argument is to say that top management influence their contexts through more or less collective processes to handle, in a practical way, the 'core problems' of organizing. For any organizers, these problems are:

1. to work out what is and might be 'going on';

2. what, if anything to do about it; and

3. translating these understandings into action.

The processes in which top management organizes in relation to issues are not one-way processes of 'perfect control'. Rather, they are processes characterized by varying degrees of mutuality, reciprocity, cooperation and conflict. These are processes which are to varying degrees, 'open-ended' as one or more participants moves around their decision-making context to identify and develop issues, and to select and implement policies. These are processes in which managers may 'move around' to make legible and coherent[22] the valuations, interests and actions of actors who could demand an interest in an issue. On the other hand, 'moving around' may be minimal, and the valuations of particular actors may be ignored, discredited, or suppressed. Through these processes, actors achieve varying degrees of influence in the 'structures' which emerge in the 'process of their projects'. In these ways, a chief executive or top management team may more or less effectively influence the degree to which processes 'converge productively' to produce policies which all can understand and find agreeable – at least for a time.

Skilful organizing processes

Hosking and Morley have developed a general model with which to appreciate the processes of organizing. The model has been informed by theory and research in disciplines such as cognitive and social psychology, political science, anthropology, and organization studies (broadly defined). It has developed from our own work on leadership,[23] negotiation,[24] and team-work.[25] However, we hope that it may be used to illuminate processes of organizing in any context, along the lines set out by Hosking (1988b).[26]

We shall continue by outlining briefly the main elements in our model, making particular use of literatures in the areas with which immediately we are concerned, that is, literatures on management, on chief executives, and on strategic decision making. We will lay out the arguments in ways which emphasize what skilful processes look like, rather than constantly reiterating the phrase 'more or less'. Our constant references to chief executives are not intended to indicate that chief executives are the only actors to which our comments apply, they simply reflect the state of the literatures, combined with our present focus on top management. We go on to illustrate our arguments using accounts obtained in interviews with chief executives, interviews designed specifically to find out what sorts of projects they organized and how and why they did so (Hosking and Mann, 1988).[27]

Organizing: The main elements in the model

The main elements in the model are networking, values and interests (including projects or issues), issue structuring, and knowing. Each has relationships of reciprocal influence with the others. For this reason we could start our description anywhere. We will being with networking and proceed in the order described.

Networking
We have said much about this and now we can be brief. Networking is a social process in which actors move around their decision-making environment to build their own understandings (cognitive processes; Chapter 4), and to mobilize influence (political processes; Chapter 5). We argue that organizing processes are more skilful when actors move around to build and mobilize relationships. More precisely, they are likely to be skilful when actors network with those with whom they are, or could be, interdependent in relation to a particular issue. Networking is central to skilled organizing, and therefore, to the model. It is the vehicle through which social knowledge is built and mobilized, more or less collectively, to define and structure issues. In this way participants create, reproduce, and change their social orderings. Some achieve more influence than others; some, more than others, add value to their own lives.

Valuing, issues, and projects

We use the terms value and valuing as we always have done – broadly to refer to 'cognitions'. The language is intended to signal the evaluative quality of descriptions. Cognitions are a mix of value and what some would call fact: they are 'appreciative' (see Part 1). Through their networking, actors are able to appreciate actual and potential changes in the status quo. Individuals and groups initiate processes of strategic decision making when they construct a change as a major issue. Should they decide that something needs to be done – to avoid a threat or create an opportunity – and take action on that basis, they may be said to have created a project; project work is a more or less collective, strategic activity.

Theorists mean different things when they refer to strategic decision making. For some, the reference is to the topic or content of decisions – usually those which shape the organization and 'its' relations with its context; top management, that is, the 'strategic apex' are assumed to be the major actors. Others use the term strategic simply to mean important (Mintzberg, Raisinghani, and Theoret, 1976). Some define as strategic, decisions which are rare, consequential, and set precedents which constrain subsequent decisions; these criteria also make strategic decisions complex (Hickson et al., 1986).

Here, the term strategic is a reference to major changes which could constitute a threat or an opportunity. The project then is a more or less social, cognitive, and political process in which actors attempt to construct the change in ways that will 'add value' to their lives. Actors create and mobilize structures in the process of projects – to protect and promote valuations and interests which are more or less widely held; this is what organizing is about. From this it follows that the project, or issue, is the basic unit of analysis in the model (Hosking and Morley, 1988).

Issue structuring

Decision processes are performed through structuring the processes by which an issue is handled within and between groups. Over time, the processes may more or less resemble an 'analytical' or 'vigilant' process (see Chapter 4). As we have seen, one reason this will be so is because actors may enter and leave the process in the sense that they may only be involved for part of the time, and may achieve effective influence only occasionally, in particular relationships, and in relation to particular descriptions (Chapter 5). For these and other reasons, descriptions of the issue will change; the 'structure in process' will be 'coherent' to the extent that it is seen by participants to reflect a consistent set of values. As we observed earlier, these processes are to varying degrees collective. They may be described in terms of the functional phases or activities of working out what is and might be 'going on'; what if anything to do about it; and translating these processes into effective action to protect, promote and/or prejudice the interests and valuations of interdependent individuals and groups.

These processes are performed within and between various kinds of groups (see Chapter 5). The groups will differ in their outlooks, their histories, their influence relations, what they define as knowledge, and in what they think important. We have argued that there are reasons, descriptive and normative, to suppose that the processes of negotiation are particularly important in the structuring of issues. Briefly, the cognitive argument, in its descriptive form, is that a chief executive does negotiate descriptions – 'inside her own head' so to speak, and with others with whom she is interdependent. The normative development of this is that by negotiating descriptions a chief executive is able better to understand the issue – from their own point of view – and from the point of view of others with whom they are interdependent. Of course this works 'both ways' in that the other actors who participate in the negotiations also are able to build their understanding of the issue.

To say that actors understand should not be taken to imply that all have reached the same 'correct' description – as it did in a unitary, managerialist perspective. Rather, our reference to understanding means that a chief executive (or any other actor) knows how others with whom they are interdependent define the issue in relation to their own values and interests, knows what 'outcomes' and processes each would value, knows who needs to be involved, knows who could mobilize influence, and how, and so on. Such knowledge helps an actor (individual or group) consistently to achieve influence over the processes through which an issue is structured in 'thought' and action. This is how they are able to structure the issue in ways which are 'legible and coherent' – at least when judged in terms of their own values.

Of course the cognitive arguments are interconnected with political ones. The political argument is that negotiation is crucial for the management of differences (see Chapter 6). It seems to be especially important as a means to achieve influence which will be accepted. When influence is achieved through negotiation, relationships between actors are more likely to be those in which they will 'invent procedures' when necessary, without bureaucratic controls or coercion. This creates and sustains a 'legible and coherent' order which is sufficiently 'open-ended' that it can create and can organize changes in the status quo.

Knowing

Networking and issue structuring depend upon and contribute to, the building of 'knowledge bases'. We prefer the term 'knowing' in order to emphasize the active, constructive qualities of these processes. We lay particular stress on what we call process knowledge . This is knowledge of how to structure issues to protect and promote interests. Process knowledge includes knowledge of who – who to go to to build understandings – and through whom to mobilize influence. Process knowledge also is knowledge of why – why for example – negotiation is so important in the structuring of cognitive and political processes.

Knowledge is more or less *practical* – different relationships make it more or less possible to translate knowledge into individual and collective action. As we argued in relation to teamworking, organizing processes are skilful to the extent that actions reflect an understanding of what will work in relation to the values and interests of participants, actual and potential.[28]

Knowledge also is in some degree *social* in the sense of being part created, reproduced, and therefore – to some extent – shared by a particular social order. Of particular importance are the processes of forming collective judgements, often at the level of tacit understandings. Particularly important are processes in which there is negotiation of order, that is, processes in which agreements are reached to resolve an equivocal issue in a particular way, that is, in a way which reflects the memories (history) of the actors and their constructions of the future. This is how actors to some extent make their contexts and make their own constraints: by negotiating descriptions and social orderings, and by a more or less collective process in which they 'enact' a particular ideology, script, or schema (see Chapter 4).

A case illustration

The model, summarized above, was translated into a series of questions concerning the main concepts and arguments. A delicate balance was sought between providing enough structure for chief executives to tell us about these processes, without providing too much. The chief executives all were Heads of State Government Departments and Bureaux operating within a Federal system of government; twenty-six were interviewed in one state, four of whom were women; two women chief executives from departments in two other states also were interviewed. Eight transcripts have been analysed in detail. [29]

In what follows, we focus on the account provided by one chief executive. We called her Fleur for reason of the frequent use she makes of floral metaphors. We also refer to the accounts of the other chief executives where a wider context facilitates interpretation. We concentrate on the more or less direct evidence Fleur provided of networking, knowing, and negotiating in the structuring of two identified issues. We asked her to think of 'major changes' which she had initiated, or which had 'in some sense happened' during her period of office: one which she, in her role of chief executive, saw as a 'threat' to her department, and the other which she saw an an 'opportunity'. We said we would ask the same set of questions about each issue; we did so, avoiding our own technical terms, having first piloted the schedule with a former chief executive in the State Government.

The opportunity – An overview
Fleur had been head of her department for two years, a department which delivered a range of services to the community. In response to our invitation to describe an 'opportunity', Fleur told us of a strategic shift in her department's activities to increase the emphasis on one particular area of

service delivery. She observed that, before she arrived in the department, she had heard that it 'was struggling' in this area. Then when she arrived she found 'everywhere I turned it was an issue . . . I had a perception in my mind that that's what was needed, so I heard those messages . . . '

She went on to describe who she talked with to build her understanding of the issue, how she 'sent out messages in every way' to signal the new priority. 'I did no work on the details'. Rather, she appointed a new Senior Planner to the programme, and kept the responsibility with the Director. An 'implementation team', which she set up 'for the reforms' in the early days, also worked with the line managers to work out the details: 'My job was to set it in motion with a broad brush. But the potential to fix it was there with their existing staff plus the person we brought in . . . who had knowledge that was not available . . . Then I left it to the Directors.'

Networking, knowing, and issue structuring

Early in the interview, before our detailed questioning on the two issues, chief executives were asked 'what are the key things someone needs to know in order to be effective in your job?' This was routinely followed by the question 'are there any key things you haven't mentioned about the wider organization and environment?' These questions immediately led a number of the chief executives, including Fleur, to talk about what we call networking. Fleur remarked as follows:

> The Federal system . . . is critical to our organization . . . In fact I have planted my little flowers throughout key Government organizations by suggesting to Ministers that they should employ them, and now they're in very senior positions throughout (the country) . . . I wouldn't actually say this very loudly, but all throughout (the country) I have planted my flowers, and that's a very important network to me in my job, because it's very good for the state.

She went on to say 'I can toss an idea around with them and then expect the funding to come in at a later date . . . '

The above extracts suggest that networking facilitates influence. The following example – which she went on to describe – is more obviously emphasizing how networks may facilitate understanding. She told us of a particular area of activity which was being discussed at the Federal level. This was an activity in which her department was involved. She knew what was being planned by the Federal Government because a senior official, whom she had long known and who was involved in the planning, would regularly ring her up for advice. She observed: '. . . and so that's subtle but it's important. It's not devious or manipulative, it's what everybody does. I mean it's getting a network, getting the best information you can. I feel comfortable using that network because they've been a part of me at some stage.'

Fleur's observation that networking is what everybody does merits further attention. One of the male chief executives remarked: 'it's a buddy network . . . it really needs a couple of new people to come along with a completely new perspective'. This illustrates networking that is not open-ended – when the 'moving around' is moving around the same points of view – when the points of view themselves are closed because of the processes through which they will be reproduced (enactment) and sustained. For organizing to be skilful an actor, directly or through others, must move around the valuations of all actors with whom they might be interdependent in relation to an issue. Another of the women chief executives (Nita) commented that her colleagues told her she should network, but that she didn't really think it was necessary. However when describing the processes of defining and structuring an opportunity she remarked that when an issue came up, then she networked, otherwise it was just a waste of time.

Another way in which we tried to get at networking was to ask questions about resources – since as we have argued – networks are potential resources for understanding and influence. In response to the question 'What do you see as resources you can build up and mobilize in your job?' some chief executives again talked about networking. Fleur talked briefly about her budget, and about people, and then said: 'why is it that some people . . . make ten phone calls . . . and others spend one phone call because their network is so good? . . . so one has to look at networks that get in information.'

We also expected that if chief executives networked, this would be apparent in their descriptions of how they identified major changes, and how they monitored them. Here, more of our chief executives answered in ways which showed networking. One prototype is found in Nita's account; Nita remember said she didn't network. When she spoke of identifying and monitoring issues, Nita emphasized written materials, procedures, and work flows. In contrast, Fleur said: 'We've got a kind of verbal monitoring with the Directors. I have, I think all of us . . . have very close links with the non-government sector . . . so we hear a lot about what's going on.' Fleur talked a great deal about live action in one way or another and went on to observe: 'I suppose my own networks are important too – people who know me tell me things – particularly the women's network.' She concluded her answer to this question by saying, 'I go to endless meetings and talk'.

In all it seems that Fleur clearly sees networking as a major resource and as a process in which influence can be achieved. She most often speaks of networking as a cognitive process – for building her own understanding – but also as a process in which she can influence the evaluative beliefs of others .

As we noted earlier, the focus of the interview was on the structuring of two changes, one of which the chief executive described (retrospectively) as a threat, and one an opportunity. Again, it was expected that networking would be evident in the processes by which each issue was structured. As it turned out, the chief executives' descriptions of a threat gave relatively little indication of networking. This may have been why the issue was described as a threat – the relationship between the actor and the issue was such that they felt they couldn't network . For example, in a number of cases there was great need for secrecy, and in another case the chief executive felt constrained by the need to appear to be in support of the Minister's policy. However, descriptions of threats and opportunities also differed in the extent to which chief executives described themselves as reacting to (threat) or creating (opportunity) the change.

Where descriptions of opportunities were concerned, the situation was very different; most of the chief executives spoke of networking in their account of the processes through which they structured their projects. Fleur described at some length the project summarized above – to shift the emphasis of her department's activities so that an area in which they previously were weak became an area of strength. We talked her through the 'structure in the process of the project'. We asked 'How did you first become aware of the need for this change?'. She replied:

> before I arrived . . . I knew on the grapevine that the state was struggling . . . .I also had a number of women (professional colleagues), one of whom was an old friend of mine who was working in the area here, who came to me and said 'your department really is the pits' . . . she was one of the many people who came to me and said, 'You've got to do something' . . . everywhere I turned it was an issue.

Chief executives were asked how they built up their understanding of the potential significance of the change. Fleur said: '[people] . . . talking to me, sending messages through the Regional Directors, through other people. They would meet me at a hundred million functions I spoke at. They were friends of mine. It came in through every network.' As we saw, her description of the further development of the project showed her as structuring the process, but not getting involved in the details. This is consistent with other researchers' findings that top management are most involved at the beginning and end of the process (Hickson et al.,1986; Heller et al., 1987).

Fleur's descriptions of the structuring of issues were very revealing of her evaluative beliefs, that is, of the valuations she had developed about the how and why of effective organizing processes. For example, she made reference to valued means such as: 'keeping responsibility with the manager of the programme . . . I mean, I come from the line, I have respect for the line, so I gave the Director permission, psychological permission, to go harder than he was going before.'

She also referred a great deal to getting appropriate knowledge structured into the issue. So, for example, when speaking of the Director of the programme she said: 'he also knew a lot of things. The knowledge was there but it needed to be released.' Then, when she decided that there was a need for someone to 'take us the next step' she made an outside appointment to bring in the appropriate knowledge. Further, she showed she realized that the 'new' actors' contributions would have to be acceptable in order for her influence to be effective. She said: 'I worked hard at having her accepted . . . I got the department to accept that we needed someone with greater knowledge'.

It appears that Fleur understood the importance of shaping and selecting networks. This is implied by the appointment, described above, which she made from outside. It also is indicated by what she had to say about the composition of the implementation team. In respect of the latter, she said they were 'people that I hand picked and trusted'.

Relationship building was also signalled as important in her answers to questions about influence and choice. When prompted on the role of the Minister she observed: 'Well, we considered it important to get an ally with the Minister and (the Minister) stayed with it all the time'. As to who had the 'strongest influence' on the policies finally implemented, she expressed the view that this came from 'the front line workers' – with whom she conducted an extensive opinion gathering exercise when she first was appointed – and the next 'would have been other people in other networks'. This sets her apart from many of the other chief executives who reported themselves as achieving the most effective influence over the policies that were implemented (see also Hickson *et al.*, 1986).

Towards the end of the interview, a series of explicit and direct questions were asked about relationships. These were: 'Relationships can sometimes be helpful – do you find this true in your job?', and 'Who are the key people you find it helpful to know?' In response to these, Fleur distinguished something like eight different 'categories of contact'. These included: those in her own department, especially her managers; people who make the decisions in the central agencies (treasury, personnel . . .); those in the Minister's circle of influence; people in similar departments in other States; 'powerful and strong friends' in the Federal government, and 'contacts in all sorts of networks'.

In answer to our question 'why is it helpful to know them?' she made explicit reference to understanding, and influence; her answers suggested that she understood the strategic importance of networking. She referred to the following: access to resources; picking up on a direction and being able to mobilize quickly when necessary; being able to 'influence the shape of directions'; and influencing the 'image of the department': 'if you have a warm relationship . . . they are more likely to think better of your department'.

In our last question we 'went fishing' so to speak. We remarked that 'studies have shown that chief executives like yourself have very little time when they are not talking with someone – in meetings – on the phone and so on. Some complain that this means they cannot do their job. What do you think?' Fleur replied:

> I am very careful about to whom I'm accessible and it's usually people who are important . . . to the way the organization runs . . . they're often junior people . . . nobody comes and chats until sometimes at about 5 o'clock when someone's had a bad day . . . and they need to tell me about it . . . as someone said to me, your role is to be the most important listener, and I think that's right.

We probably have much to learn about the skills of networking, however, Fleur's reply certainly illustrates that, to be skilled, networking does not mean talking to anyone, at any time, about anything.

Knowing

Fleur made considerably more explicit reference to knowledge that any of the other chief executives, and often did so in the context of networking. We will say something about five areas of knowing which previously we have identified as important.

Negotiation. We have argued that all actors negotiate descriptions and, to varying degrees, negotiate social order within and between groups. We also have argued that organizing processes are more likely to be skilful when participants know when, how, and why to negotiate; this is partly what it means to describe a process as 'legible and coherent'. The often tacit nature of negotiating makes the processes particularly hard to 'get at' in chief executives' accounts. We took the deliberate decision to make no explicit reference to negotiation until late on in the interview. Until then, Fleur had made many explicit references to negotiation, but these all were in relation to processes of negotiating financial resources with the treasury. We then said: 'we are interested in the extent to which your job requires negotiation as a more or less constant characteristic.' Fleur said: 'all the time really . . . it's what I do all day long . . . '. Her explanation seemed largely to focus on her belief in the need to achieve acceptable influence and the need to get others to 'invent procedures' – understandings on which we have placed considerable emphasis. Further elaborations on these themes also implied knowing when and why to negotiate.

> Well, if you're a person who doesn't make decisions – who tries to get other people to make decisions – then you have to negotiate movement. But I am very clear about what is negotiable . . . if I determine it's a good idea it's not negotiable, but what's negotiable is the implementation stretch. But that's rare though. Mostly I negotiate trades and deals and use of time, that's what it's all about . . . . I have a fundamental philosophy about balance . . . you can't kind of force a major change in one area because something goes wrong.

Capacities and demands. We argue that organizing processes are skilful when the capacities of actors are linked to the demands of their tasks. Some chief executives understand this, and attempt to make this knowledge practical, others do not. Like negotiation, this process may be relatively hard to 'get at'. There certainly were major differences between the chief executives in the degree to which this knowledge was evident in their accounts.

We already have seen in Fleur's description of the opportunity how she attempted to link capacities and demands by bringing in new expertise, giving the director 'psychological permission to go harder' and so on. Further illustrations of this process seem evident in Fleur's answer to the question 'Do you think your approach to decision making suits your department?' (we had remarked right at the start that we saw decision making as something that goes on all the time). Her reply suggested that for her, enabling was a strategy of of this kind. She replied:

> Yes . . . because it seems to have worked inasmuch as it's made the Directors be very confident and powerful in their own area, where they weren't two years ago (when she first was appointed). I mean, one measure would be what's the capacity of my next level in the organization. The final test is how they can then transfer that down to the next level.

Valuations and interests. For organizing processes to be skilful, participants must know what they themselves are trying to protect and promote – values which may be more or less widely shared. Similarly participants, including the chief executive, must understand the valuations and interests of other actors with whom they are interdependent in relation to an issue. Influential participants are likely to understand at least some valuations and interests because they themselves have participated in their structuring. Fleur nicely illustrates our argument that values need to be provoked, developed, and 'kept in' the process to make it legible and coherent to participants. She does so by her reply to our question 'what do you see as the most important things you have done in this job and why?' She described a process she initiated after her appointment when she interviewed 600 of her staff 'to see how they would like the organization to operate'. This exercise was used to identify 'problems', and therefore valuations, and was one of the processes out of which the 'opportunity' described was 'identified'. Through these processes ' . . . we got a lot of really good debate going in the organization to get our fundamental principles upon which we stand in our work'.[30]

Dilemmas. Dilemmas are endemic in strategic decision processes – these are choice situations where there are major costs (judged in relation to some values) if the policy does not change, and major costs (judged against other values) if it does. Talk of dilemmas is another way of describing what makes social realities equivocal. Dilemmas arise partly because of the participation and claims for involvement of interdependent actors whose valuations and interests – as implicated in the issue – are seen by them to conflict. However, actors also may experience dilemmas because they hold conflicting evaluative beliefs about an issue or some aspect of it (see Janis and Mann, 1977). This is illustrated by Fleur's observation that 'There's an interesting tension between being critical, being constructively critical, and being too soft and accepting poor quality work.' A little later she said: 'for each person you have to design their own, well your own set of responses to get the best response from them. And, at the same time, you have to be seen to be fair and respond to everybody in the same way.'

Issue specific knowledge. The skilful organizing of an issue requires a great deal of knowledge which is to some extent issue specific (e.g. Kotter, 1982; Gupta, 1984). We have seen that Fleur made many references to knowledge. She also raised an interesting area of uncertainty between the relative importance of knowledge of 'what' and knowledge of 'how'. She indicated that she and others were uncertain as to whether or not a chief executive had to have specialist knowledge of the department's services – what she referred to as product knowledge. She remarked that in her view, in her area, it was essential. It is perhaps relevant that Fleur had relevant 'product knowledge'. Another chief executive, who did not, also raised this uncertainty, and observed that, in her area, it probably was not essential.[31]

Last, Fleur also referred to the importance of what we call process knowledge only some of which is likely to be issue specific. Specifically, she mentioned the importance of knowing: how your department interrelates with other departments in the public service; how to work with politicians; how political processes (party and civil service) work; a chief executive's role in the political process – to implement the wishes of the Minister; the history of your department's relationships with other departments; who's 'got power', and who to influence.

Conclusion

Fleur rated her 'batting average' on major issues as 'nine out of ten'. We think she may well be right. She seemed to have a coherent and practical understanding of the cognitive, social, and political processes through which issues are identified and handled within and between groups. She articulated a clear understanding of the many ways in which networking – not just her own – but also her managers', could help build understandings and mobilize influence. She seemed clearly to understand the reasons why negotiating is a crucial qualitiy of the processes through which changes are constructed and implemented.

We have been forced constantly to focus our account of organizing in the retrospective accounts of our chief executives. Our methodology makes it impossible to track the ebb and flow of the involvements and influence of particular actors over time. Our methodology also made it difficult to track the negotiation of order (value and influence) over time, to identify the different descriptions of different actors, the processes through which identified actors achieved most effective influence, and how consistently they did so. This said, our appreciative framework seemed to make sense to the chief executives, our interpretation of their accounts seemed to make sense to them, and the perspective makes sense when judged in the context of current understandings about persons and organization. This approach makes a lot more sense than the unitary and managerialist focus on chief executives as 'great leaders', who gain the commitment of others to their own projects through their effective manipulation of beautiful values.

Notes ====

1. See also Eliott Jaques' fascinating discussion of normal psychological values and the requisite relationship between these and institutional structures. The central idea is that relationships are requisite when variety in the external environment is matched by variety in the internal systems of control. When the relationship is 'anti-requisite' the institution is said to be 'paranoiagenic' – breeding distrust and weakening social relationships (see Jaques, 1976).
2. Also see Chapter 8, in which we discuss the significance of this approach in the context of projects in engineering product design, and teamwork in general.
3. Judi Marshall's (1984) study *Women Managers* has recently come to our attention. We are interested to find the extent to which some of our key arguments concerning networking, power, and valuations, converge with hers.
4. As we noted earlier, most of these studies are of male managers. In this set, Stewart's work provides the exception, since it does include some women managers.
5. See also Kotter and Lawrence (1974); Landsberger (1962); Mintzberg (1973, 1989); Stewart (1976), and Sayles (1979).
6. See also, for example, Sayles (1964, 1979); Dalton (1959); and Kotter and Lawrence (1974).
7. Many of these may be little more than 'contacts' for so many to be sustained. See our earlier discussion of exchange processes.
8. See also Burns (1954, 1957); Kelly (1964).
9. We have borrowed this form of words from Marshall (1984). Before reading her book we would not have been able to make this point so briefly. We believe that there is much more to be said about the differences between men and women with respect to why they network.
10. Also see Chapter 4.
11. Meaning, what the chief executive thinks important.
12. Also see Peters and Waterman (1982) and Bennis and Nanus (1985), to take just two examples.
13. We have found the work of Smircich and her associates most useful (see Smircich and Morgan, 1982; Calas and Smircich, 1988).
14. This argument was illustrated in our earlier reference to the chief executive who reported that relationships are important to her because, amongst other reasons, they gave her opportunities to connect and enjoy more communal relations .
15. See Chapter 4.
16. See Neisser's (1976) account of 'ordinary seeing', which is summarized in Chapter 4.
17. See Part 2. Also see the work of Wrapp (1984) which we have described earlier in this chapter.
18. See Chapters 4, 5, and 6.
19. See Pondy (1978); Weick (1979); Smircich and Morgan (1982); Moch and Huff (1989).
20. The point about networks, therefore, is that they supplement authority relations and formalized 'organization structures': sometimes they may supplant or subvert them.
21. Uncertainty is often taken to imply that there is a 'right' answer in some set of possible

answers: the problem correctly to determine which. Equivocality makes no such assumption, but simply recognizes that social actors are confronted with multiple descriptions of reality: the problem is to 'select' that one that – at minimum – actors will not find unacceptable, or one which they cannot effectively contest.

22. See Chapter 8.

23. See Hosking (1983, 1987, 1988b); Morley and Hosking (1986); Hosking and Morley (1988). Also see Chapter 9.

24. See Morley (1986; in press, b). Also see Chapter 6.

25. See Morley (in press, a). Also see Chapter 7.

26. Also see Hosking and Fineman (1991).

27. A more detailed description of the methodology of the study and its findings will be found in Hosking (in press, a).

28. Potential because an individual or a group may demand an 'involvement' and be able to influence the process of issue structuring.

29. The study was designed, and the interviews conducted by, Dian-Marie Hosking and Leon Mann. The study was funded by a grant from The Flinders University of South Australia.

30. It has been suggested that effective groups are more self-conscious about their own performance. See the discussion of team development in Morley (1991).

31. Our own suspicion is that it is extremely important. We have given some of our reasons in Chapter 1 and in Chapter 6.

Chapter 9

Leadership processes

Introduction

We have argued that relations between person and organization must be understood as relations of mutual creation. This means recognizing that persons to some extent make their own contexts whilst also being made by them. We have emphasized a view of person as an active and social sense-maker. At the same time, we have stressed that 'not anything goes'. Rather, making sense of the equivocality of a given context – in 'thought and action' – reflects and is reflected in the relational processes between participants. Relational processes are conceptualized as social, cognitive, and political. Each process has been shown to be related to the other. What is most funda-mental about relational processes is that they are grounded in helping. All actors need the help of others in constructing their identities and their sense of social order, and need the help of others in order to act in relation to them.

Of course relational processes may be more or less helpful. We have explored how this is so through the processes of organizing projects. To do this, we developed the language of skill, leadership, and social order (or culture). The processes (cognitive, social, and political) of organizing projects were said to be more or less skilful processes in which certain sorts of cultures emerged. The language of cultures allows us to discuss the 'how' of individual and collective processes in which people construct descriptions of their contexts. In the process of constructing order, actors seek and gain support for their descriptions, relative to the descriptions of others. People and groups adjust their lines of action in relation to others. Similarly, participants show more or less willingness to move around, and in so doing, to help themselves and to help others with whom they are interdependent.

Last, the language of leadership was introduced in order further to discuss the ways in which relational processes could be more or less skilful. There are many reasons why we wish to give leadership such prominence. Put in the most general terms, the reasons lie with what we have described as the intrinsically political qualities of organizing. These we have conceptualized in terms of differences in valuing and influence. Valuing is endemic in organizing because actors have to make sense of their contexts, yet they differ from one another in their relations with their contexts such that they also differ in their valuations. Influence is endemic because actors are interdependent and because they differ in their relationships with their contexts such that some are more able than others to mobilize influence. Given these political qualities, certain questions seem to follow. These include: how is influence achieved (for example, by coercion or negotiation), by whom (only a few or by many), to reflect and support what (and whose) valuations and influence? Remember, whilst social realities are socially constructed, 'not anything goes'. This leads to the question what can 'go'? and how might we seek to appreciate the ways in which processes are more or less helpful for participants? This is where leadership comes in.

We see leadership as *a more or less skilful process of organizing, achieved through negotiation, to achieve acceptable influence over the description and handling of issues within and between groups.* Skilful leadership processes promote and support a culture of productivity. This is defined by relationships in which people see the emerging processes as: *legible*, in the sense that equivocality is understood to be reduced in recognizable and agreeable ways; *coherent*, in the sense that there is an integrated structure throughout the process; and *open-ended* in that the relationships are flexible – they can create and accommodate change. Participants are likely to differ in the extent to which they see each themselves and others consistently to influence the legibility, coherence, and openness of their culture. Further, participants are likely to see each other as achieving influence in different ways – ways which are more or less acceptable to them in that context (culture). Finally, some – or indeed all – participants may come to be perceived as making contributions which consistently achieve acceptable influence, and come to be expected to do so. *Contributions of this kind we refer to as contributions to leadership; those who make such contributions are those we define as leaders.*

Looking forward

It is important to understand that the picture of leadership laid out here is radically different from that which usually is found in the literatures of Human Resource Management (HRM) and Organizational Behaviour (OB). This should not be surprising since, as we have seen, these literatures are dominated by entitative perspectives of person and organization. In the literatures of HRM and OB individuals are set apart from one another and from their wider relational setting. Social relationships are reduced to inputs and outcomes and their human significance is reduced to potential instrumentalities for the achievement of individual gain. Leaders (persons) are emphasized rather than leadership (processes). Leadership is understood fundamentally as a means of manipulation. Leaders manipulate the instrumentalities that their relationships with non-leaders provide to pursue 'organizational' goals. As a result, and as we shall see, traditional approaches provide a very partial and restrictive perspective on leadership.

We shall continue by reviewing entitative approaches, paying particular attention to themes which highlight what is distinctive about our own perspective, and drawing upon the arguments laid out in Parts 1 and 2. This allows us to show how the social, cognitive, and political aspects of leadership have been dealt with and, in this way, to elaborate our own, very different views. Our review is not intended to be detailed and comprehensive; the interested reader can turn to a number of relatively recent texts and articles for this purpose.[1] Following our review, we focus on leadership processes which create structure in the process of projects. Our conceptual framework is outlined;[2] detailed attention then is given to the cognitive and political qualities of three major leadership processes: networking, negotiation, and enabling. We conclude that these processes, when skilfully performed, contribute to the creation of a culture of productivity.

Leaders in organizations

In the literatures of HRM and OB we find those concepts of person and of organization which we call entitative. By definition, an entitative perspective entails a sharp separation between the person and their context. Where interests in leadership are concerned, this separation is revealed in over-sharp distinctions between leaders and non-leaders – the latter being viewed as followers – and between leaders and other aspects of their context such as their group's task and the 'atmosphere' of the group (see Hosking, 1981). The result is a very partial and restrictive perspective on leadership in which treatments of the social, cognitive and political aspects of leadership are not as we would wish.

Leaders, managers, and non-managers

The literatures of OB and HRM are characterized by sharp distinctions between persons as either managers or non-managers, the former being viewed as leaders, and the latter as non-leaders. This approach is accompanied by a focus on leaders (managers) as persons rather than leadership as a process. This description needs some slight qualification in that a few theorists reject the assumption that all managers necessarily are leaders. For example, some prefer to regard managers as leaders only when they achieve influence through power bases which are independent of their formal position (Etzioni, 1965; Katz and Kahn, 1978) or when they 'do the right thing', and see themselves as leaders (Bennis and Nanus, 1985). However, such refinements are made within an entitative perspective. In the context of our present discussion it is important to note, for example, that theorists usually start from a distinction between managers and non-managers, and few have considered non-managers as leaders.[3]

In this emphasis on leaders in organization, we find an implicit dualist treatment of competence. In other words, managers are treated as though they share certain competencies which set them apart from non-managers. Few theorists abandon the restrictive and narrow focus on leaders 'in' the context of formal organization. Few attempt to separate person and process in ways which recognize that many persons, and not just managers, may make leadership contributions.[4] It is just such an approach that we take here. Our primary interest is in leadership processes. We recognize that, over time, many may make consistent contributions to leadership. Those who do so may or may not be managers. Leadership processes are not best bounded by the assumed limits of formal organization but rather must be examined in the processes of projects.

Personal inputs

The traditional distinction between person and context also is revealed in a focus on the personal characteristics of 'leaders' who, typically, are managers. Leaders' characteristics are treated as personal properties. For example, attention has been directed to personality traits and motives, as these might be reflected in the achievement of leader status and/or as possible predictors of a leader's effectiveness in promoting group and/or organizational performance (Bass, 1981; Bryman, 1986). The leader's personal characteristics are considered as inputs to a more or less complex input-output relationship. This approach permits leader effectiveness to be treated as an outcome of interactions between inputs from a leader and inputs from their context.

In the entitative approach we find little recognition of the subtle and complex ways in which social contexts may support or fail to support the development and expression of particular personalities. Yet, as we have argued, 'who a person is' depends, in a very real sense, on who they are with and why they are there. Where managers and leaders are concerned, the processes of reciprocal influence have already been illustrated in our discussions of authoritarianism, and of psychodynamic interpretations of relationships between chief executives and their organizations. It was clear that the chief executives' personalities, as reflected in their performance style, seemed only to be reflected in the performance style of the wider organization (context) when that style received social support.

The entitative perspective is reflected not just in appproaches which focus on personality, but also in those approaches which emphasize a leader's (manager's) power and influence, leadership style, leader behaviour, cognitive abilities, and knowledge. Whichever is emphasized, each is treated as the property of a leader, who is understood as independent of his or her context. Power, behaviour, style, or knowledge, are understood as a personal inputs.

Such inputs are then combined with independent inputs from the context to predict outcomes. For these reasons, an entitative perspective cannot take seriously our earlier arguments about social construction, emergent processes, and the mutuality of relationships between actor and context. When treated as a personal property, a leader's style, behaviour, power, or knowledge cannot be understood as co-constructed by leaders and other group members, yet this is precisely the approach which is required.[5]

Inputs from contexts

As we have seen, an entitative approach to person goes naturally with an entitative approach to context. For this reason it should not be surprising that, in the leadership literatures, the entitative approach is revealed, not just in the concept of person, but in the associated concept of organization. Here we put the other side of the coin, so to speak. Whether the focus is on leaders of groups, or leaders of organizations, the context within which a leader is situated is theorized and/or measured independently of the leader. This is revealed both in explicit treatments of contextual factors, but also is apparent in what is left implicit and taken-for-granted.

Dealing first with what is explicit, the typical treatment of organizational characteristics in the literatures is as objects which top managers act *on* and junior managers act *in*. So, we find what we previously have described as a physicalist approach to the qualities of contexts. Similar points can be made about the treatment of groups as the contexts for leaders and their effectiveness. Group tasks are defined as structured or unstructured independently of the leader (eg. Fiedler, 1967). Subordinates are treated as features of the leader's context and defined, for example, as mature or immature (see Hersey and Blanchard, 1977) as though this were true regardless of their relational setting.

Turning to the implicit assumptions which characterize the OB and HRM literatures, leaders and their effectiveness are understood usually in the context of formal organization. It has become commonplace to assume that leaders provide their inputs from a position of authority and therefore through power which their followers (subordinates) see as legitimate. In other words, the emphasis is on top–down influence in the context of a hierarchy of authority and responsibility. A managerialist perspective is reflected in the tacit assumption that interests are widely shared by managers and by non-managers. This is what we earlier described as a unitary perspective. If it is accepted that differences of interest may be found, it is assumed that the differences are compatible. In sum, the typical treatment of contexts sets them apart from actors and social action. It does so by adopting a unitary and physicalist perspective in which organizational structures, goals, and valuations are treated as contextual characteristics which are independent of what we call the cognitive, social, and political processes of organizing.

Our earlier discussions have shown the limitations of a perspective which rigidly sets apart person and context. In our discussions of cognitive and social processes, and of organization, we have pointed to the limitations of viewing 'organizational characteristics' as physicalist realities which exist independently of actors and social action. We have argued for a shift of emphasis to social constructions of realities – in 'thought' and 'deed'. As an illustration, the case of the Danish Television company showed that there is an important sense in which structures are constructed in and through social processes. For these reasons, and others, we reject these unitary and physicalist assumptions in favour of a pluralist perspective which emphasizes the processes through which social realities are socially constructed.

Processes as interactions between inputs and outcomes

Entitative treatments of person and organization treat their relations as interactions between independent inputs. These interactions are understood to produce lawful outcomes. The usual model is a more or less complex contingency model in which effectiveness is viewed as an output dependent on statistical interactions between (independent) inputs.[6] Leaders and their subordinates are understood as of more or less instrumental value to 'the organization'. Leaders are encouraged to consider their own actions, and their subordinates, in terms of instrumentalities and how these might be manipulated. All actors are understood to relate to one another in terms of the potential instrumental value of their relationships.

Taken as a whole, this entitative perspective of leaders in organization results in a very partial and restrictive set of understandings concerning persons, processes, and contexts. We will continue by examining traditional treatments of the social, cognitive, and political aspects of leaders and contexts. The entitative separation of person and context means that these processes are not theorized adequately. Whilst we examine these literatures it will be helpful to bear in mind what we previously have said about processes. First, organizing processes should be understood as about helping rather than grounded in the traditional view of people and relationships as a source of instrumentalities which may be manipulated for personal gain. Second, our concept of processes is that they are best understood as reciprocal and emergent. These are processes of mutual creation in which a person to some extent, makes his or her context, and vice versa.

Treatments of social processes

As we have seen, the study of leadership often has come down to the study of leaders, who they are, what they do, and with whom. 'Who they are' means managers possessing personal characteristics which set them apart from their context. 'What they do', is reduced to behaviours or activities, and 'with whom' reduced to 'contacts', classified and understood in terms of formal status (subordinate, lateral and the like). The social aspects of a leader's context often are reduced to the number, 'variety' and status (peer, subordinate and the like) of their 'contacts'.

Accounts of what leaders do may be at the level of specific behaviours such as 'offers suggestion' or 'seeks opinion' (eg. Bales, 1970). Descriptions also may be offered by using broader concepts which still can be linked to specific behaviours because of the way the categories were derived. Such concepts include, for example, 'task oriented', 'consideration', and 'initiating structure'. What 'leaders do' also may be described in very general terms, going beyond behaviours which are face-to-face (see Pondy, 1978). Descriptions of what leaders do may be yet more broad. Some, for example, refer to the many activities, systems, and procedures through which leaders might shape a setting. Examples of 'doing' here could include the various (personal and impersonal) means by which particular kinds of contribution are counted and rewarded, for example, through performance measurement and through financial controls. Other examples might be found in the different priorities given to different agenda items in management meetings (eg. Peters, 1978; Bennis and Nanus, 1985).

From our point of view, what is important about the treatment of behaviour or activity is that it is viewed as an input, made by a leader, to a context. Often what we see is the reduction of social processes to what revealingly are called 'oral interactions', referring to time spent in talking (see Yukl, 1989, p.257). Oral interactions are understood as giving and getting information (for example), and little interest is shown in the processes of social construction through which participants come to understand a leader's contributions in particular ways. In other words, a physicalist assumption is revealed in the expectation that different actors, whether they be participants or investigators should produce very much the same descriptions. This being so, if actors differ in their descriptions of their leader's behaviour, these differences are understood to reflect error variance and, perhaps, 'real' differences between subordinates in their social interactions with their leader.

The reciprocal qualities of relational processes cannot properly be considered from within the perspective described. Processes – in our sense – are not discussed. Instead, processes are reduced to connections between independent inputs and outcomes. So, for example, it simply is not possible to contemplate the different leader–subordinate relationships and how in each the processes of reciprocal influence and mutual creation emerge and are played out in different ongoing relationships. What we lack is attention to the social construction of relationships as expressed, for example, in what actors define as knowledge; in the ways they act in relation to one another; and in their collective project work. As a result, we lack sufficient attention to the creation of settings[7] – by all participants in leadership – not just leaders.

It is important to stress that what we are calling for cannot be produced by any approach which rigidly sets leaders apart from their contexts and therefore, from their relationships with other people, their relational histories, and so on. It cannot be supplied by yet another contingency model in which a leader's context is argued to influence that leader's behaviour, and/or the relationship between their behaviour and their leadership effectiveness. Rather, what is needed is a shift away from the individualistic fallacy and its emphasis on individual behaviour, stripped from sense making, to a focus on the individual and collective processes through which people make cultures and cultures make people. This necessarily means a shift from the physicalist emphasis to one in which social realities and sense making are firmly located in social relationships. The latter must be understood in ways which differ radically from the input-output model of the leadership literatures.

These arguments imply that cognitive processes must be recognized as intimately interconnected with social processes and the symbolic qualities of social interaction must get the attention they deserve. More broadly, we may say that attempts to understand the social processes of leadership must theorize these processes as intimately interconnected with cognitive and political processes. Yet when we examine the relevant literatures, it is clear that this is not the approach which usually is taken to link leadership with processes of exchange,[8] networking,[9] and negotiation[10] (see Chapter 8).

Whilst there is much of value in this literature it fails sufficiently to emphasize the processes of social construction as endemic to the processes of negotiation and exchange. Perhaps partly for this reason they fail sufficiently to move away from the traditional view of social processes as 'backwards' and 'forwards' transactions[11] between independent entities abstracted from the wider relational setting. Relationships are understood in terms of the traditional notion of instrumentalities. That relationships are grounded in helping is left unstated and undeveloped. In sum, these approaches set leaders apart from their contexts such that the interrelated social, cognitive and political processes of leadership – theorized in the very special ways we have here – cannot be discussed .

Treatments of cognitive processes

In their recent review of leadership theory and research, Fiedler and House (1988) observed that 'cognitive theories are becoming increasingly dominant in the leadership area, as in psychology in general' (p.78). As examples they cited studies of attributions: what kinds of things seem to affect how a leader describes the qualities or performance of his or her subordinates, along with how subordinates perceive their leader (e.g. Mitchell, Green, and Wood, 1981). Other examples of cognitive theories included the social information processing approach of Lord and his associates (Lord, 1985) and Fiedler's own 'cognitive resource utilization theory' (Fiedler and Garcia, 1987).

In addition to the work referred to by Fiedler and House, a cognitive focus is evident in the line of work in which plans, strategies, problem solving, 'path finding' and decision making are emphasized (e.g. Kotter, 1982; Kaplan, 1984;

Vroom and Yetton, 1973; Leavitt, 1989). Further, we should add that contingency theories of leadership, to which Fiedler and House also refer, have implicit and explicit cognitive elements. Contingency theories imply that leaders do, or should, diagnose their context so that they may adjust their behaviour appropriately (e.g. Vroom and Jago, 1988); this is the understanding aspect of their leadership. Equally, the logic of a contingency argument is that leaders influence the cognitions of others, that is, their understandings, assumptions, or 'vision'. They do this to influence the performance of those persons who are instrumental to their own goal achievement (e.g. House, 1971; Bass, 1985). As we have seen, whatever their precise details, contingency approaches view effectiveness as an outcome of leader inputs in interaction with other inputs from the leaders setting.

Much of this work has been described as 'new' (House and Singh, 1987). However, most of it is more of the same and presents a very partial and restrictive view of cognition. And yet more work of this kind has been called for, along with attention to the development of a taxonomy of leadership situations. From this point of view, contingency approaches would be judged more adequate to the extent that they appear to deal with all possible leadership settings: 'If exhaustive, or nearly so, such taxonomies would allow researchers to determine the kinds of leader behaviour and leader motivation most appropriate for each situational category' (House and Singh, 1987, p.688).

When judged in terms of the interests we wish to pursue, traditional treatments of the cognitive aspects of leadership are of little help . Many of the problems can be traced back to entitative distinctions between person and context. In other words, over-sharp distinctions are made between leaders and their contexts. Treatments of 'knowledge', or 'information' are what we have called 'physicalist'. Cognition and behaviour are emphasized at the expense of interests in intelligent social action. Cognitive processes are not linked with social processes such that it is possible seriously to pursue the question of how we know – how cognitions are formed and reformed in and about social relations. To put the point slightly differently, cognitive activity typically is treated as 'off line', so to speak, rather than 'inseparably woven into' and 'simultaneously with' action (Weick, 1983, p.222). In these literatures we find little attention to the interrelated social, cognitive, and political processes of sense making.[12]

Cognitive processes must be understood as *sense-making* processes in which many of the limits are conventional, not matters of 'right' or 'wrong' (to be defined independently of the context). When social realities are taken seriously as socially constructed, new questions are asked about how understandings are negotiated in the course of conversations. These are individual and collective processes in which actors create relationships which are more or less helpful for one another.

Treatments of political processes

Political processes are endemic to organizing. We have emphasized two essential and interrelated elements: interdependent actors differ in their relationships with their contexts[13] such that they differ in their valuations, and differ in their abilities to mobilize influence. Given this emphasis, the question is how these elements are dealt with in discussions of leadership in the OB and HRM literatures. The short answer is that they are not. The reason, broadly put, is that an entitative perspective defines political processes out of existence. It does so partly because the concept of process reduces processes to more or less instrumental input-output connections. This is the case, both in the leadership literatures, and in the literatures on organizational politics (e.g. Vredenburgh and Maurer, 1984).

The concept of what is political is also deficient. This partly is due to the ways in which the contexts of leadership have been handled, both implicitly and explicitly. So, when leadership is linked explicitly to organization it usually is taken for granted that goals and valuations[14] either are, or should be, shared by all. Similarly, when leadership is theorized in relation to groups, we find tacit assumptions about hierarchy, legitimate power, and shared valuations as characteristics of the organizational setting. In other words, we find what we earlier described as a perspective characterized by unitary and physicalist assumptions – assumptions which gloss the issue of differences in valuations and differences in influence.

Unitary and physicalist assumptions permeate the so called 'new' approaches to leadership. These include both the 'cognitive' approaches which we already have discussed, and 'charismatic' and 'transformational leadership' theories. In their review of leadership theory and research, Fiedler and House described this latter line of work as follows.

> These theories describe leaders in terms of articulating a vision and mission, and creating and maintaining a positive image in the minds of followers and superiors . . . (they) primarily address the actions of leaders that cause subordinates to *change* their values, goals, needs and aspirations. (Fiedler and House, 1988, pp.78–9)

Much the same could be said of the recently fashionable emphasis on leaders as designers of cultures (e.g. Bennis and Nanus, 1985), 'organizational character' (Peters, 1978), and 'cultures of excellence' (e.g. Peters and Waterman, 1982; see Chapter 8). Together, these literatures take for granted either that actors do share, or should share, the same valuations. This is the case, whether the valuations concern goals or structures. In the case of the latter, actors are expected similarly to perceive organizational structures, including structures of legitimate authority and power[15] and structures of value.

No discussion of political processes would be complete without examining the handling of power and influence. Perhaps the one feature that definitions and perspectives on leadership share is a focus on influence. However, the dominance of the unitary and physicalist assumptions has made it impossible to take seriously differences between actors in their ability to mobilize power. Again, the root of the problem lies with the underlying entitative concepts of persons and organization. In the case of persons, the entitative concept is reflected in the treatment of power as something possessed by a leader, leading to questions such as 'how much power should a leader have?' and what power bases and influence tactics should a leader choose to mobilize (see Yukl, 1989). In the case of organization, the prevailing entitative concept treats power as a structural characteristic (see e.g. House and Singh, 1987).

We have seen that power is not best understood, either as a property of an organization, or as the property of an individual. Rather, power must be understood as a quality of relationships. From our perspective, what is fundamental about relationships is that they are about helping in the context of interdependence. Furthermore, our arguments about valuing – that social realities are constructed socially – have very important implications for the ways in which influence must be theorized. For these reasons, our perspective on power and influence looks very different from that which dominates the literatures. We will develop these arguments by discussing leadership as a more or less skilful process through which actors create cultures which may be more or less helpful.[16]

It is astonishing that the political qualities of leadership have gone unrecognized. But it is now clear why this has been the case. Questions concerning leaders and leadership necessarily are political. This can be appreciated only when political processes are taken seriously in the manner we have described. Once the political qualities of organizing are recognized it is possible to raise questions which simply do not make sense in an entitative perspective. Now it does make sense to address issues which are moral or ethical.[17] A political perspective makes it possible to ask what valuations does a particular culture support and how open is it to other possibilities. A political perspective asks how are differences respected and how is social influence understood. These questions must be addressed.

It is only through dialogue, through what we have called conversations for action, that interdependent actors can negotiate descriptions and lines of action which they find agreeable, at least for a time. To build cultures of productivity it is essential that differences are articulated through a process of actively open-minded thinking. To build such cultures, ways must be found to respect differences which must be preserved. All participants must take responsibility to promote processes of this kind. We shall develop these arguments in our analysis of the processes through which cultures of productivity can be created.

Leadership and organizing: Structures in the process of projects

It is helpful to repeat the definition of leadership outlined at the start of this chapter: 'Leadership (is) a more or less skilful process of organizing, achieved through negotiation, to achieve acceptable influence over the description and handling of issues within and between groups.' We proposed that these processes are more skilful when they are legible, coherent, and open-ended, these being the qualities which characterize cultures of productivity. We defined as leaders, those participants whose influence consistently was found acceptable and who, as a result, came to be expected to make contributions of this kind. In other words, participants in leadership give leaders a special responsibility for structuring the processes of projects. Note that our definitions allow that many participants, or only a few may come to be described in this way.

It also is useful to reconsider our arguments about the fundamentals of relational processes as they are of crucial importance for what we want to say about networking, negotiating and enabling in relation to skilful leadership. First, social relationships are grounded in helping. Some relationships are more helpful than others. Second, we focus on relational processes, not persons and their inputs, and not outputs such as levels of production or quality of service.[18] Processes are more or less helpful. By focusing on skilful processes, questions of skill may be considered independently of the content of the processes. This is crucial as content varies with context (Hosking and Morley, 1988). Third, the relationship between person and context is one of mutual creation. Who a person is depends in some sense on who they are with and why they are there.

All of this makes leadership of vital importance, not just for a group or organization, but for society. When leaders are given special responsibility for the creation of settings this has major implications for all participants and their experiences of personhood. Our arguments about helping, responsibility, and skill imply that all participants take more or less responsibility for the process – to make it more or less helpful.[19] Last, we must emphasize that, for us, intelligent social action is a description of certain kinds of cognitive, social, and political processes.

Networking, negotiating and enabling are vehicles for the performance of leadership. They are social processes with cognitive and political aspects. They may be performed more or less skilfully. By these means actors create relationships. Through their social relations they create orderings of value and power which make sense in thought and action. In the course of their conversations, participants make commitments to particular descriptions and to particular lines of action. These commitments may be more or less helpful to collective project work. Machines are not able to act intelligently in our sense (see Chapters 1 and 4).

Networking

Networking is a process of relationship building within and between groups; it has been discussed at some length in relation to organizing and to project work. For this reason we will focus here on the cognitive and political aspects which are most relevant to leadership. Like all other relationships, social relationships may be more or less helpful to interdependent actors. It is through networking that actors organize their interdependencies and their social order more generally. Yet, as we have said, there are limits to the relationships that can be built. Networking is a social process which is vital both for negotiating and for enabling. Like those processes it has both cognitive and political aspects. Together, networking, negotiation and enabling may create and sustain cultures of productivity, or they may not.

Cognitive aspects

Social actions are equivocal and cannot be completely described. From the point of view of understanding, networking is important because it helps people build more complete and less idiosyncratic descriptions of the challenges they face. This means that they are more likely to discriminate between messages they must heed and messages they may ignore (Janis, 1989). They are also more likely to take actions which, when interpreted by others, help to contribute to a culture of productivity.

Sometimes people are highly motivated to build relationships with people who help them build organizational intelligence. However, it is quite possible to spend large amounts of time talking to other people and learn very little. Blake and Mouton (1986) have described an executive, called Frank, who 'enjoyed travelling a lot and being seen around the various operations' (p.107). He learned very little from this, however. According to his successor, 'It occupied time, made him visible, and made him look colourful. It wasn't until I saw how the problems had piled up I realized how little was going on. The situation provides a perfect answer to the question of how a person can be present while absent' (Blake and Mouton, 1986, p.108). Moving around and being visible is not enough. Building organizational intelligence requires relationships in which all participants are willing to engage in actively open-minded dialogue.

It is not clear that this point is well understood, either in the literatures on networking, or on leaders as managers of meanings. On the first, networking has been argued to be a managerial behaviour which helps the manager to 'gather information' for agenda setting and implementation (see Chapter 8). The size of the manger's 'contact network' is what is emphasized. So too is what is described as 'more aggressive' network building and 'aggressively gathering information' (Kotter, 1982, p.117, p.66). On the latter, there are dangers in building networks too aggressively. For example, Weick (1983) has argued that those who impose meanings most forcefully run most risk of generating self-fulfilling prophecies. They generate too much order and certainty because their own actions create rhetorical contexts in which their initial diagnoses are most likely to be confirmed.

Those who argue that leaders are, or should be, managers of meanings (Smircich and Morgan, 1982) or 'interpreters' (e.g. Bennis and Nanus, 1985) also would do well to pay serious attention to the processes through which this may occur. On reading the literatures it is all to easy to form the impression that leaders manage meanings through relatively simple, one-directional, causal processes, in which they impose their (superior) vision and understanding. Yet it is essential to appreciate that leaders may impose unhelpful visions and protect and promote, for example, cultures of dependence. This is why the question of skill must be put. Actively open-minded dialogue is a process essential to skilful leadership. It is this which must be recognized in any talk about the management of meaning. If leaders are to avoid traps of this kind they would do well to listen to some of the advice proffered by Grob (1984) and by Janis (1989).[20]

Returning to the argument that a large network of social contacts contributes to a manager's effectiveness it seems likely that network size may be being emphasized at the expense of the quality of relationships. It seems very unlikely that a person could have anything other than a fleeting relationship with the 'hundreds or thousands of individuals' to which Kotter referred (Kotter, 1982, p. 67). It may be that leaders develop strong relationships with a much smaller number of people who have strong networks of their own, and who act as their eyes and their ears. Examples of this kind are very evident in studies of military command. For example, Ulysses S. Grant once instructed an aide by saying that

> I want you to discuss with me freely from time to time the details of the orders given for the conduct of a battle, and learn my views as fully as possible as to what course should be pursued in all the contingencies which may arise. I expect to send you to the crucial points of the lines to keep me promptly alerted of what is taking place, and in cases of great emergency... I want you to explain my views to commanders and urge immediate action, looking to co-operation, without waiting for specific orders from me. (1987, p. 198).

There will be many occasions when leaders become dependent on other people for information and specialized skills. They will become the prisoners of such groups (Selznick, 1957) unless they create rhetorical contexts which promote actively open-minded thinking and enable people to participate fully, 'not as a technique for improving feelings but as a legitimate means of uncovering new information and problems' (Sayles, 1989, p. 218). This is why writers such as Grob (1984) ground the study of leadership in the study of dialogues which prohibit the 'mere wielding of power on behalf of static ideals' (p. 271) and encapsulate the 'essence of participatory democracy' (p. 275).

Political aspects

When viewed as a political process, networking is about creating, and influencing commitments to, particular relationships, understandings, and actions. It is important again to emphasize that our concept of networking is not the same as that which is found in an entitative perspective. We do not start from the assumption of hierarchy and the taken for granteds of formal organization: networking may be performed in the context of formalized hierarchies, just as it may be performed 'outside' them.[21] Further, our concept of networking is not grounded in traditional notions of instrumentalities, but rather, emphasizes helping.

Our interviews with chief executives revealed that many were very active in networking.[22] Only some of them networked in the ways, and for the reasons, we have described. These few valued networking for building relationships to reduce the separation and the differences which follow from hierarchy (see Hosking, in press, a). For them, networking reflected a value for rejecting conventional distinctions between work and home, for example, and between formal and informal organization. Networking was valued in its own right, not for its instrumental outcomes but for the kinds of relationships it allowed participants to enjoy. From our point of view what is crucial is that networking makes it possible for participants to understand different points of view, to negotiate descriptions, to find ways to respect differences, and to enable others. We think this is fundamental to skilful leadership processes, whatever the project.

Networking makes it possible to find ways to respect different valuations and interests and to enable relationships for example, between interdependent groups. So, for example, a social services department may try to enable their clients by giving them a real voice and role in shaping the services and relationships in which they participate. Similar points might be made about relationships between marketing, production, and research and development in the context of engineering design teams, or the relationships between management and union engaged in formal negotiations. Of course, ways must be found to handle the conflicting voices. This is one of the many reasons why negotiation (in our sense) is intimately interconnected with networking, and why both are vital in order for leadership to create and sustain cultures of productivity.

Networking has a political quality because participants influence commitments to understandings, lines of action, and relationships. Through their relationships, actors may help to promote and protect shared valuations and projects. So, for example, a person may help to promote their group's interests through their relationships with other individuals and groups. This is likely to facilitate their credibility and influence within their own group. However, our arguments about skill imply that they then must seek ways to enable other group members, for example, through processes in which understandings can be made collective. It is through such processes that the group as a whole is enabled.[23] It is through processes such as these that differences can be explored, cared for, and respected, and learning be facilitated.

Finally, we must link explicitly, the cognitive and political aspects of networking. Social action is possible only when there is sufficient consensus to coordinate lines of action. Through networking it is possible to have conversations for action. Through such conversations one or more actors can influence others to contribute, and in this way, facilitate the articulation of valuations. Through processes of actively open-minded thinking it is possible not only to articulate valuations, but to keep them in the process so that they limit what is possible. In this way, participants can negotiate the meanings of differences and agree understandings and actions. In the processes through which descriptions come to be seen as shared, participants produce social certifications of what counts as truth.[24] In these processes, it is possible for one or more actors to help disagreements to converge productively so that agreements can be reached that all can understand and accept. Processes of this kind constitute the skilful production of cultures which are coherent, legible, and open-ended.

Negotiation

The view that many of the skills of leadership are the skills of negotiation is recognized to be gaining ground (Smith and Peterson, 1988), although few have examined the process of negotiation in any detail. Negotiation is a process in which people discuss whether certain changes in their relationship are possible, and desirable. Broadly speaking, the process may be understood as one in which the participants negotiate descriptions and forge commitments to collective action based on those descriptions.

Cognitive aspects
When writers such as Bennis speak of the vision of leaders they are referring to the role of a leader as an interpreter.[25] He has argued that leaders have the capacities to create compelling visions and to forge commitments to them. However, as we have argued, leadership processes consist of conversations in which leaders help others to understand what changes in relationships are possible, and desirable.

What is important, first, is not that the leader's image of reality compels commitment but that it provides a useful frame of reference for dialogues within a group. Second, skilful leadership processes are open-ended. They are concerned with making sense of change rather than serving 'fixed notions and static ideals' (Grob, 1984, p.276).[26] Third, the kind of dialogue which is involved is very much a matter of negotiation. If a group is to perform skilfully it is important that there is constructive competition between different points of view. The culture must be such that participants are helped and supported in ways which mean that they can change their views (Janis, 1989). A culture of productivity is one in which participants are able to negotiate the acceptance of influence. Part of what this means is that those who change must be supported so that they will continue constructively to contribute to project work. Finally, there are occasions when it is important that leaders deliberately take a neutral stance, lest they bias the group process and discourage others from participating in an actively open-minded way (Janis, 1989).[27]

Skilful leadership also involves negotiation to the extent that participants reveal a practical understanding of the implications of limited capacity. They may do so by taking steps to reduce ambiguity, clarify communications, and generally slow things down, just as in skilful negotiation.[28] Arguments of this kind underlie Welford's general model of social skill (Welford, 1980).

Political aspects

Negotiating processes have a political quality because they are processes in which influence is achieved in social relations. And social relations are found between actors who differ in their relationships with their contexts such that they differ in their valuations and differ in their abilities to mobilize influence. In our discussion of power and influence we attempted to show how influence processes must be understood when the entitative separation of person and context is abandoned. The language of negotiation is intended to emphasize two themes. The first is that it is a social process involving dialogue, or what we have called conversations for action. The second, and equally necessary theme, is that for organizing to be skilful, it must be achieved through acceptable influence.

The kinds of influence which are acceptable differ with the cultural setting. When talking of skilful leadership processes, we are speaking of processes which create cultures of productivity. Such cultures cannot be created and practised through coercion. Similarly, our arguments about helping and respect in the context of difference imply that reward power has a very different quality from that found in an entitative approach. So, for example, an important feature of our understandings about rewards, in relation to influence, is that they are grounded in social relationships. They include relational messages of support and helping others to enjoy supportive relationships in which differences are respected and cared for. This will include helping others to build a practical understanding of their context. More generally, it will mean facilitating a legible, coherent, and open-ended structure in the process of a project. However, this must be done in ways which enable all participants. In other words, influence must facilitate connection rather than support the separation implied by differentiation between leaders and led.

In a culture of productivity legitimacy is negotiated in relationships. When a person's influence is accepted because they are defined as more expert, their expertise is contextualized. In other words, it is recognized that others also must be enabled to contribute and to achieve acceptable influence – through expertise – or by other means. Differences are respected by acknowledging that what counts as 'expertise' depends on the issue and the relational setting of that issue. Further, emphasis is placed on process knowledge (knowing how). Consequently, all participants are enabled to make valued contributions, whatever the content of an issue. Position power, as traditionally conceptualized, is not an acceptable basis for influence. Persons' contributions are not accepted simply because of 'who they are' in the sense of their formal position and status. Rather, in skilful processes, all participants see themselves and others as having the responsibility to contribute. By networking an actor can 'move around', and through enabling, the constraints of a particular context can, to some extent, be shaped.

To conclude, skilful leadership is achieved through negotiating acceptable influence. This is how cultures of productivity may be created, reflecting and promoting helping as a quality of social relationships .

Enabling

People need the help of others to add value to their lives in the performance of project work. If leaders are to contribute to a culture of productivity they must encourage and support contributions from others. They must show that they want to develop strong cooperative contexts in which people value and respect differences in knowledge, interest, and outlooks (Tjosvold, 1991; Hosking, in press, b). They must show that they are willing to question conventional (entitative) thinking which divides people into leaders and followers, into those who lead and those who are led.

The entitative perspective speaks of both enabling and empowerment. The sharp distinction between person and context leads to a view in which enabling or empowering others becomes one component in inventories designed to measure leadership style (see Yukl, 1989). This makes them look like matters of individual motivation. In one recent text, for example, empowerment has been described as giving people important work to do; maximizing their autonomy and discretion; giving visibility to others; acknowledging their efforts; and helping them to build strong relationships with other people (Kouzes and Posner, 1987). There is little recognition that the object of the exercise is to build relationships in which followers turn into leaders. Nor that the essence of leadership may be to encourage a certain sort of dialogue in which the identities of the leader and the led are brought continually into question (see Grob, 1984). Consequently, the concept of enabling which has been used is very different from out own.[29]

Cognitive aspects
Enabling is necessary for change.[30] People who are enabled change the ways in which they think about themselves, their relationships, and their ways of work. They develop new ideas of their potential to act inside or outside the group. Once again, however, we should beware of focusing only on the individual. What is important is the dialogue which creates shared meanings

and changes the culture of the group. It is this change in culture which allows group members to develop 'more robust, differentiated, and powerful identities in each other's eyes' (Neilsen, 1986, p.81). It is this kind of dialogue which is necessary if differences between people are to be recognized and respected. It is only when people value such diversity that groups are able to build collective strength.

This is why Grob (1984) has described enabling as a collective, 'creative activity in which the horizons of meaning surrounding the issues at hand are perpetually stretched' (p.276) He has attempted to spell out the implications of a Socratic model of leadership. In this model the object of the exercise is to create a rhetorical context in which 'all so-called truths of human knowledge and conduct must take on an ultimately provisional cast' (p.272). This means that 'Truth is now seen to reside not in a given doctrine or set of behaviors but rather in the give-and-take of critical process in which ever new perspectives on the issue in question are progressively disclosed' (p.272). From this perspective, followers 'are followers only insofar as this ability to perceive the ever widening series of perspectives in which the issue at hand must be situated is, at a given juncture, less developed than that of the leader.' (p.274). The essence of their relationship with the leader is that the dialogue promotes 'the movement of followers into leadership roles' (p.274).

There seem to be three crucial aspects to the process of enabling, from a cognitive point of view. The first is that group members, especially leaders, must recognize that they are likely to depend a great deal on the 'local knowledge' of other people.[31] Evidently, 'they draw upon local knowledge, seek it out, cherish it, and consciously accept dependence on it as part and parcel of the open, participative culture they strive to maintain' (pp.389–90). The second aspect is that group members, especially leaders, must understand 'the dynamics of constructive controversy' (Tjosvold, 1991). This is partly a matter of developing appropriate problem-solving procedures. It is partly a matter of establishing norms which support actively open-minded thinking. And it is partly a matter of recognizing that not everyone reacts in the same way to the demands of constructive confrontation There are clearly times when confrontation can be very stressful, and unless the process is very well managed the confrontation is likely to be destructive rather than constructive (Jelinek and Schoonhoven, 1990). This leads neatly to the third aspect of enabling, which means that people need help to handle the anxieties and dilemmas of group life. Neilsen (1986) has gone so far as to say that this is the leader's 'immediate task'.

Political aspects

Like the concept of networking, the concept of enabling has been wrested recently from the radical, critical literatures. It has been tamed within the traditions of HRM, where the term 'empowerment' is used instead. Empowering or enabling are now part of a new rhetoric. Leadership is still viewed as something that leaders (managers) do. Only now leaders do it by changing or 'transforming' the motives and goals of followers so that all pursue a common goal (Bennis and Nanus, 1985). Consequently, leaders are spoken of as 'enabling people', as people who are 'caring', who help others to help themselves, who help others to take responsibility for their own learning, and so on (Jaap, 1989).

Many speak of the value of distributive influence: reducing differences of power between people so that learning and commitment may be facilitated (Friedlander, 1983). Often emphasis is placed on facilitating 'patterns of more equalized interaction' and 'more equalized power' (Smircich and Morgan, 1982). The general line of argument emphasizes the negative consequences of cultures of dependency and advocates moving towards, say, a 'culture of pride' (Bennis and Nanus, 1985).

The rhetoric is deceptive. The language of caring, responsibility, and help engages our interest, seeming to offer a radical break with the traditions of HRM. From our perspective, however, what we are being offered is yet another variation on an old theme – the entitative perspective. In other words, we still find hard and fast distinctions between person and context; we still find unitary assumptions about valuations and interests; and we still find tacit but powerful assumptions that instrumentalities are what is important about social relationships.

The argument of this book has placed the language of enabling in the context of a broader perspective of organizing processes. This perspective has emphasized interdependence as a quality of social relationships. People are connected by their need for help. This is fundamental. This said, it is then possible that relationships may be characterized by separation, created and supported by hierarchies of authority, differences of tasks, rewards, rights, and so on. The theories and prescriptions in HRM and OB usually take such relationships for granted. The alternative is that relationships be viewed as about connection, not separation. The implication is that actors may look for ways to reduce separation, and may do so in ways which value and respect differences in knowledge, outlooks, projects, and the like. Unlike the authors cited above, we are not starting from the assumption of hierarchy (set by management in the form of structures and goals). These limits must be recognized as conventional. We do not take for granted the limits of what is possible – limits which others accept in the form of organizational goals and structures set legitimately by a management elite.

Enabling is about helping others to help themselves with respect to their own relational setting. It is about enabling others in relation to their own valuations and projects, and not with respect to the goals of a leader. Talk of power equalization is just another version of managerialism unless participants are helped to construct the valuational basis of their activities and relationships.

When we speak of conversations for action and cultures of productivity we are speaking of processes in which participants negotiate acceptable orderings of values and influence. In such cultures all participants take responsibility for the relational processes through which they may help and be helped. These processes are not just about power – as the language of empowering implies – they are about value. Until this is recognized the political qualities of leadership will continue to be obscured. Until the political qualities of leadership and organizing are recognized, vital questions cannot be raised. They are questions that must be put. They concern the kinds of culture we are able to create and enjoy – now and in the future.

Notes

1. Both Bryman (1986) and Smith and Peterson (1988) provide accounts of this kind. Recent review articles include those by Fiedler and House (1988) and Yukl (1989).
2. Other treatments of the framework may be found elsewhere. Some are intended to provide detailed discussion (Hosking and Morley, 1988; Hosking, 1988b); some an outline theory (Morley and Hosking, 1984, 1986; Hosking, 1987); and some situate the model in relation to particular kinds of context (Hosking, in press, a, b; Brown and Hosking, 1986; Grieco and Hosking, 1987; Morley, 1991, in press, b).
3. But see Grieco and Hosking (1987).
4. When we think of exceptions to these generalizations they are usually found outside the literatures of OB and HRM, particularly in social psychology (e.g. Gibb, 1969; Kelvin, 1970; Douglas, 1983; Brown and Hosking, 1986; Dachler, in press).
5. Of course, to achieve this it would be necessary to attend to the contribution of non-leaders (non-managers) as well as those of leaders (managers), and to do so in ways which recognize the reciprocal and emergent qualities of processes.
6. This is the fundamental model. Talk of moderator variables is simply a more complex version of the same basic model. Fundamentally, the model is one of linear, cause-effect relations, regardless of the complexities which may be introduced by reference to feedback loops and the like.
7. Not just settings but also actors. However, we are concentrating on the former in this book.
8. See Jacobs (1970); Hollander (1978); Graen and Cashman (1975); and House (1971).
9. For example, Sayles (1979). It is important to note that we are speaking of the literatures on OB and HRM. There is work within the symbolic interactionist tradition, for example, which comes closer to what we seek (Kelvin, 1970; Strauss, 1978). However, it is found outside the literatures of OB and HRM, and has not been taken up in them. Elements of what we seek are to be found in the increasing attention to the 'management of meaning' (Smircich and Morgan, 1982).
10. For example, Kaplan (1984) and Stewart (1976).
11. This is true even of the excellent work of Hollander, who emphasizes two-way influence processes. His model of 'reciprocal' influence, like most others, retains the underlying model of backwards and forwards influence, leaving little room for serious consideration of the emergent qualities of relationships.
12. There are exceptions to this general statement, and we shall make use of them in our arguments about cognitive, social, and political processes.
13. Here we mean to refer to the whole range of settings, past, present, and anticipated, of which an actor has been, and might be, a part. This is one way in which the different histories of actors may contribute to their different constructions of the present.

Similarly, two interdependent actors may have differing views about the likely future of their relationship, and this may affect their constructions. Finally, let us add that this approach avoids the narrow focus on leader-subordinate relations and does not sharply and arbitrarily distinguish work from non-work relations.

14. Sometimes the language of values is used narrowly in these literatures to refer to preferences and standards. At other times it is used more broadly to refer to what we would describe as sense making – although the perspective is individualistic. In either case the political implications go unrecognized, buried under the taken for granted assumptions of a unitary and physicalist perspective.

15. A structural approach to power and organization dominates the literatures with which we are concerned (eg House and Singh, 1987). When power is discussed in relation to persons, the usual entitative assumptions predominate so that power is treated as a personal property. When judged in relations to our interests in joining person and context, both culturalist and individualistic approaches are fallacies. Instead, we need to theorize power in relational terms (see Chapter 5).

16. Not 'strong' or 'excellent'.

17. In the OB and HRM literature such issues are rarely, if ever, addressed. The question of 'who benefits?' has been raised in organizational sociology; 'political' theorists who speak of stakeholders do so to emphasize differences of interest (see Chapter 5). Hosking has raised these issues elsewhere, in relation to leadership and organizing (Brown and Hosking, 1986; Hosking 1988b; Hosking, 1990; Hosking, in press, a). Fortunately, others are also raising these issues, both with respect to leadership, and in relation to HRM in general (see Dachler and Enderle, 1989).

18. In this way we depart from traditional theories of leadership effectiveness where the latter are regarded as outputs to be explained in terms of inputs from the leader and from the situation.

19. In other words it is not outcomes for which participants take responsibility, it is process. Participants commit themselves to making certain sorts of contributions and to enabling others to do likewise.

20. One possibility may be to announce and enforce one of the crucial aspects of the Socratic model of leadership. Essentially, this means that leaders have to show by word and deed that they are willing to open themselves to critique (Grob) and will not 'shoot the messenger' (Janis). Janis (1989) has detailed a number of specific suggestions by which such guidelines may be implemented.

21. E.g. Brown and Hosking (1986) Grieco and Hosking (1987).

22. When we refer to work with chief executives we do not wish to imply that they necessarily made contributions to leadership.

23. The sorts of things we are thinking of here include what might be described in terms of collective knowledge bases and collective memory. Hosking has described elsewhere some of the ways in which different members of extended families share their knowledge of potential employers, jobs, ways of securing houses, and the like (Grieco and Hosking, 1987). By sharing knowledge and other resources (housing, sponsorship, training) members of the family enable the network as a whole. In this way they are better able to enjoy the relationships which are important to them – adding value to their own lives and to the lives of others.

24. If one person's views are seen to predominate then their descriptions are seen as idiosyncratic, and not socially certified as valid.

25. See Bennis (1982, 1984); Bennis and Nanus (1985).

26. This is why Kelvin (1970) has argued that 'it is essential not to confuse leadership with

some rigid perpetuation of doing things the way in which they have always been done' (p.226). What is most important is that social order is flexible order. Fundamentally, leaders have to ensure that 'the general values of the group are realized, not that they are inevitably realized in only this or that particular way' (Kelvin, 1970, p227; emphasis added). In our view, one important sign of skilful leadership is a flexible social order with an 'uncommitted potentiality for change' (Bateson, 1972).

27. Blake and Mouton (1986) have argued that this is particularly likely when the leader adopts a 'paternalistic' approach to conflict. This means that conflict is seen as threatening rather than something to be valued as part of a positive force for creativity and change. The result is to stifle the expression of 'reservations and doubts, because to voice them is to express disloyalty' (Blake and Mouton, 1986, p.82). For further discussion see Tjosvold (1991) Chapter 10, plus Chapter 4 and Chapter 7 in this text.

28. See Hosking and Morley (1988). Direct evidence to support this view is hard to find, although it is consistent with analyses of the microskills of leadership (see Alban Metcalfe, 1984; Wright and Taylor, 1984). It is also consistent with descriptions of the skills of project management (see Sayles, 1989).

29. Hosking (in press, a) has argued that enabling is different in kind from the processes of networking and negotiation, because they are a fact of social life. The point is that, whereas social relations could not be formed without networking and negotiation, enabling does not necessarily happen. We believe that it is an essential aspect of leadership, and that skilful leaders will be better able to create the conditions whereby team members want to develop the competences and structure their work so that they are the right people for the job, meaning that they are willing and able to do whatever it takes to get the job done, including negotiating new relationships with other people (see Akin and Hopelain, 1986; Tjosvold, 1991).

30. The failure to respond to change is often cited as a major cause of failures to get new, competitive products to market (e.g. Jelinek and Schoonhaven, 1990).

31. Jelinek and Schoonhoven (1990) have reported that the high-technology managers in their sample were very well aware that they relied on other people for 'their detailed expertise in and familiarity with technology, markets, production realities, and all the myriad details of how to understand what is happening, and how to actually implement any plan' (p.389).

References

Abelson, R.P. (1976). Social psychology's rational man. In S.I. Benn and G.W. Mortimore (eds.), *Rationality and the Social Sciences*. London: Routledge & Kegan Paul.

Abetti, P.A. (1986). Fostering a climate for creativity and innovation in business oriented R & D organizations: an historical project. *Creativity and Innovation Network*, January-March, 4–16.

Adams, J.S. (1963). Toward an understanding of inequity. *Journal of Abnormal and Social Psychology*, 67, 422–36.

Adorno, T.W., Frenkel-Brunswik, E., Levinson, D.J. and Sanford, R.N. (1950). *The Authoritarian Personality*. New York: W.W. Norton & Company.

Akin, G. and Hopelain, D. (1986). Finding the culture of productivity. *Organizational Dynamics*, **14**, 19–32.

Alban Metcalfe, B. (1984). Microskills of leadership: a detailed analysis of the behaviors of managers in the appraisal interview. In J.G. Hunt, D.-M. Hosking, C.A. Schriesheim, and R. Stewart (eds.), *Leaders and Managers: International Perspectives on Managerial Behavior and Leadership*. Oxford: Pergamon Press.

Allison, G.T. (1971). *Essence of Decision: Explaining the Cuban Missile Crisis*. Boston: Little, Brown.

Allport, F.H. (1955). *Theories of Perception and the Concept of Structure*. New York: Wiley.

Allport, F.H. (1962). A structuronomic conception of behavior: individual and collective. *Journal of Abnormal and Social Psychology*, **64**, 3–30.

Allport, G.W. (1963). *Pattern and Growth in Personality*. London: Holt, Rinehart, and Winston.

Altemeyer, B. (1981). *Right-wing Authoritarianism*. The University of Manitoba Press.

Anguilar, F. (1967). *Scanning the Business Environment*. New York: Macmillan.

Anthony, P. (1977). *The Conduct of Industrial Relations*. London: Institute of Personnel Management.

Argyris, C. (1964). *Integrating the Individual and the Organization*. New York: Wiley.

Arnheim, R. (1962). *Picasso's Guernica: The Genesis of a Painting*. Berkeley: University of California Press.

Aronoff, J. and Wilson, J.P. (1985). *Personality in the Social Process*. Hillsdale, NJ: Lawrence Erlbaum Associates.

Aronson, E. (1969). The theory of cognitive dissonance: a current perspective. In L.Berkowitz (ed.), *Advances in Experimental Social Psychology, Volume 4*. New York: Academic Press.

Aronson, E. (1980). *The Social Animal* (Third edition). San Francisco: W.H. Freeman and Company.

Asch, S.E.(1952). *Social Psychology*. Englewood Cliffs, NJ: Prentice Hall. (All references in the text are to the paperback edition published in 1987 by Oxford University Press)

Athay, M. and Darlay, J.M. (1981). Toward an interaction-centred theory of personality. In N.Cantor and J.F.Kihlstrom (eds.), *Personality, Cognition, and Social Interaction*. Hillsdale, NJ: Lawrence Erlbaum Associates.

Atherton, W.A. (1988). Pioneers 15. William Shockley, John Bardeen and Walter Brittain: inventors of the transistor. *Electronics and Wireless World*, **94**, 273–5.

Axelrod, R. (1984). *The Evolution of Cooperation*. New York: Basic Books.

Bacharach, S. and Lawler, E. (1980). *Power and Politics in Organizations: The Social Psychology of Conflict, Coalitions, and Bargaining*. San Francisco: Jossey-Bass.

Bacharach, S. and Lawler, E.J. (1981). *Bargaining: Power, Tactics, and Outcomes*. San Francisco: Jossey-Bass.

Back, K.W. (1951). Influence through social communication. *Journal of Abnormal and Social Psychology*, **46**, 9–23.

Badawy, M.K. (1975). Organizational designs for scientists and engineers: some research findings and their implications for managers. *IEEE Transactions on Engineering Management*, **EM–22**, 134–8.

Bailey, R.L. (1978). *Disciplined Creativity for Engineers*. Ann Arbor: Ann Arbor Science Publishers.

Bakhurst, D. (1990). Social memory in Soviet thought. In D. Middleton and D. Edwards (eds.), *Collective Remembering*. London: Sage Publications Ltd.

Bales, R.F. (1970). *Personality and Interpersonal Behavior*. New York: Holt, Rinehart and Winston.

Bales, R.F. and Cohen, S.P.(with the assistance of Williamson, S.A.) (1979). *SYMLOG: A System for the Multiple Level Observation of Groups*. New York: The Free Press. London: Collier Macmillan.

Bannister, D. and Mair, J.M.M.(1986). *The Evaluation of Personal Constructs*. London: Academic Press.

Barko, W. and Passmore, W. (1986). Introductory statement to the special issue on sociotechnical systems: innovations in designing high performance systems. *Journal of Applied Behavioral Science*, **22**, 195–9

Barnard, C. (1948). *Organization and Management*. Cambridge, MA: Harvard University Press.

Barnett, C. (1963). *The Swordbearers: Studies in Supreme Command in the First World War*. London: Eyre and Spottiswoode.

Baron, J. (1988). *Thinking and Deciding*. Cambridge: Cambridge University Press.

Baron, R.A. (1986). *Behavior in Organizations: Understanding and Managing the Human Side of Work*. Boston: Allyn and Bacon.

Bartlett, F.C. (1932). *Remembering: A Study in Experimental and Social Psychology*. Cambridge: Cambridge University Press.

Bartlett, F.C. (1958). *Thinking: an Experimental and Social Study*. London: Unwin University Books.

Bass, B.M. (1981). *Stogdill's Handbook of Leadership: A Survey of Theory and Research*. New York: Free Press.

Bass, B.M. (1985). *Leadership and Performance Beyond Expectations*. New York: Free Press.

Bass, B.M. and Dunteman, G. (1963). Biases in the evaluation of one's own group, its allies and opponents. *Journal of Conflict Resolution*, **7**, 16–20.

658.3 B 317 Bass, B.M. and Barrett, G.V. (1981). *People, Work and Organizations: An Introduction to Industrial and Organizational Psychology*. Boston: Allyn and Bacon.

Bateson, G. (1972). *Steps to an Ecology of Mind*. London: Intertext.

Batstone, E., Boraston, I. and Frenkel, S. (1977). *Shop Stewards in Action*. Oxford: Basil Blackwell.

Batstone, E., Boraston, I. and Frenkel, S. (1978). *The Social Organization of Strikes*. Oxford: Basil Blackwell.

Becker, H.S. (1987). Cited in P.M.Hall, Interactionism and the study of social organization. *Sociological Quarterly*, **28**, 1–22.

658.01 B 420 Belbin, R.M. (1981). *Management Teams: Why They Succeed or Fail*. London: Heinemann.

Bennett, W.L. and Feldman, M.S. (1981). *Reconstructing Reality in the Courtroom*. London: Tavistock.

Bennis, W.G. (1982). Leadership transforms vision into action. *Industry Week*, 31 May, 54–6.

Bennis, W.G. (1984). The four competencies of leadership. *Training and Development Journal*, **38**, no. 8, 14–19.

Bennis, W.G. and Nanus, B. (1985). *Leaders*. New York: Harper and Row.

Bensinger, B. E. (1965). A creative organization. In G.A.Steiner (ed.), *The Creative Organization*. Chicago: University of Chicago Press.

Benson, J.K. (1977). Innovation and crisis in organizational analysis. *Sociological Quarterly*, **18**, 3–16.

Bergwerk, W. (1989). The role of prototypes in managing product innovation risks. *Proceedings of the Institution of Mechanical Engineers Volume 203. Part B:Journal of Engineering Manufacture*, 113–18.

Bertodo, R. (1989). Human resource deployment for design excellence. *Proceedings of the Institution of Mechanical Engineers International Conference on Engineering Design, Volume 1*. Bury St. Edmunds: Institution of Mechanical Engineers.

Biggart, N.W. (1981). Management style as strategic interaction: the case of President Reagan. *The Journal of Applied Behavioral Science*, **17**, 291–308.

Bignell, V. and Fortune, J. (1984). *Understanding Systems Failures*. Manchester: Manchester University Press (in association with the Open University).

Billig, M. (1976). *Social Psychology and Intergroup Relations*. London: Academic Press.

Billig, M. (1978). *Fascists: A Social Psychological View of the National Front*. London: Harcourt Brace Jovanovich.

Billig, M. (1989). *Arguing and Thinking: A Rhetorical Approach to Social Psychology*. Cambridge: Cambridge University Press.

Bion, W.R. (1961). *Experiences in Groups and Other Papers*. London: Tavistock.

Blake, R.R. and Mouton, J.S. (1961a). Comprehension of own and outgroup positions under intergroup competition. *Journal of Conflict Resolution*, **3**, 304–10.

Blake, R.R. and Mouton, J.S. (1961b). Competition, communication, and conformity. In I.A. Berg and B.M. Bass (eds.), *Conformity and Deviation*. New York: Harper Bros.

Blake, R.R. and Mouton, J.S. (1962). The intergroup dynamics of win-lose conflict and problem-solving collaboration in union-management relations. In M.Sherif (ed.), *Intergroup Relations and Leadership*. New York: Wiley.

Blake, R.R. and Mouton, J.S. (1986). *Executive Achievement: Making It at the Top*. New York: McGraw-Hill.

Blake, R.R., Sheperd, H.A. and Mouton, J.S. (1964). *Managing Intergroup Conflict in Industry*. Houston: Gulf Publishing Company.

Blau, P.M. (1964). *Exchange and Power in Social Life*. New York: Wiley and Sons.

Blunt, A. (1969). *Picasso's Guernica*. New York: Oxford University Press.

Bonham, M.G. (1971). Simulating international disarmament negotiations. *Journal of Conflict Resolution*, **15**, 299–315.

Bower, M. (1965). Nurturing creativity in an organization. In G.A.Steiner (ed.), *The Creative Organization*. Chicago: University of Chicago Press.

Breakwell, G. (1983). Identities and conflicts. In G. Breakwell (ed.), *Threatened Identities*. Chichester: Wiley.

Broadbent, G. (1988). *Design in Architecture: Architecture and the Human Sciences*. London: David Fulton Publishers.

Brown, H. and Hosking, D.-M. (1986). Distributed leadership and skilled performance as successful organization in social movements. *Human Relations*, **39**, 65–79.

Brown, R. (1988). *Group Processes: Dynamics Within and Between Groups*. Oxford: Basil Blackwell.

Brown, W. (1973). *Piecework Bargaining*. London: Heinemann Educational Books.

Brown, W. and Terry, M. (1975). The importance of continuity to an understanding of bargaining. Paper presented at a symposium, 'Psychology and Industrial Relations', Annual Conference of the British Psychological Society, University of Nottingham.

Bruner, J.S. (1985). Vygotsky: a historical and conceptual perspective. In J.V.Wertsch (ed.), *Culture, Communication and Cognition: Vygotskian Perspectives*. Cambridge: Cambridge University Press.

Bryman, A. (1986). *Leadership and Organizations*. London: Routledge and Kegan Paul.

Buchanan, D.A. and Huczyinski, A.A. (1985). *Organizational Behaviour – An Introductory Text*. London: Prentice-Hall International.

Buckley, W. (1967). *Sociology and Modern Systems Theory*. Englewood Cliffs, NJ: Prentice Hall.

Burns, T. (1954). The direction of activity and communication in a departmental executive group. *Human Relations*, **7**, 73–97.

Burns, T. (1957). Management in action. *Operational Research Quarterly*, **8**, 45–60.

Burns, T. (1961). Micropolitics: mechanisms of institutional change. *Administrative Science Quarterly*, **6**, 257–81.

Burns, T. and Stalker, G.M. (1961). *The Management of Innovation*. London: Tavistock.

Burnstein, E. and Berbaum, M.L. (1981). Stages in group decision making: the decomposition of historical narratives. *Political Psychology*, **4**, 531–61.

Burrell, G. and Morgan, G. (1979). *Sociological Paradigms and Organizational Analysis: Elements of the Sociology of Corporate Life*. London: Heinemann Educational Books.

Calas, M.B. and Smircich, L. (1988). Reading leadership as a form of cultural analysis. In J.G. Hunt, B.R. Baliga, H.P. Dachler, and C.A. Schriesheim (eds.), *Emerging Leadership Vistas*. Lexington, MA: Lexington Books.

Caplow, T. (1964). *Principles of Organization*. New York: Harcourt, Brace and World.

Carlson, S. (1951). *Executive Behaviour: a Study of the Work Load and Working Methods of Managing Directors*. Stockholm: Strombergs.

Carnevale, P. and Keenan, P.A. (in press). The resolution of conflict: negotiation and third party intervention. In J. Hartley and G.M. Stephenson (eds.), *Employment Relations: the Psychology of Influence and Control at Work*. Oxford: Basil Blackwell.

Carson, R.C. (1970). *Interaction Concepts of Personality*. London: George Allen and Unwin.

Chalmers, W.E. and Cormick, G.W. (eds.) (1971). *Racial Conflict and Negotiations: Perspectives and First Case Studies*. Ann Arbor: Institute of Labor and Industrial Relations, The University of Michigan-Wayne State University, and the National Center for Dispute Settlement of the American Arbitration Association.

Chamberlain, N.W. (1951). *Collective Bargaining*. New York: McGraw-Hill.

Chell, E. (1987). *The Psychology of Behaviour in Organizations*. London: Macmillan.

Cheng, J.L. (1983). Organizational context and upward influence: an experimental study of the use of power tactics. *Group and Organisation Studies*, Part 8, 337–55.

Cherns, A. (1976). The principles of sociotechnical design. *Human Relations*, **29**, 783–92.

Child, J. (1972). Organization structure, environment and performance: the role of strategic choice. *Sociology*, **6**, 1–22.

Child, J. (1977). *Organization: A Guide to Problems and Practice*. London: Harper and Row.

Child, J. (1984). *Organization: A Guide to Problems and Practice*. New York: Harper and Row.

Chin, R. and Benne, K.D. (1976). General strategies for effecting change in human systems. In W.G. Bennis, K.D. Benne, R. Chin, and K.E. Corey (eds.), *The Planning of Change* (Third edition). London: Holt, Rinehart and Winston.

Christie, R. and Geis, F.L. (eds.)(1970). *Studies in Machiavellianism*. New York: Academic Press.

Cicourel, A.V. (1973). *Cognitive Sociology*. Harmondsworth: Penguin.

Cicourel, A.V. (1976). *The Social Organization of Juvenile Justice*. London: Heinemann.

Clark, B. (1972). The organizational saga in higher education. *Administrative Science Quarterly*, **17**, 178–84.

Clark, N.K. and Stephenson, G.M. (1989). Group remembering. In P.B.Paulus (ed.), *Psychology of Group Influence* (Second edition). Hillsdale, NJ: Lawrence Erlbaum Associates.

Clutterbuck, D. (1979). R & D under management's microscope. *International Management*, February.

Cohen, G.D. (1969). *The Task-tuned Organization of Groups*. Amsterdam: Swets and Zeitlinger.

Cohen, M.D., March, J.D. and Olsen, J.P. (1972). A garbage can model of organizational choice. *Administrative Science Quarterly*, **17**, 1–25.

Collier, A. (1977). *R.D.Laing: The Philosophy and Politics of Psychotherapy*. Hassocks: The Harvester Press.

Collins, E.B. and Guetzkow, H. (1964). *A Social Psychology of Group Processes for Decision Making*. New York: Wiley.

Cooper, R.G. (1988). The new product process: a decision guide for management. *Journal of Marketing Management*, **3**, 238–55.

Coplin, J.F. (1989). Engineering design – a powerful influence on the business success of manufacturing industry. *Proceedings of the Institution of Mechanical Engineers International Conference on Engineering Design, Volume 1*. Bury St. Edmunds: Institution of Mechanical Engineers.

Craik, K.J.W. (1943). *The Nature of Explanation*. Cambridge: Cambridge University Press.

Crano, W.D. and Messé, L.A. (1982). *Social Psychology: Principles and Themes of Interpersonal Behavior*. Homewood, IL: Dorsey Press.

Crozier, M. (1964). *The Bureaucratic Phenomenon*. Chicago: University of Illinois Press.

Crozier, M. (1972). The relationship between micro and macro sociology: a study of organizational systems as an empirical approach to problems of macrosociology. *Human Relations*, **25**, 239–51.

Csikszentmihalyi, M.(1988). Society, culture, and person: a systems view of creativity. In R.J.Sternberg (ed.), *The Nature of Creativity*. Cambridge: Cambridge University Press.

Cummings, T.G. and Huse, E.F. (1989). *Organization Development and Change* (Fourth edition). St. Paul: West Publishing Company.

Dachler, H.P. (1990). Ecological thinking as a relational phenomenon: integrating the contradictory cultures of the sexes. Paper given to International Conference on Social Organisational Theory: From Methodological Individualism to Relational Formulations. St. Gallen, Switzerland, August.

Dachler, H.P. (in press). Management and leadership as relational phenomena. In M. von Cranach, W. Doise, and G. Mugny (eds.), *Social Representations and the Social Bases of Knowledge*. Bern: Haupt.

Dachler, H.P. and Enderle, G. (1989). Epistemological and ethical considerations in conceptualizing and implementing human resource management. *Journal of Business Ethics*, **8**, 597–606.

Dachler, H.P. and Hosking, D.-M. (1991). Organizational cultures as relational processes: masculine and feminine valuations and practices. *Tenth EGOS Colloquium*, Vienna, July.

Daft, R.E. and Lengel, R.H. (1986). Organizational information requirements, media richness, and structural design. *Management Science*, 32, **5**, 554–71.

Daft, R.L. and Wiginton, J. (1979). Language and organization. *Academy of Management Review*, 4, 179–92.

Dalton, M. (1959). *Men Who Manage*. New York: Wiley.

Danielsen, T. and Pankoke-Babatz, U. (1988). The AMIGO activity model. In R.Speth (ed.), *Research into Networks and Distributed Applications*. Amsterdam: North-Holland.

Davey, H.W. (1972). *Contemporary Collective Bargaining* (Third edition). Englewood Cliffs, NJ: Prentice Hall.

Davies, A.F. (1980). *Skills, Outlooks, and Passions: A Psychoanalytic Contribution to the Study of Politics*. Cambridge: Cambridge University Press.

Davis, J.H. (1969). *Group Performance*. Reading, MA: Addison-Wesley.

Davis, J.H. (1982). Social interaction as a combinatorial process in group decision. In H. Brandstätter, J.H.Davis, and G.Stocker-Kreichgauer (eds.), *Group Decision Making*. New York: Academic Press.

Davis, T. and Luthans, F. (1980). Managers in action: a new look at their behavior and operating models. *Organizational Dynamics*, **9**, Summer, 64–80.

Day, R. and Day, J. (1977). A review of the current state of negotiated order theory: an appreciation and a critique. *Sociological Quarterly*, **18**, 126–42.

De Board, R. (1978). *The Psychoanalysis of Organisations: A Psychoanalytic Approach to Behaviour in Groups and Organisations*. London: Tavistock.

De Cindio, F., De Michelis, G. and Simone, C. (1988). Computer-based tools in the language/action perspective. In R.Speth (ed.), *Research into Networks and Distributed Applications*. Amsterdam: North Holland.

De Groot, A.D. (1965). *Thought and Choice in Chess*. The Hague: Mouton.

De Rivera, J.H. (1968). *The Psychological Dimension of Foreign Policy*. Columbus, OH: Charles E. Merrill Publishing Company.

Deutsch, M., Krauss, R. and Rosenau, N. (1962). Dissonance or defensiveness. *Journal of Personality*, **30**, 16–28.

Dickson, D. (1986). Reflecting. In O. Hargie (ed.), *A Handbook of Communication Skills*. London: Croom Helm.

Dill, D.D.and Pearson, A.W. (1984). The effectiveness of project managers: implications of a political model of influence. *IEEE Transactions on Engineering Management*, **EM-3**, 138–45.

Dixon, N.F. (1976). *On the Psychology of Military Incompetence*. London: Jonathan Cape.

Dixon, N.F. (1984). Who needs enemies? *Bulletin: The British Psychological Society*, **37**, 365–72.

Dixon, N.F. (1987). *Our Own Worst Enemy*. London: Jonathan Cape.

Donaldson, L. (1985). *In Defence of Organization Theory*. Cambridge: Cambridge University Press.

Douglas, A. (1962). *Industrial Peacemaking*. New York: Columbia University Press.

Douglas, T. (1983). *Groups: Understanding People Gathered Together*. London: Tavistock.

Dreyfus, H.L. and Dreyfus, S. (1986). *Mind Over Machine: The Power of Human Intuition and Expertise in the Age of the Computer*. Oxford: Basil Blackwell.

Drory, A. and Romm, T. (1988). Politics in organizations: its perception within the organization. *Organization Studies*, **9**, 165–79.

Drucker, P. (1970). *The Effective Executive*. London: Pan Business Management.

Drucker, P. (1985). *Innovation and Entrepreneurship*. London: Heinemann.

Dunsire, A. (1978). *The Execution Process Volume 1: Implementation in a Bureaucracy*. London: Martin Robertson.

Elcock, H. (1972). *Portrait of a Decision: The Council of Four and the Treaty of Versailles*. London: Eyre Methuen.

Emery, F.E. and Trist, E.L. (1965). The causal texture of organizational environments. *Human Relations*, **18**, 21–32.

Etzioni, A. (1964). *Modern Organizations*. Englewood Cliffs, NJ: Prentice Hall.

Etzioni, A. (1965). Dual leadership in complex organizations. *American Sociological Review*, **30**, 688–98.

Evans, D.A. (1989). Design methods for one-off machines to maximise first time success. *Proceedings of the Institution of Mechanical Engineers International Conference on Engineering Design, Volume 1*. Bury St. Edmunds: Institution of Mechanical Engineers.

Farrell, D. and Peterson, J. (1982). Patterns of political behaviour in organizations. *Academy of Management Review*, **7**, 403–12.

Fayol, H. (1949). *General and Industrial Management*. London: Pitman.

Ferguson, C.K. and Kelley, H.H. (1964). Significant factors in overevaluation of own group's product. *Journal of Abnormal and Social Psychology*, **69**, 223–8.

Festinger, L. (1954). A theory of social comparison processes. *Human Relations*, **7**, 117–40.

Festinger, L. (1957). *A Theory of Cognitive Dissonance*. Stanford: Stanford University Press.

Festinger, L., Schachter, S. and Back, K.W. (1950). *Social Pressure in Informal Groups*. New York: Harper.

Fiedler, F.E. and Garcia, J. (1987). *New Approaches to Effective Leadership: Cognitive Resources and Organizational Performance*. New York: Wiley.

Fiedler, F.E. and House, R.J. (1988). Leadership theory and research: a report of progress. In C.L. Cooper and I.Robertson (eds.), *International Review of Industrial and Organizational Psychology 1988*. Chichester: Wiley.

Fiedler. F.E. (1967). *A Theory of Leadership Effectiveness*. New York: McGraw-Hill.

Fikes, R.E. (1982). A commitment-based framework for describing informal cooperative work. *Cognitive Science*, **6**, 331–47.

Fisher, R. and Brown, S. (1989). *Getting Together: Building a Relationship That Gets to Yes*. London: Business Books.

Fisher, R. and Ury, W. (1983). *Getting to Yes: Negotiating Agreement Without Giving In*. London: Hutchinson.

Forgas, J.P. (1983). What is social about social cognition? *British Journal of Social Psychology*, **22**, 129–44.

Foster, R.N. (1986). *Innovation: The Attacker's Advantage*. London: Macmillan.

Fox, A. (1966). *Industrial Sociology and Industrial Relations*. London: HMSO (Donovan Commission Research Paper 3).

Fransella, F. (ed.) (1981). *Personality: Theory, Measurement and Research*. London: Methuen.

French, J. P. Jr.and Raven, B.H. (1968). The bases of social power. In D.Cartwright and A.Zander (eds.), *Group Dynamics* (Third edition). New York: Harper and Row.

Friedlander, (1983). Patterns of individual and organizational learning. In S. Srivastava and Associates, *The Executive Mind*. San Francisco: Jossey-Bass.

Friedlander, F. and Schott, B. (1981). The use of task groups and task forces in organizational change. In R. Payne and C.L. Cooper (eds.), *Groups at Work*. Chichester: Wiley.

Friedman, H. and Meredeen, S. (1980). *The Dynamics of Industrial Conflict*. London: Croom Helm.

Friedman, M. and Rosenman, R.H. (1974). *Type A Behavior and Your Heart*. New York: Knopf.

Friend, J.K. and Jessop, W.N. (1971). *Local Government and Strategic Choice*. Oxford: Pergamon Press.

Gardner, H. (1983). *Frames of Mind: The Theory of Multiple Intelligences*. London: Heinemann.

Gardner, H.(1985). *The Mind's New Science: A History of the Cognitive Revolution*. New York: Basic Books.

Geis, F. (1978). Machiavellianism. In H.London and J.E.Exner, Jr. (eds.), *Dimensions of Personality*. New York: Wiley.

George, A.L. (1969). The operational code: a neglected approach to the study of political leaders and decision-making. *International Studies Quarterly*, **13**, 190–222.

George, A.L. (1974). Adaptation to stress and political decision making: the individual, small group, and organizational contexts. In G.V. Coeltho, D.A. Hamburg, and J.E. Adams (eds.), *Coping and Adaptation*. New York: Basic Books.

Gerson, E.M. (1976). On the quality of life. *American Sociological Review*, **41**, 793–806.

Gibb, C. (1969). Leadership. In G.Lindzey and E. Aronson (eds.), *The Handbook of Social Psychology*, 4 (Second edition). Reading, MA: Addison-Wesley.

Gioia, D. and Poole, P.P. (1984). Scripts in organizational behavior. *Academy of Management Review*, **8**, 285–91.

Glass, D.C. (1977). *Behavior Patterns, Stress, and Coronary Disease*. Hillsdale, NJ: Lawrence Erlbaum Associates.

Goffman, E. (1959). *The Presentation of Self in Everyday Life*. London: Allen Lane.

Goldhaber, G.M., Dennis, H.S., Richetto, G.M. and Wiio, O.A. (1968). *Information Strategies: New Pathways to Corporate Power*. Englewood Cliffs, NJ: Prentice Hall.

Golembiewski, R.T. (1962a). *Behavior and Organization: O & M and the Small Group*. Chicago: Rand McNally.

Golembiewski, R.T. (1962b). *The Small Group*. Chicago: University of Chicago Press.

Golembiewski, R.T. (1965). Small groups and large organizations. In J.G. March (ed.), *Handbook of Organizations*. Chicago: Rand McNally.

Gombrich, E.H. (1979). *The Sense of Order: A Study in the Psychology of Decorative Art*. Oxford: Phaidon Press.

Graen, G. and Cashman, J.F (1975). A role-making model of leadership in formal organizations: a developmental approach. In J.G. Hunt and L.Larson (eds.), *Leadership Frontiers*. Comparative Administration Research Institute, Graduate School of Business Administration, Kent State University: Kent State University Press.

Greenblatt, M., Levinson, D.J. and Williams, R.H. (eds.) (1957). *The Patient and the Mental Hospital*. New York: Free Press.

Grieco, M.S. and Hosking, D.-M. (1987). Networking, exchange and skill. *International Studies in Management and Organization*, **XVII**, 75–87.

Grob, L. (1984). Leadership: The Socratic Model. In B. Kellerman (ed.), *Leadership: Multidisciplinary Perspectives*. Englewood Cliffs, NJ: Prentice Hall.

Gross, E. (1969). The definition of organizational goals. *British Journal of Sociology*, **20**, 277–94.

Gruber, H. (1981). *Darwin on Man* (Second edition). Chicago: University of Chicago Press.

Guest, D. E. (1984). Social psychology and organizational change. In M. Gruneberg and T.D. Wall (eds.), *Social Psychology and Organizational Behaviour*. Chichester: Wiley.

Guildford, J.P. (1956). Structure of intellect. *Psychological Bulletin*, **53**, 267–93.

Guildford, J.P. (1967). *The Nature of Human Intelligence*. New York: McGraw-Hill.

Guildford, J.P. (1986). *Creative Talents: Their Nature, Uses, and Development*. Buffalo, NY: Bearly Limited.

Gulliver, P.H. (1979). *Disputes and Negotiations: a Cross-cultural Perspective*. New York: Academic Press.

Gupta, A. (1984). Contingency linkages between strategy and general manager characteristics: a conceptual examination. *Academy of Management Review*, **9**, 399–412.

Hackman, J.R. and Morris, C.G. (1975). Group tasks, group interaction process, and group performance effectiveness: a review and proposed integration. In L. Berkowitz (ed.), *Advances in Experimental Social Psychology, Volume 8*. New York: Academic Press.

Hackman, J.R. and Morris, C.G. (1978). Group process and group effectiveness: a reappraisal. In L. Berkowitz (ed.), *Group Processes*. New York: Academic Press

Hackman, J.R. and Morris, C.G. (1983). Group tasks, group interaction process, and group performance effectiveness. In H.H. Blumberg, A.P. Hare, V. Kent, and M.F. Davies (eds.), *Small Groups and Social Interaction, Volume 1*. Chichester: Wiley.

Hales, C.P. (1986). What do managers do? A critical review of the evidence. *Journal of Management Studies*, **23**, 88–115.

Hall, P. (1980). *Great Planning Disasters*. Harmondsworth: Penguin.

Hampson, S.E. (1988). *The Construction of Personality*. (Second edition). London: Routledge.

Handy, C. (1976). *Understanding Organisations*. Harmondsworth: Penguin.

Harré, R. (1979). *Social Being: A Theory for Social Psychology*. Oxford: Basil Blackwell.

Harré, R. and Secord, P.F. (1972). *The Explanation of Social Behaviour*. Oxford: Basil Blackwell.

Harré, R. (1977a). The ethogenic approach: theory and practice. In L. Berkowitz (ed.), *Advances in Experimental Social Psychology, Volume 10*. New York: Academic Press.

Harré, R. (1977b). Automatisms and autonomies: in reply to Professor Schlenker. In L. Berkowitz (ed.), *Advances in Experimental Social Psychology, Volume 10*. New York: Academic Press.

Hartley, J., Kelly, J. and Nicholson, N. (1983). *Steel Strike: A Case Study in Industrial Relations*. London: Batsford Academic and Educational Limited.

Hearnshaw, L. (1964). *A Short History of British Psychology 1840–1940*. London: Methuen.

Heller, F., Drenth, P., Koopman, P. and Rus, V. (1987). *Decisions in Organizations: a Three Country Longitudinal Study*. New York: Wiley.

Henley, S.H.A., Dixon, N.F., and Cartmell, A.E. (1977). A note on the relationship between authoritarianism and acceptance of military ideology. *British Journal of Social and Clinical Psychology*, **16**, 287–88.

Hersey, P. and Blanchard, K.H. (1977). *Management of Organizational Behavior* (Third edition). Englewood Cliffs, NJ: Prentice Hall.

Hewitt, J.P.(1979). *Self and Society: A Symbolic Interactionist Social Psychology* (Second edition). Boston: Allyn and Bacon.

Hickson, D.J., Butler, R.J., Cray, D., Mallory, G.R. and Wilson, D.C. (1986). *Top Decisions: Strategic Decision-making in Organizations*. Oxford: Basil Blackwell.

Hickson, D.J., Hinnings, C.R., Lee, C.A., Schreck, R.H. and Pennings, J.M. (1971). A strategic contingencies theory of intraorganizational power. *Administrative Science Quarterly*, **16**, 216–29.

Hilgard, E.R. (1980). Consciousness in contemporary psychology. *Annual Review of Psychology*, **31**, 1–26.

Hoffman, L.R. (1982). Improving the problem-solving process in managerial groups. In R.A. Guzzo (ed.), *Improving Group Decision Making in Organizations*. New York: Academic Press.

Hofstadter, D.R. (1985). The prisoner's dilemma computer tournaments and the evolution of cooperation. In D.R. Hofstadter, *Metamagical Themas: Questing for the Essence of Mind and Pattern*. Harmondsworth: Viking.

Hogarth, R. (1980). *Judgement and Choice*. Chichester: Wiley.

Hogg, M.A. and Abrams, D.(1988). *Social Identifications*. London: Routledge.

Hollander, E.P. (1978). *Leadership Dynamics*. New York: The Free Press. London: Collier Macmillan.

Hollins, W.J. and Pugh, S. (1989). Product status and the management of design – what to do and when. *Proceedings of the Institution of Mechanical Engineers International Conference on Engineering Design, Volume 1*. Bury St. Edmunds: Institution of Mechanical Engineers.

Holsti, O.R. (1967). Cognitive dynamics and images of the enemy. *International Affairs*, **21**, 16–39.

Holsti, O.R. (1972). Time, alternatives, and communications: the 1914 and Cuban Missile Crises. In C.F. Hermann (ed.), *International Crises: Insights from Behavioral Research*. New York: The Free Press. London: Collier Macmillan.

Homans, G.C. (1951). *The Human Group*. London: Routledge and Kegan Paul.

Homans, G.C. (1954). The cash posters. *American Sociological Review*, **19**, 729.

Homans, G.C. (1961). *Social Behavior: Its Elementary Forms*. London: Routledge and Kegan Paul.

Hosking, D.-M. (1981). A critical review of Fiedler's contingency theory. In G.M. Stephenson and J.H. Davis (eds.), *Progress in Applied Social Psychology Volume 1*. Chichester: Wiley.

Hosking, D.-M. (1983) Leadership skills and organizational forms: The management of uncertainty. Paper presented to the Sixth EGOS Colloquium, Florence.

Hosking, D.-M. (1984). On paradigms and pigs. In J.G. Hunt, D.-M. Hosking, C.A. Schriesheim, and R. Stewart (eds.), *Leaders and Mangers: International Perspectives on Managerial Behaviour and Leadership*. Oxford: Pergamon Press.

Hosking, D.-M. (1987) Leadership and organizational skills. In A.Keiser, G.Reber and R. Wunderer (eds.), *Handbook of Leadership*. Stuttgart: Poeschel Verlag.

Hosking, D.-M. (1988a). Persons, processes, and organizing. Unpublished working paper, Department of Psychology, Flinders University of South Australia.

Hosking, D.-M. (1988b). Organizing, leadership, and skilful process. *Journal of Management Studies*, **25**, 147–66.

Hosking, D.-M. (1990). Leadership processes: the skills of political decision making. In D.C. Wilson and R.H. Rosenfeld (eds.), *Managing Organization: Text, Readings, and Cases*. London: McGraw-Hill.

Hosking, D.-M. (in press, a). The organizing skills of chief executives: a strategic decision making perspective. To appear in *European Review of Applied Psychology*.

Hosking, D.-M. (in press, b). *Power, Leadership and Empowerment*. (Book 8 in Block 789, Managing Voluntary and Non-profit Enterprises.) Milton Keynes: The Open University.

Hosking, D.-M. and Fineman, S. (1991). Organizing processes. *Journal of Management Studies*, **27**, 583–604.

Hosking, D.-M. and Mann, L. (1988). The organizing skills of chief executives: a strategic decision making perspective. Paper presented at XXIV International Congress of Psychology, Sydney, Australia, August.

Hosking, D.-M. and Morley, I.E. (1988). The skills of leadership. In J.G. Hunt, B.R. Baliga, H.P. Dachler, and C.A. Schriesheim (eds.), *Emerging Leadership Vistas*. Lexington, MA: Lexington Books.

Hough, R. (1959). *Admirals in Collision*. London and New York: White Lion Publishers.

House, R.J. (1971). A path-goal theory of leader effectiveness. *Administrative Science Quarterly*, **16**, 321–38.

House, R.J. and Singh, J. (1987). Organizational behavior: some new directions for I/O Psychology. *Annual Review of Psychology*, **38**, 669–718.

Huff, A.S. (1984). Situation interpretation, leader behaviour, and effectiveness. In J.G.Hunt, D.-M. Hosking, C.A. Schriesheim, and R. Stewart (eds.), *Leaders and Managers: International Perspectives on Managerial Behaviour and Leadership*. Oxford: Pergamon Press.

Jaap, T. (1989). *Enabling Leadership* (Second edition). Aldershot: Gower Press.

Jacobs, T.O. (1970). *Leadership and Exchange in Formal Organizations*. Alexandria, VA:Human Resources Research Organization.

Janis, I.L. (1972). *Victims of Groupthink: A Psychological Study of Foreign Policy Decisions and Fiascoes*. Boston: Houghton-Mifflin.

Janis, I.L. (1982a). *Groupthink: Psychological Studies of Foreign Policy Decisions and Fiascoes*. Boston: Houghton-Mifflin.

Janis, I.L. (1982b). Counteracting the adverse effects of concurrence-seeking in policy-planning groups: theory and research perspectives. In H. Brandstätter, J.H.Davis, and G.Stocker-Kreichgauer (eds.), *Group Decision Making*. New York: Academic Press.

Janis, I.L. (1989). *Crucial Decisions: Leadership in Policymaking and Crisis Management*. New York: Free Press. London: Collier Macmillan.

Janis, I.L. and Mann, L. (1977). *Decision Making: A Psychological Analysis of Conflict, Choice, and Commitment*. New York: The Free Press. London: Collier Macmillan.

Jaques, E. (1976). *A General Theory of Bureaucracy*. London: Heinemann.

Jelinek, M. and Schoonhoven, C.B. (1990). *The Innovation Marathon: Lessons from High Technology Firms*. Oxford: Basil Blackwell.

Jenkins, R.V. (1983). Elements of style: continuities in Edison's thinking. *Annals of the New York Academy of Sciences*, **424**, 149–62.

Jenkins, R.V. and Jeffrey, T.E. (1984). Worth a thousand words: nonverbal documents in editing. *Documentary Editing*, **6**, 1–8.

Jervis, R. (1970). *The Logic of Images in International Relations*. Princeton, NJ: Princeton University Press.

Jervis, R. (1976). *Perception and Misperception in International Politics*. Princeton, NJ: Princeton University Press.

Jones, D.O. and Overton, R.A. (1988). Design auditing. Paper presented at 'Design 88', The Institution of Chemical Engineers, University of Aston.

Kahneman, D. and Tversky, A. (1979). Propsect theory: an analysis of decisions under risk. *Econometrika*, **47**, 263–91.

Kanter, R.M. (1984). *The Change Masters: Corporate Entrepreneurs at Work*. London: George Allen and Unwin.

Kapferer, B. (1972). *Strategy and Transaction in an African Factory*. Manchester: Manchester University Press.

Kaplan, R. (1984). Trade routes: the manager's network of relationships. *Organization Dynamics*, Spring, 37–52.

Kaplan, R. (1989). Trade routes: the manager's network of relationships. In H.J. Leavitt, L.R. Pondy, and D.M. Boje (eds.), *Readings in Managerial Psychology* (Fourth edition). Chicago: The University of Chicago Press.

Katz, D. and Kahn, R.L. (1978). *The Social Psychology of Organizations* (Second edition). New York: Wiley.

Kaye, K. (1982). *The Mental and Social Life of Babies: How Parents Create Persons*. London: Methuen.

Keegan, J. (1987). *The Mask of Command*. London: Jonathan Cape.

Keen, P.G.W. and Morton, M.S.S. (1978). *Decision Support Systems: An Organizational Perspective*. Reading, MA: Addison-Wesley.

Kelly, G.A. (1955). *The Psychology of Personal Constructs*. New York: Norton.

Kelly, J. (1964). The study of executive behaviour by activity sampling. *Human Relations*, **17**, 277–87.

Kelvin, P. (1970). *The Bases of Social Behaviour: An Approach in Terms of Order and Value*. London: Holt, Rinehart and Winston.

Kennedy, G., Benson, J. and McMillan, J. (1987). *Managing Negotiations* (Third edition). London: Hutchinson Business.

Kerr, S. (1983). Substitutes for leadership: some implications for organization design. In J.R. Hackman, E.E. Lawler III and L.W. Porter (eds.), *Perspectives on Behavior in Organizatons*. New York: McGraw-Hill.

Kets de Vries, M.R.F. and Miller, D. (1984). *The Neurotic Organization: Diagnosing and Changing Counterproductive Styles of Management*. San Francisco: Jossey-Bass.

Keynes, J.M. (1961). *Essays in Biography*. London: Mercury.

Kilmann, R.H. (1989). *Managing Beyond the Quick Fix: A Completely Integrated Program for Creating and Maintaining Organizational Success*. San Francisco: Jossey-Bass.

Kinder, D.A. and Weiss, J.A. (1978). In lieu of rationality. Psychological perspectives on foreign policy decision-making. *Journal of Conflict Resolution*, **22**, 707–35.

Kipnis, D., Schmidt, S.M., Swaffin-Smith, C. and Wilkinson, I. (1984). Patterns of managerial influence: shotgun managers, tacticians, and bystanders. *Organizational Dynamics*, Winter, 58–67.

Kipnis, D., Schmidt, S.M. and Wilkinson, I. (1980). Intraorganizational influence tactics: explorations in getting one's way. *Journal of Applied Psychology*, **65**, 440–52.

Kirton, M.J. (1976). Adaptors and innovators: a description and a measure. *Journal of Applied Psychology*, **61**, 622–9.

Klemp, G.O. Jr. and McClelland, D.C. (1986). What characterizes intelligent functioning amongst senior managers? In R.J.Sternberg and R.K. Wagner (eds.), *Practical Intelligence: Nature and Origins of Competence in the Everyday World*. Cambridge: Cambridge University Press.

Kochan, T.A.(1980). *Collective Bargaining and Industrial Relations*. Homewood, IL: Irwin.

Kolb, D.A. (1976). *The Learning Style Inventory: Technical Manual*. Boston: MacBer and Company.

Kolodny, H.F and Dresner, B. (1986). Linking arrangements and new work designs. *Organizational Dynamics*, **14**, 33–51.

Kotter, J.P and Lawrence, P. (1974). *Mayors in Action: Five Studies in Urban Governance*. New York: Wiley.

Kotter, J.P. (1982). *The General Managers*. New York: Free Press.

Kouzes, J.M. and Posner, B.Z. (1987). *The Leadership Challenge: How to Get Extraordinary Things Done in Organizations*. San Francisco: Jossey-Bass.

Kruglanski, A.W. and Ajzen, I. (1983). Bias and error in human judgment. *European Journal of Social Psychology*, **32**, 1134–46.

Landsberger, H.A. (1955). Interaction process analysis of professional behavior: a study of labor negotiators in twelve labor-management disputes. *American Sociological Review*, **20**, 552–8.

Landsberger, H.A. (1962). The horizontal dimension in bureaucracy. *Administrative Science Quarterly*, **6**, 299–332.

Larson, C.E, and LaFasto, T.M. (1989). *Teamwork: What Must Go Right/What Can Go Wrong*. Newbury Park: Sage.

Lawrence, P.R. and Lorsch, J.W. (1967a). Differentiation and integration in complex organizations. *Administrative Science Quarterly*, **12**, 1–47.

Lawrence, P.R. and Lorsch, J.W. (1967b). *Organization and Environment: Managing Differentiation and Integration*. Boston: Division of Research, Harvard Graduate School of Business Administration.

Lawrence, P.R. and Lorsch, J.W. (1969). *Organization and Environment*. Homewood, IL: Irwin.

Leary, T. (1957). *Interpersonal Diagnosis of Personality*. New York: Ronald Press.

Leavitt, H.J. (1989). Pathfinding, problem-solving, and implementing the management mix. In H.J. Leavitt, L.R. Pondy, and D.M. Boje (eds.), *Readings in Managerial Psychology* (Fourth edition). Chicago: The University of Chicago Press.

Lee, R. and Lawrence, P. (1985). *Organizational Behaviour: Politics at Work*. London: Hutchinson Management Studies.

Levin, P.H. (1976). *Government and the Planning Process*. London: George Allen and Unwin.

Likert, R. (1961). *New Patterns of Management*. New York: McGraw-Hill.

Linstone, H.A. (1984). Introduction. In H.A. Linstone, A.J. Meltsner, M. Adelson, B. Clary, P.G. Cook, S. Hawke, R.-E. Miller, A. Mysior, J.S. Pearson Jr., J. Shuman, L. Umbdenstock, D.Wagner and S.J. Will, *Multiple Perspectives for Decision Making: Bridging the Gap Between Analysis and Action*. New York: North-Holland.

Linstone, H.A., Meltsner, A.J., Adelson, M., Clary, B., Cook, P.G., Hawke, S., Miller, R.-E., Mysior, A., Pearson, J.S.Jr., Shuman, J., Umbdenstock, L., Wagner, D., and Will, S.J. (1984). *Multiple Perspectives for Decision Making: Bridging the Gap Between Analysis and Action*. New York: North-Holland.

Lockhart, C. (1979). *Bargaining in International Conflicts*. New York: Columbia University Press.

London, H. and Exner, J.E. Jr. (eds.) (1978). *Dimensions of Personality*. New York: Wiley.

Lord, R. (1985). An information processing approach to social perceptions, leadership, and behavioral measurement in organizations. In L.L. Cummings and B.M Staw (eds.), *Research in Organizational Behavior, 7*. Greenwich, CN: JAI Press.

Lorsch, J.W. and Lawrence, P.R. (1970). Organizing for product innovation. In G.W.

Dalton and P.R. Lawrence (eds.), *Organisational Structure and Design*. Homewood, IL: Irwin. Georgetown, Ontario: The Dorsey Press.

Lukes, S. (1974). *Power: A Radical View*. London: Macmillan.

Luthans, F. and Lockwood, D.L. (1984). Measuring leader behaviour in natural settings. In J.G. Hunt, D.-M. Hosking, C.A. Schriesheim, and R. Stewart (eds.), *Leaders and Managers: International Perspectives on Managerial Behavior and Leadership*. Oxford: Pergamon Press.

MacGregor, I.(with Tyler, R.)(1985). *The Enemies Within: The Story of the Miners' Strike, 1984–5*. London: Collins.

Mangham, I. (1979). *The Politics of Organizational Change*. London: AEB Press.

Mangham, I.L. (1986). *Power and Performance in Organizations: an Exploration of Executive Process*. Oxford: Basil Blackwell.

Mangham, I.L. and Overington, M.A. (1987). *Organizations as Theatre: A Social Psychology of Dramatic Appearances*. Chichester: Wiley.

March, J.G. and Simon, H.A. (1958). *Organizations*. New York: Wiley.

Marengo, F.D. (1979). *The Code of British Trade Union Behaviour*. London: Saxon House.

Marsh, P.D.V. (1974). *Contract Negotiation Handbook*. Epping: Gower Press.

Marshall, J. (1984). *Women Managers: Travellers in a Male World*. Chichester: Wiley.

Mason, R.O. and Mitroff, I.I. (1973). A program for research on management information systems. *Management Science*, **19**, 475–87.

Matousek, R. (1963). *Engineering Design: A Systematic Approach*. London: Blackie.

Matsumura, M. (ed.) (1987). *The Best of Japan. Innovations: Present and Future*. Tokyo: Kodansha.

McCall, G.J. and Simmons, J.L. (1966) *Identities and Interactions*. New York: Free Press.

McCall, G.J. and Simmons, J.L. (1982). *Social Psychology: A Sociological Approach*. New York: Free Press. London: Collier Macmillan.

McGrath, J.E. (1966). A social psychological approach to the study of negotiation. In R. Bowers (ed.), *Studies on Behaviour in Organizations: A Research Symposium*. Georgia: University of Georgia Press.

McGrath, J.E. (1970). *Social and Psychological Factors in Stress*. New York: Holt.

McGrath, J.E. (1984). *Groups: Interaction and Performance*. Englewood Cliffs, NJ: Prentice Hall.

McGregor, D. (1960). *The Human Side of Enterprise*. New York: McGraw-Hill.

McKelvey, B. (1981). *Organizational Systematics: Taxonomy, Evolution, Classification*. Berkeley: University of California Press.

Mechanic, D. (1962). Sources of power of lower participants in complex organizations. *Administrative Science Quarterly*, **7**, 349–64.

Meltzer, B.N., Petras, J.W. and Reynolds, L.T. (1975). *Symbolic Interactionism: Genesis, Varieties, and Criticism*. London: Routledge and Kegan Paul.

Meredeen, S. (1988). *Managing Industrial Conflict: Seven Major Disputes*. London: Hutchinson.

Meyer, M., Stevenson, W. and Webster, S. (1985). *Limits to Bureaucratic Growth*. New York: Walter de Gruyter.

Middleton, D. and Edwards, D. (eds.) (1990). *Collective Remembering*. London: Sage.

Midgaard, K. and Underdal, A. (1977). Multiparty conferences. In D. Druckman (ed.), *Negotiations: Social Psychological Perspectives*. Beverly Hills: Sage.

Might, R.J. (1984). An evaluation of the effectiveness of project control systems. *IEEE Transactions on Engineering Management*, **EM–31**, 127–37.

Might, R.J. and Fisher, W.A. (1985). The role of structural factors in determining project management success. *IEEE Transactions on Engineering Management*, **EM–32**, 71–7.

Miller, D., and Toulouse, J.-M (1986). Chief executive personality and corporate strategy and structure in small firms. *Management Science*, **32**, 1389–409.

Miller, D. Toulouse, J.-M. and Belanger, N. (1985). Top executive personality and corporate strategy: three tentative types. In R. Lamb and P. Shrivastava (eds.), *Advances in Strategic Management, Volume 4*. New York: JAI Press.

Miller, D., Kets de Vries, M.R.F. and Toulouse, J.-M. (1982). Top executive locus of control and its relationship to strategy-making, structure, and environment. *Academy of Management Journal*, **25**, 237–53.

Mintzberg, H. (1973). *The Nature of Managerial Work*. New York: Harper and Row.

Mintzberg, H. (1983). *Structure in Fives: Designing Effective Organizations*. Englewood Cliffs, NJ: Prentice Hall.

Mintzberg, H. (1989). Managerial work: analysis from observation. In H.J.Leavitt, L.R. Pondy, and D.M. Boje (eds.), *Readings in Managerial Psychology* (Fourth edition). Chicago: University of Chicago Press.

Mintzberg, H., Raisinghani, D. and Theoret, A. (1976). The structure of 'unstructured' decision processes. *Administrative Science Quarterly*, **21**, 246–75.

Miron, M.S. and Goldstein, A.P. (1979). *Hostage*. Oxford: Pergamon Press.

Mitchell, C.R. (1981). *The Structure of International Conflict*. London: Macmillan.

Mitchell, T.R. and Larson, J.R.Jr. (1987). *People in Organizations: An Introduction to Organizational Behaviour* (Third edition). New York: McGraw-Hill.

Mitchell, T.R. Green, S.G. and Wood, R.E. (1981). An attributional model of leadership and the poor performing subordinate: a test of the attributional model. In B. Staw and L.L. Cummings (eds.), *Research in Organizational Behaviour, 3*. Greenwich, CN: JAI Press.

Mitchell, T.R., Rediker, K.J. and Beach, L.R. (1986). Image theory and organizational decision making. In Sims, H.P., Gioia, D.A. and associates, *The Thinking Organization: Dynamics of Organizational Social Cognition*. San Francisco: Jossey-Bass.

Moch, M. and Huff, A. (1989). Power enactment through language and ritual. In H.J. Leavitt, L.R. Pondy, and D.M. Boje (eds.), *Readings in Managerial Psychology* (Fourth edition). Chicago: University of Chicago Press.

Morgan, G. (1986). *Images of Organization*. Beverly Hills: Sage.

Morgenstern, O. (1949). The theory of games. *Scientific American*, May, 86–9.

Morley, I.E. (1979a). Behavioural studies of industrial bargaining. In G.M. Stephenson and C.J. Brotherton (eds.), *Industrial Relations: A Social Psychological Approach*. Chichester: Wiley.

Morley, I.E. (1979b). The character of experimental studies of bargaining and negotiation. In H. Brandstätter, J.H. Davis and H. Schuler (eds.), *Dynamics of Group Decisions*. Beverly Hills: Sage.

Morley, I.E. (1981a). Negotiation and bargaining. In M. Argyle (ed.), *Social Skills and Work*. London: Methuen.

Morley, I.E. (1981b). Bargaining and negotiation. In C.C. Cooper (ed.), *Psychology and Management: a Text for Managers and Trade Unionists*. London: Macmillan/The British Psychological Society.

Morley, I.E. (1982a). Henri Tajfel's Human Groups and Social Categories. *British Journal of Social Psychology*, **21**, 189–201.

Morley, I.E. (1982b). Preparation for negotiation: conflict, commitment and choice. In H. Brandstätter, J.H.Davis and G.Stocker-Kreichgauer (eds.), *Group Decision Making*. New York: Academic Press.

Morley, I.E. (1986). Negotiating and bargaining. In O.Hargie (ed.), *A Handbook of Communication Skills*. London: Croom Helm.

Morley, I.E. (1988). Teamwork and Design. Paper presented at 'Design 88', The Institution of Chemical Engineers, University of Aston.

Morley, I.E. (1989). The formation and organisation of design teams. Lecture 16 in *Total Design: An Overview for Managers*, Design Division, University of Strathclyde.

Morley, I.E. (1990). Teamwork in engineering product design. Paper presented at Seminar on Total Design, Institution of Mechanical Engineers, London, September 28.

Morley, I.E. (1991). Building cross functional design teams. Design Productivity International Conference, Honolulu, Hawaii, February.

Morley, I.E. (in press, a). Computer supported cooperative work and engineering product design. In R. Roe and E. Andriessen (eds.), *Telematics and Work*. Hillsdale, NJ: Lawrence Erlbaum.

Morley, I.E. (in press, b). Intra-organisational bargaining. In Hartley, J. and Stephenson, G.M. (eds.), *Employment Relations: the Psychology of Influence and Control at Work*. Oxford: Basil Blackwell.

Morley, I.E. and Hosking, D.-M. (1984). Decision making and negotiation: leadership and social skills. In M.Gruneberg and T.D. Wall (eds.), *Social Psychology and Organizational Behaviour*. Chichester: Wiley.

Morley, I.E. and Hosking, D.-M. (1986). The skills of leadership. In G. Debus and H.W. Schroiff (eds.), *The Psychology of Work and Organization*. Amsterdam: North Holland.

Morley, I.E. and Pugh, S. (1987). The organization of design: an interdisciplinary approach to the study of people, process and context. In W. Eder (ed.), *Proceedings of the 1987 International Conference on Engineering Design, Volume 1*. New York: The American Society of Mechanical Engineers.

Morley, I.E. and Stephenson, G.M. (1970). Strength of case, communication systems, and the outcomes of simulated negotiations: some social psychological aspects of bargaining. *Industrial Relations Journal*, **1**, 19–28.

Morley, I.E. and Stephenson, G.M. (1977). *The Social Psychology of Bargaining*. London: Allen and Unwin.

Morley, I.E., Webb, J. and Stephenson, G.M. (1988). Bargaining and arbitration in the resolution of conflict. In Stroebe, W., Kruglanski, A.W., Bar-Tal, D., and Hewstone, M. (eds.), *The Social Psychology of Intergroup Conflict*. Berlin: Springer-Verlag.

Morris, E. (1973). *Blockade: Berlin and the Cold War*. London: Hamish Hamilton.

Murray, H.A. (1938). *Explorations in Personality*. New York: Oxford University Press.

Myers, C.S. (1924). *Industrial Psychology in Great Britain*. London: Jonathan Cape.

Myers, D.G. (1988). *Social Psychology* (Second edition). New York: McGraw-Hill.

Neilsen, E.H. (1986). Empowerment strategies: balancing authority and responsibility. In S.Srivastava and Associates, *Executive Power*. San Francisco: Jossey-Bass.

Neisser, U. (1976). *Cognition and Reality: Principles and Implications of Cognitive Psychology*. San Francisco: Freeman.

Neisser, U. (1982). John Dean's Memory: A Case Study. In U.Neisser (ed.), *Memory Observed: Remembering in Natural Contexts*. San Francisco: W.H. Freeman and Company. (Reprinted from *Cognition*, 1981, **9**, 1–22)

Newland, P.M., Powell, J.A. and Creed, C. (1987). Understanding architectural designers' selective information handling. *Design Studies*, **8**.

Nichols, R.G. (1962). Listening is good business. *Management of Personnel Quarterly*, **4**, 4.

Nisbett, R. and Ross, L. (1980). *Human Inference: Strategies and Shortcomings of Social Judgment*. Englewood Cliffs, NJ: Prentice Hall.

Nolan, V. (1987). *The Innovator's Handbook*. London: Sphere.

Norman, D.A. (1988). *The Psychology of Everyday Things*. New York: Basic Books.

Oakley, M. (1984). *Managing Product Design*. London: Weidenfeld and Nicholson.

Olsen, M.E. (1978). *The Processes of Social Organization: Power in Social Systems*. New York: Holt Saunders.

Orr, J.E. (1990). Sharing knowledge, celebrating identity: community memory in a service culture. In D. Middleton and D. Edwards (eds.), *Collective Remembering*. London: Sage.

Paine, W.S.(ed.)(1982). *Job Stress and Burnout: Research, Theory, and Intervention Perspectives*. Beverly Hills: Sage.

Papanek, V. (1984). *Design for the Real World: Human Ecology and Social Change* (Second edition). London: Thames and Hudson.

Parker, S.R., Brown, R.K., Child, J. and Smith, M.A. (1977). *The Sociology of Industry*. London: George Allen and Unwin.

Patchen, M. (1961). A conceptual framework and some empirical data regarding comparisons of social rewards. *Sociometry*, **24**, 136–56.

Pearce, J.A. and David, F.R. (1983). A social network approach to organization design and performance. *Academy of Management Review*, **8**, 436–44.

Pearson, A.W. and Gunz, H.P. (1981). Project groups. In R. Payne and C.L. Cooper (eds.), *Groups at Work*. Chichester: Wiley.

Perrow, C.A. (1967). A framework for the comparative analysis of organizations. *American Sociological Review*, **32**, 194–208.

Peston, M and Coddington, A. (1967). *The Elementary Ideas of Game Theory*. CAS Occasional Paper Number 6. London: HMSO.

Peters, T. and Austin, N. (1985). *A Passion for Excellence: the Leadership Difference*. New York: Random House.

Peters, T. and Waterman, R.H.Jr. (1982). *In Search of Excellence*. New York: Harper and Row.

Peters, T.J. (1978). Symbols, patterns and settings. *Organizational Dynamics*, **7**, 3–22.

Petroski, H. (1985). *To Engineer is Human: The Role of Failure in Successful Design*. London: Macmillan.

Petroski, H. (1987). Design as obviating failure. In G. Nadler (ed.), *1987 Congress on Planning and Design Theory: Plenary and Interdisciplinary Lectures*. New York: American Society of Mechanical Engineers.

Pettigrew, A. (1973). *The Politics of Organisational Decision Making*. London: Tavistock.

Pettigrew, A. (1977). Strategy formulation as a political process. *International Studies of Management and Organization*, **VIII**, 78–87.

Petty, R.E. and Cacioppo, J.T. (1981). *Attitudes and Persuasion: Classic and Contemporary Approaches*. Dubuque, Iowa: Wm.C.Brown.

Peyronnin, C.A. (1987). Keeping contemporary with the changing nature of interdisciplinary design. In W. Eder (ed.), *Proceedings of the 1987 International Conference on Engineering Design, Volume 1*. New York: The American Society of Mechanical Engineers.

Pfeffer, J. (1981). *Power in Organizations*. Boston: Pitman.

Pfeffer, J. and Salancik, G.R. (1978). *The External Control of Organizations:A Resource Perspective*. New York: Harper and Row.

Pondy, L. (1978). Leadership is a language game. In M.M. McCall and M.M. Lombardo (eds.), *Leadership: Where Else Can We Go?* Durham, North Carolina: Duke University Press.

Powell, J.A. (1988). Intelligent design teams design intelligent buildings. In S. McClelland (ed.), *Intelligent Buildings*. IFS Executive Briefing. Berlin: Springer-Verlag.

Prince, L. (1988). *Leadership and the Negotiation of Order in Small Groups*. Ph.D. thesis, University of Aston.

Pruitt, D.G (1971). Indirect communication and the search for agreement in negotiation. *Journal of Applied Social Psychology*, 1, 205–39.

Pruitt, D.G. (1969). Indirect communication and the search for agreement in negotiation. Indirect Communication in Negotiation Project, Working Paper II, Center for International Conflict Studies, State University of New York.

Pruitt, D.G. (1981). *Negotiation Behavior*. New York: Academic Press.

Pugh, D.S. (ed.) (1971). *Organization Theory: Selected Readings*. Harmondsworth: Penguin Education.

Pugh, S. (1981). Concept selection – a method that works. *Proceedings of the 1981 International Conference on Engineering Design*. Rome.

Pugh, S. (1983). The application of CAD in relation to dynamic/static product concepts. *Proceedings of the 1983 International Conference on Engineering Design*. Copenhagen.

Pugh, S. (1984). Further development of the hypothesis of static/dynamic concepts in product design. *Proceedings of the International Symposium on Design and Synthesis*. Tokyo.

Pugh, S. (1986). Design activity models – worldwide emergence and convergence. *Design Studies*, 7, 167–73.

Pugh, S. (1991). *Total Design*. London: Addison-Wesley.

Pugh, S. and Morley, I.E. (1988a). *Total Design: Towards a Theory of Total Design*. Glasgow: Design Division, University of Strathclyde.

Pugh, S. and Morley, I.E. (1988b). *Total Design: Some Questions and Some Answers*. Glasgow: Design Division, University of Strathclyde.

Pugh, S. and Morley, I.E. (1989). Organising for design in relation to dynamic/static product concepts. *Proceedings of the Institution of Mechanical Engineers International Conference on Engineering Design, Volume 1*. Bury St. Edmunds: Institution of Mechanical Engineers.

Putnam, L. (1985). Collective bargaining as organizational communication. In P.K. Tomkins and R. McPhee (eds.), *Organizational Communication: Traditional Themes and New Directions*. London: Sage.

Qvortrup, L. (1989). The analysis and change of computerized organizations: strtuctured analysis versus pragmatic interactionism. NETwork Workshop, 'Telematics and Work', Bad Homburg, Germany, April.

Rackham, N. and Carlisle, J. (1978a). The effective negotiator – part 1. The behaviour of successful negotiators. *Journal of European Industrial Training*, 2, no. 6, 6–10.

Rackham, N. and Carlisle, J. (1978b). The effective negotiator – part 2. Planning for negotiations. *Journal of European Industrial Training*, 2, no. 7, 2–5.

Ramsden, P. (1973). *Top Team Planning: A Study of the Power of Individual Motivation in Management*. London: Cassell.

Rasmussen, G and Zander, A. (1954). Group membership and self-evaluation. *Human Relations*, 7, 239–51.

Rice, A.K. (1958). *Productivity and Social Organisations: The Ahmedabad Experiment*. London: Tavistock.

Robbins, S.P. (1984). *Essentials of Organizational Behaviour*. Englewood Cliffs, NJ: Prentice Hall.

Robinson, M. (1989). Double level languages and cooperative working. *Cosmos Information Exchange Network*, no.6, November, 42–84.

Rose, M. (1975). *Industrial Behaviour: Theoretical Developments since Taylor*. Harmondsworth: Allen Lane.

Rubin, J.Z. and Brown, B.R. (1975). *The Social Psychology of Bargaining and Negotiation*. New York: Academic Press.

Rychlak, J.F. (1981). *Introduction to Personality and Psychotherapy: A Theory Construction Approach* (Second edition). Boston: Houghton Mifflin.

Rzevski, G. (1984). Processes within design teams. Paper presented to Workshop on Design, Economic and Social Research Council, London.

Sage, A.P. (1981). Behavioral and organizational considerations in the design of information systems and processes for planning and decision support. *IEEE Transactions on Systems, Man, and Cybernetics*, **SMC–11**, 640–78.

Sage, A.P. (1984). ARIADNE: a knowledge based interactive system for planning and decision support. *IEEE Transactions on Systems, Man, and Cybernetics*, **SMC–14**, 35–47.

Salancik, G. and Pfeffer, J. (1977). Who gets power and how they hold on to it: a strategic contingency model of power. *Organizational Dynamics*, **5**, 2–21.

Sanford, N. (1973). Authoritarian personality in contemporary perspective. In J.N.Knutson (ed.), *Handbook of Political Psychology*. San Francisco: Jossey-Bass.

Sarason, S.B. (1972). *The Creation of Social Settings and the Future Societies*. San Francisco: Jossey-Bass.

Sayles, L.R. (1964). *Managerial Behavior: Administration in Complex Organizations*. New York: McGraw-Hill.

Sayles, L.R. (1979). *Leadership: What Effective Managers Really Do and How They Do It*. New York: McGraw-Hill.

Sayles, L.R. (1989). *Leadership: Managing in Real Organizations* (Second edition). New York: McGraw-Hill.

Schattschneider, E.E. (1960). *The Semi-Sovereign People: A Realist's View of Democracy in America*. New York: Holt, Rinehart and Winston.

Schein, E.H. (1965). *Organizational Psychology*. Englewood Cliffs, NJ: Prentice Hall.

Schein, E.H. (1980). *Organizational Psychology* (Third edition). Englewood Cliffs, NJ: Prentice Hall.

Schein, E.H. (1985). *Organizational Culture and Leadership*. San Francisco: Jossey-Bass.

Schlenker, B.R. (1977). On the ethogenic approach: etiquette and revolution. In L. Berkowitz (ed.), *Advances in Experimental Social Psychology, Volume 10*. New York: Academic Press.

Schudson, M. (1990). Ronald Reagan Misremembered. In D. Middleton and D. Edwards (eds.), *Collective Remembering*. London: Sage.

Scott, B. (1988). *Negotiating: Constructive and Competitive Negotiations*. (Incorporating contributions from I. Morley, D. Sutton and J. Winkler). London: Paradigm Publishing.

Sechrest, L.J. (1983). Personal-constructs theory. In R.J.Corsini, A.J. Marsella, and contributors, *Personality Theories, Research, and Assessment*. Itasca, IL: F.E. Peacock Publishers.

Selznick, P. (1957). *Leadership in Administration: A Sociological Interpretation*. New York: Harper and Row.

Shaw, M.E. (1976). *Group Dynamics: The Psychology of Small Group Behavior* (Second edition). New York: McGraw-Hill.

Sherif, M. (1966). *The Psychology of Social Norms*. New York: Harper and Row.

Sherif, M. (1967). *Group Conflict and Cooperation*. London: Routledge and Kegan Paul.

Sherif, M. and Sherif, C.W. (1969). *Social Psychology*. New York: Harper and Row.

Sherif, M., White, B.J. and Harvey, O.J. (1955). Status in experimentally produced groups. *American Journal of Sociology*, **60**, 370–9.

Shockley, W. (1976). The path to the conception of the junction transistor. *IEEE Transactions on Electron Devices*, **ED–23**, 597–620.

Shotter, J. (1990). The social construction of remembering and forgetting. In D. Middleton and D. Edwards (eds.), *Collective Remembering*. London: Sage.

Simon, H. A. (1981). *The Sciences of the Artificial*. Cambridge, MA: MIT Press.

Simon, H.A. (1983). *Reason in Human Affairs*. Oxford: Basil Blackwell.

Sims, H.P., Gioia, D.A. and associates (1986). *The Thinking Organization: Dynamics of Organizational Social Cognition*. San Francisco: Jossey-Bass.

Slusher, E.A., Ebert, R.J. and Ragsdell, K.M. (1989). Contingency management of engineering design. *Proceedings of the Institution of Mechanical Engineers International Conference on Engineering Design, Volume 1*. Bury St. Edmunds: Institution of Mechanical Engineers.

Smart, C. and Vertinsky, I. (1977). Designs for crisis decision units. *Administrative Science Quarterly*, **22**, 640–57.

Smircich, L. and Morgan, G. (1982). Leadership: the management of meaning. *The Journal of Applied Behavioural Science*, **18**, 257–73.

Smith, K.K. (1989). An intergroup perspective on individual behaviour. In H.J. Leavitt, L.R. Pondy and D.M. Boje (eds.), *Readings in Managerial Psychology* (Fourth edition). Chicago: University of Chicago Press.

Smith, P.B. and Peterson, M.F. (1988). *Leadership, Organizations and Culture*. London: Sage.

Snyder, G.H. and Diesing, P. (1977). *Conflict Among Nations: Bargaining, Decision-Making and System Structure in International Crises*. Princeton, NJ: Princeton University Press.

Snyder, M. (1979). Self-monitoring processes. In L. Berkowitz (ed.), *Advances in Experimental Social Psychology, Volume 12*. New York: Academic Press.

Snyder, M. (1987). *Public Appearances, Private Realities: The Psychology of Self-monitoring*. San Francisco: W.H. Freeman.

Sommer, R. (1983). *Social Design: Creating Buildings with People in Mind*. Englewood Cliffs, NJ: Prentice Hall.

Stein, M.I. (1974). *Stimulating Creativity, Volume 1*. New York: Academic Press.

Stein, M.I. (1975). *Stimulating Creativity, Volume 2*. New York: Academic Press.

Steinbruner, J. (1974). *The Cybernetic Theory of Decision*. Princeton, NJ: Princeton University Press.

Steiner, I.D. (1972). *Group Process and Productivity*. New York: Academic Press.

Stephenson, G.M. (1971). Intergroup relations and negotiating behaviour. In P.B.Warr (ed.), *Psychology at Work*. Harmondsworth: Penguin.

Stephenson, G.M. (1981). Intergroup bargaining and negotiation. In J.C. Turner and H.C. Giles (eds.), *Intergroup Behaviour.*, Oxford: Basil Blackwell.

Stephenson, G.M. Kniveton, B.H. and Morley, I.E. (1977). Interaction analysis of an industrial wage negotiation. *Journal of Occupational Psychology*, **50**, 231–41.

Sternberg, R.J. (1985a). *Beyond IQ: A Triarchic Theory of Human Intelligence*. Cambridge: Cambridge University Press.

Sternberg, R.J. (1985b). General intellectual ability. In R.J. Sternberg (ed.), *Human Abilities: An Information Processing Approach*. San Francisco: W.H. Freeman.

Sternberg, R.J. (ed.) (1982). *Handbook of Human Intelligence*. Cambridge: Cambridge University Press.

Sternberg, R.J. (ed.) (1988). *The Nature of Creativity: Contemporary Psychological Perspectives*. Cambridge: Cambridge University Press.

Stewart, R. (1976). *Contrasts in Management: A Study of the Different Types of Managers' Jobs, Their Demands and Choices*. New York: McGraw-Hill.

Stewart, V. and Chadwick, V. (1987). *Changing Trains: Messages for Management from the ScotRail Challenge*. Newton Abbot: David and Charles.

Stewart, V. and Stewart, A. (1981). *Business Applications of Repertory Grid*. New York: McGraw-Hill.

Stogdill, R.M. (1974). *Handbook of Leadership*. New York: Free Press.

Strauss, A. (1978). *Negotiations: Varieties, Contexts, Processes and Social Order*. San Francisco: Jossey-Bass.

Strauss, A., Schatzman, L., Ehrlich, D., Bucher, R., and Sabshin, M. (1963). The hospital and its negotiated order. In E. Friedson (ed.), *The Hospital in Modern Society*. New York: Free Press.

Szmatka, J. (1989). Holism, individualism, reductionism. *International Sociology*, **4**, 169–86.

Tajfel, H. (1981). *Human Groups and Social Categories*. Cambridge: Cambridge University Press.

Taylor, F.W. (1923). *The Principles of Scientific Management*. New York: Harper.

Tedeschi, J.T., Lindskold, S. and Rosenfeld, P. (1985). *An Introduction to Social Psychology*. St. Paul: West Publishing Company.

Thibaut, J.W. and Kelley, H.H. (1959). *The Social Psychology of Groups*. New York: Wiley.

Tjosvold, D. (1991). *Team Organization: An Enduring Competitive Advantage*. Chichester: Wiley.

Trist, E.L., Higgin, G.W., Murray, H. and Pollock, S.B. (1963). *Organizational Choice*. London: Tavistock.

Tushman, M. and Nadler, D. (1986). Organization for innovation. *California Management Review*, **XXVII**, Spring, 74–92.

Vaill, P. (1982). The purposing of high performance systems. *Organizational Dynamics*, Autumn, 23–39.

Verba, S. (1961). *Small Groups and Political Behaviour*. Princeton, NJ: Princeton University Press.

Vickers, G.(1968). *Value Systems and Social Processes*. London: Tavistock.

Vrendenburgh, D.J. and Maurer, J.G. (1984). A process framework of organizational politics. *Human Relations*, **37**, 47–66.

Vroom, V.H. and Jago, A.G. (1988). *The New Leadership: Managing Participation in Organizations*. Englewood Cliffs, NJ: Prentice Hall.

Vroom, V.H. and Yetton, P.W. (1973). *Leadership and Decision-Making*. Pittsburgh: University of Pittsburgh Press.

Vygotsky, L. (1929). The problem of the cultural development of the child. *Journal of General Psychology*, **36**, 415–34.

Vygotsky, L. (1981). The genesis of higher mental functions. In J.V.Wertsch (ed.), *The Concept of Activity in Soviet Psychology*. Armonk, NY: Sharpe.

Waddington, D.P. (1987). *Trouble Brewing: A Social Psychological Analysis of the Ansell's Brewery Dispute*. Aldershot: Avebury.

Wagner, R.K. and Sternberg. R.J. (1986). Tacit knowledge and intelligence in the everyday world. In R.J.Sternberg and R.K. Wagner (eds.), *Practical Intelligence: Nature and Origins of Competence in the Everyday World*. Cambridge: Cambridge University Press.

Walsh, K., Hinings, B., Greenwood, R. and Ranson, S. (1981). Power and advantage in organizations. *Organization Studies*, **2**, 131–52.

Walton, R.E. and McKersie, R.B. (1965). *A Behavioral Theory of Labor Negotiations: An Analysis of a Social Interaction System*. New York: McGraw-Hill.

Walton, R.E. and McKersie, R.B. (1966). Behavioral dilemmas in mixed-motive decision-making. *Behavioral Science*, **11**, 370–84.

Warr, P.B. (1973). *Psychology and Collective Bargaining*. London: Hutchinson.

Watson, J. (1968). *The Double Helix*. New York: Signet.

Watzlawick, P., Weekland, J.H. and Fish, R. (1974). *Change: Principles of Problem Formation and Problem Resolution*. New York: Norton.

Webb, J. (1982). *Social Psychological Aspects of Third Party Intervention in Industrial Disputes*. Ph.D. Thesis, University of Nottingham.

Weber, M. (1947). *The Theory of Social and Economic Organization*. Oxford: Oxford University Press.

Weick, K.E. (1979). *The Social Psychology of Organizing*. Reading, MA: Addison-Wesley.

Weick, K.E. (1983). Managerial thought in the context of action. In S. Srivastava and Associates, *The Executive Mind*. San Francisco: Jossey-Bass.

Weigert, A.J. (1983). *Social Psychology: A Sociological Approach through Inerpretive Understanding*. Notre Dame, IN: University of Notre Dame Press.

Weisberg, R.W. (1980). *Memory, Thought, and Behavior*. New York: Oxford University Press.

Weisberg, R.W. (1986). *Creativity: Genius and Other Myths*. New York: W.H.Freeman.

Weisberg, R.W. (1988). Problem-solving and creativity. In R.J. Sternberg (ed.), *The Nature of Creativity: Contemporary Psychological Perspectives*. Cambridge: Cambridge University Press.

Welford, A.T. (1980). The concept of social skill and its application to social performance. In W.T. Singleton, P.Spurgeon, and R. Stammers (eds.), *The Analysis of Social Skill*. London: Plenum Press.

Wertsch, J. V. (1985) *Vygotsky and the Social Formation of Mind*. Cambridge, MA: Harvard University Press.

Whipp, R. and Clark, P. (1986). *Innovation and the Auto Industry: Product, Process and Work Organization*. London: Francis Pinter.

White, R.K. (1970). *Nobody Wanted War: Misperception in Vietnam and Other Wars*. Garden City, NY: Anchor Books.

Whyte, G. (1989). Groupthink revisited. *Academy of Management Review*, **14**, 40–56.

Wildavsky, A. (1979). *The Politics of the Budgeting Process* (Third edition). Boston: Little, Brown.

Wildavsky, A. (1983). Information as an organizational problem. *Journal of Mangement Studies*, **20**, 29–40.

Winham, G.R. (1977). Complexity in international negotiation. In D. Druckman (ed.), *Negotiations: Social Psychological Perspectives*. Beverly Hills: Sage.

Winham, G.R. and Bovis, H.E. (1978). Agreement and breakdown in negotiation: report on a State Department Training Simulation. *Journal of Peace Research*, **15**, 285–303.

Winkler, J. (1988). Bargaining: Part 2. Chapter 17 in B.Scott, *Negotiating: Constructive and Competitive Negotiations*. London: Paradigm Publishers.

Winkler, J.T. (1974). The ghost at the bargaining table: directors and industrial relations. *British Journal of Industrial Relations*, **12**, 191–212.

Winograd, T. and Flores, F. (1986). *Understanding Computers and Cognition: A New Foundation for Design*. Norwood, NJ: Ablex.

Wittgenstein, L. (1963). *Philosophical Investigations*. Oxford: Basil Blackwell.

Wohl, J.G. (1981). Force management decision requirements for air force tactical command and control. *IEEE Transactions on Systems, Man, and Cybernetics*, **SMC–11**, 618–39.

Wood, D. (1988). *How children Think and Learn*. Oxford: Basil Blackwell.

Wood, G. (1983). *Cognitive Psychology: A Skills Approach*. Monterey, CA: Brooks/Cole Publishing Company.

Woodward, J. (1965). *Industrial Organization: Theory and Practice*. Oxford: Oxford University Press.

Wrapp, H.E. (1984). Good managers don't make policy decisions. *Harvard Business Review*, July-August, 8–21.

Wright, P. and Taylor, D. (1984). *Improving Leadership Performance*. Englewood Cliffs, NJ: Prentice Hall.

Yukl, G.A. (1989). Managerial leadership: a review of theory and research. *Journal of Management*, **15**, 251–89.

Zachary, W.B. and Krone, R.M. (1984). Managing high creative individuals in high technology research projects. *IEEE Transactions on Engineering Management*, **EM–31** 37–40.

Zander, A. (1982). *Making Groups Effective*. San Francisco: Jossey-Bass.

Zartman, I.W. (1977). Negotiation as a joint decision process. In I.W. Zartman (ed.), *The Negotiation Process: Theories and Applications*. Beverly Hills: Sage.

Zimbardo, P.G. (1969). The human choice: individuation, reason and order versus deindividuation, impulse, and chaos. In W.J. Arnold and D. Levine (eds.), *Nebraska Symposium on Motivation 1969*. Lincoln:University of Nebraska Press.

Index

Notes, 1. All references are to organization. This word is therefore omitted from many entries.